HOW TO OBTAIN YOUR U.S. IMMIGRATION VISA FOR A TEMPORARY STAY.

The Nonimmigrant Visa Kit

By Benji O. Anosike, B.B.A., M.A., Ph.D.

Immigration Manual Volume 1

Library of Congress Cataloging-in-Publication Data

Anosike, Benji O.
Immigration manual / by Benji O. Anosike.
p. cm.
Includes bibliographical references and index.
Contents: v. 1. How to obtain your U.S. immigration visa for a temporary stay : the nonimmigrant visa kit -- v. 2. How to obtain your U.S. immigration visa for a permanent stay : the immigrant visa or green card kit.
ISBN 0-932704-52-2 (v. 1) -- ISBN 0-932704-53-0 (v. 2)
1. Emigration and immigration law--United States--Popular works. 2. Visas--United States--Popular works. I. Title.

KF4819.6.A562 2003
342.73'082--dc21

2002041610

Printed in the United States of America
ISBN: 0-932704 -52-2
Library of Congress Catalog Number:

Published by:
Do-It-Yourself Legal Publishers
60 Park Place #1013,
Newark, NJ 07102

Acknowledgments

Our profound thanks and gratitude go to the following persons and organizations: Colorado's C. James Cooper, Jr., the immigration legal practitioner and authority, the author of *The American Immigration Tapes*, and its *Form Book*, whose illustrated printed forms (and other information) are extensively reproduced in this manual (particularly in its Volume 1) for illustrative purposes; immigration lawyer and author Dan P. Danilov of Seattle, Washington, and his publisher, *Self-Counsel Press, Inc.,* from whose book, *"Immigrating To The U.S."*, a limited number of select forms are reproduced for our own illustrative purposes; lawyer and author of *The Green-Card Book,* Richard Madison of New York city, from whose publication we reproduced a few select forms or tables for their great value as illustrative tools. Others whose works proved particularly fitting, relevant and useful for the purpose of this manual and specialized readership for which it is intended, include Christopher C. Henry's *How To Win The U.S. Immigration Game* (The O'Brien Press, Dublin 6, Ireland); and the two ACLU books, David Carliner's *The Rights of Aliens* (Avon Books, 1977), and David Carliner, et al's *The Rights of Aliens and Refugees* (Southern Illinois University Press: 1990); and *The Federal Immigration Laws and Regulations*, 1998 Edition, published by West Group, and many, many others, too numerous to mention herein.

All have, in one way or the other, and by your deed, pioneering works and/or research in the field – and by your ever unselfish readiness to share and to disseminate the fruits thereof – made the present undertaking both more purposeful and easier for the present author and his publisher.

The Publisher's Disclaimer

We have, of course, diligently researched, checked and counter-checked every bit of the information contained in this manual to ensure its accuracy and up-to-dateness. Nevertheless, we humans have never been noted for our infallibility, no matter how hard the effort! Furthermore, details of most laws and procedures do change from time to time, and those pertaining to immigration are by no means exempted or immune from this rule. In deed, with particular respect to the U.S. immigration policy, the details of the rules and procedures (though not generally of the laws or basic principles) by which the processing of visa applications is carried out, and the standards of leniency or stringency by which the decisions are made, often differ from one immigration district or U.S. Consulate abroad to another. Nor, further, is this relatively short manual conceivably intended to be an encyclopedia on the subject, possibly containing or meant to contain the answers and solution to every issue on the subject.

THE READER IS THEREFORE FOREWARNED that this manual is sold with this disclaimer: the Publisher (or editors or author) does NOT make any guarantees whatsoever, or purport to engage in rendering legal or other professional services, or to substitute for a lawyer, an immigration counselor or consultant, or a personal adviser, and the like. Where any such professional help or other expert assistance is legitimately necessary in particular situations, it should be sought accordingly.

- DO-It-Yourself Legal Publishers

* Praise For *

The Previous Edition of ***"How To Obtain Your U.S. Immigration Visa."***
Here are what the **EXPERTS** say:

"...refreshing to encounter so much information about visa (laws and procedures) ... step-by-step procedures are clear and forthright ... such good research (with sample forms and illustrated sheets) that the result is a very valuable book, and because of the dearth of latest information on immigration laws, this volume(s) will be a useful addition to any library or individual seeking immigration information."

— **Vic A. Kassery,** Asst. Exec. Editor
Patrician (Radio/TV) Productions, N.Y.

"Whether prospective immigrants to the U.S. decide to hire a lawyer or do it themselves, it will help if they thoroughly understand the immigration process. This manual (provides such information) ... The steps to be taken to obtain an immigrant (or non-immigrant) visa, are outlined, including the procedures to obtain labor certification ... A useful public library book." — American Library Association's **The Booklist.**

"Information-packed guide which emphasizes both a practical understanding of how visa laws operate and how one may be obtained without a lawyer's advice ... a lot of information ... and many technical explanations of how visa standards are applied to individuals and families."

— The Midwest Book Review's **The Bookwatch**
(Book was the "Reviewer's Choice" selection of the month)

"Anosike's book is full of many positive elements ... useful contents, and index."

— **Matindale-Hubbell's Legal Publishing Preview.**

"This (2003 edition) two-volume manual is extremely useful in showing the step-by-step process for foreign nationals to qualify for a grant of entry visa into the U.S. Full descriptions are given to each kind of visa by which one can gain entry into this country... possible problem areas are brought to light ... The author even takes the reader inside the U.S. immigration office to see how things work there. A handy and unique reference."

— American Library Association's **The Booklist.**

TABLE OF CONTENTS

Chapter 5
GETTING A VISA AS A TREATY TRADER OR INVESTOR: THE E-1 AND E-2 VISAS

Chapter 6
GETTNG A VISA AS AN ACADEMIC, VOCATIONAL, OR EXCHANGE STUDENT: THE F, M, AND J VISAS

Chapter 7
GETTING A VISA AS A TEMPORARY SPECIALTY WORKER: THE H-1B VISA

Chapter 8
GETTING A VISA AS A TEMPORARY NON-AGRICULTURAL WORKER: THE H-2B VISA

Chapter 9
GETTING A VISA AS AN INDUSTRIAL TRAINEE TEMPORARY WORKER: THE H-3 VISA

Chapter 10
THE K-1 VISA: A SPECIAL ENTRY VISA FOR FIANCE(E)S ENGAGED TO MARRY U.S CITIZENS

Chapter 11
GETTING A VISA AS AN INTRA-COMPANY TRANSFEREE: THE L-1 VISA

Chapter 12
SOME SPECIALIZED TEMPORARY WORK VISA CATEGORIES FOR VARIOUS PROFESSIONALS IN THE SCIENCES, ARTS, EDUCATION, BUSINESS, ATHLETICS, ENTERTAINMENT, AND IN RELIGION: THE O, P, AND R VISAS

Chapter 13
HOW TO PROPERLY COMPLETE THE VISA APPLICATION FORM

Chapter 14
HANDLING THE ISSUE OF THE ALIEN'S INTENT: A CRITICAL DETERMINANT IN WHETHER YOU GET A VISA IN MOST NONIMMIGRANT VISA SITUATIONS

Chapter 15
THE VISA INTERVIEW

Chapter 16
ENTERING THE UNITED STATES: THE PROCESS OF GETTING ACTUALLY "ADMITTED" INTO THE COUNTRY AFTER YOU'VE GOT YOUR VISA IN HAND

Chapter 17
LEGAL GROUNDS FOR INADMISSIBILITY OF ALIENS TO THE UNITED STATES

Chapter 18
INSIDE THE U.S IMMIGRATION OFFICE: HOW THEY WORK, HOW TO GET THE BEST RESULTS IN YOUR VSA PROCESSING

APPENDICES

FOREWORD: THE PUBLISHER'S MESSAGE

Of all the mighty nations in the East or in the West
This glorious Yankee nation is the greatest and the best;
We have room for all creation and our banner is unfurled,
Here's a general invitation to the people of the world.
Come along, come along, make no delay.
*Come from every nation, come from every way.....**

So reads a passage from a 19th Century American Ballad

To All Our Readers:

The subject matter of immigration to the United States of America – the governing laws, the ways and means, and procedures by which persons may officially gain entry into, or stay in the United States – has always been a "hot", deeply felt subject for America, in deed the world, for as long as the United States has existed as a nation. In the interest of brevity, suffice it to say, simply, that the United States can legitimately lay claim to its historical reputation as a "nation of immigrants" – a nation whose citizens are overwhelmingly the sons and daughters and descendents of persons who came to United States from other lands. With the subject of immigration, one at once finds the one subject about which there's so common an experience shared by all of us AMERICANS; hence the great emotions and ambivalence with which this matter has been treated historically in America!

It requires no great intellect, therefore, for one to see that *a working knowledge of, or at least some familiarity with, the matter of who gets to be selected for admission into the country, or excluded or expelled from it, and how and why, is an issue that is of crucial interest and importance to a great many American citizens and residents, as well as foreign nationals the world over.*

What this Manual Will Do for you

HOW TO OBTAIN YOUR U.S. IMMIGRATION VISA WITHOUT A LAWYER, is primarily concerned with one fundamental but limited aspect of the immigration issue: 'the knots and bolts' of securing a U.S. entry visa; exposition of the officially prescribed requirements and procedures by which the foreign national may qualify for a visa under the laws and regulations of the immigration authorities; and the actual preparation and assembling of such requirements and its filing with the immigration authorities who grant the visa. ***In brief, with a working knowledge or mastery of the contents of this manual, YOU (any foreign national) will know what and what requirements and qualifications you need to have in order to be eligible for a grant of entry permit into the United States, or to stay in the country if already admitted; and, even more important, you will, solely by YOURSELF and without any "expert" assistance, be able to undertake all the filing procedures necessary for you to apply for and obtain the type of entry visa, immigrant or non-immigrant, which you desire and qualify***

*Quoted from "*The Rights of Aliens.* The Basic ACLU Guide to An Alien's Rights, by David Carliner (Avon Books: 1977). p.25

for. And, if you are a U.S. citizens or a permanent resident already, you will be able to determine whether or not you qualify to bring your family members to the U.S., and how to actually do so; and if you are an official of a corporation or business or institution, you will be able to master the process by which you can hire a foreign national to work for you in a vital capacity.

One fundamental premise underlies this manual: Whatever else may be said to be involved in obtaining an entry visa by which an alien can become lawfully admitted into (or to remain in) the United States, the process itself is, at its most basic level, primarily a clerical and ministerial operation, requiring no complex "legal" procedures or expertise or any specialized technical theories or knowledge of law, or one which calls for a lawyer or other such professional. Rather, all it calls for is merely a simple knowledge of the types of documentations or other evidence you need present to establish your eligibility for a given class of visa, and the ability to write up or gather such documentations for the benefit of the immigration authorities.

The National Scope – And Purpose – of This Manual

HOW TO OBTAIN YOUR U.S. IMMIGRATION VISA aims, first and foremost, at providing at "street level" to the people directly affected – namely, the aliens and foreign nationals, themselves, who seek or desire entry into or to stay in the United States – the practical tools and knowledge with which they can, themselves, seek their objectives, and in a relatively inexpensive, affordable and accessible way open to the ordinary man and woman all the world over. Similarly, the handbook is aimed at providing vital knowledge of the basics involved for the benefit of the immigration-related non-specialists engaged in various religious, civic and community organizations, voluntary agencies, non-profit organizations and other recognized public interest groups across the United States who counsel and assist aliens with various immigration-related needs and problems inside and outside the United States.

The book is published in two (2) volumes for purposes of simplicity of exposition and greater ease of comprehension of the material contents. Volume 1 deals with the procedures of obtaining the ***temporary*** type of U.S. visa – The NON-IMMIGRANT visa; and Volume 2, deals with the procedures of obtaining the ***permanent*** type of U.S. visa – The IMMIGRANT visa or Green Card.

Long-standing Recognition OF Need for a Guidebook of this Kind

This manual could not be more timely or its contents more relevant or needed for our present historical times. Even as we speak (and, even as you, the reader, probably goes through the contents herein!), the world increasingly promises to get still smaller and smaller. It's simply inevitable! With astronomical technological changes continuing – and destined – to occur all over the world and rapidly transforming the world into one "inter-related global environment," and with the historic revolutionary upheavals which have been occurring in the recent history of Asia, Eastern Europe, even in Africa and other parts of the world, which promise to sweep away (or at least chip away at) the major historical differences and barriers between social, economic and political systems among peoples and nations of the world, one thing is almost certain, namely: *the attraction and the attractiveness of the United States as the "land of opportunity" and the "last beacon of hope" for those in search of political freedom or economic betterment throughout the world, is all two likely to increase, not decrease.* The sounds and signs are all around us, and every bit of world event and evidence around the world suggest that America of the present and immediate future, is likely to see not less, but a lot more discussions and concerns centering around such immigration-related historic anxieties as the "influx" of "illegal aliens," the need for "defense of American borders" or the "amnesty program", and the issue of the "undocumented aliens", the "boat people," "refugees", and so on and so forth. This manual, it is hoped and intended, will help America – and the citizens of the world – to better understand and cope with such matters or developments, and in a more responsible and rational manner.

In deed, immigration administrators and workers, policy makers, volunteer agencies and operatives, and even legal practitioners who work in the area of immigration matters, have long seemingly recognized the crying need for a practical manual such as this book and hungered for one. And many of them, frustrated and unable to find such practical guide books or programs for use in their day-to-day work or encounters with their immigrant clients, have from time to time bemoaned the unavailability or inaccessibility of such practical materials.

Thus, as far back as 1986, C. James Cooper, Jr., a Denver Colorado immigration attorney who is one of the few and earliest among the crop of legal practitioners and experts in the field of U.S. immigration, draws a powerful but vivid portrait of the kind of reality in America's immigration world which now underlies the rationale for the publication of the present manual. Cooper sums it all up this way:

> "I have felt for a long time that there has been a need for an immigration program that would give people a better understanding about our immigration laws and policies. There are very few, if any public sources for this information.
>
> Public libraries, generally, do not.... Even if they do, it is difficult to find information on some of the "dos and don'ts" of immigration. The (U.S.) Immigration Service is very helpful in giving you the necessary immigration forms; however, they cannot legally give you advice. I have had many clients who relied on advice from well intended friends and relatives which was either misleading or misunderstood.....
>
> Qualified immigration attorneys (lawyers) are a good source of information ... However, in many cases you may only need one consultation to clarify some problem area or to get an assessment on whether you have a good chance of getting what you want or whether you should anticipate some problems....
>
> There are many things you can do by yourself without the need for any legal assistance....(and a handbook of the type will hopefully)..... guide you through some of these areas by giving you practical points on what has worked in the past and to prepare you for any potential problems.
>
> For those areas which could cause problems (from what you may discover from the knowledge you gather from your reading of the handbook), it may be worthy your time and expense to consult an attorney at least once .... As a result, you will have a better understanding about your situation and can then decide if you want to proceed (by yourself) after the consultation.
>
> (Indeed, even) if you decide you'd (rather) use the services of an attorney to prepare your entire case, [still you can benefit by reading such as guidebook, for]..... the more information you have about our immigration system, the better are your chances for getting a visa. ***Experience shows us that the most successful people are those who have the best information. I assure you, as an attorney with many years (over 40 years) of experience, that clients who have understood the immigration system and knew what to expect, were usually successful.*** This is due in large part, because such clients knew what to anticipate, and, as a result, were easily able to contribute relevant information...they were more relaxed and confident in any contacts they had with either (the) immigration or the Consulates"*

Translated, the central point is: whichever route you, the alien, intend to go, whether, on the one hand, you will choose to file for the American entry or residency visa yourself and completely pursue it by yourself; or, on the other hand, you will choose to engage the services of an immigration lawyer to do it for you in part or in whole, having this practical handbook in hand would still be to your invaluable advantage and helpfulness as a visa seeker, and might even spell the critical difference between your successfully obtaining one and your not

*Quoted from "AMERICAN IMMIGRATION TAPES" (Text). Allterra Visas, Ltd., 1986 pp. 1-2. Passage is quoted in such extensive detail as it makes the present publisher's intended point so well.

obtaining one!!

The New World of Terrorism & The New Age of U.S. Immigration Policy of The Post-September 11th 2001 Era!

In deed, even as this book is readied or goes to press, one recent, humongous, world-changing event that literally exploded on the world scene in the United States, has, in and of itself, single-handedly made the need for this manual even far more particularly timely and necessary both for the U.S. visa-seeker (present and future) and the U.S. immigration professionals and authorities: the catastrophe of September 11th 2001 and the epoch-making crashing of airplanes into the U.S. Pentagon and the famed World Trade Center twin towers in New York. Since that event, American authorities of all level – and its general public – have since learned, needless to say to their utter regrets and chagrin, that almost all of the highjackers involved in the deadly act, were foreign nationals, and that most of them had entered the country on temporary visas that had been readily and easily granted them by U.S. embassy and consulate officials largely with little or no screening or controls, or any follow-up checks after they have entered the country.

One fundamental reality is crystal clear already: namely, that in light of the heightened anxiety in America about foreigners in the wake of the event of September 11th 2001, and the general outcry among the nation's policy makers and politicians about the U.S. immigration system that is said to be "lax" and "riddled with loopholes," the immigration procedures of the U.S. will likely see many changes and tightening up in the

immediate future. They'll likely be, however, mainly in the area of greater screening, scrutiny and control of the visa granting requirement and procedures, and the monitoring of visa holders and non-U.S. citizens once they are in the country. *Whatever the nature and parameters of the future immigration policy, however, in the end simply having a copy of HOW TO OBTAIN YOUR U.S. IMMIGRATION VISA in hand, and making certain to understand and master the contents and procedures outlined therein, will still go a long way in aiding the reader to better understand the types of immigration issues that are likely to arise, anyway and how to address and handle them properly and successfully.*

Here's The Fundamental Essence and Message of This Book

In point of fact, the point of HOW TO OBTAIN YOUR U.S. IMMIGRATION VISA, should not be mis-taken or misunderstood. We emphasize that the cardinal aim of this manual is neither to debunk the actual or potential usefulness of ever employing the services of a competent immigration lawyer or other professionals in all circumstances, nor to advocate solely a do-it-yourself approach by the alien or the non-professional in all circumstances. Rather, ***the objective position of the manual is that, if equipped with a basic understanding of its workings and process, the non-lawyer and non-specialist could do just as good a job as, perhaps even a better job (and definitely a less expensive one!) than the average lawyer in applying for or securing the average U.S. visa. And it is specifically contended that this is so especially with respect to the more usual, routine types of cases which, as a rule, are generally clerical and straightforward, hardly involving any complex or technical issues of law or policy.***

Thank you all again

Do-It-Yourself Legal Publishers

Newark N.J

9/11 (2001)!

POSTSCRIPT

THE NEW IMMIGRATION ERA OF POST-SEPTEMBER 11TH 2001! A NOTE ABOUT THE PROBABLE FUTURE WAY OF DOING IMMIGRATION BUSINESS IN AMERICA

A. "LAX" U.S. IMMIGRATION SYSTEM PRIOR TO SEPTEMBER 11TH 2001?

True to its historical reputation as the "land of opportunity" and the "last beacon of hope" for people in search of political freedom or economic betterment throughout the world, American has always been known, far and wide, by friends, as well as by foes, as a free, pluralistic and open society readily welcoming of and receptiv to foreign persons and foreign ideas alike. *In deed, America's diversity, its free market economy and free-wheeling brand of democracy, are held to be the unique quality that makes America a nation distinctly different from all other countries in the modern world.*

Unfortunately, however, most likely these American realities and qualities about America would soon change. They are likely to change in terms, particularly, of the way in which America views the foreigner, especially the foreign person seeking entry into the United States, or who is already within the country. Simply summed up, the world-changing catastrophe of the now infamous September 11th 2001 crashing of airplanes into the U.S. Pentagon and the famed New York's World Trade Center twin towers by persons who turned out to be foreigners who entered the country largely on easily obtained temporary visas, has provoked such a heightened anxiety among Americans about foreigners and about the nation's immigration system and procedures. The general outcry has emerged across America among the nation's policy makers and politicians that the American immigration system is too "lax" and "riddled with loopholes," in that, it is commonly claimed, it failed to ferret out the vicious foreign highjackers. Given this prevailing mood all across the country, ***one thing certainly seems rather crystal clear already, even this early, namely: the immigration procedures of the United States will almost certainly see many changes and tightening up in the near future.***

B. THE PROBABLE CHANGES OF THE FUTURE

What, exactly, is the specific nature or the parameters of the changes that will probably come about? That remains to be seen for now (as of this writing). This much can be said with some degree of certainty, however: the changes will likely be primarily in the area of a greater screening and tightening up of the requirements and procedures of the visa granting system for visa applicants, and of the monitoring of visa holders and non-U.S. citizens who enter or stay in the country.

The new immigration law and system will probably center around immigration-control measures such as the following:

- a moratorium on issuing student visas
- establishment of an "exit lane" control – a measure which systematically matches entries by foreign students and visitors into the U.S. with corresponding exits, thereby being able to identify those who have overstayed their visas
- greater vigilance and tracking measures on foreign students and foreigners to detect those of them who have overstayed their student, tourist, visitors or temporary work visas

• creation of electronic databank on foreign students which will be accessible to U.S. law enforcement authorities

• placing vital control information on ALL visa applicants and holders on database, such as the National Crime Information Center, used by federal and local law enforcement officials, and making such information accessible to all agencies with a need to know, including the airlines

• sharing of F.B.I. crime records with the U.S. Consulates and Embassies overseas

• legal authority by federal agents to detain immigrants (non U.S. citizens) on mere suspicions of being a terrorist or having a terrorist background or intention.

• devotion of more personnel and more senior staff to the visa reviewing process by U.S. embassies and the INS

• requiring American universities and employers to keep the INS informed when a visa holder is no longer attending classes or no longer working, and when the foreign student's immigration status changes.

• instituting a mandatory waiting period in the processing of temporary visas – some 20 to 30 days – to allow the immigration staff time to check an applicant's name against lists and to run it by the foreigner's hometown authorities.

• requiring every person to apply for a visa in his country of origin as that is where his or her local authorities will be familiar with his/her past history and record

• tighter security restrictions and stricter scrutiny at crossings along the nation's international borders (Mexico, Canada, and the like), including running background checks on foreigners; and

• tighter enforcement of immigration laws and crackdown on illegal immigration and illegal aliens by the INS.

C. BUT HERE'S THE GOOD NEWS FOR ALIENS

BUT HERE'S THE OTHER SIDE OF THE STORY, THE "GOOD NEWS" PART FOR YOU, THE FOREIGN VISA-SEEKER: nothing in the kinds of measures and reforms envisaged remotely suggest that America will not still remain a "nation of immigrants" that it has always been, regardless, a nation that still welcomes and takes in foreigners, and probably in the same huge numbers as previously. Only that, this time, it will be more scrutinizing and more verifying of their backgrounds in doing so. In other words, for a foreign person, the new visa processing and granting procedures may cause a little more inconvenience than before, or take a little more time. But, in the end, if you are a qualified visa applicant (or resident alien), any way, if you have no criminal background or evil intent on America, then you still have nothing to worry about as a foreigner. You'll still get your visa to come to America, just as well, and you'll still be welcomed into America just as well; the same as you would have <u>BEFORE</u> the infamous September 11th 2001 event! ***In a word, only for the "bad guys" have the rules of the immigration game for getting an American visa or for getting admitted into or living in America really changed, in the final analysis.***

Just months before the awesome September 11th 2001 event, America city planners and governments were busy outbidding each other to attract immigrants. They offered grants and various "immigrant-friendly" incentive programs and packages to lure immigrants to their localities to help revive their economies and, as one report put it. "help restock urban neighborhood populations that shrank as the middle-class moved to the suburbs." (See a New York Times newspaper headline of May 30th 2001 below). Don't suppose that this sort of trend is necessarily going to be all dead just because of September 11!

To Fill Gaps, Cities Seek Foreigners

HEAD COUNT

Moving In From Abroad

The top 25 metropolitan areas by net international migration from 1990 to 1999 as a percentage of estimated 1999 population.

RANK	METROPOLITAN AREA	NET INTERNATIONAL MIGRATION	AS PERCENTAGE OF 1999 POPULATION	1999 POPULATION
1	Miami	337,174	15.5%	2,175,634
2	New York	974,599	11.2%	8,712,600
3	Los Angeles-Long Beach	902,097	9.7%	9,329,989
4	Orange County, Calif.	233,168	8.4%	2,760,948
5	San Diego	164,016	5.8%	2,820,844
6	Oakland, Calif.	135,027	5.7%	2,348,723
7	Houston	209,859	5.2%	4,010,969
8	Washington, D.C.	240,117	5.1%	4,739,999
9	Chicago	366,607	4.6%	8,008,507
10	Dallas	132,574	4.0%	3,280,310
11	Riverside-San Bernardino, Calif.	119,038	3.7%	3,200,587
12	Seattle-Bellevue-Everett	79,353	3.4%	2,334,934
13	Nassau-Suffolk, N.Y.	70,812	2.6%	2,688,904
14	Boston*	137,313	2.5%	5,423,689
15	Atlanta	82,580	2.1%	3,857,097
16	Denver	41,029	2.1%	1,978,991
17	Phoenix-Mesa	62,280	2.1%	3,013,696
18	Tampa-St. Petersburg-Clearwater, Fla.	42,826	1.9%	2,278,169
19	Philadelphia	91,672	1.9%	4,949,867
20	Minneapolis-St. Paul	45,981	1.6%	2,872,109
21	Detroit	68,449	1.5%	4,474,614
22	Baltimore	32,727	1.3%	2,491,254
23	St. Louis	25,310	1.0%	2,591,456
24	Cleveland-Lorain-Elyria	17,247	0.8%	2,221,181
25	Pittsburgh	8,935	0.4%	2,331,336

*Not the Boston primary metropolitan statistical area, but a group of counties that generally corresponds to the Boston area.

Source: Center for Social and Urban Research at the University of Pittsburgh, from Census Bureau estimates

INTRODUCTION: HOW TO USE THIS MANUAL

DO YOU HAVE THE RIGHT VOLUME OF THIS BOOK?

This book on U.S. immigration laws and visa procedures is organized, by deliberate and purposeful design, in two volumes. *Volume 1, How to Obtain Your U.S. Immigration Visa for a Temporary Stay: The Non-Immigrant Visa Kit,* deals with the rules and procedures for obtaining the **temporary** types of visa (see Section B.2 of Chapter 2). While Volume 2, *How To Obtain Your U.S. Immigration Visa for a Permanent Stay:* The *Immigration Visa or Green Card Kit*, deals with the same material but as it relates to obtaining the **permanent** type of visa, the visa more commonly known to immigrants and visa-seeker as the "Green Card" (See Section B.1 of Chapter 2, and Chapter 3).

This is done for a simple reason: to make the book more manageable for the reader, and to make the contents better organized and more comprehensible for the benefit of the reader.

FIRST, KNOW THE RIGHT VISA YOU QUALIFY FOR OR SHOULD SEEK

Get this right into your head, if ever you are to be successful in the end in this business: the basic rule is that you first determine the type of visa for which you qualify, and that visa – and only that – is the visa you then apply for. As a rule, if all that you did wrong is to apply for the wrong visa, in the first place, or to apply for a visa in the wrong visa category, (say, a student visa when you should have applied for a visitors, or an immigrant visa when you should have gone for a non-immigrant visa), you've just about guaranteed to lose out from the very start just for that single error alone!

Here's what you do in simple terms:

- First, determine whether you should apply for (whether you seemingly have the required qualifications for) a non-immigrant (temporary) type of visa, or for an immigrant (permanent) type. Go to Chapter 2 for the answer to this all-important question.
- Next, if you think you most likely qualify for a temporary visa and can possibly meet the requirements for one, then the book you need is Volume 1 of this manual. But if you're best suited for a permanent visa, you should go to Volume 2.
- In each of the two Volumes, the book is organized into separate chapters with each chapter devoted to a specific green card (in Volume 2), or a specific non-immigrant visa category (in Volume 1). For the Volume you pick, you may then zero in on the chapter which fits your specific situation and read those ones. And once you find that you meet substantially all the qualifications necessary for the particular visa of your choice, - and will be able to document and prove it to the U.S. immigration authorities – you may then commence the application procedures outlined in the appropriate chapters, accordingly.
- If you find you do not meet all or most of the requirements for the first visa choice you made, you may consider "going back to the drawing board" – check another kind of visa or category; you may better have the requirements for that. Or, if all else fails for the moment, rather than rush into making an application for the wrong kind of visa and possibly lose all chances of getting a U.S. visa in the future, you may consider just cooling it for now. Go back, perhaps, and consider how you can possibly change the present conditions in your life so that you can meet the prescribed requirements over time to be able to get that green card or other temporary visa you want.

HEAD COUNT

More Americans Born Abroad

In 2000, 56 million Americans, or 20 percent of the population, had either been born in a foreign country or had at least one parent who was, according to Census Bureau estimates. The question on the birthplace of parents was not asked in 1940, 1950, 1980 or 1990.

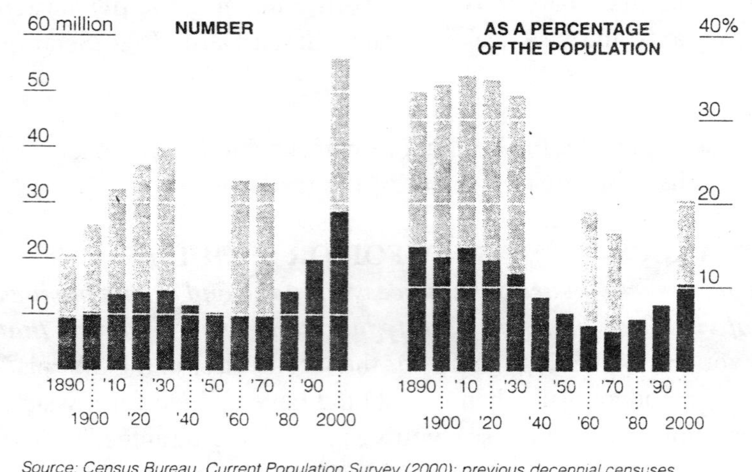

Source: Census Bureau, Current Population Survey (2000); previous decennial censuses

The New York Times

California leads in foreign-born residents, with New York second.

An Education in America

More students from around the world are attending colleges and universities in the United States.

Total international students enrolled, 1960-2001*
(as percentage of all students)

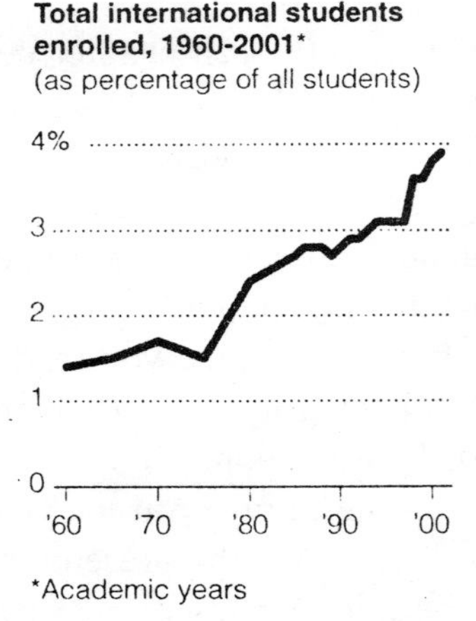

*Academic years

Institutions with highest number of international students, 2000-2001

RANK	INSTITUTION	NUMBER OF FOREIGN STUDENTS
1.	New York University	5,399
2.	University of Southern California	5,321
3.	Columbia University	4,837
4.	Purdue University Main Campus	4,469
5.	Boston University	4,443
6.	University of Texas at Austin	4,320
7.	Ohio State University Main Campus	4,035
8.	University of Michigan at Ann Arbor	4,004
9.	University of Wisconsin at Madison	3,938
10.	Northern Virginia Community College	3,877

Top 10 countries of origin, 2000-2001

RANK	COUNTRY
1.	China
2.	India
3.	Japan
4.	South Korea
5.	Taiwan
6.	Canada
7.	Indonesia
8.	Thailand
9.	Turkey
10.	Mexico

Source: Institute of International Education

The New York Times

THE NEW YORK TIMES METROPOLITAN SUNDAY, MARCH 11, 1990

Alien Students Learn More Education Is the Key

By MARVINE HOWE

It was Rap Day at John Dewey High School last week, and most of the workshops focused on sex and drugs. But in room 343, it was standing room only as students, teachers and professionals discussed the really hot topic of the times — the rights of illegal immigrant children.

Lawyers and other experts emphasized to the students that New York City's public schools are open to all young people, whether or not they are in the country legally. They also passed out Board of Education leaflets welcoming "undocumented and documented immigrants" in six languages.

"But if I can't get a job, why should I get an education?" an Asian teen-ager asked, expressing the frustration of many undocumented students. For illegal teen-agers, the 1986 Immigration Reform and Control Act has been both an opportunity and an obstacle. The act offered illegal aliens a brief amnesty in which to become legal, but also created stiff penalties for employers who hire illegals.

"Hope," responded Kathleen Jarvis, who heads the Advocates for Children's Immigrant Student Rights Project. "Eventually that law is going to change, so get your foot in the door and acquire a skill the United States needs."

Train Parents and Staff

Although figures vary widely for New York City's undocumented population, Columbia University's Center for Social Sciences conservatively estimated that after the expiration of the amnesty in May 1988, 250,000 undocumented aliens remained in the country, including 46,000 children.

The visit to John Dewey, in the Coney Island section of Brooklyn, was part of a program to help immigrant schoolchildren cope with the new system, and part of a day of discussions at the school. It was organized by the City Bar Association in New York and Advocates for Children, a nonprofit organization. They train school staff and parents, run seminars for students, and operate a telephone help line.

About 40 students signed up for the workshop. At least 80 showed up.

"There's a great need to reach out to immigrant schoolchildren who are afraid to ask for help," said Laurie Milder, director of the Bar Association's Community Outreach Law Program. She said about 60 immigration lawyers have volunteered their time.

Can They Get Financial Aid?

More than 1,000 of John Dewey's 3,000 students are foreign-born, and Ms. Milder and the other speakers faced a barrage of questions.

Are illegals entitled to go to college? Can they get financial aid? How can an illegal student get a green card — permanent resident status? If an illegal student gives birth to a child here, can the mother stay in the country?

The New York Times/Vic DeLucia

During Rap Day at John Dewey High School lawyers and other experts tried to assuage some students' fears that being undocumented immigrants would prevent them from getting jobs. Kathleen Jarvis, of the Advocates for Children's Immigrant Student Rights Project, was at right.

> Many youths are surprised to find that they can go to college.

Ms. Jarvis told them that the 17 colleges of the City University of New York are open to undocumented students and do not require a student to show a Social Security number. Later she described the case of a 17-year-old star athlete in a Brooklyn high school who had been offered athletic scholarships by 13 universities. But, because she was an illegal immigrant, from the West Indies, and all the schools insisted on having a Social Security number, she had to go to CUNY.

Undocumented students used to pay nonresident tuition, double that of residents, in the city's colleges, but now they are eligible for the residents' rate.

Undocumented students are not yet eligible for Federal or state financial aid, Ms. Jarvis said. "But we advise you to take one or two courses because you'll hear about scholarships; it's like the lottery, you've got to be in it to win it."

Robert Washington, an immigration lawyer and former teacher, told the audience that while the amnesty period was over, there were other ways to become legal. Sponsorship by a close relative or acquisition of skills listed by the Labor Department as needed in the United States. Such categories include priest, minister or religious worker, physical therapist or someone of outstanding scientific or artistic ability.

An immigration judge would probably let the undocumented mother of an American-born baby stay "because the policy has been to keep families together as a general rule," Mr. Washington said.

Ms. Jarvis later described the case of a pregnant illegal teen-ager who was thrown out of her home and moved to a shelter. Lawyers said she was entitled to some welfare benefits "because she was carrying a U.S. citizen child," Ms. Jarvis said.

After the session ended — with a burst of applause — Enid Margolies, assistant principal, gathered a dozen students to prolong the discussion.

"Now maybe there's a chance for me to continue my studies," a Haitian boy of 14 said excitedly, explaining that he had not known City University accepted undocumented students. His parents had left him with an aunt, who is a United States resident, and she was willing to adopt him but her husband was reluctant.

A Cuban boy of 17, who came here more than four years ago, asked how to get a green card "so I can study and go into the Navy."

For specific problems, the students were told to call the Immigrant Students Legal Rights Helpline at (718) 729-8866.

In the past, most calls came from school counselors, but now it is mainly students who want to go to college, Ms. Jarvis said. Since undocumented students are generally afraid to disclose their identity, they are promised confidentiality and asked only their first name, age, country of origin and school.

Chapter 1

A Brief History Of American Immigration Laws & Trend: An Overview

A. A NATION OF IMMIGRANTS

The United States of America has often been described as 'truly a nation of immigrants'. As its now generally well-known history reveals, the United States was founded by immigrants – that is, by people who were not originally from the nation. And consequently, the subject of immigration and immigration laws, have always been central to the hearts and minds of the people in the United States. The vast majority of Americans (U.S. citizens) today are descendants of parents, grandparents or great-grand-parents who themselves came to the U.S. from other lands.

B. THE BEGINNINGS OF REGULATION OF IMMIGRATION

In terms of the country's immigration history, the motivating force which compelled the original wave of immigrants (other than, of course, the slave population and indentured servants) to leave their countries to settle in the United States, was to escape deprivation and persecution in their home countries. The new continent, once discovered by people from other lands (mostly from Europe), did not take long before it become a magnet to people from different countries, as they flocked to America primarily to escape negative forces in their home countries, and as a special "land of opportunity" – a place to start a new life and to make personal sacrifices in return for political, religious, and economic freedom and betterment.

Consequently, for the first 150 years of the founding of the United States, leading us to the end of the 19th century, there was basically no structured immigration policy for the United States; there was no control or limitation on the free-flow of people into and out of the country. However, starting from 1882, all that changed.

By 1882, brought on by the Gold Rush of 1849 in California, some 300,000 Chinese laborers (among others) had found their way to America from across the Pacific Ocean, contracted for labor primarily because of their very low cheap wages. The Chinese were highly valued for the cheap labor they provided for the nation's growing innumerable construction jobs, such as the construction of the Union Pacific Railroad, but were not granted the right to become citizens. Rather, because they were distinctly different from Americans in their skin color, culture, habits and looks, they were indiscriminately subjected to widespread racial discrimination and hatred by Americans. It culminated in the passage of the first restrictive immigration law in the history of the United States – the Chinese Exclusion Act of 1882, which completely banned non-citizen Chinese from immigrating to the United States.

Since the Chinese Exclusion Act of 1882, the United States immigration policy has developed and been modified periodically to meet the changing needs or desires of the nation. A series of immigration laws have been enacted, designed to place restriction on immigration and to control the type and number of people who may enter or stay in that country.

C. HIGHLIGHTS IN U.S. LEGISLATIVE IMMIGRATION HISTORY

The following are some of the major highlights in the legislative and legal history of immigration to the United States.

1798 – the Alien Act: This gave the President authority to expel aliens who he considered to be dangerous to the peace and security of the nation. Was terminated two years later, however.

***1808 – U.S. Constitution, Article 1, Section 9*:** Constitutional amendment banned the importation of slaves.

1875 – Qualitative restrictions on immigration: Congress designated categories of aliens (communists, prostitutes, mental and physical incompetents) who were prohibited from entering the United States.

1882 – Chinese Exclusion Act: The increasing importation of low-wage Chinese labor resulted in growing public antagonism and racial hated. The law banned the future immigration of Chinese laborers into the United States and excluded them from citizenship, and remained in effect until 1943.

1892 – Amendment to the Chinese Exclusion Act: Required registration of Chinese laborers living in United States and authorized deportation if after one year they could not produce a certificate of registration.

1907 – Immigration Act: Restricted entry of immigrants over 16 years of age who were unable to read who came from central and eastern Europe, and permitted no immigration at all to the U.S. from the Asiatic Barred zone which included Orientals like China, Japan, India, Indochina, Iran, Arabia, etc. *This law marked the beginning of a great change in American immigration policy.*

1921 – First Quota law: After World War 1, with America facing economic depression and unemployment, the immigrant to America became the public scapegoat for the hard times and the mood of the country was such that Congress established the first numerical restrictions on immigration limiting the number of aliens of each nationality who were permitted into the United States to 3% of the foreign-born persons of that nationality living in American during the 1910 census, and allowing a total of approximately 350,000 to immigrate annually. (Aliens residing for one year in an independent country of the Western Hemisphere prior to admission to the United States, were exempt from the quota.)

1924 – National Origins Act: The 1921 law, which had been enacted as a temporary measure, was made permanent by this statute. For the first time, Congress established permanent numerical restrictions on immigration of aliens to the United States from all parts of the world, except the Western Hemisphere, under a ceiling of 150,000 per year, with national quotas based on the ethnic composition of the United States in the 1920 census. Prospective immigrants were required to obtain a sponsor in the United States and a visa from an American consulate abroad. Further restrictions were placed on Asian immigration, particularly prohibiting the immigration of all aliens who were ineligible for U.S. citizenship.

The object of the law was expressed to be "to arrest a trend toward a change in the fundamental composition of the American stock" – that is, not simply to limit immigration of certain aliens (e.g. those from southern and eastern Europe), but to favor certain kinds of immigrants (e.g. western Europeans) and keep out others completely (e.g.

Asians were completely excluded).

1940 - Alien Registration Act: All aliens in the United States were required to register and be fingerprinted. The exclusion and deportation of criminal and subversive groups was expanded.

1943 – Repeal of the Chinese Exclusion Act of 1882: Residents of China were now permitted to immigrate to the United States.

1945 – War Brides Act: With the end of World War II, the American immigration door was again to open – but this time, not so wide, and only for some carefully selected groups of aliens. By this law, Congress meant to facilitate the union and immigration of 118,000 alien spouses and children of members of the U.S. armed forces who had fought and married or fathered children overseas.

1948 – Displaced Persons Act: This legislation provided for the admission of 400,000 refugees from Germany, Italy, and Austria to the United States. These were mostly persons who had been displaced during the war from other countries (Poland, Romania, Hungary, the Baltic, Ukraine and Yugoslavia) and had been placed in refugee camps in these countries.

1952 – Immigration and Nationality Act (commonly called the MacCarran-Walter Act): This is the Basic immigration law of the United States, as we know it, although frequently amended. This legislation provides for family reunification, protection of the domestic labor force and the immigration of persons with needed skills. This law consolidated and codified under a single statute, all laws relating to immigration to the United States. It provided by national origins a quota system, and unrestricted numerical immigration to the U.S. from Western Hemisphere countries.

1953 – Refugee Relief Act: When the communist Iron Curtain fell on eastern Europe, by this law an additional 214,000 refugees from communist countries were admitted to the United States.

1965 – Immigration and Nationality Act Amendments: The racially-biased national origins quota system was repealed by this legislation. Basically, these amendments introduced two basic ways of becoming an American immigrant – by family relationship to an American citizen or immigrant, and by the employment and skills needs of the U.S. Thus, a new, eight-category *"preference system"* was instituted to reunite family relationships and admit aliens with talents or job skills on a "first come, first served" basis in each category. The new law provided an annual limitation of 170,000 for immigrants from Eastern Hemisphere (Asia, Europe and Africa), and applicants from this group were subject to a preference system, and had a quota limit of 20,000 per country; immigrants from North and South America, on the other hand, had a quota limit of 120,000 and applicants were not subject to the preference system. Spouses and children of U.S. citizens and parents of citizens over 21 were exempt from numerical ceilings. Requirements for labor certifications were instituted to control the admission of skilled or unskilled foreign workers. As a separate category, an annual admission of 10,000 refugees was authorized. *With this law a new phenomenon began to emerge in the U.S. immigration system: application of admissions policies without regard to national and racial origins.*

Not too long after these amendments were enacted, the impact of the new immigration policy began to be felt even worldwide. In the United States, for example, skilled workers, who had a higher "preference" under the law than unskilled workers, immigrated more easily and in greater numbers to the United States, and highly trained professionals (doctors, lawyers, engineers, scientists, accountants, nurses, teachers, etc) departed their home countries for the United States in large numbers, and caused a "brain drain" in their home countries around the developed and developing countries.

1976 – The Immigration and Nationality Act Amendments of 1976: The aim of this law was to eliminate the inequities in the existing law between Eastern and Western Hemisphere. Hence, it extended the eight-category preference system' to all Western Hemisphere countries, together with 20,000 per country limited according to eight-category preference system which gave priority to persons having:
Close family ties with family relatives already in the United State; (b) Labor skills in short supply in the United States; (c) Refugee status..

However, additional numbers of refugees could be brought into the United States above the numerical limitations by approval of the Attorney General, as in the case of Indo-China refugees.

1978 Law - the 95th Congress made sweeping changes in immigration legislation, and these became effective in October 1978. The separate immigration quotas for Eastern and Western Hemispheres were eliminated and replaced by a worldwide numerical limitation of 290,000 persons annually. Children of one U.S. and one non–U.S. parent are now able to retain U.S. citizenship without ever living in the United States, and naturalization is now made possible for anyone who is 50 years of age and has been a legal permanent resident for 20 years. The British colony of Hong Kong was allowed a yearly quota of 5,000 immigrants into the U.S. Changes were also made in the regulations governing the adoption of foreign children and the status of refugees.

1980 – New Refugee Act: This was basically in reaction by Congress to the flood of refugees to the U.S., from two areas of the world: the Indochina with the end of the Vietnam War, and Cuba with the declaration of Fidel Castro in 1980 that the Port of Mariel was open to anyone who wanted to leave. The law basically removed the preferential treatment of refugees from the Communist countries and redefined a refugee more literally as being simply someone who fears persecution in his or her home country based on religious or political beliefs, race, national origin, or ethnic affiliation. (Later, by the immigration Act of 1990 – see below – the refugee policy of the U.S. was further expanded; a refugee was now defined to include a person fleeing war or natural disasters, such as earthquakes, flood, etc).

Congress eliminated the seventh preference and allotted 6% of this numerical allocation of worldwide visa numbers to the second preference. Distinctions in the definitions of "refugee" and "asylum" provide for new procedures for those people to become permanent residents in the United States. A limit of 50,000 refugees was authorized by Congress to enter the United States in 1980, 1981, and 1982. The annual worldwide limitation on visa numbers for immigrants to the United States was reduced to 270,000 persons.

1986 – Immigration Reform and Control Act of 1986: The law, more commonly known as the Amnesty Law, opened the U.S immigration still wider: it legalized the legal status of aliens who were already in the United States without legal status since January 1982, while at the same time trying to control the future influx of illegal aliens into the nation. The law established the following measures:

(a) Civil and criminal sanctions/penalties imposed against all employers who knowingly hire illegal aliens.
(b) Illegal aliens who resided in the U.S. prior to January 1, 1981 were granted amnesty and allowed to apply for legalization of their status as permanent residents in the U.S; and
(c) Spouses of U.S. Citizens and Permanent Alien Residents were accorded "conditional" Resident Status, and

after 24 months of obtaining the immigrant visa, must apply to the INS for permanent resident status if the marriage is bona fide and not terminated by divorce. Changes were made in the law to prevent fraudulent marriages by aliens in order to acquire immigration benefits.

1990 - The Immigration Act of 1990: This is probably the most comprehensive overhaul of the U.S. immigration law by Congress since 1965. The law provided a huge increase in the number of aliens that could enter the country annually (700,000 in each of the years 1992 to 1994, and 675,000 from 1995 onwards). *But, even more importantly, the law solidified a policy shift in the nation's basic U.S. immigration objective:* the thrust of the policy would be to emphasize attracting persons who possess certain desirable or preferred occupational skills or economic resources. To be sure, the law still maintains the traditional immigration policy of providing for the unification of families and close relatives of U.S. citizens, and, though to a lesser extent, of permanent resident aliens. But the primary, dominant emphasis was to attract aliens who have the education, occupational skills or money to contribute to and to enhance the economic growth and well-being of the U.S. Thus, the law, now for the first time ever, established a specific category of permanent visa meant for millionaire entrepreneurs and investors who establish or invest in new job creating enterprises. And, as anticipated, the new law has been hugely successful in the area of attracting doctors, lawyers, engineers, scientists, accountants, nurses, teachers, inventors and other such highly skilled professionals to the United States.

1996 - Illegal Immigration Reform and Immigrant Responsibility Act (IIRAIRA): The law, designed primarily to stem the flow of illegal immigration to the U.S., contains some of the toughest provisions ever enacted by Congress in immigration matters. For example, under this law, immigrants living in the United States who have been long-term law abiding citizens of the nation, may still be subject to deportation, and an immigrant's dependents such as his or her spouses and children, who may have inadvertently exceeded or violated his or her visa status, is readily deportable.

Chapter 2

All The Different Types Of Visas By Which One Can Gain Entry Into The U.S: The Immigrant & Non-Immigrant Visas

A. WHAT IS A VISA?

A visa is, in a word, a document issued to an alien person (i.e., a foreign person or non-national of the U.S.) by the responsible U.S. government agency, which authorizes the alien person to lawfully enter the United States. This authorization would usually be stamped in your (the alien's) passport by an America consul (a U. S. government officer) in a U.S. Embassy abroad, or an immigration agency official within the United States. This formality merely conforms with the common procedure in international law.

Under the international law which applies, as well, to virtually every country in the world, in order to lawfully enter the United States from another country (with the possible exception of Canada and certain "exempted" countries which are, by special arrangement, exempt from this rule)*, every person must, in addition to having a passport from his/her own home country, be granted a "visa" from an American Embassy or Consulate – that is, a U.S. government's (written) permission – allowing him to enter the U.S. If you enter the United States with a valid visa – with the proper permission – you are called a "legal" alien by the U.S. immigration authorities. On the other hand, if you were to enter the country without a valid visa – without the proper documents showing the required government permission – you are called an "illegal" alien or "undocumented alien," and would face a lot of difficulties at the hands of the U.S. government authorities in trying to live and function in the United States.

Under the immigration laws and regulations of the United States, the term "ALIEN" is used to denote "any person not a citizen or a national of the United States." In other words, every person applying for entry to the United States – unless he or she is a U.S. citizen or a national – is an "alien" under the parlance of the U.S. immigration authorities.

B. THE TWO MAJOR BROAD GROUPS OF U.S. VISAS

In the broadest term, there are TWO kinds of visas that an alien person can receive from the U.S. Embassy or Consulate in order to gain admission into (or to remain in) the United States: either an IMMIGRANT type of visa, or a NON-IMMIGRANT type of visa.

**See pp 14–15 for a list of such countries*

1. The Immigrant Type of Visa

The IMMIGRANT type of visa is the visa for the alien who is intent on entering the United States for permanent stay or residence there. With this kind of visa, you are given an unlimited amount of time; the legal right to live and work permanently in the country. There is only ONE kind of immigrant visa (also called "permanent residency visa" or the "green card"), and it is the type of visa which, once obtained, has no other classification or conditions attached to it.

There are two or three basic ways by which to secure a "green card" (the name by which the immigrant visa is popularly known): through having a family relationship to a U.S. citizen such as being married to a U.S. citizen, or through having an employment relationship or labor certification for an employment in the United States (see Chapter 3 for the full details). However, for our purposes here in this chapter, what is important for you to know, is that regardless of the avenue by which you obtain a green card, *all Green Cards are exactly the same in terms of the rights and privileges they confer on the holder of the card; they confer upon you an unlimited right to work and live in the U.S. for as long as you wish, whether permanently or otherwise.* One other major distinction which applies between the immigrant type of visa and the non-immigrant type, is that the number of immigrant visas issued by the U.S. government each year, is limited by a quota, while the number of non-immigrant visas issued in the various categories, is unlimited by law or any quota.

TYPES OF U.S. VISAS AVAILABLE

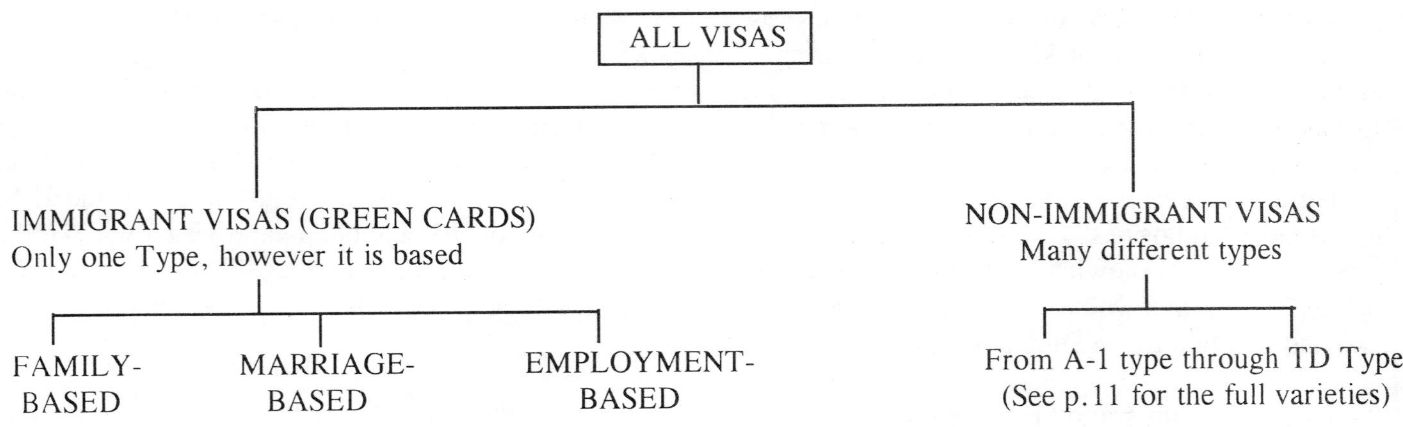

2. The Non-Immigrant Type of Visa

The NON-IMMIGRANT type of visa, on the other hand, is the visa for the alien who is intent on entering and staying in the U.S. for a temporary period of time and for limited purposes (such as to visit or to do business or study, and the like). With this kind of visa, you are given the legal right to stay in the U.S. for a temporary period of time with limited rights.

Unlike the immigrant visa, which has only one classification, there are, however, many different types and classes of Non-immigrant visas and each type has its own set of qualifications and rights and conditions in terms of the duration of the visa and the rights and privileges to which the card holder is entitled, or the activities he/she may or may not lawfully engage in. On the average, unlike the immigrant visas, which can take months or even years to obtain because of the quota requirements, non-immigrant visas can usually be obtained very quickly.

C. THE DIFFERENT TYPES OR CLASSES OF NON-IMMIGRANT VISA AVAILABLE

There are, in all, about 56 different "classes" (types) into which the non-immigrant visa category is divided. (See Figure 2 - 1 below).

As previously stated, there are a variety of types of non-immigrant visas for the reason that each type is issued for a specific and different purpose. Consequently, when you are issued a non-immigrant visa of a specific kind or the other, the government, assuming simply that you will perform the applicable specific activity while you are in the United States, will merely issue you a specialized visa authorizing that particular activity (paying a visit, or undertaking a course of study, for example), and no other activity. Furthermore, in contrast to an immigrant type of visa, which is in all instances absolutely permanent in character, all non immigrant visas have one major thing in common: they are all temporary in character, granted only for a specific period of time deemed reasonable to have completed the authorized activities for which that type of visa is granted. As an alien involved in a visa application or processing for a nonimmigrant type of visa with a U.S. Embassy (or Consulate), you will often hear the Embassy officials refer to such classifications in shorthand by a symbol composed of a letter followed by a number.

The following chart provides a summary of all the nonimmigrant U.S. visa classifications or types that are available.

Figure 2-1

VISA CLASSIFICATION SYMBOL	CLASS (TYPE) OF NON-IMMIGRANT VISA	MAXIMUM ADMISSION PERIOD
A-1	High foreign government officials, such as ambassadors, public ministers, consular officers or career diplomats, and their immediate family members	Duration of status
A-2	Other foreign government officials or employees and their immediate families	Duration of their status
A-3	Personal attendants, servants or employees of A-1 or A-2 visa holders, and their immediate families	1 year
B-1	Temporary Visitors for business	6 months
B-2	Temporary Visitors for pleasure or tourism	6 months
C-1	Alien travelers in immediate and continuous transit through the U.S.	Not more than 29 days

C-2	Alien traveler in transit to or from the United Nations Headquarters	Duration of status in transit to U. N.
D-1	Crewmen (sea or air) remaining with vessel or aircraft	Time carrier is in port not to exceed 29 days from arrival
D-2	Crewmen (sea or air) discharged from vessel or aircraft arrival	Not to exceed 29 days from
E-1	Treaty trader, his spouse or children, if accompanying of following to join him	2 years
E-2	Treaty investor, his spouse or children accompanying or following to join him	Duration of status
F-1	A student coming to pursue a full course of study at a qualified institution	Duration of status
F-2	The Spouse or minor child(ren) of the F-1 alien	Same as in F-1
G-1	Designated principal resident representative of a foreign government coming to the U.S. to work for an international organization and his/her staff members and immediate families	Duration of status
G-2	Other representatives of foreign governments coming to the U.S to work for an international organization, and their immediate families	Duration of status
G-3	Representatives of foreign governments and their immediate families who would ordinarily qualify for G-1 or G-2 visas except that their governments are not members of an international organization	Duration of status
G-4	Officers of employees of international organizations and their immediate families	Duration of status
G-5	Attendants, servants and personal employees of G-1 through G-4 visa holders, and their immediate families	1 year
H-1B	Alien temporary worker of some distinguished merit or ability coming to perform exceptional service or services requiring such qualities, and/or to work in a specialty occupation requiring at least a bachelor's degree or its equivalent in on-the-job experience.	2 years with possible 1 year extension up to 5 years
H-2A	Temporary agricultural workers coming to the U.S to fill positions for which a temporary labor shortage of American workers had been recognized and declared by the U.S Department of Agriculture	2 years
H-2B	Temporary workers of various kinds coming to the U.S. to perform temporary jobs of skilled or unskilled labor for which there is a shortage of available qualified American workers	2 years
H-3	Temporary trainee worker coming as "Industrial Trainee"	Length of program
H-4	Spouses or minor children of H-1B, H-2A, H-2B or H-3 visa holders	Duration of H-1B, H-2A, or H-2B or H-3 alien
I	Bona fide representative of foreign press, radio, film, or other information media, coming solely to engage in such vocation, and his spouse or minor child(ren) if accompanying or following to join him	1 year
J-1	So-called "Exchange Visitor": a bona fide student, scholar, trainee, teacher, professor, research assistant, specialist, leader in a specialized field of knowledge or skill, or similar person, coming to participate in a program designated	

	by the U.S. Secretary of State for the purpose of pursuing such activity.	Duration of status
J-2	Spouse and minor children of J-1 alien, if accompanying or following to join him.	Same at J-1 alien
K-1	Alien fiancées and fiancés of U.S. citizens coming to the U.S. for the purpose of getting married.	90 days
K-2	Children of K-1 aliens	Same as K–1 alien
L-1	Intra-company transferees who work as managers, executives or persons with specialized knowledge.	1 year interval extend-able to 3 years.
L-2	Spouses and minor children accompanying or following to join L-1 alien	Same as for L-1 above
M-1	Vocational or other nonacademic students	Duration of status, but generally 1 year
M-2	Immediate family members of an M-1 visa holder	Same as for M-1 alien.
N	Children of certain special immigrants	Varied
'NATO alien'-1	Principal permanent representatives of member states to North Atlantic Treaty Organization or NATO, including subsidiary bodies who are resident in the U.S., and resident official staff members, secretaries general, assistant secretaries general, and executive secretaries of NATO, other permanent NATO officials of similar rank, or their immediate families.	Duration of status
NATO-2	Other representatives to NATO member states, including any subsidiary bodies, its advisers and technical experts of delegations, members of Immediate Articles 3, 4 UST 1796 families; dependents of members of armed forces entering in accordance with the Status-of-Forces Agreement or in accordance with the Protocol on Status of International Military Headquarters; members of such a force, it issued	Duration of status
NATO-3	Officials clerical staff accompanying representatives of NATO member states, including any subsidiary bodies, or their immediate families	Duration of status
NATO-4	Official of NATO, other than those who can be classified as NATO-1, or their immediate families	Duration of status
NATO-5	NATO "expert," or member of a civilian component, other than officials who can be classified as NATO-1, accompanying or attached to a force under the NATO, and their dependants.	1 year
NATO-6	Members of civilian components accompanying forces entering in accordance with provisions of the NATO Status-of-Forces Agreement; members of civilian components attached to or employed by allied headquarters under the Protocol on Status of International Military Headquarters set up pursuant to the North Atlantic Treaty, and their dependents	1 year
NATO-7	Attendants, servants or personal employees of aliens of NATO-1 through NATO-6 classes, or their immediate families	1 year
O-1	Aliens of extraordinary ability in the sciences, arts, education, business or athletics	2 years with possible 1 year extensions up to 5 years.

O-2	Accompanying aliens of O-1	Same as O-1 alien
O-3	Spouses or children of O-1 or O-2 visa holders	Same as O-1 alien
P-1	Internationally recognized athletes and entertainers	Duration of program
P-2	Artists or entertainers in reciprocal exchange programs	Duration of program
P-3	Artists and entertainers coming to the U.S. to give culturally unique performances in a group	Duration of program
P-4	Spouses or children of P-1, P-2 or P-3 visa holders	Same as for P-1, P-2, or P-3 alien
Q-1	Participants in international cultural exchange programs	Duration of program
Q-2	Immediate family members of Q-1 visa holders	Same as or Q-1 alien.
R-1	Ministers and other aliens in religious occupation	2 years
R-2	Spouses or children of R-1 visa holders	Same as R-1 alien
S-1	Certain aliens supplying critical information relating to a criminal organization or enterprise	Duration of need or status
S-2	Certain aliens supplying critical information relating to terrorism	Duration of need or status
S-3	Immediate family members of S-1 or S-2 visa holders	Same of S-1 alien
TN	NAFTA professionals	1 year
TD	Spouses or children of NAFTA professionals	Same as TN alien

D. A FEW SPECIAL CASES WHEN ALIENS MAY BE EXEMPTED FROM HAVING A VISA FOR ENTRY INTO THE U.S.

In other chapters of this manual, we shall outline in great detail the applicable qualifications and requirements needed, as well as the procedures, for applying for and obtaining each of the various types of visas outlined in Section B and/or C above. However, for your immediate information, you should note that under a relatively new agreement between the U.S. government and some 21 countries or so, there are situations when citizens of a few select countries are allowed to come to the United States without first obtaining a visa, providing the interested person meets certain minimal conditions.

THE VISA WAIVER PROGRAM

Under a special program called the VISA WAIVER PILOT PROGRAM which was started by the U.S. Department of State's (DOS) in 1989, applicants for U.S. visas from certain approved countries (see list below) who are clearly temporary visitors requiring a tourist visa, are allowed to enter the U.S. as tourists without having or using visa. All that they require are a passport from their home country and a round-trip ticket. And, upon their arrival at a U.S. port of entry, the U.S. Immigration and Naturalization Service will readily admit them without any questions.

1. Countries Which Are Covered In the Visa Exemption Program

As a matter of U.S. policy, countries included or includable in the Visa Waiver Program usually demonstrate certain basic common characteristics: they would generally have a low rate of refusals of tourist visa applications, and would have evidence of very few violations of the U.S. immigration laws, particularly with regard to over-staying their visa and working illegally in United States.

As of this writing, the following countries are included among the countries whose citizens and passport holders are exempt from having a visa in order to enter the United States:

Andorra
Argentina
Austria
Australia
Belgium
Brunei
Denmark
Finland
France
Germany
Great Britain
(United Kingdom)
Holland
(Netherlands)
Iceland
Ireland
Italy
Japan
Liechtenstein
Luxembourg
Monaco
New Zealand
Norway
San Marino
Slovenia
Spain
Sweden
Switzerland

NOTE: Under the Visa Waiver Program, the U.S. Department of State, which is the policy administrator of the program, is authorized to expand or to decrease the number of countries eligible for the program from time to time. Furthermore, as a rule, visa application rules and procedures may change from time to time, and at times visa application procedures may differ from one U.S. consulate to the next. Hence, it is always wise – and hereby strongly advised – that you check with your U.S. consulate to be sure that your country is currently included among the list of visa exempt countries before you set out on your travel.

2. The Minimum Conditions Required

To be eligible to come to the U.S. without first obtaining a visa under the visa waiver program, you only need to meet the following conditions:

- You (the person seeking entry into the U.S.), have to be planning to come to the United States for a duration not more than 90 days;
- there are no reasons, or "grounds of exclusion" (usually meaning criminal convictions), why you should not be admitted to the United States;
- you will be flying on a *participating* airline (check to see if an airline is participating before you pay for your ticket);
- you will be able to show a round ticket at the time of your departure out of your country and arrival in a U.S. port of entry as evidence that you are simply visiting and will return to your country not later than 90 days.

THE NEW YORK TIMES SUNDAY
FEBRUARY 24, 1980
SPOTLIGHT

He Gets Visas for the Famous

By SUSAN HELLER ANDERSON

Robin Laurance

Richard D. Fraade, immigration lawyer

LONDON — Well-heeled, well-educated and wanting a piece of America, hundreds of thousands of foreign business executives, professionals, skilled workers and heavy investors emigrate annually to the United States. In contrast to the impoverished or persecuted refugees who have historically flocked to American shores, they sport Savile Row suits and Vuitton luggage.

On hand to help them through the complicated entry process is a fast-growing group of legal professionals — the immigration lawyers. More than 1,200 attorneys are engaged solely in this specialty, which until five years ago was all but ignored in law schools.

One immigration lawyer is Richard D. Fraade of Beverly Hills and — since early this year — London. Attorney for some of the world's most prominent would-be Americans, Mr. Fraade is believed to be the first of the lawyers to open an office in London, the scene of much immigration activity. The United States Embassy's visa office on Grosvenor Square is the world's busiest and expects to issue a million visas in fiscal 1980, a 30 percent increase over 1979.

Under American law, every visiting alien must have a visa. About 80 percent of the visas issued here are for tourists and present little problem. The rest go to persons who want to work, either temporarily or permanently, and these people must enter a lengthy and complicated process that can take months and often years. The immigration lawyer finds ways to facilitate this process.

Parts of the immigration system are fraught with scandal and red tape. Some lawyers have mastered it by skirting the law, but no such charges have been made against Mr. Fraade and Embassy officials here say that immigration lawyers can perform a useful service.

"When Elton John comes to the U.S., he needs a temporary work permit," Mr. Fraade explained. "He's not going to queue up on Grosvenor Square." Of the more than 500 active clients on Mr. Fraade's books in Beverly Hills 90 percent are European.

Mr. Fraade's services have been employed by Roger Vadim, the film director, Joe Bugner, the boxer, Diana Dors, the actress, musicians Oscar Peterson and the Little River Band, Columbia Pictures, the University of Southern California, model agencies run by Eileen Ford, Wilhelmina and Johnny Casablancas, and virtually all of the toney French restaurants in Los Angeles. He has engineered temporary work permits for dozens of servants to the stars. Other clients are large employers of skilled workers, such as the California-based aircraft and silicon chip industries.

Describing himself as a "Europhile and Anglophile in particular," Mr. Fraade attires himself in English pin stripes and shirts bought from the international peacocks' shop, Turnbull and Asser. "I'm a suitoholic," he confessed. Having descended from Russian immigrants "of the pushcart variety," and having lived abroad, he said, helps him to identify with his clients. Shortly after he was born in Oklahoma City in 1942 his parents moved to New York, then, after the war, to Düsseldorf. "That gave me the introduction to Europe that marked me," said Mr. Fraade. The family later went West and Mr. Fraade was graduated from the University of California at Los Angeles. He attended Brooklyn Law School. "When I graduated in 1968 immigration law was not taught," he recalled.

"To stay out of the Army I taught school in Bedford Stuyvesant," he said, "then went into the special prosecutor's office under New York State Attorney General Louis Lefkowitz in 1970. Meanwhile, I continued traveling to Europe."

"Through friends I met girls coming to New York who wanted to work as models," he said. He moonlighted by shepherding their visa applications through the Labor and Justice Departments. In 1975 he returned to California, passed the bar and set up the immigration department for a large law firm. He started his own practice last August in Beverly Hills.

Last month he placed a discreet ad in the London Financial Times announcing the opening of his London office. He got enough responses to indicate there was a potential market here for his services. "Coming to England is a logical extension of what's been happening in my practice," he said.

"I charge a flat fee," Mr. Fraade said, "from $3,000 to $7,500 depending on the case. The lower figure is more usual. I also try to do some pro bono work taking immigrant cases for no fee." In London the fee is slightly higher.

For immigrant visas, priority is given to relatives of United States citizens. Only two categories apply to immigrants wishing to work who have no American relatives. The sixth-preference category — skilled and semiskilled workers — has a backlog of six to eight months. The third preference — professionals, scientists and artists — has no backlog. "Vadim is clearly third preference," Mr. Fraade said. "But a top chef? The law's not so clear." Some 90 percent of his clients seeking permanent residency are in the third- or sixth-preference categories and his job is often to convince visa officers of the validity of their claims. "Here the advocacy role can be helpful," said Alan Gise, United States consul general here.

Investors, however, are not given preference and, because the flow of immigrants is now so heavy that quotas are often filled by the preference categories alone, prospects are dim. Mr. Fraade has a solution.

On his latest trip he saw a client in Frankfurt whom he described as a top German industrialist. "He's convinced Europe is in a state of moral, economic and political decay and that Russia will take over. He won't make any more capital investments in Europe," Mr. Fraade said. "He wants to emigrate to America, the last bastion of capital enterprise. The structuring of a business affiliate lets him come on an E-2 Treaty-Investor visa — the next best thing to a green card." A "green card," which is in fact blue and white, is a permanent resident's permit.

Consular officials admit to mixed feelings about immigration lawyers but concede that, for corporations and investors in particular, they are useful. "The system is set up so no one should require a lawyer," Mr. Gise noted. "But in practice if you are an investor the immigration lawyer prepares the papers, oversees the transfer of funds, sees that requirements are met." Mr. Fraade has a client who wants to set up a subsidiary in California, which requires incorporation in that state. While his Beverly Hills office begins the incorporation procedure his brother Robert, in London, gathers the personal documents necessary for the client's visa, perhaps saving months.

Chapter 3

The Various Types Of Non-Immigrant Visas Available: An Overview

A. THERE ARE MANY DIFFERENT TYPES OF NON-IMMIGRANT VISAS

In Chapter 2, we explain that while there are a great many types of U.S. visas available, all visas fall into only Two broad classes – either an IMMIGRANT type of visa, commonly called the Green Card, or a NON-IMMGRANT type of visa. And, basically, the difference between the two types of visa, is that the Immigrant type of visa (more commonly known as the Green Card, although the visa is not really Green), gives the holder the right to live and work in the U.S. indefinitely for as long as he or she wants, while the Non-Immigrant types of visa would give the holder the right to come to the U.S. for a specific purpose for a short period (usually not less than 6 months or more than a few years), and, in certain cases, depending on the type of nonimmigrant visa, to accept certain types of employment while there in the U.S. In a word, the immigrant visas are PERMANENT in nature, while the Nonimmigrant visas are TEMPORARY.

B. THE SELECTED NON-IMMIGRANT VISA CLASSES WE SHALL ADDRESS IN THIS MANUAL

As is also explained in Chapter 2 (see Sections B.2 and C. thereof), unlike the immigrant visa, all of which are only of one type, there are many different varieties ("classes") of Non-Immigrant visas and each type has its own set of requirements for qualification, the specific rights and privileges it offers its holder, as well as its specific duration and expiration date, and the activities which the holder of the visa may or may not lawfully engage in.

There are, in all, about 56 or so such different "classes" of immigrant visas, most of which are listed in the summary listing on Chart 2 at p. 11.

As a practical matter, we cannot possibly cover in any meaningful details all the available nonimmigrant visa classifications. Hence, in this book, we shall limit ourselves only to the treatment of the most important and most commonly used nonimmigrant visa classifications, those that are of interest to, and are used in great numbers by, the largest number of people applying for non-immigrant visas. We leave out those types of nonimmigrant visas which are very specialized or used mostly by very limited classes of people (e.g. the A-1 type of visa for foreign government officials, the in-transit C-1 visa, crewmen D-1 or D-2 visa, the NATO alien visa, and the like).

Starting from the Chapter 4, we shall discuss in each chapter of the manual, one specific class of non-immigrant visa (or some two or more related classes, where applicable), setting forth in detail the specific and specialized procedures for filing for the particular visa classification, and the eligibility standards and qualifications that apply for obtaining it.

Here are the non-immigrant visa classes that we shall discuss in the succeeding chapters. They are listed below in the order in which they will be treated in the manual, namely, both by name and by the short-hand symbols by which they are more popularly called by the immigration officials:

1. Temporary Visitors – B-1 and B-2 visas (see Chapter 4)
2. Treaty Traders – E-1 and E-2 visas (Treated in Chapter 5)
3. Academic Students – F-1, F-2 visas (Treated in Chapter 6)
4. Temporary Specialty Workers – H-IB visas (Treated in Chapter 7)
5. Temporary Workers in Non-agricultural Occupations – H-2B visas (Treated in Chapter 8)
6. Temporary Trainees – H-3 visas (Treated in Chapter 9)
7. Exchange Visitors – J-1 visas (Treated in Chapter 6)
8. Alien Fiancées or Fiancés of U.S. Citizens – K-1 and K-2 visas (see Chapter 10)
9. Intra-company trasfees – L-1 and L-2 visas (Treated in Chapter 11)
10. Vocational students – M-1 and M-2 visas (Treated in Chapter 6)
11. Aliens of extraordinary ability in the Sciences, Arts, Education, Business and Athletics – 0-1, 0-2, and O-3 visas (Treated in Chapter 12)
12. Internationally recognized athletes, entertainers and artists – P-1, P-2, P-3, P-4 visas (Treated in Chapter 12)
13. Ministers, Religious Workers & Other Aliens in Religious Occupations – R-1, R-2 visas (Treated in Chapter 12)

Chapter 4

Getting A Visa As a Business Or Tourist Visitor: The B-1 And B-2 Visas

A. WHAT IS A B-1 OR B-2 VISA

The B type of visa is by far the visa used by the largest number of non-immigrants applying to go to the United States. Indeed, the great majority of foreign persons who enter the U.S. every year do so through the use of a visitors' visa or B type visa, and are granted the visa either for business purposes (B-1 visa), or for tourism and pleasure (the B-2 visa). Like all non-immigrant visas, B visas are, of course, granted only to those applicants who are seeking entry into the U.S. for a limited, temporary period of time, and who will, while in the U.S. continue to maintain a permanent status abroad. Generally, B-1 visas are available to visitors who are making a business trip, while B-2 visas are for those coming as tourists and other purposes. Sometimes, however, the American Consulate which issues the visa in a particular country will issue a B-1/B-2 visa which covers visits made for business or pleasure, or a combination of the two purposes.

According to the U.S. Foreign Affairs Manual, it is the explicit policy objective of the U. S. Government that the processing of the visitor's visa applications be expedited for "the facilitation of international travel [is very important] both for its cultural and social advantage to the world and for its economic significance". Nevertheless, it has equally been true that over the years, an increasing number of temporary visitors have used the devise of the nonimmigrant visa as an avenue by which to enter the U.S. only to remain permanently as overstays. For this reason, the immigration authorities have had to lay down a number of restrictions and strict criteria for admission, the aim of which being to attempt to limit the granting of temporary visitors only to those persons who are really bona-fide nonimmigrants and would actually stay in the U.S. only temporary.

B. WHO QUALIFIES

Basically, to qualify, you (the alien applicant) must be able to establish the following to the U S. visa officer's satisfaction:

(i.) that you have a permanent residence in your foreign county to which you would return and have no intention of abandoning (see Chapter 14 on the critical issue of the alien's "intent");

(ii.) that you intend to enter the U.S. only for a temporary period of specifically limited duration;

(iii.) that you are doing so "'to engage solely in legitimate activities relating to business or pleasure" (see Chapter 14 on the critical issues of the alien's "intent");

(iv.) that you have the necessary financial capacity to conduct a business or pleasure trip in the U.S., and have a round trip ticket available; and

(v.) that you are not otherwise disqualified (excludable) from entering the U.S. for criminal or reasons. (see Chapter 17).

The fundamental rule relating to the granting of this visa is simple: that under no circumstances may the holder of this visa (B type of visa) engage in activities which will result in financial compensation of any kind – wages, tips, fees, commissions, etc. The following, for example, have been considered acceptable activities for visitors for pleasure (B-2) applicants: tourism, social visits to relatives and friends, visits for health purposes or to participate in amateur sports or music contest and like activities, providing no payment is given for such participation, trip to visit schools in the U.S. as a prospective student, or to appear as a party or witness in a legal proceeding. And such activities as the following have been considered acceptable activities for visitors for business (B-1) applicants: taking of commercial orders in the U.S. for a specialized product or service to be filled in a foreign country, negotiating in conferences or seminars of scientific, business or professional nature, visiting to install or repair machinery or equipment which was purchased overseas or to train others for such activities, and the undertaking of independent research, participation in Board of Directors meetings or in professional athletic events involving payment limited to the prize money.

Common Factors Typically Considered In Deciding Whether a B Visa Could Be Granted.

In making the determination as to whether to qualify an applicant as a visitor, the U.S. consular officer often uses a "profile" as aid in determining whether a person might be a poor risk for receiving a B-1 or B-2 visa. Here are the kinds of factors the consular officials would generally consider:

i. Are the arrangements you (the alien visa applicant) have made for meeting the expenses of your visit and your return passage sufficiently adequate to make it unnecessary for you to have to obtain employment in the U.S.?

ii. Might you have to work for pay while in the U.S. or attend a school full-time?

iii. Are your financial arrangements in any way dependent on assurances that relatives or friends in the U.S. will provide all or part of your financial support? If so, are there "forceful and compelling" ties existing between you and such sponsors which would lead the consular official to believe that the sponsors' assurances will in deed be undertaken?

iv. Does it seem that you have "specific and realistic plans" for undertaking those things for which you are applying to make the visit, or, on the other hand, are your intentions merely "vague and uncertain"?

v. Is the period of time for which you are planning to visit consistent with the stated purpose of your trip? And have you established with "reasonable certainty" that you will leave the U.S. upon completion of the stated purpose of your trip?

vi. Is there any indication that you (the applicant) gave conscious consideration to your proposed period of stay, or are your intentions simply expressed in terms of remaining in the U.S. for the maximum time the U.S. authorities will allow, or for the period for which friends and relatives have invited you?

vii. Are you the principal wage earner for your family? If so, can you satisfactorily explain how your spouse and children will be provided for in your absence, and why you would wish to be separated from the family for a lengthy period of time, if it so applies?

viii. Do you have reasonably permanent and well-paying employment or business, or social or family relationships in your homeland significant enough to make you want to return home?*

As is the case in most visa application situations, it is upon YOU (the visa applicant) that the whole burden falls to prove and demonstrate to the satisfaction of the consular and immigration authorities, that you have no intention of abandoning your foreign residence for good and that you will depart the U.S. voluntarily at the end of your authorized stay.

C. APPLICATION PROCEDURES FOR A VISA

1. Determine Where You Are To File:Is It Abroad,Or In The U.S.?

Except, perhaps, for the visitors' visa, which obviously has to be applied for from outside the United States, virtually every other non-immigrant type of visa may be applied for either from the U.S. consulate outside the United States, or from within the U.S. at an Immigration and Naturalization Service (INS) office. The overwhelming majority of nonimmigrant visa applications, however, are filed at consulates abroad. This is so primarily because most nonimmigrant visa application cases simply don't qualify for U.S. filing.

---

*If, for example, you are young, single and without permanent employment in your home country (e.g. a recently graduated student), expect to find it really difficult, probably impossible, to be issued a visa, no matter what financial guarantees are made on your behalf by a U.S. sponsor. Likewise, aliens with immediate family members permanently residing in the U.S. might have to demonstrate substantial ties to their home country to assure visa issuance.

What options are open to you in terms of choosing to file abroad or in the United States? In the first place, if you are already physically present in the U.S. illegally, then in such a case consular filing is the ONLY option for you. An alien in such a circumstance, is not eligible to process what is known as a "status" application – meaning an application to change from one nonimmigrant status to another nonimmigrant status. On the other hand, if you are already in the U.S. legally on some other type of nonimmigrant visa, then you qualify to apply for a specific other nonimmigrant visa you might want at an INS office inside the U.S., using a procedure known as a "change of status" which technically says that you are switching from one nonimmigrant status to another.

Basically, assuming you are physically present already in the U.S., you may apply for a non-immigrant visa status from within the U.S. ONLY IF you meet the following conditions:

- You are physically present already in the U.S.
- You are either filing the paper work for a visa petition simultaneously, or have already received an approved petition.
- You entered the U. S. legally.
- You did not enter the U. S. as a visitor without a visa under the Visa Wavier program.
- You have never worked illegally in the U.S.
- The date on your 1-94 card (the card the border inspectors give you whenever you enter the U.S. which states the period of stay for which you are authorized) has not passed.
- You are not otherwise legally inadmissible to the U.S. and none of the bars to changing status apply to you (see Chapter 17).

Assuming you are physically present in the U.S., and that you meet the above listed conditions, then you may file for your nonimmigrant visa at an INS office in the U.S. But if otherwise, then you have only one place to file – at the U.S. consulate in your home country.

2. Inquire About Your Local U.S. Consulate's or INS's Filing Policy Procedures

Generally speaking, the procedures and requirements for a visa, as well as the nature and extent of the documents which will be required in support of a visa application, vary and differ significantly among U.S. consulates overseas (see Chapter 18, Section A, for more on this). For example, for many Consulates in many countries (e.g. those in London and Canada), your visa applications may be processed by mail, and you can also simply walk into the office with your supporting documents and complete your application forms and documents there and then, and be issued your visa on the spot the same day, while for others, you'll have to submit your paperwork in advance, and then come back by an appointment for a personal interview several weeks later before you may get your visa.

Hence, before ever you commence your visa application, the first thing you should do is to phone or otherwise contact your area's U.S. consulate (or INS, if applicable) and ask about their specific local visa policies and procedures, such as any special forms or procedures for submission of papers that the consulate may utilize, and about what type of supporting documentation it may require, etc. (See Chapter 18 Sections A and B, for more on the subject of variations in policies and practices among consulates and INS offices)

A complete list of all the U.S. consulates around the world, and of the INS offices in the U.S., are outlined in Appendices, A and B respectively.

NOTE: As a rule, as much as possible, unless there are some extraordinary or unavoidable reasons why you may not do so (such as being resident in some other country for a long time, or having a permanent job or assignment there), ***you should always try to choose your home country as the place to file for your visa application.*** True, under the law presently existing (it's very likely, though, that this will probably change soon in the wake of the revolutionary September 11 2001 event), you are allowed to apply for a non-immigrant visa at any U.S. consulate of your choice. As a practical matter, however, usually your case is more likely to get a more speedy treatment and greater consideration when filed at the consulate in your place of origin, as this will make your background easier to verify and thus make your application and your underlying motivation for going outside your home to apply less subject to suspicion and concern in the minds of the consular officers.

In any event, you should know that the practice of "consulate shopping" by visa applicants is strictly frowned upon by immigration officials, as to them, such an act automatically "sets off a bell" that the applicant might have avoided his home country for a reason, and that he probably had or would have trouble of some sort with the immigration authorities in his home country.

Finally, please note that, in any case, in general if you have ever overstayed your visa in the U.S. or been present or stayed in the U.S. unlawfully, or if an immigration judge or INS official has ever determined that you were at some point in the past unlawfully present in the U.S., then you are prohibited under the current Immigration Law Amendments and Regulation of 1966 from engaging in what is known as a "third country national" or TCN visa processing – that is, applying for a visa at a U.S. consulate which is not located in one's own home country. And, in such a case, your only option is that you must return to your home country to apply from the consulate there.

3. Basic Forms Used

i. Prepare the following:

- Optional Form OF-156. As a visa applicant who files for a visa at a U.S. consulate overseas, the consulate will usually provide you with their required "optional forms" and the instructions for completing them, and such forms are designated by a prefix "OF" preceding a number, as in OF-156.
  (See illustrated sample of Form OF-156 on p. 177)

NOTE: The proper completion of this form is by far the single most important and primary thing you can do in any non-immigrant visa application which will determine ultimately whether you get the visa or not. For that reason, we set forth in one chapter, Chapter 13, a detailed, step-by-step process by which to properly complete this form, and the underlying considerations by which to answer the questions asked or to provide the information required therein. Please refer immediately to Chapter 13.

*ii. General Supporting Documents For Most Nonimmigrant Visa Situations**

- A valid PASSPORT for each applicable alien issued by the alien's (i.e., the visa applicant's) country. (This is used primarily to serve as proof of the alien's identity and nationality)
- POLICE CERTIFICATE (a certificate by the police or the appropriate law enforcement authorities in the foreign country, reporting what their record shows, if any, regarding the alien), and/or REPORT OF FINGERPRINTING (use FORM ID-258 or FD-258, sampled on p. 179). (Fingerprinting or police certificate applies only to applicants 14 years of age or older. The fingerprinting may be made either at a U.S. consulate, or a local police or other enforcement department, and the fingerprint card and report are duly filled out and signed by the authorized official).
- Two (it may be more) passport-size PHOTOGRAPHS of each alien applying, showing a full front view of the facial features. The reverse side of each photo must be signed (full names) by the alien submitting each application. [see Chapter 18, Section F, for the proper photo specifications and dimensions required by the immigration authorities]
- REPORT OF MEDICAL EXAMINATION. (This exam must usually be done at the proper time directed by the consulate, and by a doctor or medical facility specifically designated to the alien for this by the Consular office)
- Documentary EVIDENCE OF CLOSE FAMILY RELATIONSHIP to an accompanying relative (usually a spouse or minor children), where this applies – evidence such as marriage certificates, birth certificates, sworn declarations by witnesses of birth and family relationship, and the like.

***NOTE:** Some of the supporting documents listed here may not apply or be required for your own particular visa classification or in your own particular case or consulate, and are only listed here as a general all-inclusive guide. Ultimately, the best source of what would specifically be required in a given case, is your consular official, and he will usually advice you of such details at the appropriate time.

- PROOF OF THE ALIEN'S FINANCIAL STATUS: Some evidence showing that you (the principal aliens) are of sufficient financial means, enough that you will not seek to work in the U.S. (e.g. a letter from your prospective hosts in the U.S. stating the trip's purpose and possibly assuring your financial needs while you are in the U.S., an already purchased round trip ticket, your bank statements, and any other financial or property documentations.)
- Documentation appropriate to establish your maintenance of a residence in your home
- The appropriate FILING FEE – the proper amount required will be given the applicant by local U.S. consulate or INS
- PROOF OF THE ALIEN'S FINANCIAL STATUS: In most non-immigrant visa applications, generally one critical, indeed central, element, is that you MUST be able to convince the consulate officers that were you to be allowed to come to America, once you arrive in the U.S. you are not likely to seek employment or go public welfare, or that you will not simply disappear into the country and never return to your home country upon the expiration of your visa. In other words, you must be able to offer such facts and information – a good enough documentation — as are sufficient to convince the consular officer (or the INS) that you (the principal alien or aliens), are of sufficient financial means that you can remain in the U.S without working. And, even when the nonimmigrant visa you seek is the type which legally allows you to work or to be employed or have a business, such as an E or H visa, frequently you'll still be expected to have the intent to eventually leave the U.S. when the business for which you're originally given the visa is completed.

Documentations such as the following will generally be appropriate and helpful:

--Documents showing ownership of real property in your home country

--Documents showing that you are leaving behind in your home country some close family members (a spouse, children, etc), or a profitable business or major property.

NOTE: Some of the supporting document listed here may not apply or be required for your own particular visa classification or in your own particular case or consulate, and are only listed here as a general all-inclusive guide. Ultimately, the best source of what would specifically be required in a given case, is your consular official, and he will usually advice you of such details at the appropriate time.

--Documents, such as a letter or sworn statements from your employer, showing that you have a permanent job with a well-known employer in your home country, and that you have that job still waiting for you when you return to your home country (should include relevant particulars about the job: how long the alien has been employed, and in what capacity, his /her position, salary structure, known marital and family status, his character, etc.

--Your personal bank statements from your bank in your home country or the U.S., and other financial statements

--Evidence of your current sources of income

--Proof of financial support, such as a letter from your relatives or prospective hosts in the U.S. inviting you to visit, stating your trip's purpose and that you are welcome to stay with them, and, most importantly, possibly assuring that they'll fully meet your financial needs while you're in the U.S.

--Completion of the Form 1-34, *Affidavit of Support*, by the relative host, who must be either a U.S. citizen or Green Card holder, guaranteeing that he or she (or both spouses whenever either of the parties is a married person) will take financial responsibility for you. (see sample copy of Form 1-34 on p.173)

--An already purchased round ticket for the trip

- FOR BUSINESS-RELATED VISIT. If the trip is for business purposes, a letter from your foreign employer explaining the reason for your U. S. trip

NOTE: Generally, documents submitted to the U. S. Consulate for visa application purposes must be the originals, or, in the absence of that, the official government certified copies. Documents submitted to the INS, on the other hand, may be merely photocopies, expect that you must have the original available ready to produce them for verification at the request of the INS officials. Government certified copies of documents must clearly bear a visible and verifiable official government seal and stamp of authentication certifying that the document is a true and actual copy of the document. Documents which are not in English language, should be translated into English to expedite your application, and the person making the translation should enter a statement at the end of the translation and sign it, certifying something to the effect that "the translated document from the . . ? . . language to English, is accurate and complete." (Refer to Chapter 18 for more an the proper document preparation measures and procedures to follow).

4. File The Forms & Supporting Documents With The U. S. Consulate

Upon your completion of the application forms and assembling of the necessary supporting documents, the next order of business on your path to applying for your U. S. entry visa, is for you to "file" the papers with (i.e., to summit them to) the appropriate U. S. government agency for processing-you submit them to the CONSULAR OFFICER in charge of the non-immigrant visa section at the U.S. consulate or Embassy in your (i.e. the alien applicant's) home country. Depending on the specific procedures followed in the particular consulate where your application is filed (if you have followed the advice of Section C.2 above, you shall have probably known already what such procedures would actually be), you may be required to submit your papers on an advance appointment say a week or so beforehand, or you may simply walk into the consulate office with your necessary supporting documents, fill out your application form(s) there and then, and be issued your nonimmigrant visa all on the same day. Or, as with some consulates, such as London (these are relatively fair, though), your visa application could even be processed by mail. (List of U. S. consulates worldwide is set forth in Appendix A).

What happens next upon your filing your application papers with the Consular visa processing officer. The consular officer will conduct a quick preliminary check of your application and the submitted supporting documents concerning their format and contents to see that your submissions are at least complete and that the forms are completely filled out. The Consular officer will usually require you to come to the consulate personally when you need to "execute" (i.e. sign) the application form(s) in his presence. The Consular officer may tell (or inform you by mal) you that certain necessary information or documentations are missing or improperly or incompletely filled in. If that should happen, don't even worry about it. Simply request the officer to tell you specifically what needs to be corrected or supplied, and make a note of that. Then you'll need to make the corrections or obtain the missing documents and resubmit the papers accordingly.

In any case, assuming that the papers submitted seem at least complete and in order enough to be accepted, you will pay the consular officer the applicable filling fee, if any, and the officer will assign a "case number" to your application. (Make sure you collect a receipt of filing from the officer, for your records).

The Consulate may or may not require an interview in your case before deciding on your visa issuance. Now, the Consular officer will at this stage probably give you (or later send you) a list of the instructions on the rest of the procedures still ahead to be undertaken: when and where to appear for the formal visa interview, if any is to be had in your case; how and where to take the medical examination, if any is applicable or not already taken; whether you are to complete FORM G-325A (the standard Biographic Information form used mostly in immigrant visa cases to conduct security clearances); and a list of any further documenations not already submitted which the consular officer may deem necessary or appropriate in your particular case, and what have you.

5. Attend The Visa Interview, If One Is Required In Your Case

Whether you are doing a U. S. filling or a consulate filing, a face to face personal interview with the visa processing officials may or may not be required in your case before the authorities render their final decision on your visa issuance. In any event, if a visa interview is required in your particular case, you will be so notified by the visa processing office. Upon your assembling together all the items required by the consulate or the INS, whichever one is applicable, you will appear on the appointed date, time and place set for the interview and undergo one with the designated interviewer. The visa processing officials will promptly render a final decision on your application, but only AFTER such interview.

(Turn to Chapter 15 for the full procedures involved in this all-important step in any nonimmigrant (as well as immigrant) visa application – the visa interview).

6. Final Approval Of Your Visa Application

In the end, assuming that everything is in order with your visa application – basically, that you have, for example, all the proofs and documentation require to show your eligibility for the visa applied for, and that there's nothing that makes you inadmissible under the U. S. Immigration law, such as having some serious criminal or terrorist record or potential, or a contagious, communicable disease – your application for a visa will be approved. You will be issued your visa. The U. S. consul in charge of visa issuance (if a consulate filing abroad), will usually stamp the approved visa that applies in your case (say, a B-1 and /or B-2 visa, in the case of the visitor's visa, or the E-1 or E-2, in the case of a treaty trader or investor) in your passport. If you got your visa through a U. S. filing, upon approval of your visa application, you are given a visa "status," and not an actual visa. (Under the law, only a Consulate may issue visa, and not the INS). This may be stamped in your passport and you will receive from the INS a *Notice of Action* Form 1-797 indicating the dates for which your status is approved, with a new 1-94 card attached at the bottom of the form.

*7. **Now, Get Formally "Admitted" Into The U.S. at a Port of Entry***

As a holder of a non-immigrant type of visa, you will normally be authorized to stay in the U.S. for a specific period of time, depending on the type and classification of the nonimmigrant visa involved. For example, for a B visa, you are normally authorized to stay in the U.S. for 6 months with the possibility of multiple extensions upon future application, while for an E-1 or E-2 visa, the authorized period of stay is 2 years at a time, with the possibility of extension or renewal of the visa for additional one- or two-year periods, and so on with respect to other types of nonimmigrant visas. And, when you enter the U.S. from a foreign country with your visa, at that time you will be given a 1-94 card, which will be stamped with the dates showing your authorized stay. Then, each time you exit and re-enter the U.S., you will get a new 1-94 card with a new period of authorized stay affixed thereto.

BUT HERE'S THE MAIN ISSUE OF IMPORTANCE YOU SHOULD NOTE HERE: before you can be actually allowed entry into the U.S. even with your approved and issued visa in hand, you must first be formally "admitted" into the country – that is, you have to successfully pass through some strict formalities involved in a procedure called the "inspection and admission" process into the United States. Turn to Chapter 16, *Entering The United States: The Process of Getting Actually Admitted Into The Country After You've Got Your Visa In Hand.*

*8. **What To Do If Your Visa Application Is Denied***

What if, in the end, for whatever the reason, your visa application is turned down and you are denied a visa? Turn Chapter 5, *Section G.8. What To Do If Your Visa Application Is Denied (p. 35).*

Chapter 5

Getting A Visa As A Treaty Trader Or Investor: The E-1 And E-2 Visas

A. WHAT IS AN E-1 OR E-2 VISA.

Th E-1 and E-2 visas, more formally called the TREATY TRADER and TREATY INVESTOR visas, respectively, are the most important nonimmigrant visas issued by the U.S. consulates worldwide. These visas are, in a word, meant for the business-oriented aliens who want to came to the United States in order to direct and develop the operations of a business in which they shall have invested substantial funds or in which a sizeable trade takes place.

The E type visas are a highly unique visa. For, though they are a non-immigrant type of visas, they are, nevertheless, viewed as the closest thing, within the nonimmigrant classification, to the immigrant (i.e. permanent resident) visa. The visa authorizes an initial duration of 2 years stay and there is no limit to the total combined amount of time that the alien may remain in the U.S. with the proper extensions so long as he continued with the original employer. An alien having a treaty trader (E-1) or a treaty investor (E-2) status, need not maintain a domicile in a foreign country, as one would be required to do under most other nonimmigrant categories. Furthermore, there is no requirement that the E visa holder's intended stay in the U.S. should be temporary, which means that a holder of an E visa may stay in the U.S. for an indefinite period of time so long as he or she continues to maintain the business enterprise for which he had secured the visa*. Equally worthy of note, is the fact that the E visa is typically issued for up to 4 or 5 years, depending on the treaty country involved. The initial period of stay is limited to one year but an unlimited number of extensions is possible in two-year increments.

B. WHO QUALIFIES FOR E TYPE VISA

Do you qualify for an E type visa? Here are the basic requirements you are to meet:

i. You (i.e., the alien applicant for the visa) must be a "national" (that is, a citizen, but not necessarily a native) of a country with which the U.S. has signed a treaty for trade and navigation (see list of such countries in Section C and D below).

ii. You should be able to prove to the consular and immigration officials that you have the intent in good faith, and will be able, to depart the U.S. upon the termination of your visa status.

iii. The trade you seek to carry on must be on a "substantial" scale and international in scope, principally between the U.S. and your foreign country, and carried on by you (the alien) on your own behalf or as agent of a foreign person or company so engaged.

---

*In theory: this means that as an alien treaty trader or investor, you can avoid the expense of having to maintain two residences. You should note, however, the warning sounded by experienced immigration experts and lawyers regarding this. It is recommended that, in light of the attitude and working philosophy of the U.S. consulate visa officers, the prudent approach for the alien would be to be able to show that he does, in fact, continue to maintain a foreign residence as well as other close contacts with the home country. This way, you (the alien) will be better able to establish the "temporary intent" element, asserting that your interest in acquiring the U.S. enterprise is purely financial.

iv. The company which you represent shall have been incorporated under law or be otherwise formally registered for business purposes within the foreign treaty country of which you are a citizen.

v. With respect to an E-1 visa, more than 50% of the trade involved must take place between your country and the U.S.

vi. You (the alien visa applicant) must be actively managing either your own business or your employer's; if in the person's or company's employ, such employer or company must have the same nationality as your (the treaty country), with at least 50% of U.S. organization owned by nationals of your (the treaty) country; you must be employed in a supervisory or executive capacity, or if employed in lesser capacity, you should have specialized skills or qualifications such that your services are essential to the operations of your company or employer.

C. TREATY TRADER OR E-1 VISA

The E-1 visa, called the TREATY TRADER visa, is meant for aliens of a treaty country who are engaged in a "substantial" volume of trade with the United States. The trade transactions cover "the exchange, purchase, or sale of goods" of all tangible commodities of merchandise, excluding money, securities and negotiable instruments, as well as "the exchange, purchase, or sale of services," such as banking, insurance, transportation, communication and data processing, advertising, accounting, design and engineering, management consulting and tourism. For the trade transactions to be deemed "substantial," they need not be individually large so long as they are numerous and the total percentage volume of trade is sufficient to at least support the alien in the United States.

The applicant for an E-1 visa can be either the owner of the qualifying business or company, or the key employee, depending on whether or not it is you who own the company.

LIST OF THE E-I TREATY COUNTRIES

As of this writing (if uncertain at a particular time you apply, you can always check with your local U.S. consulate), the countries with which the United States has entered into the appropriate treaty qualifying them for E-1 visa (trade) privileges, are the following:

Argentina	Austria	Belgium
Bolivia	Brunei (Borneo)	Bulgaria
China	Colombia	Costa Rica
Denmark	Estonia	Ethiopia
Finland	France	Germany
Greece	Honduras	Iran
Ireland	Israel	Italy
Japan	Korea	Latvia
Liberia	Luxembourg	The Netherlands
Nicaragua	Norway	Pakistan
Paraguay	The Philippines	Spain
Sultanate of Muscat and Oman		Switzerland
Thailand	Togo	The United Kingdom
Vietnam	Yugoslavia	

D. TREATY INVESTOR OR E-2 VISA

In contrast to the E-1 visa which is meant for trade purposes by and between the ~~an~~ alien's treaty country and the United State, the treaty investor visa (E-2) is meant for an alien of a treaty country who is to enter the U.S. to develop and manage a business enterprise for which he (she) has invested or is committed to invest an amount of capital that is of "substantial" nature and not "marginal". In other words, the applicant for an E-2 visa can be either the owner of the qualifying business or company or a key employee, depending on whether or not it is you who owns the company.

LIST OF E-2 TREATY COUNTRIES

As of this writing (if uncertain, you can always check with your local U.S. consulate), the following are the countries with which the United States has signed a treaty qualifying them for E-2 treaty investor privileges:

Argentina	Austria	Australia
Belgium	Bulgaria	China
Colombia	The Czech Republic	Costa Rica
Ethiopia	France	Germany
Honduras	Iran	Ireland
Italy	Japan	Korea
Liberia	Luxembourg	The Netherlands
Norway	Oman	Pakistan
Paraguay	The Philippines	Slovakia
Spain	Sweden	Switzerland
Suriname	Thailand	Togo
The United Kingdom	Vietnam	Yugoslavia

E. BASIC REQUIREMENTS FOR E-1 AND E-2 VISAS COMPARED

As compared to the treaty trader or E-1 situation, the qualifications for an E-2 visa are essentially identical to those enumerated above for the E-1, except that the treaty investor applicant needs to show that he is entering the United States for the sole purpose of investing a "substantial" amount of capital, or that he has so invested such already; that the business enterprise in which he has made, or intends to make such investment, is actual, and is a genuine bona-fide business either already existing or in the process of formation, and not merely a fictitious paper operation.

The guideline given by the U.S. Foreign Affairs Manual, states that, in general, whether an alien's investment qualifies as "substantial investment", would depend on the type of business, the nature of the business operation required, and whether the investment has already been made or is simply in the process of being made. ***The central question to be determined here by the examining consular or immigration official in making such determination, is essentially this: does the type of investment offered by the particular alien applicant in the particular line of business, seem to be "substantial" within the context of the particular business, in relation to the kind of funds which would ordinarily be necessary to effectively operate in that type of business?***

For example, a business enterprise involving a heavy marine construction, would obviously require millions of dollars of investment, since every individual piece of equipment alone (barges, cranes, tugboats, etc) is quite costly. In contrast to that, an investment in a wholesale distribution business for which the inventory, the warehouse space, and a few office furniture, are the only capital investment that may be required, might require a capital investment of, say, $75,000 or so. And in this later case, the U.S. visa officer abroad would very likely require from the alien an investment of at least 90% of the expected $75,000 cost required for the business, while for the more heavily capitalized company, a lesser percentage requirement for the alien investor is probably likely from the U.S. visa officer.

The Foreign Affairs Manual provides, for the benefit of consular and immigration examiners, two tests by which such determination should be attempted: (1) the "relative" test, wherein the amount invested by the alien should be weighted against the total value of the particular enterprise in question (more appropriate when investment is in an ongoing established business); or (2) the so-called "proportionality" test, wherein the amount invested by the alien should be weighted against the amount normally considered necessary to establish a viable enterprise of the type contemplated (more applicable when the alien is in the process of investing in a brand new business).

Here Is a summary of the eligibility requirements for an E-2 visas as established by the U.S. Department of State, and INS regulations and other rules:

- In situations involving the start-up of a new enterprise where the enterprise is being developed from the scratch by the alien investor, the determination of whether or not a particular amount of capital is to be deemed "substantial" will primarily be based on a comparison of the size of other businesses of similar type.
- A gauge of the overall size of the business, as well as of the number of employees contemplated for the business, will play a significant part in making a determination of whether or not the investment is substantial.
- In a newly developed start-up business situation, the business does not have to be functioning before the visa is issued the alien; however, the alien must establish that the investment is committed, that it is of such magnitude as to ensure the successful operation of the enterprise and to support the likelihood that the alien investor will successfully develop and direct the enterprise.

Substantiality of a given investment is very often determined by the use of a "proportionality" or "relative" test, using these two methods:

(a.) In the case of the acquisition of an enterprise that is already in existence and functioning, the capital invested by the alien must be proportional to the total value or cost of the particular business enterprise as follow:

- For an enterprise having an acquisition cost of $100,000.00 or less, the required percentage of capital investment should be between 90-100%.
- For a business acquisition cost of between $100,000.00 to $500,000.00, the required percentage of capital investment should be between 60-75%.
- For an acquisition cost of between $500,000.00 and $3,000,000.00, the required percentage of capital investment should be over 50%.
- When and where the amount invested is over $1,000,000.00, the investment will probably be presumed substantial as a consequence merely of its size, even though it may not approximate the recommended percentages

(b.) In the case of "start-up" enterprises involving the creation of a brand new business by the alien, the capital invested must be an amount normally considered necessary to establish a viable business enterprise of the type contemplated.

- As a general guideline, one 'rule-of-thumb' is that the minimum amount of cash required to meet the test of substantiality is $ 100,000 U.S., as long as that amount is proportional to the cost of acquisition of the business, and, generally speaking, to many U.S. consuls, an investment of less than this might seem insubstantial. (According to the U.S. Foreign Affairs Manual, most E-2 visas are granted, not to large foreign corporations requiring multi-million dollar investments, but to businesses requiring relatively small investments, such as grocery stores or restaurants).
- The alien investor must be prepared to present documentary proof that the funds invested (or to be invested) are the investor's own funds – a paper trail documenting the origin and/or ownership of the funds from the bank account in the home country to the United States. Loan proceeds that are guaranteed by the personal credit of the alien will count as part of the alien's own personal capital requirement, as long as the loan is not also collaterallized by the acquired assets.
- Aside from the normal requirement of being able to establish ownership and control of the enterprise (at least 51 % thereof), the alien must be prepared to present sufficient proof that he is entering the U.S. to actively <u>direct</u> and <u>manage</u> the investment and enterprise: obviously, if the alien does not need to be physically present in the United States in order to manage and control the investment, then of course the visa would be unnecessary!
  NOTE: Technically, the alien need not prove that he (she) is an "executive" or "manager," but merely that he is in a position to direct and manage the enterprise – that is, that he is in a position to be in control of the enterprise.
- Unlike the situation with the L-1 visa, alien inventors can qualify for the E-2 visa without having previously conducted business in a particular legal entity (a corporate entity) in the home country, even if they have previ-

ously operated or intend to operate in the future as a sole proprietor. Furthermore, the alien investor is not required to prove that he is an "executive" or "manager", but merely to prove that he is in a position to direct and manage the enterprise, meaning that he simply is in control of the enterprise. (The distinction immediately eliminates many of the technical problems traditionally involved in proving the status of "executive" or "manager".)

- The alien's capital investment is not limited only to his cash investment in to the enterprises; valuable tangible assets, such as equipment, fixtures, inventory, as well as intangibles, such as patent rights, royalty, and other contract rights, are also valid assets usable in the valuation of the alien's investment so long as they can be objectively appraised.
- The investment must be an active enterprise, as opposed to a passive investment (e.g. investments in stocks, bonds, mutual funds, etc); the key purpose of E-2 visa is to bring key people into the U.S. whose presence is required to actively direct and manage the business enterprise, and if an investment is one that does not require the personal involvement of the investor, the E-2 visa would not be the proper visa for that person.
- You must be able to put together, and to submit, A COMPREHENSIVE BUSINESS PLAN to establish that the enterprise will not be a "marginal" one – meaning that it will be one that will be capable of generating more than enough income to financially support the alien investor and his family, or alternatively, one that has the present or future capacity to make "significant economic contribution" in its local area of operation within 5 years of the start of business. A significant economic contribution can be demonstrated, for example, by showing (with some documentary evidence) that the alien could rehabilitate a troubled business and thereby saving the jobs of, or creating employment for, many U.S. citizens and residents.

F. NATIONALS OF OTHER COUNTRIES WHO QUALIFY FOR THE E-2 VISA

Aside from, and/or in addition to, the countries previously listed above as signatories to E-2 visa treaty with the U.S., there are other countries whose nationals are also eligible to apply for the E-2 treaty investor privileges by virtue of some other treaties or agreements existing between their countries and the United States. As of this writing, the following countries have signed bilateral accords known as BILATERAL INVESTMENT TREATIES (BIT) with the United States which accords nationals of those countries the same eligibility rights to apply for E-2 treaty investor visas:

Albania	Argentina	Armenia
Azerbaijan	Bangladesh	Belarus
Bulgaria	Cameroon	Congo
Croatia	Czech Republic	Ecuador
Egypt	Estonia	Finland
Georgia	Grenada	Ireland
Jamaica	Jordan	Kazakhstan
Kyrgyzstan	Latvia	Moldavia
Mongolia	Morocco	Panama
Romania	Russia	Senegal
Slovak Republic	Sri Lanka	Trinidad
Tobago	Turkey	Tunisia
Ukraine	Zaire	

And, finally, under the bilateral agreement signed in 1994 between the United States and Canada and Mexico, called the *North American Free Trade Act or NAFTA,* all the provisions and requirements that apply to E-1 and E-2 treaty applicants now apply to Canadian and Mexican citizens.

G. APPLICATION PROCEDURES FOR A VISA

1. Determine Where You Are To File: Is It Abroad, or In the U.S.?

For an E visa, you may file an application either in the United States, if you are physically present there already, or at a U.S. consulate abroad, providing you meet the required conditions for filing in either place. See Section C.1 of Chapter 4, and follow exactly the same details contained therein in determining whether you qualify to file at an INS office in the U.S., or at a U.S. consulate abroad.

2. Inquire About Your Local U.S. Consulate's or INS's Visa Filing Policies And Procedures

Turn to Section C.2 of Chapter 4 (p. 19) and apply here the same details contained therein, See, also, Chapter 18 Sections A and B, for more on the issue of variations in visa filing policies and practices among consulates and INS offices

3. Application Forms Used

i. *Prepare The Following Basic Forms:*

- Optional Form OF-156, *NONIMMIGRANT VISA APPLICATION.* This form is required ONLY IN overseas filings with a U.S. consulate. Generally, if your visa application is filed at a U.S. consulate in a foreign country, the consulate will usually provide you (the alien) with their required "option forms" complete with the instructions for completing them, and such forms are designated by a prefix "OF" preceding a number, as in OF-156. (See illustrative sample of Form OF-156 on p.177)

NOTE: FORM OF-156 is the basic application form which the vast majority of non-immigrant visa applicants will encounter. The proper completion of this form is, by far, the single most important and primary thing you can do in any nonimmigrant visa application which will determine ultimately whether you get the visa or not. For that reason, we set forth in one chapter, Chapter 13, the detailed, step-by-step instructions by which to properly complete the form, and the underlying considerations by which to answer the questions asked or to provide the information required therein. Please refer immediately to Chapter 13.

- Form 1-129 and the E SUPPLEMENT, *Petition For Nonimmigrant Worker.* This form is the form used in U.S. filings with the INS. (See sample of Form 1-129 on pp. 162, 165 and 168, and use the supplement E of the Form).
- Form 1-539, *Application To Extend/Change Nonimmigrant Status.* This form is applicable ONLY IF it is a U.S filing and only for accompanying relatives of the principal alien applicant, if any. Only one application form is needed for an entire family. But all accompanying relatives, if more than one, should be listed on the form. (see sample of Form 1-539 on p. 183).

NOTE: Form 1-126, which is the previous version of the current form 1-129E, is shown on p. 160, while the previous version of Form 1-539 (Form 1-506) is shown on p. 183. Both of these older versions of the forms in current use are reproduced here for illustrative purposes, namely, to illustrate the visa filing procedures in an actual case previously filed and successfully processed for the same type of visa, material generously made available courtesy of C. James Cooper, Jr., a long-time veteran Denver Colorado immigration lawyer and specialist. See "EXPLANATORY NOTE" on p. 37.

Note, also, that under the system in current use, the latest version of the Form 1-129 has various "supplements" to the basic form, each for particular nonimmigrant classifications – E, F, H, L, O, P, R, etc. And all you have to do is complete the basic Form 1-129 and simply tear out and use the supplement that applies to your visa category.

ii. General Supporting Documents For Most Nonimmigrant Situations*

- Form 1-94, Arrival-Departure Record Card, the small white card which shall have been issued you (each alien) on your entering the U.S. submit one for each applicant, including any accompanying relatives. (Note that if the

*NOTE: Some of the supporting documents listed here may not apply or be required for your own particular visa classification or in your own particular case or consulate, and are only listed here as a general all-inclusive guide. Ultimately, the best source of what would specifically be required in a given case, is your consular official, and he will usually advice you of such details at the appropriate time.

departure date stamped on your 1-94 card has already passed, you are not eligible to file in the U.S.)

- A valid PASSPORT for each applicable alien issued by the alien's (i.e. the visa applicant's) country. This is meant primarily to serve for proof of the alien's identify and nationality.
- POLICE CERTIFICATE – a certificate by the police or other appropriate law enforcement authorities in the foreign country, reporting what their record shows, if any, regarding the alien; and/or a REPORT OF FINGERPRINTING (use FORM ID-258 or FD-258, stamped on p. 179. (Finger printing or police certificate applies only for applicants 14 years of age or older. The fingerprinting may be made either at a U.S. consulate or a local police or other enforcement department, and the fingerprint card and report are duly filled out and signed by the authorized official).
- Two (it may be more) passport-size PHOTOGRAPHS of each alien applying, showing a full front view of the facial features. The reverse side of each photo must be signed (full names) by the alien submitting each application. [See Chapter 18, Section F, for the proper photo specifications and dimensions required by the immigration authorities]
- REPORT OF MEDICAL EXAMINATION (This exam must usually be done, at the proper time directed by the consulate or the INS, and by a doctor or medical facility specifically designated to the alien for this by the Consular or INS office)
- Documentary EVIDENCE OF CLOSE FAMILY RELATIONSHIP to an accompanying relative (usually a spouse or minor children), where this applies – evidence such as a civil marriage certificates, birth certificates to verify a parent/child relationship; sworn declarations by witnesses of birth and family relationship, and the like.
- PROOF OF THE ALIEN'S FINANCIAL STATUS: In most non-immigrant visa applications, generally one critical, indeed central, element, is that you MUST be able to convince the consulate (or INS) officers that were you to be allowed to come to America, once you arrive in the U.S. you are not likely to seek employment or go on public welfare, or that you will not simply disappear into the country and never return to your home country upon the expiration of your visa. In other words, you must be able to offer such facts and information – good documentation – that are sufficient to convince the consular officer (or the INS) that you (the principal alien or aliens) are of sufficient financial means, that you can remain in the U.S. without working. And, even when the visa nonimmigrant visa you are applying for is the type which legally allows you to work or to be employed or have a business, such as an E or H visa, frequently you'll still be expected to have the intent to eventually leave the U.S. when the business for which you're originally given the visa is completed.

Documentations such as the following will generally be appropriate and helpful:

- - documents showing ownership of real property in your home country
- - documents showing that you are leaving behind in your home country some close family members (spouse, children, etc), or a profitable business or major property
- - documents, such as a letter or sworn statements from your employer, showing that you have a permanent job with a well-known employer in your home country, and that you have that job still waiting for you when you return to your home country (it should include relevant particulars about the job: how long the alien has been employed there and in what capacity, his/her position, salary structure, future prospects with the company, know marital and family status, his character, etc.)
- - your personal bank statements from your bank in your home country or the U.S., and either financial statements
- - evidence of your current sources of income
- - proof of financial support, such as a letter from you relative or prospective hosts in the U.S. inviting you to visit, stating your trip's purpose and that you are welcome to stay with them, and, most importantly, possibly assuring that they'll fully meet your financial needs while you're in the U.S.
- - completion of the Form 1-134, *Affidavit of Support*, by the relative's host, who must be either a U.S. citizen or Green Card holder, guaranteeing that he or she (or both spouses whenever either of the parties is a married person) take financial responsibility for you. (See sample copy of Form I-134 on p.173)
- -an already purchase round trip ticket for the trip.

- FOR BUSINESS-RELATED VISIT: if the trip is for business purposes, a letter from your foreign employer explaining the reason for your U.S. trip. (This may not be necessary for an E type of visa).

NOTE: Generally, documents submitted to the U.S. consulate for visa application purposes must be the originals, or, in the absence of that, the official government certified copies. Documents submitted to the INS in U.S filing, on the other hand, may be merely photocopies, except that you had better have the original available and ready to produce them for verification to the INS officials. Government certified copies of documents must clearly bear a visible and verifiable official government seal and stamp of authentication certifying that the document is a true and actual copy of the document. Documents which are not in English language, should be translated into English to expedite your application, and the person making the translation should enter a statement at the end of the translation and sign it, stating something to this effect that: "the translated document from the ... language to English, is accurate and complete." (Refer to Chapter 18 for more on the proper documents preparation measures and procedures to follow).

iii. Supporting Documentations Specific to "E" Visa Classes

In addition to such documents as are applicable to you listed under 3(ii) immediately above, the following may be necessary.

For the Treaty Trader (E-1) case:

- Evidence indicating the nationality of the person or persons who own the stock, or the principal amount, of the business of the foreign company constituting the trading or investing entity. [In general, see items cited, for example, in Explanatory Note, p. 37]
- Proof of the nationality of the alien (or aliens) seeking the E visa (he does not have to be a citizen or national of the U.S. or a U.S. permanent resident), such as the passport, showing that you are a citizen of one of the trade treaty countries, and documents indicating where such aliens are currently living, such as a sworn affidavit from each stating their places of residence.
- A statement of unequivocal intent to return to his home country when his E status ends.
- Invoices showing purchase prices for goods, equipment or machinery transferred to the U.S. for use in the business enterprise.
- Invoices showing that substantial volume of trade exists between the U.S. enterprise and the foreign business or company in the alien's country, the number of transactions, and whether there is a continuous course of trade.
- Evidence showing that the qualifying business is actually owned by a citizen (or citizens) of one of the trade treaty countries. If you and/or any of the owners are presently living in the U.S., you must show proof that such persons hold a valid E-1 visa, such as copies of their passports and their Form 1-94 cards.
- If qualifying business is a corporation, then submit copies of the Articles of Incorporation, copies of all stock certificates, plus a notarized statement (affidavit) signed by the Secretary of the corporation listing the names of all shareholders for all shares issued to date, and the number of corporate shares owned by each. (To qualify, you or other nationals of the treaty country must own at least 50% of the qualifying business).
- If the qualifying business is not an incorporated business, then present appropriate legal papers proving the existence and ownership of the company, such as partnership agreements, certificates of business registration, business licenses, notarized statements on the company's business letterhead from the owner(s) of the company certifying the names, addresses and other particulars of the company's owners, and in what percentages they own it.
- If you are not personally the majority owner of the company, then you'll need to submit evidence that you meet the "key employee" definition for your role in the company – that is, that you qualify as an "executive", a "supervisor", or a "key employee" of the company as defined by the INS – such as a detailed (preferably notarized) statement from the sponsoring business specifying the duties you'll undertake, the number and kind of employees you will supervise, the nature and kind of essential knowledge or experience you possess and how it will be used in your employment with the company, etc [see documents listed on pp. 191, 195, 196, for examples of the

proper kinds of documents]

- Documentary evidence that the qualifying business is real, that it is an ongoing, active and existing business – letters from the bank or bank statements of the qualifying company showing the average account balance of the business, credit agreements with suppliers, invoices of commercial activities, leases or deeds for the business premises used by the company, tax returns and payroll tax returns filed for the past 2 years, if the business has been in operation for some time.
- For a newly formed business for which no tax return may have been filed, you may simply submit a detailed business plan, including detailed financial projections for at least five years
- Copies of all import and export documents for the previous 12 months (purchases or sale orders, bills of lading and customs entry documents, contracts with foreign suppliers, the qualifying company's balance sheet, etc), to prove that more than 50 percent of the company's total trade consist of commerce between the alien's treaty home country and the U.S.
- The qualifying company's financial statement for the past two years (if applicable) from accountants, such as profit and loss statements and balance sheets.
- Records of bank wire transfers showing monies transferred to the U.S. from overseas for the use of the business or investment.
- Photographs of the business enterprise showing the alien engaged in the conduct of the business

For Treaty Investor (E-2) case:

- In general, the same class of documents which are listed immediately above for the E-1 situation: documentation appropriate to establish that the alien visa applicant possesses the required funds; that he (or she) actually invested or is in the process of investing the required money in the business; that the business actually exists and has all the necessary licenses and other requirements to lawfully operate, and that he is a principal manager in the company – in a word, any and all appropriate documentation helping to establish to the consulate or INS official that the alien meets the conditions for getting an E-2 visa discussed earlier in this Chapter in Section E above, that he or she does, in fact, intend to establish a bona-fide investment (or trade) company on a substantial scale. [see sample documentations listed in "EXPLAINATORY NOTE" on p. 37]

4. File The Forms and Supporting Documents With the U.S. Consulate or the INS

Upon your completion of the application forms and the assembling of the necessary supporting documents, the next order of business in the process of applying for your U.S. non-immigrant entry visa, is for you to "file" the papers with (i.e., to submit them to) the appropriate U.S. government agency for processing – either to the U.S. CONSULATE or EMBASSY in your (i.e., the alien applicant's) home country, or to the U.S. Immigration and Naturalization office in the United States. Which of the two places could you file? Basically, you are to file at an INS office inside the U.S., if you are already in the U.S. <u>legally</u> on some other type of nonimmigrant visa, using the procedure known as "change of nonimmigrant status". And, you will have to file at a U.S. consulate in your home country, if you are physically present there, or if you have been or are now working or living <u>illegally</u> in the U.S. (see Section G.1 above, and Section C.1 of Chapter 4 (p. 19) for more on the factors which will determine in which of the two locations you may file)

If your application is a U.S. filing, here is what you do: simply send your application papers (the forms and photocopied documents) by mail to the Immigration and Naturalization Service (INS) Regional Service Center for the area covering the intended place of business. Be sure to enclose the appropriate filing fee (it's $130 as of this writing), payable in checks or money orders. Always send the papers <u>by certified mail</u> with return receipt requested, so that you can retain the receipt as your proof that they were received. There are only 4 such INS Regional Service Centers spread across the U.S., and are <u>not</u> the same thing as the INS local offices. [see Appendix B for the list of these centers and their addresses]

For U.S. Consulate filing in a foreign country, depending on the specific procedures followed in the particular consulate where your application is field (if you have followed the advice of Section G.2 above, you shall have already known what those procedures would actually be), you may be required to submit your papers on an advance appointment set a week or so beforehand, or you may simply walk into the consulate office with your necessary supporting documents, fill out your application form(s) there and then, and be issued your nonimmigrant visa all on the same day. Or, as with some consulates, such as London (these are relatively few, though), your visa application could even be process by mail. (List of U.S. consulates worldwide is set forth in Appendix A)

WHAT HAPPENS NEXT, upon your filing your application papers with the U.S. consulate or the INS? In the case of U.S. filing, you'll likely receive from the INS, within a week or two of your mailing the application papers, a written notice of confirmation that the papers are being processed. The notice will also give you the immigration "file number" assigned to your case, and approximately when you are to expect a decision. If some material defects or omissions are found in the papers, such as unsigned forms or missing information or documents or the payment, the INS will probably return the entire application papers to you with a note or a Form 1-797, stating what corrections need to be made or what additional documents or pieces of information need to be supplied. Or, in some cases, the INS may simply retain the papers already submitted but issue a request, in the form of a Form 1-797, for additional documents or information that is needed. And in such an event, all you'll need to do is simply supply the additional data required and promptly mail them (along with the Form 1-797 and the rest of the file, if applicable) back to the INS office.

In the case of a Consular filing, basically a similar scenario applies. The consular officers will conduct a quick preliminary check of the application and supporting papers you submitted to see that your submissions are at least complete and that the forms are completely filled out. And if there are any essential information or documents that are missing or improperly or incompletely filled out, the consulate will notify you, and you'll be given the opportunity to make the corrections or to submit the missing documents. And, assuming that the papers you submitted seem at least complete and in order enough to be accepted, you will pay the consular officer the applicable filing fee, if any, and the officer will assign a "case number" to your application. At this stage, the consular officer will properly give you (or send you) a list of instructions on the remainder of the visa procedures that are still ahead to be undertaken: when and where you are to appear for the formal interview, if any is to be had in your case; how and where you are to take the medical examination, if any is applicable or not already taken, whether you are to complete Form G-325A (the standard Biographic Information form used mostly in immigrant visa cases to conduct security clearances); and a list of further documentations not already submitted which the consular officer may deem necessary or appropriate in your particular case, and so on.

5. Attend The Visa Interview, If One Is Required In Your Case

Whether you are doing a U.S. filling or a consulate filing, a face-to-face personal interview with the visa processing officials may or may not be required in your case before the authorities render their final decision on your visa issuance. In any event, if a visa interview is required in your particular case, you will be so notified by the visa processing office. Upon your gathering together all the items required by the consulate or the INS, whichever one is applicable, you will appear on the appointed date, time and place set for the interview and undergo one with the designated interviewer. The visa processing officials will promptly render a final decision on your application, but only AFTER such interview.

(Turn to Chapter 15 for the full procedures involved in this all-important step in any nonimmigrant as well as immigrant visa application – the visa interview).

6. Final Approval of Your Visa Application

In the end, assuming that everything is in order with your visa application – basically, that you have, for example, all the proofs and documentation required, and that there's nothing that makes you inadmissible under the U.S. immigration law, such as having some serious criminal or terrorist record or potential, or a contagious, communicable disease -- your application for a visa will be approved. You will be issued your visa. The U.S. consul in charge of visa issuance, will usually stamp the approved visa that applies in your case (say the E-1 or E-2 visa, in the case of the Treaty Trader or Investor applicant visa) in your passport.

7. Now, Get Formally "Admitted" Into The U.S. at a Port of Entry

As a holder of a non-immigrant type of visa, you will normally be authorized to stay in the U.S. for a specific period of time depending on the type and classification of the nonimmigrant visa involved. For example, for a B visa, you are normally authorized to stay in the U.S. for 6 months with the possibility of multiple extensions upon future application, while for an E-1 or E-2 visa, the authorized period of stay is 2 years at a time, with the possibility for extension or renewal of the visa for additional one- or two-year periods, and so on. And when you enter the U.S. with your visa at the time you will be given a 1-94 card, which will be stamped with the dates showing your authorized stay. Then each time you exit and re-enter the U.S., you will get a new 1-94 card with a new period of authorized stay affixed thereto.

BUT HERE'S THE MAIN ISSUE OF IMPORTANCE YOU SHOULD NOTE HERE: before you can be actually allowed entry into the U.S. even with your approved and issued visa in hand, you must first be formally "admitted" into the country – that is, you have to successfully pass through some strict formalities involved in a procedure called the immigration "inspection and admission" process into the United States. Turn to Chapter 16, *Entering The United States: The Process of Getting Actually "Admitted" Into The Country After You've Got Your Visa In Hand.* (p.118).

8. What To Do If Your Visa Application Is Denied

What if, in the end, for whatever the reason, your visa application is turned down and you are denied a visa? Is there anything you can do? Yes, there are a few things you can do. In the first place, for most nonimmigrant visa category cases, there are two points during the visa processing at which your visa request process could possibly be stopped – first, at the initial "petition" phase of the visa processing, and then at the "application" phase.

(a) What You Can Do In The Petition Phase

In the "petition" phase (that first phase of the visa filing procedures, you recall from the earlier part of the chapter, which generally involves the alien's U.S. employer or sponsor, and which is primarily executed in the U.S.), if the petition is denied, your U.S. sponsor will get a written *Notice of Denial* from the INS. The notice will contain a statement of the reasons for the denial and explanation of how to appeal, or it could contain a request for additional evidence (Form 1-797) requesting specific information or documentation. A common reason why most petitions are usually denied, is that the alien's job qualifications for the visa desired are poorly documented, and that the prospective U.S. employer left out some necessary documents.

What remedy is open to you? One option is for the U.S. employer to make a formal appeal of the denial. If this path is chosen by the U.S. employer, then he/she must be sure to make the appeal within 30 days of the date on the Notice of Denial. The appeal is directly filed with the same INS office that issued the Notice of Denial, and with a filing fee of $110. The INS, in turn, will then forward the appeal papers to the Administrative Appeals Unit of the central INS office in Washington D.C. for its consideration. The employer should expect a decision by that Unit by mail in about 6 months or more. And, should the appeal to the INS be again denied, (fewer than 5% of all such appeals are said to be successful), the next step open to the U.S. employer at this stage, would be for the U.S. employer to now file an action in a federal court and to appeal the case through the U.S. judicial system.

Experts widely experienced in such immigration matters strongly advise, however, that the best course of action to take, would be to avoid filing an appeal of a petition denial altogether. Rather, they say, a better approach would be for the U.S. petitioner to write a letter to the same INS office and request simply the "reopening" of the case. This measure, technically, is known as a "Motion to Reopen". You pay $110 to the INS (in a check or money order) to file this letter ("motion") with the INS. In general, using the Motion to Reopen approach, these experts say, would be more effective than filing a formal appeal, for a number of reasons. For one thing, to file an appeal would have meant, in effect, making an argument to the INS that its own reasoning and judgement was wrong. The INS does not particularly like this. And making such argument with the agency is difficult to do with any degree of success (only fewer than 5% of all such appeals are successful.) Rather, it would probably be more effective with the INS for the petitioner to simply file a new or improved petition better prepared than the first. The U.S. employer and petitioner can, for example, simply improve on the first paperwork that had been submitted, say, by supplying some necessary documents that may have been left out but which have since been located, or new documents or facts and information which better explain the alien's qualifications or issues raised for the denial, or more or other documents that eliminate the reason the petition had failed.

(b) What You Can Do In The Application Phase

It is with respect to the denial of the visa request in the "application" phase of the nonimmigrant visa processing that an appeals or challenge is most critical and difficult. This is so more particularly in the consular visa processings, which is where the vast majority of nonimmigrant visa applications are processed, any way.

If your visa application is denied, the consular officer will inform you (the alien) of the reason for the denial, usually verbally as a written statement of visa decisions is not normally provided in nonimmigrant cases. For what reasons may your application have been turned down? It could be on any number of bases – for lack of evidence (in the opinion, of course, of the U.S. consular officer in charge) about a particular point of the application, or because the consular officer does not believe that your investment (in the case, for example, of an E-2 or L-1 visa) is substantial enough, or that, in the opinion of the consular officer, you are inadmissible, or simply that the consular officer just does not believe that you intend to return to your home country, and so on.

What remedy is open to you at this stage as an alien whose nonimmigrant visa application is denied? As a practical matter, the reality is that when a consulate turns down a nonimmigrant (or even immigrant) visa application, there is really no way to make a formal appeal of that decision, although you are free to reapply for the visa for as many times as you wish. For all practical purposes, whether you are granted a visa or not granted one, is really entirely up to the U.S. consulate officers (or the INS officers, if applicable). To be sure, U.S. immigration procedures provide for some ways of appeal of consular decisions. But, as one veteran immigration expert aptly put it, in practice, the reality is that "the time, the expense and likelihood of failure of such appeals render them useless for all but the most important visa applications for permanent residency."*

Consequently, here's the simple but realistic approach that are judged the most effective in nonimmigrant visa application appeals. Simply study the reasons the consular (or the INS) officer tells you are the basis for denying your application. Then, see if indeed you can realistically gather and supply what it will take to remedy the reason(s) given. Is it for a lack of evidence about a particular point in your application, for example? Or, because of doubts or questions about your job qualifications for the visa desired, or doubt about whether you'll ever return to your home country? Then simply gather more evidence and documentation that will better clarify and strengthen your position in that regard and resupply them to the consular officer – e.g., more (or better) evidence of your ties to your home country that makes it more likely that you'll return, more (or better) evidence of the substantialness of your investment, for an E-2 visa application, for example, and so on.

---

*Christopher E. Henry, in *How To Win The U.S. Immigration Game*, p. 48

EXPLANATORY NOTES

(To illustrate The E, H and L Visa Cases employed in the manual)

1. These **EXPLANATORY NOTES** offer some helpful visa filing procedures and specifics with respect to the E, H and L visa classifications discussed in Chapters 5, 7-9, and 11 respectively. As has been emphasized in various sections of this manual (see, for example, Chapter 13 Section A, and Chapter 18, Sections A, B & C), the immigration forms are generally notorious for frequently changing. Consequently, several sample forms reproduced and used in this manual for illustrative purposes may have long been superseded by a revised newer edition of the same forms. Nevertheless, we employ many of the older, outdated forms here for illustration because the same basic principles still underlie all such forms, whether old or new. The older forms employed herein for illustrating the various types of visas discussed in the manual, possess one unique and fitting quality for our purpose in this manual: they are true actual forms (and the related actual documentations) which have been previously filed and successfully used and processed in obtaining the nonimmigrant visa involved. Reproduced herein by courtesy of C. James Cooper, Jr. Esq. a renowned Denver, Colorado immigration law specialist. the personal and business names, addresses and other identifying details of sorts have been deleted on these sample Cooper forms and documentations, but merely out of concern to protect the privacy of the parties involved.

2. **THE H-1B VISA**. (Discussed in Chapter 7). The particular Form I-129B reproduced on pp. 162-4, was filed specifically for an H-1 VISA (the equivalent of the current H-1B visa) for the position of an apparel Accounts Executive for a Hong Kong-based beneficiary (alien). Among the qualifications possessed by the beneficiary, are a Bachelor's Degree in Business Administration, an Associate Degree from the Fashion Institute, and work experience, the alien's qualifications were documented by submission of (among other things) copy of the Englewood Colorado employer's letter of offer of employment to the Hong Kong based alien (see p.192), an itemized job description of the position in question (see p.193, as well as certified copies of the alien's degree and transcripts, etc.

(See also p. 199 for anther excellent sample EMPLOYER LETTER illustrative of the type of covering letter used in support of H-1 (i.e. H-1B) visa petitions. Here, the alien, originally from India, had entered the U.S. in August 1983 on an F-1 (i.e. nonimmigrant) visa as a student. Then after receiving his Master's Degree in Computer and Information Science and getting some practical training and work experience, the alien got a job offer from a company in Ft Collins, Colorado, for a <u>temporary</u> position as a Software and Development Engineer, which meant that he needed an H-1B visa. The prospective employer filed a petition (Form I-129B) for him for an H-1B visa. At the same time the employer filed the petition, the alien applied to change his status from F-1 (student), to an H-1 (temporary worker), by filing Form I-506.)

NOTE: However, if this alien had gained entry already into the U.S., and is "in legal status" under another non-immigrant category (say, as a student, for example), the alien would, in addition, have to file an Application to change his/her status on Form I-506, along with the Form I-129B petition. (If the alien was <u>NOT</u> in legal status, then he would have been ineligible to apply for the H-1B visa from within the U.S., and would have had to designate a Consulate in a foreign country where he would apply for the H-1B visa from.)

3. **THE H-2B VISA** (Discussed in Chapter 8). The particular Form I-129B reproduced on pp. 165-7, was filed specifically for an H-2 VISA (i.e. for H-2B visa under current classifications) a Mexican national whose job in the U.S. would be to train United State workers in the act of hand wiping tin on copper ware for a Denver Colorado Company. Documentations submitted with the I-129B petition in support for the H-2B visa request, (read Form I-129H under the revised, current version), included: i) letter of Labor Certificate approval

from the U.S. Department of Labor's office, (see pp. 201, 204, 205, for examples of such certification); ii) the application form used in applying for the labor certification, Form ETA 750A only (see p.165); and iii) the Employer's Letter, a so called " Business Necessity" letter (see p. 194), among other documentatons. (Another sample BUSINESS NECESSITY LETER is set forth on p. 203, for your information).

4. THE H-3 VISA (Discussed in Chapter 9). The particular Form 1-129B reproduced on pp. 168-170 (read, Form 1-129H under the revised, current version), was filed specifically for an H-3 TRAINEE VISA for one Andreas, a Swiss national who was then resident in Longmont Colorado, but on J- 1 visa. The alien (he first applied for a Waiver of the 2-year requirement for the J-1 holders and was granted the waiver) was to be given business training in the management of the lumber business. Documents submitted with the I-129B petition for this H-3 visa request, included, among others, letter of employment/training from the sponsor (see p. 195), which clearly shows the general scope of the training, and more particularly, that the program has both classroom instruction as well as on-the-job training components.

5. THE L-1 VISA (Discussed in Chapter 11) the particular Forms 1-129B (read, Form 1-129L under the revised, current version) reproduced on pp. 162, 165, 168, were filed specifically for an L-1 INTRA-COMPANY TRANSFEREE VISA for an alien person who has been working in Bangkok, Thailand, as a Manager for a parent company there. The L-1 visa was to allow this employee to come to and remain temporarily in the U.S. (Denver, Colorado) for a period of 3 years for the purpose of setting up the subsidiary located in Denver and training U.S. workers for the subsidiary. Documents submitted with the I-129B petition for this L-1 visa request, included, among others, the following: **(i)** letter of employment from the U.S. petitioner-employer (see pp. 196); **(ii)** a brochure of the company's product; **(iii)** numerous invoices and orders; **(iv)** certified copy of the certificate of incorporation of the business in the State of Colorado; **(v)** certificate of stock ownership of the U.S. subsidiary; and **(vi)** other documentations to show the corporate relationship between the U.S. company in Colorado and foreign parent company in Thailand.

6. THE E-1/E-2 VISA (Discussed in Chapter 5). The particular Forms 1-506 (read, Form 1-539 under the revised, current version of the form) reproduced on p. 181, and Form 1-126 (read, form 1-129E under the revised current version of the form), reproduced on p.160, were specifically filed in a successful actual application made for an E-2 TREATY INVESTOR'S VISA for Jules Renaud, a French West Indian alien who happened to have come into the U.S. on a B-2 (i.e., Tourist-Visitor's) visa, but then decided to invest in and work as a specialty cook in a restaurant in Duranja, Colorado. This, then, meant that he had to apply for change of his visa status from B-2 to an E-2 (i.e. INVESTOR'S) visa.

This particular case exemplifies a situation where the investor has some specialised knowledge and would be working in a minor technical capacity, rather than a managerial or executive capacity. Among the documents submitted in support of this particular petition, were: 1) supporting letter from the principal investors in the restaurant, a husband-and-wife team (see pp. 197 & 198); ii) the foreign investor's Form 1-94, Arrival-Departure Record, which has been issued him by the Immigration Services at the time of his entry into the U.S.; iii) an AFFIDAVIT (sworn statement) by the owners of the restaurant supporting the proposed investment by the alien (see p. 198); and other documents, such as a certified copy of deed to the restaurant building, the wine list and menu, media review of the restaurant, etc. (Form 1-539, *"Application for Extension of Temporary Stay,"* was apparently not submitted (or necessary) in this particular instance.)

Chapter 6

Getting A Visa As An Academic, Vocational Or Exchange Student: The F, M, And J Visas

A. THE THREE MAIN CLASSES OF EDUCATIONAL VISAS

The following nonimmigrant visas which share the common purpose of providing education and/or vocational skills to foreign persons, will be discussed in this chapter:

1. The academic student visa, or "F" visa
2. The vocational student visa, or "M" visa
3. The foreign exchange student visa, or "J" visa

B. THE ACADEMIC STUDENT OR "F" VISA

1. Nature Of The F-1 Students' Program

The F-1 visa is the visa provided to the alien person who seeks to enter the United States for the purpose of engaging in a full-time academic course of study. The F nonimmigrant class applies to the principal alien, and he (or she) is admitted in F-1 status, while his accompanying spouse and minor children, if applicable, are admitted in F-2 status. The visa extends to persons enrolled at any level of education, from elementary school through the post-graduate and doctoral levels of university education. The F visa, however, does not apply to vocational school students or others enrolled in skills-oriented, non-academic courses of studies. Second, an F visa is not granted for just one specific course of study, but for a student's broad, comprehensive academic program, which may include several consecutive diplomas or degrees and which, with extensions granted, may last for one or two decades or so.

The alien student for an F-1 visa must, however, apply for, and upon enrollment, be engaged in an educational course of study that provides academic training (as opposed to a purely vocational type of training). And a vocational, or business or other types of school whose curriculum is basically non-academic, would not support an F visa at the hands of the U.S. consular officers. Furthermore, an F visa applicant must be accepted for a full-time course of study at an approved American school, and must continue in that full-time status for the visa to remain valid. The fact that the student is free from school activities during normal vacation periods, even for a long two-or-three-month break during the summer, does not interrupt this full-time status. Determination that a student is or is not enrolled in a full-time course of study, is based on two criteria:

- The number of academic credits or hours for which the student is scheduled each semester (for post-secondary school studies)
- The actual length of time which it takes the student to complete the course of study. For example, if a student is enrolled in a baccalaureate degree program which normally takes 4 years to complete, and takes the required number of credits each semester required in order to qualify as a full-time student but nevertheless fails to complete the degree within the normal time period (plus approximately a year's grace period), the F visa may be cancelled.

As an F-1 visa student, however, you are restricted to the original program for which your visa is granted. However, you can transfer from one school to another or from one academic program to another by obtaining the permission of the U.S. Immigration and Naturalization Service which usually entails a simple procedure of notifying the INS of a proposed change. You may work legally in a part-time job on campus, but are prohibited from working off campus, except that you may do so with special permission from the INS under special circumstances, such as when such a job would provide practical training for your field of study. Accompanying relatives (wife and children) may stay with you in the U.S., but are not permitted to work.

An F-1 visa application for you to study at a publicly funded elementary school or adult education program or secondary school, will not be approved by the immigration authorities. However, with respect only to public secondary schools, such may be approved providing you prepay the full cost of the program. Furthermore, you may not obtain an F visa to study at a private secondary or elementary or adult education program, and then transfer to a publicly funded school. Any alien student who violates either one (or both) of the last two regulations face a stiff penalty: he or she will be inadmissible to the U.S. for 5 years. In addition to the principal course of study, an alien student may also be authorized to do practical training program during the normal course of the alien's academic studies for a total combined period not to exceed 12 months, including time spent in the practical training, for summer vacations, mid-semester breaks, etc. Essentially, all that are required are the following: that the practical training be related to the alien's main educational course of study in the United States, and that the alien student be unable to receive such practical training in his home country. (In general, certification by the school official of the U.S. institution that such practical training sought by the student will benefit his academic training, will normally be sufficient. Nevertheless, the alien applicant should still be fully prepared to present good documentary proof to the U.S. consul to this effect).

2. Who Qualifies For an F-1 Visa

Basically, to qualify for an F-1 nonimmigrant student visa, you must be able to demonstrate the following elements to the satisfaction of the U.S. consular officer by adequate evidence and documentation:

i. that you have a residence in a foreign country which you have no intention of abandoning;
ii. that you are a "bonafide student qualified to pursue a full course of study" in the U. S.;
iii. that you seek to enter the U.S. "temporarily and solely for the purpose of pursuing such a course of study at an established institution of learning in the United States," one approved by the U.S. Attorney General for attendance by nonimmigrant students;
iv. that you will, in fact, engage in a "full course of study" in the U.S.;
v. that you have sufficient money or financial support* for at least the first year so that you won't need to engage in employment in the U.S.;
vi. that you will be able to understand the English language well enough as to be able to carry out your studies; and most importantly,
vii. that you intend to leave the U.S. upon completion of your course of study.

Briefly summed up, there are really essentially two-related bases which cause applications for F visas to be denied: not being able, on the part of the prospective student applicant, to convince the consular officer that at a minimum he (or she) will have the means to financially support himself in the American school for a period of one year without resorting to employment, and that the prospective student, if given admission into the U.S., will leave the United States upon completing his stated course of study, and that he would not, instead, seek employment and remain permanently in the U.S. thereafter. *Hence, you had better be prepared to present substantial evidence to the consular officer demonstrating your intent to return to your home country – e.g. evidence of your ties to your home country, of availability of employment in your home country in the field of your intended specialization. And you had better be equally prepared to demonstrate to the consulate officials that you can pass the financial "means test" alright. The dollar amount that will be required will not be the same for each applicant, but will depend on such factors as these:*

---

*In determining whether adequate financial support is available to you, you are permitted to count such funds, if any, as you are to derive from sources such as fellowships or work study programs from the U.S. school, scholarship or assistantship grants, such as research projects, or lecturing or performance of other academic functions. Students will, however, need to attach certification from the institution that they will also pursue a full course of study in addition to these other activities.

- The amount of the tuition cost at the applicant's intending school
- Whether or not the applicant will have room and board supplied by the school (or, for example, by a relative with whom the student will reside).
- The general cost of living where the school is located
- Whether or not the applicant will be accompanied by a spouse and/or children for whom the student will have to provide, since under the rules a spouse who accompanies the student will not be authorised to accept employment in the U.S.
- The nature and amount of the prospective student's expected sources and means of support – his own cash funds, the expected amount of tuition or stipends to be provided through scholarships and grants either by American institutions or by private governmental institutions in the applicant's own country, and by fellowships and normal work-study programs (these forms of employment are permitted for the F visa holder)
- Money or other support (such as room and board) which will be provided by relative either in the student's own country or in the U. S., if any.

3. Proof Of Temporary Intent By The Alien Prospective Student

Probably the biggest stumbling block for aliens applying for the F visa, is the requirement under the U.S. immigration procedures that an alien applying for a nonimmigration visa demonstrate a purely temporary "intent". The U.S. Department of State and the INS are wary, and not entirely for unfounded or far-fetched reasons, that individuals applying as students may simply be entering the U.S. merely to immigrate permanently to the United States in circumvention of the normal immigration visa process, and will disappear into the U.S. job market as soon as they leave the airport. Consequently, the consular officers closely scrutinize for evidence of immigrant intent in non-immigrant visa applications such as for F-1 visa.

The following step, among others, will be some of the helpful ways of convincing the consular officer that the alien student actually has a "temporary" intent.

- Proof by the alien, by tangible documentations, of his/her continuing ties to his/her home country – through such things as family photographs and/or other information showing membership in various civil and social organizations, proof that the alien has a job available or reserved for him at home to which he will return at the completion of his schooling, or other evidence of ties to the home country.
- Proof that the alien has sufficient funds to pay for the educational program as well as his (her) maintenance for the duration of the program.
- Proof that the funds are <u>currently</u> available and not based on any future hopes or projections, and, most importantly, that the <u>alien</u> himself, or through the family, has the required funds. (Where the alien's family or close friends or relatives are to provide the funding in part or in whole, or to provide the room and board, a strong affidavit of support to that effect must be provided by them, backed by proof of their own financial standing and stability). [See Chapter 14 for a full discussion of the whole issue of overcoming the critical "alien intent" problem in nonimmigrant visa applications generally]

C. THE VOCATIONAL STUDENT OR "M" VISA

The "M" nonimmigrant visa is the type of visa issued to the foreign student who is specifically limited to undertaking a full course of VOCATIONAL training, as opposed to pure academic education. (The M-1 is for the principal alien, while the M-2 visa applies to his or her spouse and minor children). For the educational program to qualify, the vocational training program must be undertaken in an established vocational or other recognized nonacademic institution. Training in programs such as the following, for example, has been considered acceptable for vocational students: training to qualify as an automobile mechanic, welder, secretary, computer programmer, television repairing, book-keeping, health care technician, and so on.

ELIGIBILITY FOR M-1 VISA

What qualifications are required of you to be eligible for an M visa? Basically, the requirements for qualification for an M-1 visa are essentially the same as those for the F-1 as set forth in Sections B.2 and B.3 above, but with just one exception: the M-1 applicant must intend to study at a VOCATIONAL or nonacademic institution. Thus, as a vocational, as opposed to academic student, you will have to apply on a Form 1-20M-N (instead of on the Form 1-20A-B which is used for the F-1 academic student visa).

NOTE: As a rule, the consular officer, however, will not usually qualify you for an M vocational student status unless you can demonstrate that the vocational training you seek is not available in your own country, and that the particular training or skill you seek to acquire is needed in your country. It's somewhat of significance for M-1 applicants to note, further, that the M category of students was carved out of the F student category by the Congress in June 1982 and made a separate category in its own right, for this specific reason: to permit closer INS supervision over students whose programs were essentially vocational in nature. The INS had felt that vocational students required shorter periods of time to complete their programs, and that because of the difficulty involved for the INS in separating out vocational students from other students, it was difficult to determine whether such students had over-stayed beyond the period required to complete their vocational training. In addition, the INS felt it needed a way of separating out the vocational student applicant since many of them had often enrolled in programs which involved skills and training which could not readily be put to use in the student's home country, thereby increasing the likelihood that such students would remain in the U.S. and seek employment upon completion of their programs. *Hence, generally the central concern of the INS in regard to the M visa applicant, is to police closely the conditions for entry and maintenance of status of such persons.*

Like the F-1 visa, the M-1 visa is issued for the estimated length of time it will take to complete the proposed program of study. However, generally academic programs involving F-1 students are considered to last longer than vocational or non-academic programs involving the M-1 student, and M-1 students are generally given a period lasting no loner than one year.

As an alien student (whether F-1 or M-1), once you're admitted to the U.S. you may remain in student status for up to the maximum stay allowed you (the date indicated on your Form 1-20 for academic student, or 1-20M for vocational students), plus a 60-day (only 30 days for M-1 students) grace period, provided you remain "in status" – i.e., that you remain enrolled in an approved program of studies, and maintain full-time student status and do not become inadmissible or deportable. However, when your student status expires because your maximum allowed time is up, the school you are attending is required to report to the INS that you're no longer enrolled. However, if you wish so you can apply to the designated school official of your school (the application must be made within 30 days of the Form 1-20 expiration date) for an extension of stay. And you'll probably get your extension, provided you can show that you still remain in your student status, and that you are still enrolled in an approved program, and that there is good reason why it is taking you that much time to complete your studies.

D. FOREIGN EXCHANGE STUDENT or "J" VISA

1. Basic Nature of J-1 Program

The exchange student visa, the so-called "J-1" visa, has been characterized by one expert as "the most difficult type of students visa" for the alien to obtain. The central source of this "difficulty" has to do with the fact that a special restriction exists with regard to exchange students (as well as exchange visitors, who come just as well, under the J nonimmigrant visa categories for business and industrial trainees), which does not apply to other nonimmigrant categories. Thus, under a unique legal restriction which applies to no other nonimmigrant categories, the J-1 visa holder must return to his or her home country for a period of at least 2 years immediately upon completing his or her original academic program.

In brief, what this requirement means, in practical terms, is this: that the J-1 visa holder who has spent any time at all living in the United States, cannot apply to change or adjust his status to a Permanent Resident status as an immigrant; nor can he even apply to change his status from the "J-1" nonimmigrant status to another nonimmigrant status, such as an L or H visa – until and unless he shall have first gone back to his country and lived there for the required two-year period immediately following his authorized period of study in the U.S. when the U.S. training shall have been completed.

The professed rationale and intent behind the exchange student or visitor program, is said to be primarily to help the so-called "third world" countries to implement or speed up their economic development by providing them with professionals of high skills and training which the foreign student could take back to go and assist in developing his or her native country's underdeveloped conditions. With such professed mission in mind, the U.S. immigration officials have generally had a policy of strict enforcement of the 2-year foreign residency requirement in most instances. The rule applies as well to exchange visitors who fall under these categories: those whose programs have been financed, in whole or in part, by the U.S. government, or by their own governments, or those who are nationals of countries that the U.S. Information Agency has determined to require the skills and services of persons with the alien's special training. Informed by the reality that the primary purpose of the J visa is to encourage sponsorship of Third World persons into the U.S., neither the United States nor the foreign country would often want the foreign exchange student to remain in the United States at the completion of the training program since this would then be simply self-defeating for the program.

2. Possible Waiver Of The Requirements

Under a provision of the Immigration Act (Section 212(e) thereof), however, the J-1 visa holder is allowed to avoid the 2-year foreign requirement, and may also immediately adjust his status to a permanent resident in the U.S. under one condition: if he applies for and is able to receives a WAIVER from the Department of Justice's INS. Such a waiver may be granted under the following conditions: (i) if the J-1 alien can show that he (or she) is married to a U.S. citizen or lawful permanent resident, and that departure from the U.S. would bring "exceptional hardship" upon the alien's spouse (or upon a minor child of the alien, who must be either a U.S. citizen or permanent resident), or (ii) if the alien can establish that he would be subject to persecution "on account of race, religion or political opinion" if he were to return to his country; or (iii) if the aliens home country gives a "no objection" statement in writing to the U.S. Secretary of State stating that it has no objection to such a waiver being granted to the alien; and (iv) if a waiver is requested by a U.S. government agency on behalf of the exchange alien, on the grounds that retaining the alien will be beneficial to the United State security interests or to that public good.

Readers should note, however, that most of these situations are somewhat rare or untenable. Take for example, the no-objection letter. The U.S. government is not bound by such letters, and is even of far less effect or influence to the United States government if the government will be paying all or most of the foreign exchange student's costs. Furthermore, the no-objection letter is not applicable to exchange students who apply as foreign medical graduates. In all circumstances, the waiver is adjudicated by the U.S. Attorney General's Office, and is generally granted "upon the favorable recommendation" of the USIA supporting a waiver, which is oftentimes based on the request of a U.S. Government agency or the INS. (To apply for a waiver, the alien files Form 1-612, *"Application For Waiver of the Foreign Resident Requirement,"* with the INS)

3. Foreign Nationals Who Use or Seek The J Visa Essentially Fall Into Four Groups:

i. Students seeking to pursue graduate or post-graduate program at a U.S. University;
ii. Scholars and other experts, often University professors, seeking to undertake research or train others in their skills;
iii. Foreign medical school graduates who must have at least passed Parts 1 and 11 of the National Board of Medical Examiners Examination or the Foreign Medical Graduate Examination in Medical Sciences (FMGEMS);
iv. Persons from business or industrial organizations who seek to come to the U.S. to receive training in particular occupational skills, or in a particular company's method and techniques, or an introduction to U.S. business or industrial techniques.

4.Who Qualifies For J-1 Visa

How do you qualify to receive a J-1 visa? Essentially, with a few minor differences the requirements you need to demonstrate to the local U.S. Consular Officer in your home country, are the same as those required for the F-1 student situation (Section B.2 & B.3 above).

The J-1 visa assumes, however, that the alien student will be actively engaged in on-the-job training under circumstances similar to regular employment. In other words, it is expected that the U.S. employer to whom the J-

1 alien is attached for training will be gaining some productive benefits from the alien employee's activities, even though the main purpose of the alien's presence in the U.S. is to gain on-the-job practical training. A U.S. company or institution designated by the U.S. Information Agency as an exchange visitor program sponsor, has eligibility to sponsor foreign employees as exchange visitors. There are over 1,500 USIA approved programs in existence which are authorized to sponsor J-1 visa applicants. And a current listing of exchange visitor programs is obtainable from: United States Information Agency, Office of the General Counsel, 4th and C streets, S.W., Washington D.C. 20457.

The J-1 visa is very often used in bringing "au pairs" to the U.S. Like the F-1 or M-1 visa holder, the J-1 visa alien is required to have enough money to cover his expenses while in the U.S. But, unlike the F-1 alien, the J-1 visa alien, generally a job trainee, must be employed on a full-time basis, with compensation equal to at least the prevailing minimum wage. Hence, for most J-1 students, the usual requirement that the alien must firmly establish his ability to cover all expenses in the U.S., is usually an easy one to meet. Most importantly, the purpose of the training must be to improve the alien's job or professional skills and abilities for use in his or her home country. Consequently, PROBABLY THE SINGLE MOST ESSENTIAL ELEMENT FOR A SUCCESSFUL J-1 VISA APPLICATION IS THIS: the alien applicant must show, physically and by intent, that he (she) continuously maintains a foreign residence to which he intends to return after his training, and must display no indication whatsoever that he harbors any intention to remain in the United States on a permanent basis. If, for example, you are studying, or training to prepare yourself for an occupation for which there are no jobs available in your home country, you'll probably be giving yourself away to the U.S. immigration officials, neither the INS nor the U.S. consulate officer is likely to believe that you are planning to go back there to your own country at the end of your studies in the U.S.

E. HOW TO APPLY FOR AN F, M, or J VISA

1. Where You May File Your Application: Is It Abroad or In The U.S.?

You may, depending on whether you meet the required conditions, apply for any of the educational visas in either the U.S. consulate in your home country, or in the United States. If you meet the following conditions, you may apply from within the U.S. But if otherwise, then the place for you to file will be in your home country:

- You are physically present already in the U.S.
- You have been accepted as a student by a U.S. government approved school (a USIA-approved exchange visitor program sponsor, in the case of the J-1 visa applicant), and the school or program sponsor has given you a Certificate of Eligibility
- You had entered the U.S. legally and did not enter as a visitor without a visa under the visa waiver program.
- You have never worked illegally in the U.S.
- The date on your 1-94 card has not passed, and
- You are not legally inadmissible on any of the grounds outlined in Chapter 17

2. Inquire About Your Local U.S. Consulate's or INS's Filing Policies And Procedures

Turn to Section C.2 of Chapter 4 and apply here the same details contained therein. See, also, Chapter 18, Sections A and B, for more on the subject of variation in policies and practices among different consulates and INS offices). A complete list of U.S. Consulates around the world, and of the INS offices in the U.S., are in Appendices A and B respectively.

3. Application Forms Used

First, under the educational visa application procedures, with respect to the F-1 and M-1 visas before you even begin to apply for those, you shall have FIRST applied to and been accepted by an "accredited" school in the Unites States which is approved by the U.S. Attorney General for foreign student attendance. And with respect to the J-1 visas, before you may apply for those, you must have FIRST located a U.S. sponsor (it could be an academic institution or a business enterprise) that is approved by the U.S. Information Agency, which administers the applicant's intended J-1 exchange visitor program. In the case of the J-1 visa application, such government approved exchange visitor programs (or their sponsors) are generally impossible to find outside the normal business or academic channels. Hence, as a practical matter, unless you are a university student or a recent foreign graduate (particularly one in the technical or medical professions), or one associated with a business which itself has connections to potential approved U.S. sponsors, you will probably find it impossible to find a suitable J-1 visa sponsor, or one which is USIA-approved. On the other hand, with regard to F-1 and M-1 visas, as a practical matter, schools which qualify as accredited schools approved by the U.S. Attorney-General for the purpose of the F-1 and M-1 visas, are very common, and include all elementary, secondary and post- secondary educational institutions, all schools listed in the U.S. Department of Education Publications, or secondary schools operated by a college or university listed in the said publications. Most private institutions with established reputation and recognizable names are almost probably approved. Nevertheless, when applying for enrolment in an educational institution, unless it is a public institution, you should always inquire, anyway, just to be sure that the private institution is in fact one approved by the U.S. Attorney General's office.

Upon your being accepted by the institution, the institution returns to you (the alien student) a part of the form that you had completed. Form 1-20A-B in the case of the F-1 and M-1 student, and Form 1AP-66, in the case of the J-1 student, with the first page of the form completed by the institution. This form, which is sent you by the institution, is what is known as the *Certificate of Eligibility.* And only then, AFTER – and if – you shall have received this Certificate of Eligibility, may you now apply to the immigration authorities for your educational visa*.

i) Prepare The Following Basic Forms

• Form 1-20 A-B, *Certificate of Eligibility For Nonimmigrant (F-1/M-1) Student Status*

This form applies only for F-1 and M-1 applicants. It is provided by the U.S. school you are to attend after you shall have directly applied to the school and been accepted and met their other requirements (such as paying all or part of the tuition in advance). You will play no part in completing this form, other than for you to submit it to the U.S. consulate or the INS and to sign it upon submitting it to them. (NOTE: make sure that the consular (or INS) official returns this form to you in the end as you would be expected to present it to the immigration admission officers when you appear at the U.S. point-of-entry) [see sample of Form 1-120 A-B on p. 155]

• Form 1AP-66, *Certificate of Eligibility For Exchange Visitor (J-1) Status.*

This form applies only for J-1 applicants. You obtain this form from a U.S. company or institution approved and designated by the U.S. Information Agency as an Exchange Visitor Program Sponsor authorized to sponsor J-1 visa applicants. (see Section D.4 above for the address of the USIA which maintains a free list of such USIA-approved sponsors). This form (Form 1AP-66) will be completed in its entirety by the J-1 sponsor, and will then be returned directly to the visa applicant. The applicant will then present the form to the U.S. consulate (or INS) at the time of the application, and the applicant is then to sign it in the presence of the consulate official. (see sample of Form 1AP-66 on p. 159)

• Form OF-156, *Nonimmigrant Visa Application*

This form is required ONLY IN overseas filings with a U.S. consulate. Generally, if your visa application is filed at a U.S. consulate in a foreign country, the consulate will usually provide you with their required "optional forms," complete with the instructions for completing them, and such forms are designated by a prefix "OF" preceding a number, as in OF-156. (see illustrative sample of Form OF-156 on p. 177)

NOTE: Form OF-156 is the basic application form which the vast majority of nonimmigrant visa applicants will encounter. The proper completion of this form is, by far, the single most important and primary thing you can do in any nonimmigrant visa application which will determine ultimately whether you get the visa or

*Under the immigration rules, the mere presentation by the student of a valid Certificate of Eligibility, is to be treated as a "prima facia evidence" – that is, as a probable cause to believe – that the student will engage in a full course of study in the U.S. and that the institution in question is an accredited school duly approved by the Immigration and Naturalization Service (INS) for attendance by foreign students. It should be noted, however, that such evidence alone is not always accepted as final or conclusive by the consular or immigration personnel, and that they may a times (as they are entitled to do under the law) make their own independent determination on the issue.

not. For that reason, we set forth in one chapter, Chapter 13, a detailed, step-by-step instructions by which to properly complete the form and the underlying considerations by which to answer the questions asked or to provide the information required therein. Please refer immediately to Chapter 13.

- Form 1-134. *Affidavit of Support* for you and each accompanying relative.

This form applies essentially to the F-1 and M-1 student. It is optional and not necessarily required, in that an applicant may consider getting one or more of his relatives or friends (they must be U.S. citizens or Green Card holders) to provide this for him for the purpose proving that he has the financial means to support himself for his studies (or for participating in the exchange program) for at least one year without having to resort to unlawful employment in the U.S. (Sample of form is on p.173)

- Form 1-539, *Application To Extend/Change Nonimmigrant Status.*

This form is applicable only in a U.S. filing and to accompanying relatives of the principal alien applicant. Only one application form is needed for an entire family. (See sample of Form 1-539 on p. 183)

ii) Supporting Documents:

- Same documents as those listed in Chapter 5, Section G.3 (ii) thereof under "General Supporting Documents for Most Nonimmigrant Situations," may apply here. (see p. 30)

In addition, the following may be particularly necessary and helpful.

- Documentation appropriate to establish that sufficient funds are or will be available to you to cover all expenses during the entire period of your study in the U.S. (Example: AFFIDAVIT OF SUPPORT preferably from the applicant's relatives, such as the parents. (See sample of this form in p. 173)

NOTE: Note, however, that the financial status of the person furnishing this affidavit is often closely evaluated by the consular officer to establish the person's ability to provide the support, and to probe the depth of his obligation and commitment to the applicant.

- Documentation appropriate to establish that you (the alien) have "successfully completed a course of study equivalent to that normally required of an American student seeking enrolment at an institution at the same level" – school transcript, diplomas, awards, etc.
- Substantial evidence, particularly with regard to your ties to your country, in proof that you intend to depart the U.S. upon completing your studies. (Examples: evidence of availability of employment in the alien's home country in the field in which the alien is undertaking studies, evidence of strong family ties in his home country to which he is likely to return).

F. FINAL STEPS IN CONCLUDING THE SECURING OF THE VISA

When you've filed your initial application papers with either the U.S. consulate in a foreign country, or the INS in the United States (Sections E.1, E.2, and E.3 above), the immigration officials will go to work on the application, and take you through a series of steps and procedures that are required for the processing of your visa till the approval of your visa is granted. The remainder of the steps and procedures you'll need to undergo in the processing of your visa application from this point on till the end when you (the alien) actually receive the visa in hand, and till when you even get admitted into the U.S., are essentially the same as those outlined in Chapter 5 beginning from Section G.4 thereof. Hence, turn to Chapter 5 at Section G.4, *"File The Forms and Supporting Documents with the U.S. Consulate or INS office"* (p. 33). And finish up the rest of your visa processing as provided there, starting precisely from there.

Chapter 7

Getting A Visa As A Temporary Specialty Worker: The H-1B Visa

A. THE THREE DIFFERENT CLASSES OF THE H VISA

The temporary worker or trainee classes of visa – the "H" and "L" types of visas – are among the most popular and commonly applied for nonimmigrant visa categories by aliens. Basically, this category falls into four main classifications, three of which fall under the "H" classification, with the last one falling under the "L" classification. The following are the three H-type visa classifications:

(i.) The H-1B or Specialty occupation temporary worker
(ii.) The H-2B or Temporary non-agricultural worker
(iii.) The H-3 or Industrial trainee temporary worker

The dependants – that is, the spouse and minor children – accompanying or following to join the principals under each "H" category, are classified as having the H-4 status. Such relatives are granted the H-4 visas simply by providing proof of their relationship to the principal alien. H-4 aliens are not permitted to work, however, except that the children are allowed to go to school.

B. THE H-1B VISA OR SPECIALTY OCCUPATION TEMPORARY WORKER ALIEN

In this Chapter, we shall address the H-1B category of nonimmigrant visa. The number of visas which can be issued under this category is subject to changes by Congress from time to time, depending on the prevailing job skills needs of the economy. For the fiscal 1998 year, for example, there was a quota of 65,000 visa allotted to the H-1B category. In November 2000, Congress bowing to the intense pressure by high-tech companies to be allowed to hire skilled foreigners, particularly computer programmer and software engineers, raised the number of H-1B visas which the INS would be able to issue to 195,000 per year, up from the then existing 115,000 yearly figure.

C. THE RIGHTS AND PRIVILEGES CONFERRED BY H-1B VISA

Basically, if you are an alien interested in working temporarily in the United States for three to five years, and know of an American business which would be willing to sponsor you, then you are good candidate for an H-1B visa. The H-1B visa authorizes you (the alien) to work legally for the person or business who acted as your sponsor into the U.S. for the H-1B visa; the alien may travel in and out of the U.S. (or he may remain continuously in the country) until the expiration of his H-1B status. However, while the H-1B alien may work legally in the U.S., he is restricted to working only for one specific employer – to just the employer who sponsored the H-1B alien into the United States. And if you wish to change jobs from your original sponsor to another U.S. employer, then you must apply for and secure a new H-1B visa altogether from the INS.

H-1B status lasts for no more than 6 years, though it must be renewed after the first 3 years. Then, you must return to your home country (unless, of course, you can in the meantime meet the eligibility requirements which would have allowed you to change to another nonimmigrant visa category or to apply for an immigrant visa). Accompanying relatives may stay in the U.S. with the H-1B alien, but may not work, unless they qualify for a work visa independently in their own right.

D. WHO QUALIFIES FOR THE H-1B VISA

Briefly summarized, to qualify for an H-1B visa, here are the basic qualifications:

1. You (the applying alien) must have first had a specific job offer from a "qualified" U.S. employer for work to be performed in the United States. And such U.S. employer (it can be a company or an individual) has to be willing and able to act as the petitioner who sponsors you in filling for and getting the H-1B visa.
2. You must be coming to the U.S. to perform for the employer the kind of services which qualifies as "specialty occupation" – defined as an occupation requiring highly specialized knowledge normally acquired through a university education. Or, you must be a distinguished fashion model. If the particular job or occupation is one which usually requires a license or some other official or professional certification by the U.S. State in which you will be working in order to practice your particular occupation (e.g. law, medicine, architecture, teaching, accounting, etc), then you must also have obtained the right license or certification in addition to your educational credentials.

In other words, for the purposes of an H-B visa qualification, the position offered can't be just any type of job, it must be of such caliber that it really requires the skills of a highly educated person. That is to say, it is not enough in such a situation, that the foreign employee is a professional; the job itself must be one which is usually filled by a professional. If the architects in the example used below in the Section D, were being hired, instead, to perform primarily non-professional duties, the application for H-1B visa would fail. Specialty jobs which require a university degree would qualify, such as the following: a nuclear scientist, a certified public accountant, an architect, engineer, lawyer, physician, surgeon, and school and college teacher, computer systems analyst, physical therapist, chemist, pharmacist, medical technologist, hotel manager (large hotels), and upper level business managers. Lately, in the early 21st century, jobs primarily in the high-technology industries have come to be among those most identified with the H-1B visa category, such as computer programmers and software engineers.

3. The job must be such that it usually requires a bachelors degree or higher degree (or the equivalence in work experience) as the minimum requirement for entry into the position, or a bachelor's degree as the common requirement to the industry in parallel positions among similar organizations; or the nature of the specific duties of the position is such that they are so specialized and complex that it can be performed only by a person with at least a bachelor's degree. Or, where the alien lacks the university degree, then he must have its equivalence in work experience. Under the INS procedures, three years of responsible work experience is considered equivalent to one year of university education, meaning that with at least 12 years of work experience, an alien with no university education may possibly qualify for an H-1B visa.

4. The job offered you (the alien) by the U.S. employer must be paying at least the "prevailing wage" that is generally paid workers for your type of job in that particular geographic area of the U.S.

5. The alien must possess the general educational or professional credentials or job experience required to meet the general standards outlined above. But, <u>in addition</u>, he must also have the correct background and abilities that match the specific job he is offered. For example, if you are a qualified Certified Public Accountant, but are offered a position managing a computer software company in the U.S., you will not be considered eligible for an H-1B visa because you lack a background in computer software business which is the related background for the job you are supposed to do. Or, for another example, let's say you are a prominent business person but lack a university degree, you will generally not be granted an H-IB visa, even though you may have had a substantial on-the-job experience. Rather, a better suited educational training visa instead of that, would be the O-1 visa. Likewise, if you are, for example, an athlete or entertainer, you are unlikely to be granted an H-IB visa; rather, you stand a better chance of securing an O or P visa, in stead of the H-IB visa.

6. Finally, an important qualification is that the alien must not simply have a qualified U.S. employer. But the U.S. employer must sponsor the alien for an H-IB visa. Basically, the U.S. employer does so by first filing what is known as an "attestation" *(also known as a Labor Condition Application)* with the U.S. Department of Labor (DOL), essentially certifying that the services of the alien are essential to the American enterprise, and that the alien as well as other American workers, are being treated fairly. (To file an attestation, the U.S. employer simply completes DOL's Form ETA-9035 and submits it to a regional office of the DOL. See p. 189 for a sample of the form and filing procedures. A list of the addresses of the Department of Labor offices is in Appendix C).

E. THE ATTRACTIVE ASPECTS OF THE H-IB VISA

This visa is a highly sought after one because, unlike many other types of visas in the non-immigrant category, the position that is filled by the H-1B visa alien can be a PERMANENT position. With respect to the H-1B visa, it is only the U.S. employer's need for the alien (but not the position itself) that is required to be temporary. To put it another way, under the unique rules pertaining to H-1B visa procedures, the job offer made an alien by a prospective American employer must be envisioned as being *temporary* – as far as the H-IB applicant is concerned. That is to say, the job itself need not be temporary, only the employer-employee relation. Sounds a bit confusing? You're probably wondering, for example, why any employer or company would be willing to hire anyone, any way, more especially from a foreign country, whom it didn't intend to keep and who didn't intend to stay on? But this, nevertheless, is the preeminent requirement for obtaining an H-1 visa, and one which is required to be adhered to strictly if the application is to succeed!

Here's one illustrative example cited by Christopher E. Henry, a New York immigration lawyer. An architecture firm in the U.S. specializes in renovating victorian-design mansions in New England and expects to continue to do so indefinitely. They need architects who have had prior experience in doing this type of work, but there aren't many in U.S. So, they advertise for help in London. The jobs which they are offering are, or could be, permanent in nature quite alright; but they must envision only a temporary relationship with the foreign employee in hiring them.

Furthermore, a major advantage of the H-IB visa is that with respect to the H-IB visa the Immigration Service recognizes what is known as "dual intent", which says that while the sponsoring companies and the alien employees envision only a temporary relationship, they are, nevertheless, legally permitted to apply for the IMMIGRANT kind of visa (the permanent residency or Green Card) for these same employees under the employment-based Third Preference category, even while these aliens are working in the U.S. in their H-1B status. And, in fact, this is actually the basic route by which many foreign persons attain their permanent residency in the United States!

NOTE: As a rule, H-1B visa applications made by the alien without a university degree are subjected to far greater scrutiny than for those with a degree. Consequently, persons without a degree who are contemplating applying for an H-1B visa would probably be well-advised to apply directly for an employment-based Third Preference immigrant visa (the Green Card or permanent residency visa), instead. Why? Because the requirements are essentially the same (see Chapter 15 of Volume 2, especially Section D thereof)*, and yet with a Green Card an alien is far better off than simply getting an H-IB visa which is only a temporary worker's visa, in that, with such a Green Card, you can live and work in the U.S. for as long as you wish, and can change employers at will without having to receive permission from, or to notify the immigration

*One possible difference is that the Third Preference job would require a Labor Certification from the Department of Labor (DOL), while the H-1B job would require merely that the alien's U.S. employer and H-1B sponsor file an attestation with the DOL.

service, and so on.

On the other hand, you should also consider the central reality that, realistically, it is probably easier to get a U.S. employer to sponsor you for an H-1B visa than for a Green Card since it is generally a lot faster and easier to obtain an H-1B visa, and, furthermore, with a H-1B visa you can get into the U.S., and once you are in the country with a work permit, it is usually easier to find an employer willing to sponsor you for a Green Card (or other avenues for securing one).

F. HOW TO FILE FOR THE H-1B VISA

Briefly summarized, an application for an H-1B visa is a two-part process. In the first place , the alien visa applicant must have a specific job offer from a "qualified" American employer for work to be performed in the U.S.

The U.S. employer (he may be a company or an individual) will then act as the petitioner and sponsor for the alien in getting the H-1B visa. The business or individual, in order to act as the alien's sponsor for the H-1B visa petition, must first file an "attestation" with the U.S. Department of Labor (DOL). Once this has been done, from this point on the act of getting an H-1B visa is a two-part process. First, the U.S. employer, as the formal petitioner for the visa, files the "petition" for the visa on the alien's behalf with the Immigration and Naturalization Service (INS). Then, secondly, the alien himself (and the accompanying relatives, if any) now files the actual visa "application" with either the INS (if he's already in the U.S. in some other type of nonimmigrant visa and meets other conditions for it), or in a U.S. consulate abroad, if the alien is living outside the U.S.

1. STEP ONE: THE VISA "PETITION" PHASE

a. The U.S. employer who is able and willing to sponsor the alien H-1B visa-seeker, makes a specific job offer to the alien, and completes and files the DOL's Form ETA-9035 (known as the "attestation" or Labor Condition application) with the required office of the DOL in the United States. (See p. 191 for a sample copy of this form. A list of the addresses, phone numbers and fax numbers of the Dept of Labor offices is in Appendix C).

To file for the attestation, the U.S. employer simply mails or faxes the Form ETA-9035 to the DOL regional office. Upon the acceptance of the attestation, the DOL returns to the employer one of the original ETA-9035 forms, with a DOL endorsement stamped thereon.

b. The U.S. employer, upon receiving from the DOL its endorsement of the attestation application, completes the petition form for the H-1B visa on the alien's behalf – Form 1-129 and the H supplement. The U.S. employer then submits the said Form 1-129H, *Petition for a Non-immigrant Worker,* to one of the four INS regional office centers in the U.S. covering the intended employer's place of business. (All H-1B visa papers in the PETITION phase are filed in the U.S. with the INS centers). See sample of Form 1-129 on pp. 162, 165 & 168. Add supplement H of the form.

NOTE: Form 1-129B, which is the previous version of the current Form 1-129H, is shown on pp. 162, 165 & 168. This earlier version of the current form is reproduced here for illustrative purposes to illustrate the actual visa filing procedures in an actual case previously filed and successfully processed for the same type of visa, material obtained courtesy of C. James Cooper, Jr., a long-time veteran Denver, Colorado immigration lawyer and specialist. See "EXPLANATORY NOTES" on p. 37

Note, also, that under the system in current use, the latest version of the Form 1-129 has various "Supplements" to the basic form, each for particular nonimmigrant classifications – E, F, H, L, O, P, R, etc. And all you have to do is complete the basic Form 1-129 and simply tear out and use the supplement that applies for your visa category.

Supporting Documents For Visa Petition

U.S employer-petitioner attaches the following supporting documents to the petition forms:

- A copy of DOL endorsed attestation, Form ETA-9035
- IN GENERAL, gather and provide the kinds of documentations which will apply in providing that alien's qualification under the particular employment specification to which the alien belongs, as set forth in Section D above.
- JOB VERIFICATION DOCUMENTS from the U.S. employer to prove that the business entity actually exists, and that it can afford to employ and to pay the alien the required salary, and that it earns sufficient income to be able to do so. You may provide, for example, the company's U.S. tax returns for the past 2 years. Or, bank statements for the company and the balance sheet, plus the profit and loss statements, may be submitted. Publicly held corporations and larger, better known companies that are nationally or internationally known, may generally not have to produce such documents; for such companies the corporate annual reports would usually suffice.
- EVIDENCE OF JOB OFFER and that the job is a professional level one: supporting letters or written offer of employment or sworn affidavits from the alien's U.S. petitioner-employer, giving the alien's job specifications, salary, and facts as to whether the employment is long term or permanent (see samples of such a letter on pp. 192, 200, 202). You may include a separate statement giving a detailed description of all job functions, with an explanation of how and why it is generally held by, say, highly experienced and degreed people, and how and why advanced knowledge and education (or the particular knowledge and the level of education you claim is required by the specific visa classification involved) are essential to the performance of the job function. Written affidavits from experts, such as educators in the field or other employers in similar business, stating that the kind of job at issue is normally held by highly qualified, experienced or degreed persons of the kind sought by the present U.S. employer-petitioner.
- EVIDENCE OF THE ALIENS'S JOB EXPERIENCE, OR THAT HE IS A PROFESSIONAL: Letters or affidavits from the alien's previous (and/or present) employers, professors or professional colleagues
- Certified copies of CERTIFICATES, DIPLOMAS, SCHOOL TRANSCRIPTS, and other documents and proofs of educational qualification, job skills or professional status for the job or position claimed. (see samples of this on pp. 189-190, 196-199).
- SWORN AFFIDAVITS FROM CREDIBLE AUTHORITIES OR EXPERTS in the alien's field of expertise testifying from their personal knowledge or evaluation that the alien has the special technical training or specialized experience claimed – e.g. the skill to use a particular machine or to speak a foreign language that such a job calls for.
- PUBLISHED MATERIALS BY OR ABOUT THE ALIEN in newspapers, magazines, professional journals, etc.
- PROOF OF PROFESSIONAL LICENSES, membership in professional societies, achievement awards, and the like.
- CERTIFICATE AWARDS from trade union or technical schools, apprenticeship schools, etc.
- LICENSES or trade union certificates.
- Enclose the appropriate filing fees. The current amount for this as of this writing is $130, if no change of status is being requested, and $155, if change of status is requested. Send payment in a check or money order.

NOTE: If the alien had been educated outside the U.S. in a foreign country, it is not uncommon for the INS to request that a credentials evaluation be made by an accredited academic evaluation service in the U.S. before such credentials could be accepted for immigration purposes. (See Chapter 18, Section G for pointers on this)

c. Approval of the Visa Petition

When the sponsoring U.S. employer completes the application forms and the necessary supporting documents, the employer "files" the papers with (i.e. he submits them to) one of the four INS regional service centers in the U.S. which cover's the area of the intended employer's business. The papers should be mailed to the INS office by certified mail, with return receipt requested, so that you can retain the receipt as proof that the package was received. (See Appendix B for the addresses of the INS offices nationwide).

NOTE: The Form 1-129, which is the actual petition for all employment-related nonimmigrant visas, is required to be completed not by the alien, but always by the alien's prospective U.S. employer. You should note, however, that nothing in the immigration rules stops you (the alien) from helping out your U.S. employer with the paperwork involved. In fact, it is generally expected and highly advisable that you do so in order to lessen the inconvenience and time factor on the sponsoring employer and to facilitate his willingness to act as the visa sponsor. Generally, for example, it is not uncommon to find that it is the alien who would fill out the forms and prepare most of the papers involved, and simply have the employer check them over for factual accuracy and then sign them.

You (i.e. employer) will receive from the INS, within a week or two of the mailing, a written notice of confirmation that the papers are being processed. The notice also gives you the immigration "file number" assigned to the case, and approximately when you are to expect a decision. If some material defects or omissions are found in the papers, such as unsigned forms or missing information or documents or the payment, the INS will probably return the entire application paper to you (the prospective U.S. employer) with a note or a Form 1-797, *Notice of Acton,* telling him or her what corrections need to be made, or what additional documents or pieces of information need to be supplied. Or, in some cases the INS will simply retain the papers already submitted but issue a request, in the form of a Form 1-797, for the additional items that are needed. And, in such an event, all you'll need to do is simply supply the additional data required and promptly mail them (along, with the Form 1-797 and the rest of the file, if applicable) back to the INS office.

The employers' H-1B petitions are usually approved by the INS within some 3 to 8 weeks. Upon such approval, the INS sends the employer a *Notice of Action* Form 1-797 showing that the petition has been approved. Where the alien visa beneficiary is residing abroad, or where the alien otherwise intends to undertake the second phase of the visa processing abroad (see STEP Two below), the INS will also notify the U.S. consulate of the alien's choice designated in the petition papers, and forward a complete file of the case to that consulate to enable its further processing of the visa request.

2. STEP TWO: THE VISA "APPLICATION" PHASE

Once the original "petition" filed by the U.S. employer has been approved by the INS – and only then – the second phase of the H-1B visa application can then be commensed. Here's the important point: this second phase is called the "application", and is undertaken primarily BY THE ALIEN, rather than by the U.S. employer.

(a) Where You May File The Application: Is It Abroad,Or In The U.S.

You (the alien visa-seeker) may, depending on whether you meet the required conditions for it, apply for the H-1B visa at the U.S. consulate in your home country, or at the INS office in the U.S. The conditions you must meet in order to be eligible to file in the U.S. are the same conditions as are outlined in Chapter 4, Section C.1 (p. 19). Otherwise, then you have to file in a U.S. consulate abroad.

(b) Inquire About Your Local U.S. Consulate's or INS's Visa Policies and Procedures

Turn to Section C.2 of Chapter 4 and apply here the same details contained therein. See, also, Chapter 18, Sections A and B, for more on the subject of variations in visa processing policies and practices among different consulates and INS offices. A complete list of U.S. Consulate around the world, and of the INS offices in the U.S., are in Appendices A and B respectively.

(c) Form and Documentations Used

i. prepare the following forms

- Optional Form OF-156, *Nonimmigrant Visa Application.* This form is required ONLY WHEN AN OVERSEAS FILING with a U.S. consulate is involved. Generally, if your visa application is filed at a U.S. consulate in a foreign country, the consulate will usually provide you (the alien) with their required "option forms" complete with the instructions for completing them, and such forms are designated by a prefix "OF" preceding a number, as in OF-156. (see illustrative sample of Form OF-156 on p.177).

NOTE: OF-156 is the basic application form which the vast majority of non-immigrant visa applicants will encounter. The proper completion of this form is, by far, probably the single most important and primary thing you can do in any nonimmigrant visa application which will determine ultimately whether you get the visa or not. For that reason, we set forth in one chapter, Chapter 13, the detailed, step-by-step instructions by which to answer the questions asked or to provide the information required therein. Please refer immediately to Chapter 13.

- Form 1-539, *Application To Extend/Change Nonimmigrant Status.* This form is applicable only if it is a U.S. filing that you are doing, and for accompanying relatives of the principal alien applicant, if any. Only one application form is needed for an entire family, except that if there's more than one accompanying relative, each should be listed on the form. (sample of Form 1-539 is on p.183).

ii. Supporting Documents To Attach

For the supporting documents, turn to Chapter 5, Section G.3 (ii) [p.30] and attach for your supporting documents the same kinds of documents listed under "General Supporting Documents For Most Non-immigrant Situations". Except that you should note, however, that for the H-1B visa, documentation relating to proof of the alien's financial status would not generally be relevant or required.

(d) File The "Application" Papers With The U.S. Consulate or The INS, As Applicable

Turn to Section G.4 of Chapter 5 (p.33) and follow here the same procedures outlined therein to file your visa application.

(e) Attend The Visa Interview, If One Is Required In Your Case

Whether you are doing a U.S. filing or a consulate filing, a face to face personal interview with the visa processing officials may or may not be required in your case before the authorities render their final decision in your visa issuance. In any event, if a visa interview is required in your particular case, you will be so notified by the visa processing office. Upon your gathering together all the items required by the consulate or the INS, whichever one is applicable, you will appear on the appointed date, time and place set for the interview and undergo one with the designated interviewer. The visa processing officials will promptly render a final decision on your application, but only AFTER such interview.

[Turn to Chapter 15 for the full procedures involved in this all-important step in any nonimmigrant (as well as immigrant) visa application - the visa interview].

(f) Final Approval of Your Visa Application

In the end, assuming that everything is in order with your visa application – basically, that you have, for example, all the proofs and documentation required to show your eligibility for the visa applied for, and that there's nothing that makes you inadmissible under the U.S. Immigration law, such as having some serious criminal or terrorist record or potential, or a contagious, communicable disease – your application for a visa will be approved. You will be issued your visa. The U.S. consul in charge of visa issuance (if a consulate filing abroad is involved), will usually stamp the approved visa that applies in your case (say, a E-1 or E-2 visa, in the case of the treaty trader or investor) in your passport. If you got your visa through a U.S. filing, upon approval of your visa application, you are given a visa "status", and not an actual visa. (Under the law, only Consulates may issue visas, and not the INS). This may be stamped in your passport, and you will receive from the INS a *Notice of Action* Form 1-797 indicating the dates for which your status is approved, with a new 1-94 card attached at the bottom of the form.

(g) Now, Get Formally "Admitted" Into The U.S. at a Port of Entry

As a holder of a non-immigrant type of visa, you will normally be authorized to stay in the U.S. for a specific period of time, depending on the type and classification of the nonimmigrant visa involved. For example, for a B visa, you are normally authorized to stay in the U.S. for 6 months with the possibility of multiple extensions upon future application, while for an E-1 or E-2 visa, the authorized period of stay is 2 years at a time, with the possibility of extensions or renewal of the visa for additional one- or two-year periods, and so on with respect to other types of nonimmigrant visas. And when you enter the U.S. from a foreign country with your visa, you will at that time be given a 1-94 card, which will be stamped with the dates showing your authorized stay. Then, each time you exit and re-enter the U.S., you will get a new 1-94 card with a new period of authorized stay affixed thereto.

BUT HERE'S THE MAIN ISSUE OF IMPORTANCE YOU SHOULD NOTE HERE: before you can be actually allowed entry into the U.S. even with your approved and issued visa in hand, you must first be formally "admitted" into the country – that is, you have to successfully pass through some strict formalities involved in a procedure called the "inspection and admission" process into the United States. Turn to Chapter 16, "*Entering The United States: The Process of Getting Actually Admitted Into The Country After You've Got Your Visa In Hand.*" *(p. 118)*

(h) You May Be Denied A Visa. What Can You Do?

What if, in the end, for whatever the reason, your visa application is turned down and you are denied a visa? Turn to Chapter 5, Section G.8 "*What To Do If Your Visa Application Is Denied*" (p. 35)

Chapter 8

Getting A Visa As A Temporary Non-Agricultural Worker: The H-2B Visa

A. WHAT IS THE H-2B VISA OR TEMPORARY NON-AGRICULTURAL WORKER ALIEN?

The H-2B visas are granted to both skilled and unskilled workers who are found to be in short supply in the United States. Basically, the visa is for an alien who is coming to the U.S. for a temporary or seasonal nonagricultural job with a U.S. employer. The need for the alien employee must be TEMPOPARY, even though the job itself may not be of temporary nature. The H-2B visa applies to aliens whose skills or occupation do not rise to the level of an H-1B applicant. Compared to H-1B visas, which are intended for university-educated workers, the H-2B visa holder may be either skilled or unskilled worker.

The H-2B visa is subject to a quota restriction of the number which can be issued every year. For the fiscal 1998 year, for example, there was a quota of 66,000 visas allotted by Congress to the H-2B category.

B.THE RIGHTS AND PRIVILEGES CONFERRED BY AN H-2B VISA

With the H-2B visa, the alien may travel in and out of the U.S. (or he may remain continuously) until the expiration of his H-2B status. The H-2B visa holder may work legally in the U.S., but only for one specific employer – for just that employer who sponsored him or her into the U.S. And if the alien wishes to change jobs, he must then apply for and secure a completely new H-1B visa. The visa is initially approved for up to only one year, with additional one year extensions permitted up to a maximum of 3 years. Thereafter, you (the H-2B visa holder) must return to your home country and wait for at least one year before you may apply for another H-2B visa (unless, of course, you can in the meantime meet the eligibility requirements which would have allowed you to change to another nonimmigrant category or to apply for an immigrant visa).

C. WHO QUALIFIES FOR THE H-2B VISA

As stated above, to qualify for a visa under the H-2B category, an alien need not necessarily have any specific or unique skill or ability. Indeed, he need not have any skill or ability per se – he (she) may be skilled, or semi-skilled or totally unskilled. What is of relevance here, is that the position the H-2B applicant seeks to fill be temporary in nature, and that the job in question be one for which there is a demonstrated shortage of available American workers, as officially certified by the U.S. Department of Labor. Persons like seasonal laborers, workers on short-term business projects and those who come to the U.S. as trainers of other workers and even professionals like entertainers who cannot meet the requirements for the O or P visas (Chapter 12 of this manual), commonly get the H-2B visa. An entertainer with specific bookings, for example, would be considered a "temporary" a position as that has most of the attributes – the bookings are a one-time occurrence, they meet a seasonal need or fulfill an intermittent but not regular need of the employer.

The Basic Requirements for Qualification For an H-2B Visa

To qualify for an H-2B visa, here is a summary of the basic requirements:

1. Job Offer Must be One of The Appropriate Nature

The applying alien must first have a specific job offer from a U.S. employer to perform a nonagricultural work inside the U.S. that is either temporary or seasonal in nature. And this U.S. employer has to act as the petitioner who sponsors the alien in getting the H-2B visa.

For the job to qualify, the job you are offered can't be just any position. Rather, it must be one that meets the legal definition of a "temporary" or "seasonal" position. With respect to the "seasonality" of a job, it is relatively easy to understand what kind of jobs are seasonal. Simply put, if the need for an employer is seasonal or intermittent, then the job qualifies as seasonal. Professional minor-league baseball players, for example, would be a common example of employees who do seasonal work. Job temporariness, on the other hand, is a little harder concept to grasp for the reason that it is viewed by the law in a very different way. There are two parts to the "temporariness" concept which are relevant. First, the position that the alien is filling has to be of a temporary nature, and secondly, the company's need for the designated position itself (the employer's need for the alien employee) must also be temporary even though the job itself may not be of a temporary nature. In other words, the term "temporary" refers to the employer's need for the duties performed by the position, regardless of whether the underlying position itself is permanent or temporary. Because the H-2B visa is issued for a duration of one year at a time, under the rules for the granting of the H-2B visa for a job to be considered "temporary", the period of the employer's need for the services must generally be one year or less. A common type of job usually viewed as temporary by the INS for H-2B purposes, are those tied to a specific project of the employer, such as building a housing project. The alien employer's job in such a case is regarded as terminated once the project is completed.

Another common situation where the job is viewed a temporary for H-2B purposes (i.e., where both the need for the position as well as the position itself are viewed as temporary), is in a training position since training positions involve spending a limited time teaching others how to carry out specific procedures or how to use special equipments. An example of this would be where a U.S. employer starts a new manufacturing operation and requires the assistance of a foreign expert who can train the U.S. employer's workers and give consulting advice to the management on the running and administration of the new operation. Thus, in this example, the position (the foreign expert's) is temporary in that it has a defined beginning and end; and the need for the position is temporary since the employer's need for the position will terminate with the completion of the job.

NOTE: The mere designation of a position's or job's termination date does not meet the proof of "temporariness" to the Immigration and Naturalization Service. Rather, in other to support the visa petition, the employer must provide operational evidence showing the projected termination of the position as well as the employer's need for the position.

2. Alien Must Possess The Correct Background

Another requirement for being granted an H-2B visa, is that you (the applying H-2B alien) must have the correct background and abilities for the specific job you have been offered, even though under the basic rules governing the H-2B eligibility the visa can be issued to unskilled as well as skilled workers. For example, if you are a qualified bookkeeper, but are after a position of managing a restaurant, you will not qualify for an H-2B visa because you lack specific background in restaurant business.

3. There Should Be No Qualified Americans Available For The Position

There must be no qualified Americans willing or able to take the job you have been offered. As previously stated, an important feature of the H-2B visa application, is that the U.S. employer is required to file a request with the U.S. Department of Labor asking for the DOL's Temporary Labor Certification as a prerequisite to the filing of the H-2B petition. And, in the process of doing this, if the U.S. employer is to successfully obtain the Temporary Labor Certificate, he must prove to the DOL that there are no U.S. workers available in the location of the job placement who are willing and able to perform the required work at the prevailing wage rate. In addition, the U.S. employer will need to prove that the employment of the alien worker(s) will not adversely affect the U.S. labor market.

4. Alien Must Show Absolute Intent To Return To His/Her Home Country

The H-2B visa is meant to be temporary and not permanent. Indeed, in legal terms, if at all you have in mind to take up permanent residence in the United States, the H-2B visa is not for you and you are (legally) ineligible for that visa. In light of this, at the time of your applying for the H-2B visa, the fundamental presumption and precondition, is that the alien must intend to return to his home country upon the expiration date of the visa. Hence, a major requirement for the beneficiaries of an H-2B visa petition, is presentation of proof that their intention in entering the U.S. is temporary, not permanent. Obviously, it will be difficult for the immigration officials to read minds to determine who among the applying aliens genuinely intend to stay or return to their home countries. Therefore, as an H-2B visa applicant, you should be prepared to show documentary and objective proofs, that you meet this key requirement.

D. SOME BASIC DIFFERENCE BETWEEN THE H-1B AND H-2B

1. Basically, the H-1B visa could be deemed as the professional level temporary workers' visa, while the H-2B visa is the non-professional level equivalent. Unlike the H-1B visa, which allows an employer to hire foreign professionals temporarily without having to prove that a shortage of U.S. workers exists, such proof is required, in deed even crucial, in the successful filing of an H-2B visa application, as a major prerequisite for the prospective employer before an application for an H-2B visa could be made is that the prospective U.S. employer must first file for and meet the Labor Certification requirement of the Department of Labor to certify that a shortage of American workers exists for the kind of foreign labor the American employer is intending to hire.

2. On the one hand, the H-2B visa application could be said to be less restrictive in general terms, than is the H-1B visa, in that the alien employee's credentials (his/her degrees, experience, training etc) are not as closely scrutinized and are generally not as central to the success of an application in an H-2B case. On the other hand, however, the amount of time and paperwork an application for H-2B visa consumes, because such an application has to go through the Department of Labor certification, is frequently a real problem for both the American employer and the foreign employee. For the American employer, because of the amount of time it takes to get an approval, ranging from several weeks in some states to several months or more in others, it is hard for such companies to plan for their personnel needs when dealing with such constraints. And for the foreign employee, all things considered, applying for an H-2B visa is generally not in his best interests. This is primarily because the H-2B visa holder is not allowed to do an "adjustment of status" – i.e., to change from his temporary nonimmigrant status to a permanent residence or green card holder while in the United States. Hence, it may often appear far better for the alien to simply apply for employment-based Second or Third preference Green Card directly from his country (see, for example, Chapter 2 of this present manual, and Chapter 14 & 15 of Volume 2). Such application may take two or three years, but, if successful, will at least enable you to live and work in the U.S. on a permanent basis and to work where and when you choose, without having to apply and reapply for various visas and extensions for the rest of your life in the U.S.*

NOTE: It's not that if you have an H-2B visa you cannot file to get a green card to adjust the H-2B visa to a permanent residence alien status. But the point is that you should note, however, that as a practical matter, for most aliens it is nearly impossible to successfully adjust the H-2B visa to a permanent residency status. Why? This is because, since the H-2B visa, like most nonimmigrant visas, is intended for those who plan to return home once their jobs or other activities in the U.S. are completed, an application made for a green card by a H-2B alien, would, in effect, amount to making a statement that he never really intended to leave the U.S. in the first place. Therefore, it would ordinarily be almost impossible for such a person to obtain a Green Card as an H-2B visa holder since the INS will generally view such an application as a strong evidence that you had always intended to get a green card, any way, when you originally applied for the H-

---

*Readers interested in the processes of filing for Green Card applications under the employment Second and Third preference categories, should consult the Volume 2 of this manual at Chapters 14 and 15 respectively.

2B visa, and that you will not return home if you are unable to secure a green card before your H-2B visa expires. Such a position would frequently be just about impossible to overcome in the eyes of the INS officials, and should your application for a green card be denied, your existing H-2B status can almost certainly be taken away as well, leaving you with no valid U.S. visa of any kind.

Unlike the H-1 visas, no "dual intent" is recognized for the H-2B visas. And the point is that the H-2B visa holder can apply for permanent residence quite alright while working in the U.S. in the H-2B status base on labor certification. But, he may only do so when the H-2B visa shall have expired, and he shall have spent a period of not less than 6 months outside the U.S. before he may be granted any additional visa.

Finally, is it your current employer who first sponsored you for the H-2B visa that is also to sponsor you for the green card? If that is so, then, watch out, for there is a grave danger associated with that. Under the INS regulations, if an alien has an approved Labor Certification for which he was sponsored by the same employer who had petitioned for his H-2B visa, then the H-2B visa is subject to automatic revocation. Hence, unless you have another sponsoring employer completely different from the original H-2B visa sponsor to sponsor you for a green card, you had better forget changing your status to a green card from an H-2B visa status.

3. Finally, there's one other important area of difference between the H-IB and H-2B visas. Unlike the H-1B employment positions, any jobs offered the H-2B visa applicant is required to be absolutely temporary – not just as far as the employee is concerned, but also as far as the employer is concerned. For example, let's say a mining company in Montana finds miners in short supply for its workforce needs. Such a company still can't bring in foreign miners on H-2B visas, even if each miner were to stay for only a year or two, because the job itself isn't temporary (unless, of course, the company is planning to close down the mine when the alien workers' visa expire!).

E. HOW TO FILE FOR THE H-2B VISA

Briefly summarized, making an application for an H-2B visa is a THREE-PART process. First, the prospective U.S. employer who wants to employ the alien, files an application to the local Department of Labor (DOL) to obtain a Labor Certification which is to state that the DOL has so determined that no qualified U.S. workers can be found to fill the job which is being offered to the foreign employee. Second, upon approval of the employer's application by the DOL, the employer then makes another application, this time to the U.S. Immigration and Naturalization Service (INS) – this one is known as the visa "petition". Finally, if the INS approves the employer's petition, the foreign employee, himself, then applies for the H-2B visa. In this, he may do so either at his local U.S. consulate abroad, or at an INS office in the U.S., if he's already present in the U.S. and meets the required conditions for a U.S. filing. The consular (or INS) officials then make the final decision on whether the visa is to be granted or not.

1. STEP ONE: THE TEMPORARY LABOR CERTIFICATION PHASE

(a). Basically, to file for a Temporary Labor Certificate, the U.S. employer who accepts to and is able to sponsor the alien H-2B visa-seeker, makes a specific job offer to the alien, and completes the Department of Labor's Form ETA-750, Part A only, *The Offer of Employment.* (Only the part A is required for the H-2B visa). The U.S. employer then files this form with the local Department of Labor Office, which is a part of the state government, for the state office nearest the employer's place of business. There's no uniformity in operating methods among the various state employment agencies. Hence, before you file the Temporary Labor Certificate application papers, a simple phone call to your nearest state employment agency office will usually tell you where and how to file this form in your area.

IMPORTANT: This application process may not begin more than 120 days (45 days for entertainment industry related workers) before the alien employee is needed. Form ETA-750A is reproduced in p. 185, 187. (See "EXPLANATORY NOTE" on p. 37).

NOTE: For persons seeking Temporary Labor Certificate for entertainment industry performance and nonperformance workers, the application process differs in a few details. The applications are not filed with the local state employment office, but with one of the three DOL designated regional offices for the processing of entertainment industry workers:

(1) Alien Employment Certification Office
N.Y. State Dept. of Labor
1 Main St., Rm. 501
Brooklyn N.Y. 11202
Phone: 718-797-7223

(2) Alien Temporary Labor Certification Unit
Texas Employment Commission
TEC Building
Austin TX 78778
Phone: 512-397-4814

(3) Los Angeles Certification Office
California Employment Development
156 West 14th St.
Los Angeles, CA 90015
Phone: 213-744-2105

(b). Upon the approval of the application, the DOL will send the U.S. employer a decision granting the Temporary Labor Certification. (Temporary Labor Certification is considered to be only advisory. And therefore, even when such certification is denied by the DOL, an H-2B visa petition may still be filed with the INS, except that in such a situation you should be prepared to convince the INS that the DOL was wrong in its decision).

2. STEP TWO: THE VISA "PETITION" PHASE

(a). The U.S. employer, upon receiving the approved Temporary Labor Certification, now completes the petition for the H-2B visa on the alien's behalf – Form 1-129, and the H supplement. The U.S. employer then submits the completed Form 1-129H, *Petition For a Non-immigrant Worker*, to one of the 4 INS regional office centers in the U.S. for the one covering the intended employer's place of business. (All H-2B visa papers in the visa PETITION phase are required to be filed in the U.S. with the IN S centers). [See sample of Form 1-129 on pp. 162, 165 & 168, then add, the supplement H of the form].

NOTE: Form 1-129B, which is the previous version of the current form 1-129H,* is shown on pp. 162, 165 & 168. This earlier version of the current form is reproduced here for illustrative purposes, to illustrate the actual visa filing procedures in an actual case previously filed and successfully processed for an H-2B visa, material obtained courtesy of C. James Cooper, Jr., a long-time veteran Denver, Colorado immigration lawyer and specialist. See "EXPLANATORY NOTES" on p. 37.

Note, also, that under the procedures in current use, the latest version of the Form 1-129 has various "supplements" to the basic form, each for particular nonimmigrant classifications – E, F, H, L, O, P, R, etc. And all you have to do is complete the basic form 1-129 and simply tear out and use the supplement that applies to your visa category.

Supporting Documents For Visa Petition

U.S. employer-petitioner attaches the following supporting documents to the petition forms:

- The approved (the original copy) of the Temporary Labor Certifications. This is actually the Form ETA-750, Part A, returned by the DOL to the employer with a red and blue approved stamp affixed thereto. (Only the original of this, and not a photocopy, is to be submitted).
- Copies of all documentations that were submitted in the original filing for the Temporary Labor Certification
- EMPLOYER'S STATEMENT OF NEED – statement containing a full and detailed explanation of why the job

is temporary, and if the need is temporary or intermittent, whether the need is expected to occur again (see samples of such documents on pp. 194, 203).

• Documents showing evidence that the alien employee has the minimum education and experience, the skills or abilities called for in the advertisements and job description listed on the Form ETA-750A, and the manner by which such qualifications were acquired. (See samples of this on p. 193)

• In general, supply similar kinds of documentation outlined for the H-IB visa situation, as listed in Chapter 7, Section F.1(b) [p. 51].

• Enclose the appropriate filling fees. The current amount for this is $130, if no change of status is being requested, and $155, if change of status is requested. Send the payment in a check or money order.

(b.) Approval of the Visa Petition

Upon the sponsoring U.S. employer's completion of the application forms and the necessary supporting documentations, the employer "files" the papers with (i.e. he submits them to) one of the four INS Regional Service Centers in the U.S. which covers the area of the intended employer's business. The papers should be mailed to the INS office by certified mail, with return receipt requested, so that you can retain the receipt as proof that the package was received.

NOTE: The Form 1-129, which is the actual petition for all employment-related nonimmigrant visas, is required to be completed, not by the alien, but always by the alien's sponsoring U.S. employer. You should note, however, that nothing in the immigration rules stops you (the alien) from helping out your U.S. employer with the paperwork involved. In fact, it is generally expected and highly advisable that you do so in order to lessen the inconvenience and time factor on the sponsoring employer and to facilitate his willingness to act as your visa sponsor. Generally, for example, it is not uncommon to find that it is the alien who would fill out the forms and prepare most of the papers involved, and simply have the employer check them over for factual accuracy and then sign them.

You (i.e. employer) will receive from the INS, within a week or two of the mailing, a written notice of confirmation that the papers are being processed. The notice will also give the immigration "file number" assigned to the case and approximately when you are to expect a decision. If some material defects or omissions are found in the papers (unsigned forms or missing information or documents, or the payments, etc), the INS will promptly return the entire application papers to you (the prospective U.S. employer) with a note or a Form 1-797, *Notice of Acton,* telling him or her what corrections need to be made or additional documents or pieces of information need to be supplied. Or, in some cases, the INS will simply retain the papers already submitted but issue a request, in the form of a Form 1-797, for the additional items that are needed. And, in such an event, all you'll need to do is simply supply the additional data required and promptly mail them (along with the Form 1-797 and the rest of the file, if applicable) back to the INS office.

The employer's INS H-2B petitions are usually approved by the INS within some 3 to 8 weeks. Upon such approval, the INS sends the employer a *Notice of Action* Form 1-797 showing that the petition has been approved. Where the alien visa beneficiary is presently residing in a foreign country, or where the alien otherwise intends to undertake the third phase of the visa processing abroad (see STEP THREE below), the INS will also notify the U.S. consulate of the alien's choice designated in the petition papers, and forward a complete file of the case to that consulate to enable its further processing of the visa request.

3. STEP THREE: THE VISA "APPLICATION" PHASE

Once the original "petition" filed by the U.S. employer has been approved by the U.S. INS – and only then – the third phase of the H-2B visa application can be commenced. HERE'S THE IMPORTANT POINT: this third phase is called the "application", as opposed to the "petition", and is undertaken primarily by the ALIEN, rather than by the U.S. employer.

(a) Where You May File The Application: Is It Abroad,Or In The U.S.?

You (the alien visa-seeker) may, depending on whether you meet the required conditions for it, apply for the H-2B visa at the U.S. consulate in your home country, or at the INS office in the U.S. The conditions you must meet in order to be eligible to file in the U.S. are the same conditions as are listed in Chapter 4, Section C.1 [p. 19]. Otherwise, then you have to file in a U.S. consulate abroad.

(b) Inquire About Your Local U.S. Consulate's or INS's Visa Policies and Procedures

Turn to Section C.2 of Chapter 4 and apply here the same details contained therein. See, also, Chapter 18, Sections A and B, for more on the subject of variations in visa processing policies and practices among different Consulates and INS offices.

(c) Forms and Documentations Used

i. Prepare the following forms

- Optional Form OF-156, *Nonimmigrant Visa Application*. This form is required ONLY WHEN AN OVERSEAS FILINGS with a U.S. consulate is involved. Generally, if your visa application is filed at a U.S. consulate in a foreign country, the consulate will usually provide you (the alien) with their required "Optional Forms" complete with the instructions for completing them, and such forms are designated by a prefix "OF" preceding a number, as in OF-156. (see illustrative sample of Form OF-156 on p. 177).

NOTE: OF-156 is the basic application form which the vast majority of non-immigrant visa applicants will encounter. The proper completion of this form is, by far, probably the single most important and primary thing you can do in any nonimmigrant visa application which will determine ultimately whether you get the visa or not. For that reason, we set forth in one chapter, Chapter 13, detailed, step-by-step instructions by which to properly complete the form and the underlying considerations by which to answer the questions asked or to provide the information required therein, please refer immediately to Chapter 13.

- Form 1-539, *Application To Extend/Change Nonimmigrant Status*. This form is applicable only if it is a U.S. filing that you are doing, and only for accompanying relatives of the principal alien applicant, if any. Only one application form is needed for an entire family, except that if there's more than one accompanying relative, each should be listed on the form. (sample of Form 1-539 is on p.183).

ii. Supporting Documents To Attach

For the supporting documents, turn to Chapter 5, Section G.3 (ii) at [p.30] and attach as your supporting documents the same kinds of documents listed therein under "General Supporting Documents For Most Non-immigrant Situations". TAKE NOTE OF THIS, HOWEVER: that to the U.S. immigration officials the most central documentation you'll need to provide for the H-2B visa filing, are documents and related ones which would establish your intent to leave the U.S. when your visa status expires – namely, evidence such as those showing that your ties to your home country are so strong that you will be highly motivated to return to the country and the people, the assets and connections, you left there (e.g. deeds verifying your ownership of a home or other real property, letters and sworn statements from you and/or others explaining that close relatives are being left behind, or from a company showing that you have a good, well-paying job waiting for you upon your return from U.S., and similar kinds of evidence or documentation as are listed under "Proof of the Alien's Financial Status" in Chapter 5, Section G.3 (ii) [p. 31].

(d) File The "Application" Papers With The U.S. Consulate or The INS, As Applicable

Turn to Section G.4 of Chapter 5 (p.33) and follow here the same procedures outlined there to file your visa application.

(e) Attend The Visa Interview, If One Is Required In Your Case

Whether you are doing a U.S. filing or a consulate filing, a face-to-face personal interview with the visa processing officials may or may not be required in your case before the authorities render their final decision in your visa issuance. In any event, if a visa interview is required in your particular case, you will be so notified by the visa processing office. When you shall have gathered together all the items required by the consulate or the INS, whichever one is applicable, you will appear on the appointed date, time and place set for the interview and undergo one with the designated interviewer. The visa processing officials will promptly render a final decision on your application, but only AFTER such interview.

[Turn to Chapter 15 for the full procedures involved in this all-important step in any nonimmigrant (as well as immigrant) visa application – the visa interview].

(f) Final Approval of Your Visa Application

In the end, assuming that everything is in order with your visa application – basically, that you have, for example, all the proofs and documentation required to show your eligibility for the visa applied for, and that there's nothing that makes you inadmissible under the U.S. immigration law, such as having some serious criminal or terrorist record or potential, or a contagious, communicable disease – your application for a visa will be approved. You will be issued your visa. The U.S. consul in charge of visa issuance (if it's a consulate filing abroad), will usually stamp the approved visa that applies in your case (say the a B-1 and/or B-2 visa, in the case of the visitors visa, or the E-1 or E-2, in the case of treaty trader or investor) in your passport. If you got your visa through a U.S. filing, upon approval of your visa application, you are given a visa "status", and not an actual visa. (Under the law, only consulates may issue a visa, and not the INS). This may be stamped in your passport, and you will receive from the INS a *Notice of Action* Form 1-797 indicating the dates for which your status is approved, with a new 1-94 card attached at the bottom of the form.

(g) Now, Get Formally "Admitted" Into The U.S. at a Port of Entry

As a holder of a non-immigrant type of visa, you will normally be authorized to stay in the U.S. for a specific period of time, depending on the type and classification of the nonimmigrant visa involved. For example, for a B visa, you are normally authorized to stay in the U.S. for 6 months with the possibility of multiple extensions upon future application, while for an E-1 or E-2 visa, the authorized period of stay is 2 years at a time, with the possibility of extensions or renewal of the visa for additional one- or two-year periods, and so on with respect to other types of nonimmigrant visas. And, on your entering the U.S. from a foreign country with your visa, you will at that time be given a 1-94 card, which will be stamped with dates showing your authorized stay. Then, each time you exit and re-enter the U.S., you will get a new 1-94 card with a new period of authorized stay affixed thereto.

BUT HERE'S THE MAIN ISSUE OF IMPORTANCE YOU SHOULD NOTE HERE: before you can be actually allowed entry into the U.S. even with your approved and issued visa in hand, you must first be formally "admitted" into the country – that is, you have to successfully pass through some strict formalities involved in a procedure called the "inspection and admission" process into the United States. *Turn to Chapter 16, "Entering The United States: The Process of Getting Actually Admitted Into The Country After You've Got Your Visa In Hand." (p. 118)*

(h) You May Be Denied A Visa. What Can You Do?

What if, in the end, for whatever the reason, your visa application is turned down and you are denied a visa? Turn to Chapter 5, Section G.8 *"What To Do If Your Visa Application Is Denied"* (p. 35)

Chapter 9

Getting A Visa As An Industrial Trainee Temporary Worker: The H-3 Visa

A. WHAT IS THE H-3 VISA OR INDUSTRIAL TRAINEE TEMPORARY WORKER ALIEN?

The H-3 visa is offered to qualified foreign persons who are coming to the U.S. for the purpose of participating in an established on-the-job occupational training program provided by an American company. The visa anticipates that the alien's primary activity in the U.S. will be acquiring training; that the alien will not be engaged in "productive" employment, even though some degree of productive employment may often be necessary so long as it is inconsequential in nature or merely incidental to the training.

As an H-3 visa alien, you are restricted to training with and working only for the U.S. company or employer under whose sponsorship you entered the United States. If you wish to change training program, you must get a different H-3 visa. The H-3 visa is initially approved for the documented length of time necessary to complete the training program, which usually means a limit of 18 to 24 months. It is technically possible to extend the visa beyond the 2-year period, but a request for such an extension will usually be met with skepticism by the INS. There are no quota restrictions for the H-3 visa. Accompanying relatives of the principal H-2 alien may stay in the U.S. with him or her, but are not permitted to work, unless, however, they obtain permission from the INS to do so in their own right.

B. WHO QUALIFIES FOR THE H-3 VISA

To meet the INS standards for qualifying for an H-3 visa, you must have a specific offer from a U.S. company or U.S. government agency to participate in a job training program. (The U.S. company must have filed a preliminary petition with the INS to participate in an established training and/or educational program). The job training you (the alien) are invited to fill can't be just any occupation: it must be one that will further the alien's career in his home country; the training program must have a formal structure, such as a curriculum, books and study materials; the actual training of the alien person cannot anticipate an eventual job offer by the U.S. employer for the alien; and the prospective alien trainee must personally not have had access in his home country to the same kind of training being sought in the U.S. The training may be existing in your home country, but so long as you can show that you, personally, do not have access to it, you qualify.

By way of a summary, to qualify for a visa under the H-3 category, here are basically the three key essentials:

i. the alien must be coming to the U.S. to participate in a bona fide established training program under an America company;

ii. the alien must be able to show that the skill or training he or she will receive in the United States is not readily available in his or her home country or elsewhere; and

iii. the alien must show that any employment aspects of his undertaking is merely incidental to the training activities, that the training and his stay in the United States is for a temporary period, and that he intends to leave the U.S.

to apply the benefit of his training in the own country after the program is completed.

Many large U.S. corporations (industrial establishments, organizations, firms, etc.), in the fields of agriculture, commerce, finance, government, transportation, and the professions, often have training programs which involve both classroom instruction and on-the-job training. A typical H-3 candidate, for example, would be, say, an alien from an agriculturally backward Third World country who wishes to learn some of the American agricultural techniques and technologies for increasing crop production which have made the United States so pre-eminent in the world in agricultural productivity.

In making a determination as to whether an alien qualifies for an H-3 classification, a number of principles have been established over the years by which the Immigration and Naturalization Service officials assess the applicants. In sum, however, *the most significant consideration for an H-3 program seems to boil down to this: that an alien trainee not engaged in what is termed "productive employment", if such employment will displace an American resident. The Immigration Service's overriding concern is that the alien trainee not be performing productive employment, as opposed to (and in the guise of) genuine job training. Hence, as a rule, if the INS authorities should believe that the amount of productive employment involved in a given program is excessive in comparison to the job training or instruction to be received, the petition will usually be denied.*

Hence, to ensure approval of his H-3 petition, the petitioning U.S. employer must typically be ready to back up his petition with adequate supporting documents. The employer must document the following: that an actual training program exists; that the program involves considerable hours of classroom instruction as well as of on-the-job training without supervision; that the training is not for the purpose of recruiting and training aliens merely to staff U.S. firms, but would actually provide the alien with training which is unavailable outside the U.S.; that the training is purposeful (is actually meant to impart skills or experience), and not just incidental to giving an alien productive employment.

Training programs involving H-3 visas generally exist in two situations: a U.S. company with branches in foreign countries would train foreign employees in its U.S. branches before sending them to work overseas; or, a U.S. company wishing to establish a beneficial business relationship with a foreign company would bring in some of the foreign company's personnel and teach them about the American business, and these foreign personnel then develop personal ties with the U.S. company.

NOTE: As a practical matter, most people are unable to secure the H-3 visa for the reason that the INS qualifications for the training programs are very strict and there are few training programs that meet such standards.

C. HOW TO FILE FOR THE H-3 VISA

Briefly summarized, once an alien has been offered a training position by a U.S Company, filing for an H-3 visa is a TWO-PART process. First, the prospective U.S. employer who wants to train the alien, acts as the alien's sponsor; he makes a written application (it's called the "petition" in this phase) to the Immigration and Naturalization Service at one of the four INS Regional Service Centers in the U.S., to demonstrate that a qualifying formal training position has been offered to the alien, and that the said training meets all the requirements set forth in Section B above. And if the INS approves the employer's petition, the foreign trainee himself (and the accompanying relatives, if any), then applies for the H-3 visa. This second phase of the H-3 visa processing, is undertaken by the alien himself, and is called the "application" phase. In this, the alien may carry this out either at his local U.S. consulate abroad, or at an INS office in the U.S., if he's already present in the U.S. and meets the required conditions for a U.S. filing. The consular (or INS) officials then make the decision on whether the visa is to be granted or not.

1. STEP ONE: THE VISA "PETITION" PHASE

(a) The U.S. employer (or company) who is willing and able to sponsor the alien H-3 trainee, upon offering a training position to the alien, now completes the petition for the H-3 visa on the alien's behalf – the Form 1-129, and the H supplement. The petitioning U.S. employer then submits the completed Form 1-129H, *Petition For a Non-Immigrant Worker,* to one of the 4 INS Regional office centers in the U.S. covering the intended employer's place of business (All H-3 visa papers in the PETITION phase are required to be filed in the U.S. with the INS centers). [see sample of Form 1- 129 on p. 162, 165 & 168.]

NOTE: Form 1-129B, which is the previous version of Form 1-129H*, is shown on pp. 162, 165 & 168. This earlier version of the current form is reproduced here for illustrative purposes, to illustrate the actual visa filing procedures in an actual case previously filed and successfully processed for the H type of visa, material obtained courtesy of C. James Cooper, Jr., a long time veteran Denver, Colorado immigration lawyer and specialist. See "EXPLANATORY NOTES" on p. 37.

Note, also, that under the procedures in current use, the latest version of the Form 1-129 has various "Supplements" to the basic form, each meant for particular nonimmigrant classifications – E, F, H, L, O, P, R, etc. And all you have to do is complete the basic Form 1-129 and simply tear out and use the supplement that applies to your visa category.

Supporting Documents For Visa Petition

U.S. employer-petitioner attaches the following supporting documents to the petition forms:

- Documentations appropriate to establish that an actual bona-fide training program exists with a U.S. employer, and that the program involves both considerable hours of classroom instruction and on-the-job training without supervision. (see "Explanatory Note" on p. 37, item #4)
- A statement describing the kind of training that is to be given the alien and setting forth the number of hours that will be devoted, each to classroom instruction and to on-the-job training without supervision; the position or duties for which this training will prepare the alien trainee; a full explanation as to why it is claimed that such training cannot be obtained in the alien's country, the manner in which the alien came to the attention of the U.S. employer, and how he (she) was selected.* (see sample on p. 195)
- Proof of the alien's maintenance of a residence in his home country, and of his intention not to abandon it but to return to his home country after the U.S. training.
- Letters or affidavits from leaders of industry, government officials or university administrators, stating their familiarity with the alien, and that they are acquainted with the intended training program in the U.S. and that similar training is not available in the alien's home country and/or that the alien has no access to it.
- Letter from the alien's present employer in his home country explaining how and why the U.S. training will further the alien's career in his home country; a letter from a company in the alien's home country offering the alien a job based on his completion of the training in the U.S.; letter or written statements from industry leaders, government officials or university administrators or professors in labor-related fields, certifying that there is a demand in the alien's country for persons with the type of training the alien will receive in the U.S.
- Letters from the alien's employer in the foreign country describing the nature, length of stay, and salary history

---

*The INS Examination Handbook directs immigration examiners to scrutinize H-3 petitions closely for the reason that there is a high incidence of fraud experienced in such petitions. It cites the following as what should serve as the "warning signs" for examiners in evaluating H-3 petitions: (1) a proposed training program which deals in generalities with no fixed schedule, objectives or means of evaluation; (2) an elaborate proposed training program that is incompatible with the nature of the U.S. employer's business; (3) a training program on behalf of an alien who appears to already possess substantial expertise in the proposed field or in another field; (4) a training program in a field for which there would be little or no need in the alien's native country; (5) a training program in which the U.S. employer claims no American will be displaced but for which no one can be found in the U.S. to fill the position; (6) a training program in which the salary is far above the minimum wage level.

of the alien's present and/or previous employment, and describing how, perhaps, the alien's special background, qualifications and work experience, will fit perfectly into the nature of the training he will receive in the U.S.

- Certified copies of the alien's diplomas, school transcripts, etc.

Enclose the appropriate filing fees for a visa petition. The current amount for this as of this writing (it changes often) is $130, if no change of status is being requested, and $155, if change of status is requested. Send the payment in a check or money order.

b. Approval of the Visa Petition

When the sponsoring U.S. employer (trainer) completes the application forms and the necessary supporting documentations, the employer "files" the papers with (i.e., he submits them to) one of the four INS Regional Service Centers in the U.S. which covers the area of the intended employer's business. The papers should be mailed to the INS office by certified mail, with return receipt requested, so that you can retain the receipt as proof that the package was received.

You (i.e., employer) will receive from the INS, within a week or two of the mailing, a written notice of confirmation that the papers are being processed. The notice also gives the immigration "file number" assigned to the case, and approximately when you are to expect a decision. If some material defects or omissions are found in the papers (unsigned forms or missing information or documents, or payment, etc), the INS will probably return the entire application paper to you (the prospective U.S. trainer or employer), with a note or a Form 1-797, *Notice of Acton,* telling him or her what corrections need to be made, or what additional documents or pieces of information need to be supplied. Or, in some cases the INS will simply retain the papers already submitted but issue a request, in the form of a Form 1-797, for the additional items that are needed. And in such an event, all you'll need to do is simply supply the additional data required and promptly mail them (along with the Form 1-797 and the rest of the file, if applicable) back to the INS office.

The employers' INS H-3 petitions are usually approved by the INS within some 3 to 8 weeks. Upon such approval, the INS sends the employer a Notice of Action Form 1-797 showing that the petition has been approval. Where the alien visa beneficiary is presently residing in a foreign country, or where the alien otherwise intends to undertake the second phase of the visa processing abroad (see STEP Two below), the INS will also notify the U.S. consulate of the alien's choice designated in the petition papers, and forward a complete file of the case to that consulate to enable its further processing of the visa request.

2. STEP TWO: THE VISA "APPLICATION" PHASE

Once the original "petition" filed by the U.S. trainer/employer has been approved by the U.S. – and only then – the second phase of the H-3 visa application can then be commenced. HERE'S THE IMPORTANT POINT: this second phase is called the "application", as opposed to the "petition", and is undertaken primarily by the ALIEN, rather than by the U.S. employer.

(a) Where You May File The Application: Is It Abroad,Or In The U.S?.

You (the alien visa-seeker) may, depending on whether you meet the required conditions for it, apply for the H-3 visa at the U.S. consulate in your home country, or at the INS office in the United States. The conditions you must meet in order to be eligibility to file in the U.S. are the same conditions as are listed in Chapter 4, Section C.1 [p. 19]. Otherwise, then you have to file in a U.S. consulate abroad.

(b) Inquire About Your Local U.S. Consulate's or INS's Visa Policies and Procedures

Turn to Section C.2 of Chapter 4 (p. 20) and apply here the same details contained therein. See, also, Chapter 18, Sections A and B, for more on the subject of variations in visa processing policies and practices among various consulates and INS offices.

(c) Forms and Documentations Used

i. Prepare the following forms

- Optional Form OF-156, *Nonimmigrant Visa Application.* This form is required ONLY WHEN AN OVERSEAS FILING with a U.S. consulate is involved. Generally, if your visa application is filed at a U.S. consulate in a foreign country, the consulate will usually provide you (the alien) with their required "optional forms" complete with the instructions for completing them, and such forms are designated by a prefix "OF" preceding a number, as in OF-156. (see illustrative sample of Form OF-156 on p. 177).

NOTE: OF-156 is the basic application Form which the vast majority of non-immigrant visa applicants will encounter. The proper completion of this form is, by far, probably the single most important and primary thing you can do in any nonimmigrant visa application which will determine ultimately whether you get the visa or not. For that reason, we set forth in one chapter, Chapter 13, a detailed, step-by-step instructions by which to answer the questions asked or to provide the information required therein. Please refer immediately to Chapter 13.

- Form 1-539, *Application To Extend/Change Nonimmigrant Status.* This form is applicable only if it is a U.S. filing that you are doing, and only for accompanying relatives of the principal alien applicant, if any. Only one application form is needed for an entire family, except that if there's more than one accompanying relative, each should be listed on the form. (sample of Form 1-539 is on p. 183).

ii. Supporting Documents To Attach

For the supporting documents to attach, turn to Chapter 5, Section G.3 (ii) [p.30] and see the listing outlined therein under "General Supporting Documents For Most Nonimmigrant Situations" for the kinds of supporting documents to provide. Except that, you should take note of this, however: that for the H-3 visa filings documentation relating to proof of the alien's financial status would not generally be central or required.

(d) File the "Application" Papers With the U.S. Consulate or The INS, As Applicable

Turn to Section G.4 of Chapter 5 (p.33) and follow here the same procedures outlined there to file your visa application

(e) Attend The Visa Interview, If One Is Required In Your Case

Whether you are doing a U.S. filing or a Consulate filing, a face-to-face personal interview with the visa processing officials may or may not be required in your case before the authorities render their final decision on your visa issuance. In any event, if a visa interview is required in your particular case, you will be so notified by the visa processing office. When you shall have gathered together all the items required by the consulate or the INS, whichever one is applicable, you will appear on the appointed date, time and place set for the interview and undergo one with the designated interviewer. The visa processing officials will promptly render a final decision on your application, but only AFTER such interview.

[Turn to Chapter 15 for the full procedures involved in this all-important step in any nonimmigrant (as well as immigrant) visa application – the visa interview].

(f) Final Approval of Your Visa Application

In the end, assuming that everything is in order with your visa application – basically, that you have, for example, all the proofs and documentation required to show your eligibility for the visa applied for, and that there's nothing that makes you inadmissible under the U.S. immigration law, such as having some serious criminal or terrorist record or potential, or a contagious, communicable disease – your application for a visa will be approved. You will be issued your visa. The U.S. consul in charge of visa issuance (if it's a consulate filing abroad), will usually stamp the approved visa that applies in your case (say, a B-1 and/or B-2 visa, in the case of the visitors visa, or the E-1 or E-2, in the case of a treaty trader or investor) in your passport. If you got your visa through a U.S. filing, upon approval of your visa application, you are given a visa "status", and not an actual visa. (Under the law, only a consulate may issue a visa, and not the INS). This may be stamped in your passport, and you will receive from the INS a Notice of Action, Form 1-797, indicating the dates for which your status is approved, with a new 1-94 card attached at the bottom of the form.

(g) Now, Get Formally "Admitted" Into The U.S. at a Port Of Entry

As a holder of a non-immigrant type of visa, you will normally be authorized to stay in the U.S. for a specific period of time, depending on the type and classification of the nonimmigrant visa involved. For example, for a B visa, you are normally authorized to stay in the U.S. for 6 months with the possibility of multiple extensions upon future application, while for an E-1 or E-2 visa, the authorized period of stay is 2 years at a time, with the possibility of extension or renewal of the visa for additional one- or two-year periods, and so on with respect to other types of nonimmigrant visas. And when you enter the U.S. from a foreign country with your visa, you will at that time be given a 1-94 card, which will be stamped with the dates showing your authorized stay. Then, each time you exit and re-enter the U.S., you will get a new 1-94 card with a new period of authorized stay affixed thereto.

BUT HERE'S THE MAIN ISSUE OF IMPORTANCE YOU SHOULD NOTE HERE: before you can be actually allowed entry into the U.S. even with your approved and issued visa in hand, you must first be formally "admitted" into the country – that is, you have to successfully pass through some strict formalities involved in a procedure called the "inspection and admission" process into the United States. Turn to Chapter 16, *"Entering The United States: The Process of Getting Actually Admitted Into The Country After You've Got Your Visa In Hand." (p. 118).*

(h) You May Be Denied A Visa. What Can You Do?

What if, in the end, for whatever the reason, your visa application is turned down and you are denied a visa? Turn to Chapter 5, Section G.8 *"What To Do If Your Visa Application Is Denied."* (p. 35).

Chapter 10

The K-1 Visa: A Special Entry Visa For Fiance(e)s Engaged To Marry A U.S. Citizen

A. WHAT IS A K-1 VISA

The K visa is singularly unique. Officially, it is classified as a NONIMMIGRANT visa. However, in reality, it is almost like an immigrant visa, if not exactly one. Hence, we are devoting here a separate chapter solely to discussing the eligibility standards and the procedures involved in obtaining the K visa.

The K visa is, in a word, for the alien living abroad who is a fiance or fiancee engaged to marry a United States citizen. The object of the K visa is to enable its alien holder who is a fiance or fiancee of a U.S. citizen engaged to marry the citizen, to gain entry into the U.S. SOLELY for the purpose of that alien marrying the U.S. citizen. If the alien is granted a visa, he of she must enter into the marriage with the U.S. citizen WITHIN 90 days of his or her entry into the U.S.; otherwise, the visa shall expire and the alien fiance or fiancee must return to his or her home country. No extensions are given on a K visa, the sole exception being in cases of illness or other like unforeseen emergencies; and no change of status to other categories, immigrant or nonimmigrant, is permissible for the K visa holder or the minor children accompanying such K visa holder, if any.

The K nonimmigrant category is unique in one major respect, namely: it differs from any other nonimmigrant classification in that it is the only nonimmigrant visa about which it is clear from the time of its issuance, and at the time of the alien's entry into the U.S. at the border, that the alien nevertheless intends to remain in the U.S. PERMANENTLY. (Under a provision of the Immigration Marriage Fraud Amendments of 1986, however, all K non-immigrants upon marrying the U.S. citizen spouse, are first subject to a 2-year period of "conditional permanent' residence, before they may secure permanent residency status).

B. HOW THE K-1 VISA WORKS

If you are an alien person engaged to or intending to marry a U.S. citizen, you will, with a K-1 visa, be able to come to the U.S. for the purpose of marrying the U.S. citizen; your U.S. citizen fiancee or fiance may bring you to America (he/she is to file a petition for you from the U.S.) by asking for you to be granted an entry visa into the U.S. for the sole purpose of undertaking the marriage – the K-1 visa. And, then, once you are granted a K-1 visa, if you also have any unmarried children who are under 21 years of age, they too would qualify for a visa, called the K-2 visa. With their K-2 visa, such children can accompany you to the U.S.; and further more, you can, as well, apply for a green card to have a permanent residence status in the U.S. once you actually get married to your U.S. citizen fiancee or fiance down to road.

C. THE UNIQUENESS AND BENEFITS OF THE K-1 VISA

K-1 visa is unique in that, though it is a nonimmigrant visa quite alright, once the K-1 visa holder gets married to the U.S. citizens, the visa can almost automatically be converted into a permanent residence visa or green card. The visa, while being issued by the U.S. Consulate abroad to the fiancee of a U.S. citizen, is perfectly understood to be a temporary visa that requires that the alien person contract an intended marriage within 90 days of his/her entry into the U.S. Yet, the visa just as clearly presumes that, once the marriage is contracted, the alien person will then apply for a permanent visa to the U.S. and will adjust his/her immigration status in the U.S. to a permanent residency status. In fact, the K-1 visa has no other real value or purpose – other than, in other words, to serve as a preliminary step to getting a permanent resident visa. In deed, most couples, in apparent recognition of this reality, do not generally apply for the K-1 visa. Instead, they simply get married and then apply directly for the green card. For example, if you (a U.S. citizen) were to marry your alien fiancee (or fiance) in her country, you can simply file a petition for her for a green card to bring her in as "an immediate relative," a procedure that is much quicker, easier and less expensive. (No round trip expense, at least!) In consequence, as a practical matter, there is really one situation when the use of a K-1 visa is most proper and advisable: namely, when there is some good reason why the marriage between the two parties cannot take place either in the U.S. or in the alien's home country (e.g. the U.S. citizen is sick and bedridden or cannot take the time off to go abroad to marry, etc).

D. HOW TO QUALIFY FOR A K-1 VISA

Briefly summarized, to qualify for a K-1 visa, here are the basic requirements:

- the U.S. citizen, who must be the petitioner for the K-1 visa on the alien fiance(e)'s behalf, must establish that he/she is in deed a U.S. citizen.
- both parties in the couple, must establish that they are legally free and able to marry. (Each must be single and of legal age, and where either one has been previously married, proof of the termination of the marriage must be provided.)
- the alien fiance(e) must demonstrate genuine intention to actually marry the U.S. citizen within 90 days after entry into the U.S.
- the parties must establish that they have physically met and personally seen each other within the past 2 years prior to filing the visa petition. Except, however, that, in the case of those persons for which marriages are customarily arranged, or whose religious principles and practice prohibit couples from meeting before marriage (or where such a meeting would cause exceptional hardship), the requirement of pre-marital meeting may be waived for such persons, upon application. However, for such a waiver to be granted, the couple would need to make a showing to the U.S. Consular officer that both parties will be following as well all the relevant religious customs of the marriage.

E. HOW TO FILE FOR THE K-1 VISA

To file for a K-1 visa for your alien fiancee or fiance, follow these steps and procedures exactly in the same order and chronology in which they are listed below:

1. You (the U.S. citizen and petitioner) complete and sign these papers:

- Immigration Form I-129F, *Petition For Alien Fiance(e)*. (See sample of this form on p. 171)
- Form G-325A: *Biographic Information*, for each person. Both the petitioner and the alien fiance(e) and accompanying children, if any, are to complete and sign this form. (See sample of this form on p. 180)
- Form I-134, *Affidavit of Support* (see the sample on p. 173), made out, signed and sworn to by the sponsoring U.S. citizen, whereby the petitioner promises that he (she) will financially support the alien and ensure that he (she) does not become a "public charge" to the U.S. government if admitted to the U.S. A cover sheet to this form carries detailed instructions and a list of the supporting documents (employment

certification, statement of earnings, bank records, evidence of property ownership, etc) to be attached to this affidavit.

- COLOR PHOTOGRAPHS of the petitioner and the alien fiancé(e) that were taken within 30 days before the filing of the visa petition (see Chapter 18, Section F for specification of the exact type and style of the photo that's acceptable to the INS).
- PROOF OF AMERICAN CITIZENSHIP for the visa petitioner: birth certificate, certificate of citizenship or naturalization, U.S. passport, etc.
- DIVORCE DECREE/DEATH CERTIFICATES: Proof showing that any previous marriage in which either the petitioner or the alien were involved, if any, had been legally terminated.
- AFFIDAVIT by the U.S. citizen stating facts and information about how the fiancé and the fiancée met, how and why they decided to be married to each other, and their plans for the marriage and a married life together.
- PROOF that the U.S. citizen and the alien fiancé(e) have personally met each other within the past 2 years: photographs, videos, plane tickets, letters, etc.
- PROOF that the parties have an intention to marry within 90 days after the alien fiancé(e) arrives in the U.S.: personal letter from the parties themselves, letters from the religious or civic authority who will officiate at the marriage ceremony or a wedding, long-distance telephone bills, receipt showing advance payment made for reservation of the place where the wedding reception will be held, printed engagement or wedding invitation cards, etc.
- THE FILING FEE – it's $80 as of this writing, to be made out in the form of a money order or certified check, made payable to the "Immigration and Naturalization Service."

2. File The Completed Petition Forms and Papers

Now, you, the American citizen (variously called the "sponsor" or the "petitioner" in this process), are to file the visa petition for your alien fiancé(e). Simply, you sign the completed petition forms and submit them, along with the necessary supporting documents that are required, to the U.S. Immigration and Naturalization Service's regional office for the area in which you reside. (See Appendix B for the addresses of the INS). You may submit the above items in person by hand; or you may mail them, by certified mail with return receipt requested, and preserve the receipt of mailing.

NOTE: DO not sent the ***originals*** of the documents needed at this time. Only sent the photocopies for now. Retain the originals until the point when you're specifically asked to present them for inspection and verification.

F. FINAL STEPS IN CONCLUDING THE SECURING OF THE K-1VISA

Upon your filing the petition papers with the INS office (Section E above), the INS will consider the petition, and, assuming that everything is in order, it will likely approve the visa petition. It will send you (as well as the alien beneficiary of the petition and the U.S. Consulate office in the foreign country where the alien is presently located) a written notification of the preliminary approval of the initial visa petition, called a NOTICE OF ACTION Form 1-797. (See Chapter 4 at Section C and D thereof, for the detailed procedures of how this works). ***But the important thing to note is that thereafter, from this point on in the Visa processing, all further steps required for concluding the visa processing now shift to the visa-seeker, THE ALIEN himself or herself, and the U.S. Consulate office in the foreign country where the alien is located.*** The Notice of Action Form 1-797 will contain instructions for the next steps that will need to be taken, including a listing of the additional information or documentation required to be supplied for the concluding phase of the visa processing.

The remainder of the procedures and steps called for in the processing of the alien fiancé(e)'s K-1 Visa from this point on till the end when the alien actually has the visa in his/her hand, are essentially the same as those outlined from Chapter 4, Section C thereof. Hence, turn to Chapter 4 Section C, *The Application Phase: Upon the Approval of the sponsor's "Petition," Then it is the Alien, who Must Now File An "Application" For the Actual Visa* (p. 19). Have the alien visa applicant finish up the remainder of the visa processing starting precisely from there.

NOTE: At the conclusion of the visa filing process and all the additional paperwork by the alien fiancé(e) at the American Consulate in his or her home country, the American Consul in charge of visa affairs there, upon being convinced that the American citizen and the alien fiancé(e) are genuinely engaged to be married and that they will likely marry upon the alien's arrival in the U.S., will grant the K-1 visa. The Consul will simple stamp the alien fiancé(e)'s passport with a K-1 visa. And if you (the alien) have any accompanying minor children (they must be under 21 years of age) for whom you have also requested a visa, the Consul will also stamp their passports with a K-2 visa, meaning that they are dependent upon the K-1 visa holder for their immigration status. *Your K-1 Fiancé(e) visa is, however, a NONIMMIGRANT Visa and only accords you [the alien fiancé(e)] a nonimmigrant status since, by it, you are simply promising to marry an American citizen.* You haven't married him or her yet. However, there's one immediately advantage of having the K-1 visa (aside, obviously, from your gaining entry into the United State): upon your arrival in the U.S., you can apply at once for an Employment Authorization card which will enable you to start working at once legally.

Finally, note that as a K-1 visa holder, one principal precondition upon which the granting of your K-1 visa is based, is that you must, under the U.S. immigration law, get married to your U.S. citizen fiancé(e) WITHIN 90 days after you've arrived in the U.S. The rule is that if a K-1 fiancé(e) fails to marry his or her American fiancé(e) within the prescribed 90 days, or ever, the INS would start deportation proceedings against the K-1 alien as well as all the minor children who accompany the K-1 alien, if any; and if the K-1 fiancé(e) were to marry someone else other than his/her American petitioner, the K-1 alien (and any minor children who accompany the K-1 alien) will lose the right to receive a green card.

On the other hand, if you follow through with the INS preconditions for granting you the K-1 visa and proceed to actually marry your American fiancé(e) within the required 90-day period – as the overwhelming numbers of K-1 fiancé(e) who come into America every year actually do-there's just one more step you'll need to take to finalize the securing of your green card. And that is: you must file the immigration Form 1-485 with the local INS office in the area where you live in the U.S. in a procedure known as "*Adjustment of Status*." You'll probably have a "conditional", Permanently residency status at this point. But at the end of your two years into the marriage, you can file to remove the conditional element and to convert to a permanent residence. (See Chapter 6 Section H for the procedures for removal of the conditional element for a green card which is based on marriage).

Chapter 11
Getting A Visa As An Intracompany Transferee: The L-1 Visa

A. WHAT IS THE L-1 VISA OR INTRA-COMPANY TRANSFEREE

The L-1 visa, formally called the INTRA-COMPANY TRANSFEREE visa, has been called by experts "one of the most flexible and sought after temporary visas which provide for employment, and one of the most useful non-immigrant visas available to employees of foreign companies." Among immigration experts, this visa is commonly viewed as probably the best among the group of four employment-related nonimmigrant temporary visas, which range from the H-1B, to H-2B, H-3 and L-1 visas. The specific purpose of the Immigration and Naturalization Act of 1970 which established the L-1 visa, is to ease the way for large international companies to transfer key foreign employees and personnel to the United States for tours of duty there so as to strengthen international trade with other countries of the world; to facilitate the transfer of the key employees to the U. S. from companies that are affiliated with or related to U.S. corporations. Consequently, in the law creating the L-1 program, Congress used a broad, unambiguous language which made it apparent that small business entities, even individual investors and companies that are composed of no more than two or three individuals, could take advantage of the L-1 visa as well.

With an L-1 visa, an alien can be transferred to the U.S. and legally work there for a company that is a branch, subsidiary, affiliate or joint venture partner of a company that already employs the alien outside of the U.S. And you can remain there and travel in and out of the U.S., or remain there continuously, for the duration of your L-1 visa. However, as an alien L-1 visa holder, you are restricted to working only for the U.S. company or employer who acted as your L-1 sponsor, a company which must be a branch, subsidiary, affiliate or joint venture partner of the company which already employs you outside the U.S. The L-1 visas are initially approved for only up to three (3)years, but extensions of 2 years at a time may be granted until the alien has been in the U.S. for a total of 7 years, for aliens who qualify as a manager or executive, and a total of 5 years only, for those who qualify as having "specialized knowledge." Accompanying relatives of the L-1 alien are granted the L-2 visas; L-2 visa holders may stay in the U.S. with the principal alien, but may not work, unless, however, they can get work authorization in their own independent right. There are no quota restrictions for the L-1 visa.

B. WHO QUALIFIES FOR THE L-1 VISA

Simply, stated, you qualify for an L-1 visa if all three of the following elements are present:

(i.) you (the alien) are seeking to enter the U.S. for a temporary period of time;

(ii.) the primary purpose for such entry into the U.S. is for you to perform services of a managerial or executive nature, or services involving specialized knowledge; and

(iii.) such services are to be performed with the same company or an affiliate or subsidiary of the company with which you have been employed overseas for one year (or more) immediately preceding the time of your visa application.

To put it differently, you qualify for an L-1 visa if you have been continuously employed outside the U.S. as a manager, executive, or a person with specialized knowledge, in an overseas company – defined simply as a company physically located outside the U.S. for at least one year out of the last three years immediately prior to your entry into the U.S. – and are transferred to the U.S. to be employed in a similar position you held in the foreign country. The U.S. company to which you are transferring, meaning the U.S. company that is to employ you in the U.S., must be the one acting as your sponsor for the L-1 visa, and must be a branch, subsidiary, affiliate or joint venture partner of the company that already employs you outside the U.S., and the foreign company that is already employing you outside the U.S. must remain in operation as a viable business entity through out the period that you have the L-1 visa. And, if the foreign business entity that's currently employing the alien should cease to exist or to function as a viable business entity, the alien's L-1 status is immediately in jeopardy.

C. W HO QUALIFIES AS A MANAGER, AN EXECUTIVE, OR PERSON WITH SPECIALIZED KNOWLEDGE

A central question involved in application for an L-1 visa, is this: how do you define who qualifies under the key terms "manager," "executive," or a person with "specialized knowledge," in this specific context? For our purpose here, it is important for readers to know that the definition of who qualifies under each of those three positions is more structured and restricted under the immigration rules, than their normal meanings.

1. Who Qualifies As A Manager

A person qualifies as a manager, if he has all of the following characteristics; if he or she:

- manages the company or a department of the company;
- supervises and controls the work of other supervisory, professional or managerial employees, or manages an essential function within the company, or a department or subdivision of the company. (Note that, in other words, a mere supervisor does not qualify as a "manager" here; rather, for a first-line supervisor to qualify in this context, he must be supervising persons of professional caliber).
- has the authority to hire and fire the persons under his (her) supervision. If no other employees are supervised, he must function at a senior level within the organization;
- is a person who exercise the official discretion and authority to establish goals and policies, and to make decisions concerning the day-to-day operations of that portion of the organization or function for which he (she) has responsibility; and
- receives only general supervision from higher executives, board of directors or stockholders.

2. Who Qualifies as an Executive

An executive is defined as a person who has all of the following characteristics:

- Who directs the management of the organization (the company) or a major part of it.
- Who establishes the goals and policies of the organization or a major part of it.
- Who has wide discretionary authority on major decisions concerning the company.
- Who receives only general supervision or direction from higher level executives, a board of directors or the shareholders of the organization

NOTE: You should take note that if you either meet the eligibility requirements for an L-1 visa or now have an L-1 visa, you can equally obtain a permanent resident Green Card under the employment-based First Preference Category with virtually the same qualifications - namely, by being qualified as a manager or an executive, having been employed as a "priority worker" employee by a qualified company outside the U.S. for at least one year, and seeking entry into the U.S. for the purpose of taking a similar position with an American branch, affiliate or subsidiary of the same company. Readers interested in exploring obtaining a Green Card by this avenue, should refer to Chapter 13 of Volume 2 of this manual, written by the same author and published by Do-It-Yourself Legal Publishers.

3. Who Qualifies As A Person With Specialized Knowledge

A person with specialized knowledge is defined as a person who has the following characteristics:

- Special or unique knowledge that specifically concerns the petitioning employer company's product, service, research, equipment, techniques or international marketing methods or management; or an advanced level of knowledge or expertise in the company's processes and procedures.
- Special knowledge is knowledge which is different from, or exceeds, the ordinary or usual knowledge of an employee in a particular field. And a specialized knowledge professional is a person who has specialized knowledge and is a member of the profession.

By way of a summary, it should be stated that, notwithstanding all of the specific and precise definitions stated above, we are still dealing here, as with most matters concerning visa processing and procedures, with a matter which, in the final analysis, still depends highly on the subjective discretion, personal judgment and disposition, of the particular consular or immigration officer who handles your visa application! And this reality is more especially true with respect to positions that fall under the so-called "grey area" – that is, those involving lower-level type of managers or executives, as differentiated from the top management types of positions when the status may be more readily easy to categorize – positions such as foreman, office managers, and the like, as opposed to positions like the principal partners or the directors or officers of a corporation.
Consequently, the above definition should always be regarded primarily as a guideline by which to attempt a determination of what is needed.

Here's one immigration expert's rather vivid but concise definition of the above-named three key terms, which may be helpful:

"Show me a person who can hire and fire employees (whom he supervises and controls). And I will show you a Manager. On the other hand, show me a person who has authority to sign company checks and to make policy decisions, and I will show you an Executive. Show me a person who has proprietary knowledge (i.e., that type of knowledge which is unique to or used in a particular business, e.g., customer lists, trade secrets or a secret recipe) which is essential to the operation of a business, and I will show you a person with Specialized Knowledge."*

D. BLANKET L-1 VISA: A SPECIAL, PRIVILEGED CASE FOR LARGE COMPANIES

Under the L-1 visa rules, qualified large U.S. companies that are branches, subsidiaries or affiliates of foreign companies, may obtain what is known as a "blanket" L-1 visa status. With a blanket L-1 status, the qualifying U.S. company is given a general ("blanket") approval that permits it to transfer foreign employees to their related U.S. companies instead of applying on an individual basis for each transferee, thus eliminating for the U.S. company much of the time, paperwork and expense required in processing each case individually. Even though the foreign company from which the employees are transferring has several U.S.-based branches, subsidiaries or affiliates (joint venture partnerships do not qualify for the blanket L-1 visa privilege), it need only obtain just one blanket L-1 petition for all of its related U.S. companies.

The blanket L-1 visa requirements are somewhat stiff and the procedures are not commonly or generally

---

*C. James Cooper. Jr., an eminent Denver Colorado immigration lawyer and specialist in his *The Immigration Tapes (Text)*.

employed. However, there are enormous benefits for a company which qualifies and can obtain this status. For one thing, only a one-time application is required to receive a blanket L-1 status. And, with the L-1 visa privilege, a company is at liberty to bring in key employees into the U.S. as it needs, directly bypassing the individual petition process of the INS and the delays and expenses involved. Hence, if a company has the need for one, and is able to meet the requirements for it, it is certainly worth it seeking to obtain a blanket L-1 status.

Note that it is the U.S. company itself (and not the alien employee or the foreign-based branch, subsidiary or affiliate) that qualifies for, or can petition and receive the blanket L-1 status. The L-1 visa is available under the blanket program to managers and executives of the qualifying blanket L-1 company, as well as those employees considered to be specialized knowledge professionals. However, in the blanket L-1 visa context, the "specialized knowledge" category differs from the one for plain individual L-1 applicants: for employees of companies with blanket L-1 status, an individual employee (the alien) must have the usual specialized knowledge required of all L-1 visa applicants. But, in addition, he (she) must further be a member of the professions as the term is defined in the immigration law. Thus, such occupations as the following, among others, have been specially designated by immigration law as professional positions: architects, engineers, lawyers, physicians, surgeons, teachers in elementary and secondary schools, colleges, academics or seminaries, registered nurses, accountants, computer systems analysts, physical therapists, chemists, pharmacists, medical technologists, hotel managers, fashion designers, commercial airline pilots of large air crafts and upper-level business managers. In general terms, the term "Profession" is more liberally defined to include any occupation that requires theoretical and practical knowledge to perform it in fields such as architecture, the physical and social science, business and the arts, often requiring completion of a university education, such as a bachelor's degree (or higher education) as a minimum requirement for entry to the occupation.

A U.S. company qualifies for a blanket L-1 petition if it meets the following requirements:

- The petitioning U.S. company to which the foreign employee is to be transferred is a branch, subsidiary or affiliate (the joint venture partnership does not qualify) of a company physically located outside the U.S.
- Both the U.S. company and the related outside company are engaged in actual trade or the rendering of services
- The U.S. company has been actively doing business for at least one year
- The U.S. company has a total of at least three branches, subsidiaries or affiliates, even if some of the three are located outside the U.S.
- The U. S. company (and any related U.S. companies) must have:
  - - successfully obtained L-1 visa for at least 10 of its employees during the past 12 months
  - - combined annual sales of not less than $25 million, or a combined total of at least 1,000 employees working in the U.S.

E. THE ATTRACTIVE ASPECTS OF THE L-1 VISA

One great attraction of the L-1 visa comes from the fact that it is easier for the intra-company transferee, if he is an executive or a manager, to change his (or her) status to a Permanent Resident (Green Card) status if his U.S. company can show that it needs his services permanently. The ease of changing to such permanent residency status, stems from several factors: for one thing, such a Transferee (if an executive or a manager) is not required to get a labor certification from the U.S. Department of Labor as to whether or not there is a shortage of labor; secondly, unlike the situation with respect to other nonimmigrant temporary worker categories (e.g. the H-1 category), the L-1 visa holder need not maintain a domicile in a foreign country, as long as his intent and the intent of the employer is for his (the alien's) services to be utilized in the United States temporarily. Furthermore, the alien may have served in one capacity in foreign country and yet fill a different position in the United States. Nor is the alien required to be employed on a full-time basis by his would-be employer in the U.S. Finally, the initial approval period for the L-1 transferee is three years, and may be extended in increments of one year.

As is the case in virtually all nonimmigrant visas, an important consideration for the L-1 visa, as well, is the question of the alien's "intent." In theory, here as well, it is required that the intention of the sponsoring U.S. employer as well as that of the alien employee, be one, not of permanent employment or permanent stay in America, but temporary. Nevertheless, THERE IS ONE IMPORTANT THING TO NOTE IN THIS REGARD IN THE SPECIFIC CONTEXT OF THE L-1 VISA: ***namely, that in practice, in the context of the L-1 visa procedures, the issue of "intent" has been largely altered and eliminated as a problem for the alien – one other important reason for the attractiveness of the L-1 visa to most seekers of the nonimmigrant visa.***

Here's how it works out in the context of the L-1 visa. Under the L-1 procedures, an alien employee is allowed to have what is known as "dual intent" – that is, the alien employee and the intended U.S. employer may have the present intention that the alien will remain in the U.S. on a temporary basis, while at the same time having an intention for the alien to file a petition for a permanent residency visa at some point in future. This condition will be acceptable to the Immigration and Naturalization Service (INS), providing only that it is proven to the INS that both the employer and the employee agree that the employee will return abroad if the permanent residency visa is not approved by the time the period allowed by his L-1 visa shall have expired.

As one expert* summarizes it, here's what the "dual intent" concept says, in effect;* what it is saying is that both the alien employee and U.S. employer agree that: "It is my (the alien's) intention to remain in the United States on a temporary basis during the period of time that my L-1 visa is valid. I may decide to remain in the United States as a permanent resident by filing an application for a permanent visa, but I agree that I will depart the United States in the event that the L-1 visa expires before I obtain my permanent visa."

Typical of those who use the L-1 visa, are executives of foreign-based parent organizations needing to travel to the United States frequently to oversee the operations of their U.S. subsidiaries. Frequently, multinational companies with subsidiaries or branch offices in both the U.S. and a foreign country have need to transfer their executives or those with specialized expertise in and out of the United States, enabling such executives to readily make multiple trips in and out of the United States to oversee business operations or problems as the need arises. Also, under the Immigration Act of 1990, managers, partners, and other high-level employees of large, prominent international accounting firms (those that are part of an international accounting organization with internationally recognized names) qualify for the L-1 visas.

F. HOW TO FILE FOR THE L-1 VISA

Briefly summarized, once an alien employee stationed in a foreign country has been offered a job transfer to the U.S., the task of filing for an L-1 visa is a two-part process. First, the U.S. employer company to which the alien is to be transferred, acts as the alien's sponsor; it makes a written application (it's called a "petition" in this phase) to the U.S. Immigration and Naturalization Service at one of the four INS Regional Service Centers in the U.S., to demonstrate that the U.S. company requires the alien's service and that the alien and the company meet all the requirements set forth in Sections B, C and D above. And if the INS approves the U.S. entity's petition, the foreign employee himself (and the accompanying relatives, if any), then applies for the L-1 visa. This phase two of the L-1 visa processing, which is undertaken by the alien himself, is called the "application" phase. This time, the alien may carry this out either at his local U.S. consulate abroad, or at an INS office in the U.S., if he's already present in the U.S. and meets the required conditions for a U.S. filing. The consular (or INS) officials then make the decision on whether the visa is to be granted or not.

---

*Ramon Carrion, a Clearwater Florida immigration attorney, and author of *U.S. Immigration Guide*, p.128

1. STEP ONE: THE VISA "PETITION" PHASE

(a) There are two different types of L-1 visa petitions that could be applied for – individual L-1 visa, and so-called blanket L-1 visa. The INDIVIDUAL L-1 petition is the one you file for when a company intends to transfer one or merely a few employees to the U.S. on an infrequent basis, while the BLANKET L-1 visa petitions are the petitions already on file for big corporations that transfer large numbers of employees to the U.S. on a regular basis yearly. A company which qualifies under a blanket L-1 status, shall have had on file with the INS an approved blanket L-1 status to cover all of the company's potential transferees.

Hence, if your current foreign-based or non-U.S. employer wants to transfer you to the U.S., and already has an approved blanket petition on file with the INS (simply ask the U.S. company whether it has this), then simply obtain from the employer three copies of a document known as a *Certificate of Eligibility,* INS Form 1-129S, and a copy of the Notice of Action, INS Form 1-797, that shows that an approved blanket L-1 petition has been obtained, and proceed directly to STEP TWO below.

However, assuming that your current foreign-based or non-U.S. employer does not already have an approved blanket petition status (and does not qualify for or wish to apply for one), you'll probably need to file for the individual L-1 visa petition – the petition for just each potential transferee. In such a case, the U.S. employer company, upon offering the prospective alien transferee a job transfer to the U.S., now completes the petition for the L-1 visa on the alien's behalf – the Form 1-129, and the supplement L. The petitioning U.S. employer then submits the complete Form 1-129L, *Petition For A Non-immigrant Worker*, to one of the 4 INS Regional Office centers in the U.S. for the one covering the intended employer's place of business. (All papers in the visa PETITION phase are required to be filed in the U.S. with the INS centers).

[see sample of Form 1-129 on p. 162, 165 & 168, and use the Supplement L of the form].

NOTE: Form 1-129B, which is the previous version of the current Form 1-129L, is shown on p. 162. This earlier version of the current form is reproduced here for illustrative purpose, to illustrate the actual visa filing procedures in an actual case previously filed and successfully processed for the same type of visa, material obtained courtesy of C. James Cooper, Jr., a long time veteran Denver, Colorado immigration lawyer and specialist. See "EXPLANATORY NOTES" on p. 37.

Note, also, that under the procedures in current use, the latest version of the Form 1-129 has various "supplements" to the basic form, each meant for a specific nonimmigrant classification – E, F, H, L, O, P, R, etc. And all you have to do is complete the basic form 1-129 and simply tear out and use the supplement that applies to your visa category.

Supporting Documents For The Visa Petition

U.S. employer-petitioner attaches the following supporting documents to the petition forms:

- Documentatons appropriate to establish that the alien is a bona fide nonimmigrant intending to stay in the U.S. only for a temporary period (e.g., proof of alien's maintenance of a residence, a wife/husband and children, real property and other assets in his home country, and other proof that he has no intention of abandoning his home country).
- Documentations or evidence showing that: qualifying corporate branches and qualifying employment positions are involved in the transfer; that the U.S. subsidiary or affiliate has physical premises to operate its business (a lease or deed to an office space); that the petitioning U.S. business entity and the overseas business are related as branches, subsidiaries or affiliates, and how, with the proper verifications duly attached (e.g. the last annual foreign federal or provincial tax return for the corporation, incorporation papers for both the foreign and U.S. corporations clearly showing shared ownership by the two, current profits/loss statement for the foreign corporation, etc) [For examples, see items cited in "Explanatory Note" on pp. 37-8].

• Evidence (attach a resume) showing the experience of the alien to assure that he or she has filled one of the qualifying positions outside the U.S. for the required one year period and a description of the capacity in which he/she was employed overseas; detailed statement from both the U.S. and non-U.S. employers explaining the alien's specific duties, the kinds and number of employees supervised by him, his powers, authority and responsibilities as a manager or executive person, and if the petition is based on the alien's specialized knowledge, include detailed statements, as well, describing the nature of the specialized knowledge possessed and how it will be used in the U.S. job.

• Evidence regarding the employer's intent to employ that alien in the U.S. temporarily, and a description of what capacity the alien would be employed in.

• Evidence showing the total number of shares issued, the classes of stock ownership, the owners of the issued stock, and the percentage of ownership for each stock holder. (If possible, attach on Organization Chart showing the alien's standing in the overseas company's line of authority and another flow chart showing the connection with the U.S. company). [see "Explanatory Note" on pp. 37-8, and sample letter on p. 196]

• A supporting letter by the U.S. subsidiary or affiliate, requesting the alien employee's transfer, and giving a full explanation (the "business necessity" letter) of why it is necessary that the particular worker be transferred, and his essentiality to the survival, well-being and progress of the U.S. company [see sample letter on p. 196.]

• A letter from the non-U.S. company stating that the alien was employed there for at least one of the past 3 years, copies of wage statements received or tax returns filed by the alien in his home country for the most recent years.

• Documentary evidence showing that both the U.S. and the non-U.S. companies are financially sound and currently actively engaged in trade or the rendering of services – tax returns of the U.S. and non-U.S. companies for past 2 years; annual shareholders reports of the U.S. and non-U.S. companies, if a publicly held company; accountant's financial statements, including profit and loss statements and balance sheet of the U.S. and non-U.S. companies for the latest 2 years, payroll records of both the U.S. and the non-U.S. companies for the past 2 years; reference letter from the Chamber of Commerce for the non-U.S. company; letters from banks and bank statements giving the average account balance of the U.S. business; copies of the company's article of incorporation, or of partnership agreements, or other documents of legal charter.

• In general, provide documents which identify the owners of both the U.S. and the non-U.S. companies and showing that there's commonality of ownership between them – e.g., similar kinds of documents listed for the E visa filings under Chapter 5, Section G.3 (iii) on p. 32.

Include These SPECIFIC/(ADDITIONAL) Documents, If Filing a Blanket L-1 Petition

• If the U.S. company's claim for eligibility for blanket L-1 visa petition is based on its related U.S. companies having a combined sales of at least $25 million in the past year, provide the company's annual income tax returns, audited accountants profit and loss statements and balance sheets, or annual report to the shareholders

• If the U.S. company's claim for eligibility for blanket L-1 visa petition is based on the company having more than 1,000 U.S. employees, provide the most recent quarterly State unemployment tax return and federal employment tax return Form 940.

• If the U.S. company's claim for eligibility for blanket L-1 visa petition is based on the company having obtained at least 10 L-1 visas for its employees in the past 12 months, provide copies of the Notice of Action Form 1-797 for each of the claimed approved employees.

Enclose the appropriate filing, fees for a visa Petition. The current amount for this is $130, if no change of status (i.e., Step Two below, if U.S. filing only) is being requested, and $155, if change of status is being requested.

(b.) Approval of the Visa petition

When the sponsoring U.S. employer has completed the application forms and the necessary supporting documentations, the employer "files" the papers with (i.e., he submits them to) one of the four INS Regional Service Centers in the U.S. which cover the area of the intended employer's business. The papers should be mailed to the INS office by certified mail, with return receipt requested so that you can retain the receipt as proof that the package was received.

NOTE: The Form 1-129, which is the actual petition for all employment-related nonimmigrant visas, is required to be completed, not by the alien but always by the alien's sponsoring U.S. employer. You should note, however, that nothing in the immigration rules stops you (the alien) from helping out your U.S. employer with the paperwork involved. In fact, it is generally expected and highly advisable that you do so in order to lessen the inconvenience and time factor on the sponsoring employer and to facilitate his willingness to act as your visa sponsor. Generally, for example, it is not uncommon to find that it is the alien who would fill out the forms and prepare most of the papers involved, and simply have the employer check them over for factual accuracy and then sign them.

You (i.e., employer) will receive from the INS, within a week or two of the mailing, a written notice of confirmation that the papers are being processed. The notice will also give the immigration "file number" assigned to the case, and approximately when you are to expect a decision. If some material defects or omissions are found in the papers (unsigned forms or missing information or documents, or the payment, etc), the INS will promptly return the entire application paper to you (the prospective U.S. employer) with a note or a Form 1-797, *Notice of Action,* telling him or her what corrections need to be supplied. Or, in some cases, the INS will simply retain the papers already submitted but issue a request, in the form of a Form 1-797, for the additional items that are needed. And, in such an event, all you'll need to do is simply supply the additional data required and promptly mail them (along with the Form 1-797 and the rest of the file, if applicable) back to the INS office.

The employer's INS L-1 petitions are usually approved by the INS within some 3 to 8 weeks. Upon such approval, the INS sends the employer a Notice of Action Form 1-797, showing that the petition has been approved. Where the alien visa beneficiary is presently residing in a foreign country, or where the alien otherwise intends to undertake the second phase of the visa processing abroad (see STEP TWO below), the INS will also notify the U.S. consulate of the alien's choice designated in the petition papers, and forward a complete file of the case to that consulate to enable its further processing of the visa request.

2. STEP TWO: THE VISA "APPLICATION" PHASE

Once the original L-1 "petition" filed by the U.S. employer has been approved by the U.S. – and only then – the second phase of the L-1 visa application can be commenced. HERE'S THE IMPORTANT POINT: this second phase is called the "application," as opposed to the "petition," and is undertaken primarily by the Alien, rather than by the U.S. employer.

(a) Where You May File The Application: Is It Abroad, Or in the U.S.?

You (the alien visa-seeker) may, depending on whether you meet the required conditions for it, apply for the L-1 visa at the U.S. consulate in your home country, or at the INS office in the U.S. The conditions you must meet in order to be eligible to file in the U.S. are the same conditions as are listed in Chapter 4, Section C.1 [p. 19]. Otherwise, then you have to file in a U.S. consulate abroad.

(b) Inquire About Your Local U.S. Consulate's or INS's Visa Policies and Procedures

Turn to Section C.2 of Chapter 4 (p. 20) and apply here the same details contained therein. See, also, Chapter 18, Sections A and B, for more on the subject of variations in visa processing policies and practices among various consulates and INS offices.

(c) Forms and Documentations Used

i. Prepare the following forms

Optional Form OF-156, *Nonimmigrant Visa Application.* This form is required ONLY WHEN AN OVERSEAS FILING with a U.S. consulate is involved. Generally, if your visa application is filed at a U.S. consulate in a foreign country, the consulate will usually provide you (the alien) with their required "optional forms" complete with the instructions for completing them, and such forms are designated by a prefix "OF" preceding a number, as in OF-156. (see illustrative sample of Form OF-156 on p. 177)

NOTE: OF-156 is the basic application form which the vast majority of non-immigrant visa applicants will encounter. The proper completion of this form is, by far, probably the single most important and primary thing you can do in any nonimmigrant visa application which will determine ultimately whether you get the visa or not. For that reason, we set forth in one chapter, Chapter 13, the detailed, step-by-step instructions by which to properly complete the form and the underlying considerations and to answer the questions asked or provide the information required therein. Please refer immediately to Chapter 13.

- Form 1-539, *Application To Extend/Change Nonimmigrant Status.* This form is applicable only if it is a U.S. filing that you are doing, and only for accompanying relatives of the principal alien applicant, if any. Only one application form is needed for an entire family, except that if there's more than one accompanying relative, each should be listed on the form. (sample of Form 1-539 is on p.183).

ii. Supporting Documents To Attach

For the supporting documents, turn to Chapter 5, Section G.3 (ii) [p. 30], and see the listing outlined therein under "General Supporting Documents For Most Nonimmigrant Situations" for the kinds of supporting documents you may have to provide.

In addition, if your situation is one involving a U.S. employer that has an approved L-1 blanket status, you should be sure to secure a document called a Certificate of Eligibility, Form 1-129S, from the U.S. company and to submit it (or the original copy of the Notice of Action Form 1-797, if you only filed for the individual L-1 petition), along with the rest of the supporting papers.

(d) File The "Application" Papers With the U.S. Consulate or The INS, As Applicable

Turn to Section G.4 of Chapter 5 (p. 33), and follow here the same procedures outlined therein to file your visa application.

(e) Attend The Visa Interview, If One Is Required In Your Case

Whether you are doing a U.S. filing or a consulate filing, a face to face personal interview with the visa processing officials may or may not be required in your case before the authorities render their final decision in your visa issuance. In any event, if a visa interview is required in your particular case, you will be so notified by the visa processing office. When you've gathered together all the items required by the consulate or the INS, whichever one is applicable, you will appear on the appointed date, time and place set for the interview and undergo one with the designated interviewer. The visa processing officials will promptly render a final decision on your application, but only AFTER such interview.

[Turn to Chapter 15 for the full procedures involved in this all-important step in any nonimmigrant (as well as immigrant) visa application – the visa interview].

(f) Final Approval Of Your Visa Application

In the end, assuming that everything is in order with your visa application – basically, that you have, for example, all the proofs and documentation required to show your eligibility for the visa applied for, and that there's nothing that makes you inadmissible under the U.S. Immigration law, such as having some serious criminal or terrorist record or potential, or a contagious, communicable disease – your application for a visa will be approved. You will be issued your visa. The U.S. consulate in charge of visa issuance (if a consulate filing abroad), will usually stamp the approved visa that applies in your case (say, a B-1 and/or B-2 visa, in the case of the visitor's visa, or the E-1 or E-2; in the case of the treaty trader or investor) in your passport. If you get your visa through a U.S. filing, upon approval of your visa application, you are given a visa "status" and not an actual visa (under the law, only consulates may issue visa, and not the INS). This may be stamped in your passport, and you will receive from the INS a Notice of Action Form 1-797 indicating the dates for which your status is approved, with a new 1-94 card attached at the bottom of the form.

(g) Now, Get Formally "Admitted" Into The U.S. at a Port of Entry

As a holder of a nonimmigrant type of visa, you will normally be authorized to stay in the U.S. for a specific period of time, depending on the type and classification of the nonimmigrant visa involved. For example, for a B visa, you are normally authorized to stay in the U.S. for 6 months with the possibility of multiple extensions upon future application, while for an E-1 or E-2 visa, the authorized period of stay is 2 years at a time, with the possibility of extensions or renewals of the visa for additional one or two year periods, and so on with respect to other types of nonimmigrant visas. And on your entering the U.S. from a foreign country with your visa, you will be given a 1-94 card, which will be stamped with dates showing your authorized stay. Then, each time you exit and re-enter the U.S., you will get a new 1-94 card with a new period of authorized stay affixed thereto.

BUT HERE'S THE MAIN ISSUE OF IMPORTANCE YOU SHOULD NOTE HERE: before you can be actually allowed entry into the U.S. even with your approved and issued visa in hand, you must first be formally "admitted" into the country – that is, you have to successfully pass through some strict formalities involved in a procedure called the "inspection and admission" process into the United States. Turn to Chapter 16, *"Entering The United States: The Process of Getting Actually Admitted Into The Country After You've Got Your Visa In Hand."* *(p. 118)*

(h) You May Be Denied A Visa. What Can You Do?

What if, in the end, for whatever the reason, your visa application is turned down and you are denied a visa? Turn to Chapter 5, Section G.8 *"What To Do If Your Visa Application Is Denied"* (p. 35)

Chapter 12

Some Specialized Temporary Work Visa Categories For Various Professionals In The Sciences, Arts, Education, Business, Athletics, Entertainment, And In Religion: The O, P, And R Visas

A. THE SPECIALIZED WORK VISAS COVERED IN THIS CHAPTER

In this Chapter, we shall cover the requirements for qualifying for, and the visa filing procedures thereof for, some three highly specialized temporary work visas created by the Immigration Act of 1990 – the O, P, and R visas.

(i.) The "O" visa is the visa classification by which aliens of extraordinary ability in the sciences, arts, education, business and athletics, may be given a temporary visa for entry into the U.S.

(ii.) The "P" visa is the visa classification by which internationally recognized entertainers and artists may be given a temporary visa for entry into the U.S.

(iii.) The "R" visa is the visa classification that similarly offers entry rights into the U.S. by religious Ministers, and other aliens in religious occupations.

All of the above-designated three visa classifications are quite narrow in scope, however, and all three of them possess a basic common denominator among them, namely, they all require a prior job offer from a U.S. employer.

B. THE O-1 VISA: ALIENS OF EXTRAORDINARY ABILITY IN THE SCIENCES, ARTS, EDUCATION, BUSINESS AND ALTHETICS

1. What Is The O-1 Visa

While the P visa (to be considered in the Sections C to G below) is the visa category for alien persons of outstanding or extraordinary ability in the fields of athletics and entertainment, the O-1 visa, on the other hand, is designated for aliens of outstanding or extraordinary ability in the fields of science, arts, education, and business. These visas allow you (the alien) to work legally in the U.S. for an employer but only and solely for your visa sponsor. If you wish to change jobs, you must get a new visa.

The initial duration of the O, P and R visas, is 3 years. In all instances, the duration of the visa should be sufficient for the completion of the events or activity but for no longer than 3 years. However, extensions of stay are granted only in order to complete the events or activity.

2. Requirements For O-1 Visa

(a.) Qualifying In Science, Education, Business or Athletics Sub-category

To qualify for an O-1 visa in the areas only of science, education, or business or athletics – that is, not including the arts – here are the basic requirements:*

- You (the alien) must be able to show that you are coming to work in the U.S. in a field of science, education, or

*See The Administrative Code of Federal Regulations for the essential information about these standards.

business in which you possess some "extraordinary ability," and that you received a "sustained national or international acclaim" and recognition in such a field of endeavors.

- You can establish this by: Demonstration of receipt of a major internationally recognized award, such as a Nobel Prize; OR,
- If you have accomplished at least three of the following, with all due documentations thereof:
- Documentation of your (the alien's) receipt of nationally or internationally recognized prizes or awards for excellence in the field of endeavor.
- Documentation of your (the alien's) membership and association in the alien's field of expertise and which requires outstanding achievement for membership as judged by recognized national or international experts in their disciplines or fields.
- Published material in professional or major trade publications or major media about the alien, relating to the alien's work in the alien's field of expertise, which shall include information such as the title, date and author of such published material, and any necessary translation into English.
- Evidence of the alien's participation on a panel or individually, as a judge of the work of others in the field or in an allied field of specialization.
- Evidence of the alien's original scientific scholarly or business-related contributions that are of major significance in the field.
- Evidence of the alien's authorship of scholarly articles in the professional journals or other major media in the field.
- Evidence that the alien has been employed in a critical or essential capacity for organizations with distinctive reputation.
- Evidence that the alien has commanded and/or commands a high salary or other remuneration for services evidenced by contracts or other reliable evidence.

(b.) Qualifying In The Arts Sub-category

To qualify for an O-1 visa in the area only of the Arts – defined as any field of creative activity, including but not limited to fine, visual, culinary and performing arts – here are the basic requirements:*

You (the alien) must be able to show that you are coming to the U.S. to perform in a field of the arts in which you possess "extraordinary ability," and that you have received recognition as being prominent and having attained extraordinary achievement in your field of endeavor.

You can demonstrate this by this:

- Evidence (documentations) showing that the alien has been nominated for, or has been the recipient of, significant national or international awards or prizes in the particular field, such as an Academy Award, an Emmy, a Grammy, or a Director's Guild Award; or, alternatively, by showing at least three of the following forms of documentation:

i. Evidence that the alien has performed and will perform services as a lead or starring participant in productions or events which have a distinguished reputation as evidenced by critical reviews, advertisements, publicity releases, publications, contracts, or endorsements;

ii. Evidence that the alien has achieved national or international recognition for achievements, evidenced by critical reviews or other published materials by or about the alien in major newspapers, trade journals, magazines, or other publications;

---

*See, for example, The Federal Register, Vol.57, No.69, April 9, 1992, for the essential information

iii. Evidence that the alien has performed in a lead, starring, or critical role for organizations and establishment that have a distinguished reputation evidenced by articles in newspapers or trade journals;

iv. Evidence that the alien has a record of major commercial or critically acclaimed successes, as evidenced by such indicators as title, rating, standing in the field, box office receipts, credit for original research or product development, motion picture or television ratings, and other occupational achievements reported in trade jounals, major newspapers, or other publications;

v. Evidence that the alien has received significant recognition for achievements from organizations, critics, government agencies, or other recognized experts in the field in which the alien is engaged. Such testimonials must be in a form that clearly indicates the author's authority, expertise, and knowledge of the alien's achievements; or

vi. Evidence that the alien has commanded or now commands a high salary or other substantial renumeration for services in comparison to others in the field, as evidenced by contracts or other reliable evidence.

If the above standards or criteria do not readily apply to the alien's situation, the alien may submit alternative but comparable evidence in order to establish the alien's eligibility.

(c.) Qualifying in the Motion Picture and Television Industry Sub-category

To qualify for an O-1 visa in the area of motion picture and television industry, here are the basic requirements:

- You (the alien) must be able to show that you are coming to America to work in an area of the motion picture or television industry in which you posses extraordinary ability.

You can demonstrate this by:

- Evidence (documentations) showing that the alien has been nominated for, or has been the recipient of, significant national or international awards or prizes, such as an Academy Award, an Emmy, a Grammy or a Director's Guild Award. Or, alternatively, you can present evidence of at least <u>three</u> of the following achievements:
- Performing (presently, or in the past or future) in a lead or starring role in a production or event having a distinguished reputation
- Aquiring national or international recognition, as demonstrated by letters, published materials, critical reviews and print media articles of acclaim
- Perform (presently, in the past or future) in a lead, starring or critical role for an organization of distinguished stature
- Performing in a role or production having a major commercial or critically acclaimed successes, as evidenced by such indicators as good box office receipts or television ratings
- Attainment of significant recognition for accomplishments from organizations, critics, government agencies, or recognized experts in the industry
- Commanding or having commanded a high salary or other substantial remuneration, as evidenced by contracts or other reliable evidence

Now, if the above standards or criteria do not readily apply to the alien's situation, the alien may submit alternative but comparable evidence to establish his/her eligibility.

O-1 visas are issued only for the time needed to complete a particular event, tour or season.

3. The O-2 Visas: Support and Assisting Persons To O-1 Visa Holders

O-2 visas are for the aliens who work as essential support personnel of O-1 athletes and entertainers – the persons who accompany and/or assist the O-1 alien in the performance. O-2 visas are not available in the fields of science, business or education. The O-2 visa worker must be an integral part of the actual performance of the O-2 visa artist or athlete and must also have critical skills and experience with the O-1 alien that are not general in nature and cannot be readily performed or replicated by a U.S. worker. In the case of O-2 visa aliens who assist persons in the movie and television industry, such persons must have a pre-existing and long-standing working relationship with the O-1 alien, and where filming is required both inside and outside of the U.S., he/she (the O-1 visa alien) must be deemed necessary for the purposes of maintaining continuity of filming and a successful production.

O-2 visa holders are not allowed to pursue permanent residence (the Green Card) while in nonimmigrant O status. (This differs, on the other hand, directly with the O-1 and O-3 aliens who are, on the other hand, permitted to do so while in their nonimmigrant O status). The O-2 aliens must show that they have intent to depart the U.S. and that they maintain a residence abroad to which they plan to return. The law also requires that the Immigration and Naturalization Service consult with the labor organizations on an advisory basis on the question of the O-2 alien's importance to the O-1 alien visa holder prior to issuance or denial of the visa, but with only labor organizations experienced in the skill involved.

4. The O-3 Visas: Accompanying Relatives of O-1 and O-2 Visa holders

Dependent family members (spouses and unmarried children under age 21) of O-1 and O-2 visa holders, are issued O-3 visa. The O-3 visa holder is allowed to remain in the U.S., and may seek permanent residence while in O-3 status, but are not authorized to work.

C. THE P-1 VISA: VISA FOR OUTSTANDING ALIEN ATHLETES, ATHLETIC TEAMS, AND ENTERTAINMENT COMPANIES

1. The Two Main Classes In the P-1 Visa Category

P-1 visas are available for two principal types of internationally recognized persons or teams:

- - athletes or athletic teams who compete at an "internationally recognized level of performance" for a long and continuous period of time, and
- - Entertainment companies (or entertainers who perform as part of a group) that have received international recognition as "outstanding" for a "sustained and substantial period of time".

NOTE: Notice that, unlike the O visa which is always based on the qualifications and capabilities of the individual alien applicant, the P-1 visas can be issued based on the qualifications and capabilities of a team or group.

2. Requirements For The P-1 Visa

(a) Qualifying In the Athletic Sub-category

To qualify for a P-1 visa in the area of ATHLETICS, here are the basic requirements:*

i. An alien athlete must have an internationally recognized reputation as an international athlete, or he or she must be a member of a foreign team that is internationally recognized. The athlete or team must be coming to the United States to participate in an athletic competition which has a distinguished reputation and which requires participation of an athlete or athletic team that has an international reputation.

ii. If for an athletic team, provide evidence proving that the team, as a unit, has achieved international recognition in the sports. Each member of the team is accorded P-1 classification based on the international reputation of the team. If the visa is sought for an athlete who will compete individually or as a member of a United States team,

*See The Federal Register. Vol.57. No.69. April 9, 1992. for the essential rules and regulations establishing these standards.

provide evidence prooving that the athlete has achieved international recognition in the sport based on his or her reputation

A petition for a P-1 athlete or athletic team shall include:

a. A tendered contract with a major United States sports league or team, or a tendered contract in an individual sport commensurate with international recognition in that sport; and

b. Documentation of at least Two of the following:

- Evidence of having participated previously, to a significant extent, in athletic events with a major United States sports league;
- Evidence of having participated in international competition with a national team;
- Evidence of having participated previously to a significant extent, with a United States college or university in intercollegiate competition;
- A written statement from an official of a major United States sports league or an official of the governing body of the sport which details how the alien or team is internationally recognized;
- A written statement from a member of the sports media or a recognized expert in the sport detailing how the alien or team is internationally recognized;
- Evidence that the individual or the team is internationally ranked, if international ranking is applicable; or
- Evidence that the alien or the team has received a significant honor or award in the sport.

(b) Qualifying in the Entertainment Field Sub-category

In the case of persons in the entertainment industry, individual entertainers are not accorded a P-1 visa to perform as individuals separate and apart from a group. Rather, a P-1 visa is accorded only to a GROUP to perform as a unit based on the international reputation of the GROUP

To qualify for a P-1 visa in the area of entertainment, here are the basic requirement:

i. Evidence that the entertainment group has been internationally recognized as outstanding in the area of entertainment for "a sustained and substantial period of time" – generally a period of at least one year.

ii. At least 75 percent of the members of the group must be an integral part of the group for at least one year, and must provide functions integral to the group's performance. (This one-year requirement is for performers only; it does not apply to support personnel, and does not apply to anyone who works for a circus in whatever capacity whatsoever)

A petition for a P-1 visa for the members of an entertainment group shall include:

- Evidence that the group, under the name shown on the petition, has been established and performing regularly for a period of at least one year. (The INS may waive the one-year group membership requirement for an alien new member if he/she is replacing an ill or otherwise unexpectedly absent but essential member of the group, or if the new member will be performing a critical role of the group's operations)
- A statement listing each member of the group and the exact dates for which each member has been regularly employed by the group.
- The evidence that the group has been internationally recognized as outstanding in the discipline, may be demonstrated by the submission of evidence of the group's nomination or receipt of significant international awards or prizes for outstanding achievement in its field, or by at least three of the following different types of documentation:

- - Evidence that the group has performed and will perform as a starring or leading entertainment group in the productions or events which have a distinguished reputation as evidenced by critical reviews, advertisements, publicity releases, publications, contracts, or endorsement;

- - Evidence that the group has made an outstanding international achievement in its field as evidenced by reviews in major newspapers, trade journals, magazines, or other published materials;
- - Evidence (by way of articles in newspapers, trade journals and publications, or testimonials) that the group has performed and will perform services as a leading or starring group for organizations and establishments that have a distinguished reputation;
- - Evidence that the group has a record of major commercial or critically acclaimed successes, as evidenced by such indicators as ratings, standing in the field, box office receipts, record, cassette, or video sales, and other achievements in the field as reported in trade journals, major newspapers, or other publications;
- - Evidence that the group has achieved significant recognition for accomplishments from organizations, critics, government agencies, or other recognized experts in the field. Such testimonials must be in a form that clearly indicates the author's authority, expertise, and knowledge of the alien's achievements; or
- - Evidence (by way of written contracts or other reliable proof) that the group has commanded or now commands a high salary or other substantial remuneration for services comparable to other similarly situated in the field.

D. SPECIAL PROVISIONS FOR ALIEN CIRCUS PERSONNEL AND CERTAIN ENTERTAINMENT GROUPS

In the case of entertainment groups, the one-year group membership requirement is not applicable to alien circus personnel who perform as part of a circus or circus group. That is, circus personnel do not need to have been a part of the circus group or organization for one year in order to qualify for a P-1 visa. Provided, however, that the particular circus that the alien(s) are coming to join is one that has been recognized nationally as being outstanding for a long period of time.

Also, in the case of certain entertainment groups, namely, those which have been recognized nationally as having a sustained, long-term outstanding national reputation, the Immigration and Naturalization Service may consider other types of evidence or waive the "international" recognition requirement under these circumstances: if some "special circumstances" would make it difficult for their group to prove their international reputation. Such special circumstances would be, for example, when an entertainment group is unable to demonstrate recognition beyond the borders of more than one country due to such factors as having only limited access to news media, or problem based on the group's geographical location. This provision is designed for the purpose of aiding entertainment groups which may be quite talented and recognized in their own country or region but who do not yet have an international acclaim or recognition for one reason or the other.

E. P-2 VISAS: FOR PARTICIPANTS IN RECIPROCAL EXCHANGE PROGRAMS

The P-2 visas are for artists and entertainers, individually as well as a part of a group, who came to U.S. to participate and perform under a reciprocal exchange program between U.S.-based and foreign-based organizations that are engaged in temporary exchange of artists and entertainers. The P-2 visa classification covers all essential support personnel. The U.S. artist or entertainer or group being exchanged must, as well, have skills and terms of employment comparable to that of the alien person coming to the U.S.

To qualify as a legitimate reciprocal exchange program, for purposes of a P-2 visa, legitimacy of the program must be proven by a formal, written agreement, and a labor union must have either played a major role in the exchange negotiations or have agreed to the exchange.

F. P-3 VISAS: FOR PERFORMERS IN CULTURALLY UNIQUE PROGRAMS

The P-3 visas are for artists and entertainers who come to the U.S., either individually or as part of a group, to perform or otherwise participate "under a program that is [considered] culturally unique."

To qualify for a P-3 visa, here are the basic requirements:

1. Presentation of evidence that the alien's coming to the U.S is for the purpose of participating, by way of developing, performing, coaching, or teaching, in a cultural event or events that will further the development or understanding of his art form
2. Evidence as well as demonstration of credentials, showing that he or his group possess authentic skills and knowledge in performing, presenting, coaching or teaching the unique or traditional art form
3. Evidence that his performance or his group's performance is indeed "culturally unique," as evidenced by reviews in newspapers, journals or other published materials.

The essential support personnel of P-3 aliens are required to seek the same P-3 visa as well. The P-3 alien support person should present documentation showing what consultation had been had with a U.S. labor organization having expertise in the area of the alien's skills, a copy of the contract of employment with the alien, and a statement detailing why the support alien is essential to the principal alien's role.

G. P-4 VISAS: FOR ACCOMPANYING RELATIVES OF OTHER P VISA HOLDERS

The P-4 visa is applicable to accompanying relatives of any P-1, P-2 or P-3 visa worker. P-4 visa holders are permitted to remain in the U.S., but may not work unless granted special work authorization in their own right.

Temporary Intent Requirement For P Visa Alien; Duration of stay.

The duration of stay under both P-2 and P-3 visa is the time needed for specific performance or event. The P-1 athletes, however, may be allowed a duration of stay of up ten years. This provision is made in consideration of the fact that many professional athletes are required or encouraged to sign multi-year contracts with the team organizations for which they play. The P visa applicants must maintain a residence in their home country (or other foreign countries) to which they intend to return.

H. THE R-1 VISA: VISA FOR RELIGIOUS WORKERS

The R-1 visa is the nonimmigrant religious worker visa category; it is available for an alien person who has been a member of a legitimate religious denomination for at least 2 years, and has a job offer from an affiliate of that same religious organization in the U.S. to work for it in America. People who are members of the clergy as well as lay religious workers are equally eligible for the R-1 visa. The R-1 visa (which, of course, is a nonimmgrant visa), is very similar to the immigrant visa (Green Card) category for special immigrant religious workers discussed in Chapter 16 of the other volume of this title, the Volume 2*. In fact, the criteria for qualifying for the nonimmigrant R-1 visa are almost exactly the same as those for qualifying for the immigrant visa category for religious workers. Hence, in general, one who qualifies for the R-1 visa would have been equally qualified for the special immigrant religious worker visa, and may well be better advised to apply directly for the immigrant visa (Green Card) category**. The few principal differences between the R non-immigrant religious worker visa and the immigrant religious worker visa, are as follow: the R visa category has a five-year limitation and unlike the immigrant category, it is not necessary that the R-1 visa worker be employed by the religious organizatiion before

---

* See Chapter 16, Section B of How To Obtain Your U.S. Immigration Visa, Volume 2

** Note, however, that as of this writing under the law establishing the immigrant religious worker category, that visa category (unless renewed or extended by an act of Congress) expires on October 1, 2000; the R visa category, on the hand, will continue to apply indefinitely.

getting the visa. They need only have been members of the religious organization.

1. The Requirements For An R-1 Visa

(a) *The criteria for classification of an R religious worker are:** *

- Proof that the alien is a member of a religious denomination that has an authentic, bona fide nonprofit, religious organization in the United State.
- Proof that the religious denomination and its affiliate, if applicable, are exempt from taxation, or are one that qualifies for, tax-exempt status.
- Proof that the alien has been a member of the organization for two years immediately preceding application for a visa or for admission to the U.S. (NOTE that, unlike an applicant for a special immigrant visa as a religious worker, an applicant for the non-immigrant R visa needs only to have been a member of the organization for the required 2-year period and need not to have been engaging in ministerial, vocational, or occupational activities in addition to membership.)
- Proof that the alien is entering the United States solely to carry on the vocation of a minister of that denomination; OR that, at the request of the organization, the alien is entering the United States to work in a religious vocation or occupation for that denomination or for an organization affiliated with the denomination, whether in a professional capacity or not; OR that the alien is the spouse or child of an R-1 non-immigrant who is accompanying or following to join him or her, and
- Proof that the alien has resided and been physically present outside the United States for the immediately prior year, except for brief visit for business or pleasure, if he or she has previously spent five years in this classification.

NOTE: Only individuals authorized by a recognized religious denomination to conduct religious worship and to perform other duties usually performed by authorized members of the clergy of that religion, may be classified as ministers of religion. Evidence that a person qualifies as a minister of religion is normally available in the form of official ecclesiastical recognition, such as certificates of ordination, licenses, formal letters of conferral, etc. The following, for example, may be considered to be ministers of religion: a deacon of a recognized denomination, practitioners and nurses of the Christian Science Church, commissioned officers of the Salvation Army, an authentic Buddist monk.

(b) *Characteristics of a Religious Denomination.*

To qualify as an authentic "religious denomination," an organization will generally have the following elements or comparable indications of its bona fides:

- Some form of ecclesiastical government.
- A recognized creed and form of worship.
- A formal code of doctrine and discipline.
- Religious services and ceremonies.
- Established places of religious worship.
- Religious congregations.

(c) *Requirements for a nonprofit organization.*

To qualify as a true U.S. "nonprofit organization," an organization must meet the following criteria as described in the Internal Revenue Code of 1986:

- No part of the net earnings of the organization may benefit any private shareholder or individual;

*Reproduced from 69 Interpreter Release 412. April 6, 1992

- No substantial part of the organization's activities may involve propagandizing or otherwise attempting to influence legislation;
- The organization may not participate or intervene in any political campaign, including publishing or distributing statements on behalf of (or in opposition to) any candidate for public office.

Evidence that the religious denomination, or its affiliate qualifies as U.S. nonprofit religious organization, is usually presented (by the alien or by his/her U.S. employer) in the form of: (1) a certificate of tax-exempt status issued by the Internal Revenue Service; or (2) in the absence of that, documentation demonstrating that the organization would qualify for tax exemption, if such status were sought.

(d) ***Certification from employing religious organization.***
An authorized official of the specific organizational unit of the religious denomination or affiliate which will be employing or engaging the R-1 alien applicant in the United State, must prepare a letter certifying the following:

- That if the alien's religious membership was maintained (in whole or in part) outside the United States, the foreign and United States religious organizations belong to the same religious denomination.
- That immediately prior to the application for the non-immigrant visa or application for admission to the United State, the alien has been a member of the religious organization for the required two-year period.
  That (as appropriate):
- If the alien is a minister, he or she is authorized to conduct religious worship for that denomination and to perform other duties usually performed by authorized members of the clergy of that denomination. (The duties to be performed should be described in detail.)
- If the alien is a religious professional, he or she has at least a United States baccalaureate degree or its foreign equivalent; such a degree is required for entry into the religious profession.
- If the alien is to work in a nonprofessional religious vocation or occupation, he or she is qualified in that vocation or occupation. (Evidence of such qualifications may include, but need not be limited to, evidence establishing that the alien is a monk, nun, or religious brother or sister, or that the type of work to be done relates to a traditional religious function.)
- Detailed statement of the arrangements made for payment for services to be rendered by the alien, if any, including the amount and source of any salary, a description of any other types of compensation to be received (including housing, food, clothing and any other benefits to which a monetary value may be affixed) and a statement whether such payment shall be in exchange for services rendered.
- The name and location of the specific organizational unit of the religious denomination or affiliate for which the alien will be providing services within the United States.
- If the alien is to work for a bona fide organization that is affiliated with a religious denomination, a description of the nature of the relationship between the affiliate and the religious denomination.

R-2 Aliens (spouses and defendant of the R-1 aliens) are not authorized to accept employment. R-2 aliens are permitted to study during their period of stay in the U.S.

2. Temporary Intent Requirement for R Visa Alien; Duration of Stay

There is no requirement that applicants for R visa establish that they have a residence in a foreign country which they have no intention of abandoning. However, the R nonimmigrant is limited to a total period of stay not to exceed 5 years, with the initial period of admission of not more than 3 years. The alien's stated intention to depart the U.S. when his/her status ends, is normally sufficient to satisfy that requirement, in the absence of any specific indication or evidence that the alien's intent is to the contrary. Upon the expiration of the initial 3-year period of stay, an extension may be authorized for a period of up to 2 years, on application to and approval by the INS Service Center which has jurisdiction over the alien's place of employment in the U.S.

I. HOW TO FILE FOR THE O, P, R, VISA

Briefly summarized, once a qualifying alien has been offered a job in his field of ability by a U.S. company, employer, or institution, the process of filing for an O, P, R, visa, is a TWO-part process. First, the prospective U.S. employer who wants to employ the alien, acts as the alien's sponsor; he makes a written application (it's called the "petition" in this phase) to the U.S. Immigration and Naturalization Service at one of the four INS Regional Service Centers in the U.S., to demonstrate that the prospective alien meets all the requirements set forth in Section B.2 above, or in Section B.3, B.4, or C.2, E, F, or H.1, as the case may be. And if the INS approves the employer's petition, the foreign person himself (and the accompanying relatives, if any), then applies for the visa. This phase two of the visa processing, is undertaken by the alien himself, and is called the "application" phase. In this, the alien may carry this out either at his local U.S. consulate abroad, or at an INS office in the U.S., if he's already present in the U.S. and meets the required conditions for a U.S. filing. The consular (or INS) officials then make the decision on whether the visa is to be granted or not.

1. STEP ONE. THE VISA "PETITION" PHASE

(a.) The U.S. employer (or company) who accept to and is able to sponsor the alien O, or P or R visa applicant, upon offering a position of a high enough level or appropriate nature to the alien, now completes the petition for the visa on the alien's behalf – the Form 1-129, and the O/P/Q/R supplement. The petitioning U.S. employer then submits the completed Form 1-129O/P/Q/R, *Petition for Nonimmigrant Workers,* to one of the 4 INS Regional Service Centers in the U.S. for the one covering the intended employer's place of business. (All O, P, R visa papers in the visa PETITION phase are required to be filed in the U.S. with the INS centers). [see sample of Form 1-129 on pp. 162, 165 & 168, and use the supplement O/P/Q/R of the form.] See Appendix B for list of all INS offices in the US.

NOTE: Form 1-126, which is the previous version of Form 1-129, is shown on pp. 162, 165 & 168, while the previous version of today's Form 1-539 (Form 1-506) is shown on p. 183. These older versions of the form in current use are reproduced here for illustrative purpose, to illustrate the actual visa filing procedures of an actual case previously filed and successfully processed for the same type of visa, material obtained courtesy of C. James Cooper, Jr., a longtime veteran Denver Colorado immigration lawyer and specialist. See "EXPLANATORY NOTE" on p. 37. Note, also, that Form 1-129 under current use comes in several "supplements," each meant for a specific nonimmigrant category – E, F, H, L, O, P, R, etc. And all you do is simply tear out and use the supplement that applies to you.

Supporting Documents For Visa Petition

U.S. employer-petitioner attaches the following supporting documents to the petition forms:

General For O & P Visas

- Copy of a written employment contract by U.S. employer with the alien, containing details on the terms of the alien's employment, his (her) job duties, salary, and other benefits and compensation, the tour schedule, if applicable
- A written statement giving details of the nature and identity of the U.S. employer and the nature of the business or profession engaged in and its operations, the specific events or activities (athletics, entertainment, arts, etc) in which the alien will be engaged in, and how and why his participation is essential.
- Official transcripts of academic degrees, diploma, certificate, or similar academic record from a college or university, showing that the alien has a U.S. baccalaureate degree or advanced degrees or a foreign equivalent,

relating to his area of claimed 'extraordinary ability' (for O visas)

• Evidence of license to practice the profession, or certification for a particular profession (for O visas)

• Written articles by or about the alien about their success or achievements in their business, trade or profession, testimonials and letters of recommendation from renowned members of the alien's peer group; public records and report describing awards or prizes given the alien as, say, an outstanding entrepreneur or business leader or executive, annual reports of the alien's company

• Evidence (such as letters from current or former employers) showing that the alien had, say, 10 years of full-time experience in the field for which he is being sought; evidence (i.e. letters from present or former employers) that he has commanded a high salary or other exceptional ability (at least $US 75,000 to $US $1 00,000 per year), and explaining the alien's importance to his previous employers

• Evidence of membership by the alien in professional associations

• Evidence of recognition for achievements and significant contribution to the alien's industry or field by peers, government entities or educational, professional or business organizations

• FOR A PERFORMING ARTIST, for example: you may present playbills, reviews, magazine articles and awards, showing your national and/or international acclaim and credibility as a performing artist (a classical guitarist, lead singer etc), or as a popular actor or actress in the cinema, theatre, etc

• FOR AN ARTIST OR ART DEALER OR EXPERT (painters, sculptors, authors or writers, arts exhibitionist, etc): you may present critical reviews by or about the alien and/or his/her work in cultural or art magazines or cultural pages of newspapers, reporting awards or prizes won by the alien in national competitions, and discussing the alien's abilities as a painter, sculptor, nationally recognized author or writer,

• FOR A SCIENTIST, for example: you may present articles in the alien's professional or academic field, in magazines and newspapers, scientific journals, by and about the alien about his research work; books and reports of critical acclaim published about the alien's scientific research or study, and evidence of awards, prizes or fellowships earned by the alien.

Special For O and P Visas

For all O and P visa petitions, you must include a "consultation report" (a written opinion) from an appropriate peer group, labor union, and/or management organization, concerning the nature of the work to be done by the alien and his qualifications. The consultation report can simply be a letter from the U.S. consultant organization (see the footnote below for information on how to obtain such qualified consultant organizations) stating that it has no objection to the alien being granted the visa, and may, in addition, give its assessment of the reputation of the alien and/or his team and an explanation of the nature of the events in the U.S., and its opinion as to whether or not the alien is essential to the performance and why. For O-2 cases and P-1 petition cases, the consultation report must include a statement of whether or not U.S. workers are readily available for the kind of job for which the alien is being employed; P-2 consultation report must include statement about the existence of a viable exchange program, and P-3 consultation report must include an assessment of the cultural nature of the performances and certify that the event or activities are essentially cultural in nature, and an explanation of why they fit properly into the P-3 classification.*

---

*The list of organizations maintained by the INS which supply consultation reports, include the following: American Federation of Musicians and American Guild of Musicians, both in New York city (for instrumental and other musicians); Actors Equity Association of New York city (for stage managers and all nonmusical performers in live productions); Screen Actors Guild of Hollywood, California and New York City, and American Federation of Television and Radio Artists of New York city (for all nonmusical performers in film and electronic media); International Alliance of Theatrical State Employees and Moving Picture Machine Operators of New York City and Hollywood California; International Brotherhood of Electrical Workers, Washington D.C. and National Association of Broadcast Employees and Technicians, Bethesda, Maryland (for all directors of photography, technical and Craft personnel); and Writers Guild of America in West Hollywood, CA. and New York city (for writers in film and electronic media).

Special For R Visas, Provide:

- All diplomas, certificates and transcripts showing your academic and professional qualifications (e.g., certificate of ordination or authorization to conduct religious worship as a member of the clergy, diploma from religious institutions, or other written proof that the alien is qualified in a religious vocation or occupation).
- Letter from the sponsoring religious organization in the U.S. detailing its organizational structure, number of followers in both the U.S. and your home country, facts about your job offer in the U.S., including the job title, duties, salary, qualification requirements, and duration of the employment, etc, and showing that the job or services you will perform are of a religious or professional nature.
- Letter from authorized official of the religious organization in the alien's foreign country, which verifies the alien's membership in the organization for at least 2 years; and if by any chance the alien had worked in the past for the organization, then provide details as well of the kind of religious work and employment he (she) has had therein.
- Written proof that the religious organization (or an affiliate) which will employ the alien in the U.S., is a bona fide nonprofit religious organization, and is exempt from taxation by the U.S. Internal Revenue Service; such proof as may be required from the religious organization to show its nonprofit status.

Enclose the appropriate filing fees for the visa Petition. The current amount for this as of this filing (it changes often) is $130, if no change of status is being requested, and $155, if change of status is requested. Send the payment in a cheek or money order.

(b.) Approval of the Visa petition

Upon the sponsoring U.S. employer's completion of the application forms and the necessary supporting documentations, the employer "files" the papers with (i.e., he submits them to) one of the four INS Regional Service Centers in the U.S. which covers the area of the intended employer's business. Preferably, the papers should be mailed to the INS office by certified mail, with return receipt requested, so that you can retain the receipt as proof profit that the package was received.

NOTE: The Form 1-129, which is the actual petition for all employment-related nonimmigrant visas, is required to be completed, not by the alien but always the alien's sponsoring U.S. employer. You should note, however, that nothing in the immigration rules stops you (the alien) from helping out your U.S. employer with the paperwork involved. In fact, *it is generally expected and highly advisable that you do so on order to lesson the inconvenience and time factor on the sponsoring employer and to facilitate his willingness to act as your visa sponsor.* Generally, for example, it is not uncommon to find that it is the alien who would fill out the forms and prepare most of the papers involved, and simply have the employer check them over for factual accuracy and then sign them.

You (i.e. employer) will receive from the INS, within a week or two of the mailing, a written notice of confirmation that the papers are being processed. The notice will also give the immigration "file number" assigned to the case and approximately when you are to expect a decision. If some material defects or omissions are found in the papers (unsigned forms or missing information or documents, or the payment, etc) the INS will promptly return the entire application papers to you (the prospective U.S. employer) with a note or a Form 1-797, *Notice of Action,* telling him or her what corrections need to be made or additional documents or pieces of information need to be supplied. Or, in some cases, the INS will simply retain the papers already submitted but issue a request, in the form of a Form 1-797, for the additional items that are needed. And, in such an event, all you'll need to do is simply supply the additional data required and promptly mail them (along with the Form 1-797 and the rest of the file, if applicable) back to the INS office.

The employer's INS O, P or R visa petitions are usually approved by the INS within some 3 to 8 weeks. Upon such approval, the INS sends the employer a Notice of Action, Form 1-797, showing that the petition has been approval. Where the alien visa beneficiary is presently residing in a foreign country, or where the alien otherwise intends to undertake the second phase of the visa processing abroad (see STEP Two below), the INS will also notify the U.S. consulate of the alien's choice designated in the petition papers, and forward a complete file of the case to that consulate to enable its further processing of the visa request.

2. STEP TWO: THE VISA "APPLICATION" PHASE

Once the original "petition" filed by the U.S. employer has been approved by the U.S. – and only then – the second phase of the O, P or R visa application can be commenced. HERE'S THE IMPORTANT POINT: this second phase is called the "application," as opposed to the "petition", and is undertaken primarily by the ALIEN, rather than by the U.S. employer.

(a) Where You May File The Application: Is It Abroad, Or In The U.S.?

You (the alien visa-seeker) may, depending on whether you meet the required conditions for it, apply for the O, or P or R visa at the U.S. consulate in your home country, or at the INS office in the U.S. The conditions you must meet in order to be eligible to file in the U.S. are the same conditions as are listed in Chapter 4, Section C.1 [p. 19]. Otherwise, then you have to file in a U.S. consulate abroad.

(b) Inquire About Your Local U.S. Consulate's or INS's Visa Policies and Procedures

Turn to Section C.2 of Chapter 4 (p. 20) and apply here the same details contained therein. See, also, Chapter 18, Sections A and B thereof, for more on the subject of variations in visa processing policies and practices among different consulates and INS offices.

(c) Forms & Documentations Used

i. Prepare the following forms

- Optional Form OF-156, *Nonimmigrant Visa Application.* This form is required ONLY WHEN AN OVERSEAS FILING with a U.S. consulate is involved. Generally, if your visa application is at a U.S. consulate in a foreign country, the consulate will usually provide you (the alien) with their required "optional forms" complete with the instructions for completing them, and such forms are designated by a prefix "OF" preceeding a number, as in an OF-156. (see illustrative sample of Form OF-156 on p.177).

NOTE: OF-156 is the basic application form which the vast majority of non-immigrant visa applicants will encounter. The proper completion of this form is, by far, probably the single most important and primary thing you can do in any nonimmigrant visa application which will determine ultimately whether you get the visa or not. For that reason, we set forth in one chapter, Chapter 13, detailed, step-by-step instructions by which to properly complete the form and the underlying considerations by which to answer the questions asked or to provide the information required therein. Please refer immediately to Chapter 13.

- Form 1-539, *Application To Extend/Change Nonimmigrant Status.* This form is applicable only if it is a U.S. filing that you are doing, and only for accompanying relatives of the principal alien applicant, if any. Only one application form is needed for an entire family, except that if there's more than one accompanying relative, each should be listed on the form. (sample of form 1-539 is on p.183).

ii. Supporting Documents To Attach

For the supporting documents, turn to Chapter 5, Section G.3 (ii) [p.30], and see the listing therein under *"General Supporting Documents For Most Nonimmigrant Situations"* for the kinds of supporting documents you may have to provide.

(d) File The "Application" Papers With The U.S. Consulate or the INS, As Applicable

Turn to Section G.4 of Chapter 5 (p.33) and follow here the same procedure outlined therein to file your visa application.

(e) Attend The Visa Interview, If One Is Required In Your Case

Whether you are doing a U.S. filing or a consulate filing, a face-to-face personal interview with the visa processing officials may or may not be required in your case before the authorities render their final decision on your visa issuance. In any event, if a visa interview is required in your particular case, you will be so notified by the visa processing office. Upon your gathering together all the items required by the consulate or the INS, whichever one is applicable, you will appear on the appointed date, time and place set for the interview and undergo one with the designated interviewer. The visa processing officials will promptly render a final decision on your application, but only AFTER such interview.

[Turn to Chapter 15 for the full procedures involved in this all-important step in any nonimmigrant (as well as immigrant) visa application – the visa interview].

(f) Final Approval Of Your Visa Application

In the end, assuming that everything is in order with your visa application – basically, that you have, for example, provided all the proofs and documentation required to show your eligibility for the visa applied for, and that there's nothing that makes you inadmissible under the U.S. immigration law, such as having some serious criminal or terrorist record or potential, or a contagious, communicable disease – your application for a visa will be approved. You will be issued your visa. The U.S. consul in charge of visa issuance (if it's a consulate filing abroad), will usually stamp the approved visa that applies in your case (say, a B-1 and/or B-2 visa, in the case of the visitor's visa, or the E-1 or E-2, in the case of the treaty trader or investor) in your passport. If you got your visa through a U.S. filing, upon approval of your visa application, you are given a visa "status," and not an actual visa. (Under the law, only Consulate may issue a visa, and not the INS). This may be stamped in your passport, and you will receive from the INS a Notice of Action, Form 1-797, indicating the dates for which your status is approved, with a new 1-94 card attached at the bottom of the form.

(g) Now, Get Formally "Admitted" Into The U.S. at a Port of Entry

As a holder of a non-immigrant type of visa, you will normally be authorized to stay in the U.S. for a specific period of time, depending on the type and classification of the nonimmigrant visa involved. For example, for a B visa, you are normally authorized to stay in the U.S. for 6 months with the possibility of multiple extensions upon future application, while for an E-1 or E-2 visa, the authorized period of stay is 2 years at a time, with the possibility of extensions or renewals of the visa for additional one- or two- year periods, and so on with respect to other types of nonimmigrant visas. And when you enter the U.S. from a foreign country with your visa, you will at that time be given a 1-94 card, which will be stamped with dates showing your authorized stay. Then, each time you exit and re-enter the U.S., you will get a new 1-94 card with a new period of authorized stay affixed thereto.

BUT HERE'S THE MAIN ISSUE OF IMPORTANCE YOU SHOULD NOTE HERE: before you can be actually allowed entry into the U.S. even with your approved and issued visa in hand, you must FIRST be formally "admitted" into country – that is, you have to successfully pass through some strict formalities involved in a procedure called the "inspection and admission" process into the United States. Turn to Chapter 16, *"Entering The United States: The process of Getting Actually Admitted Into The Country After You've Got Your Visa In Hand."* (p. 118)

(h.) You May Be Denied A Visa. What Can You Do?

What if, in the end for whatever the reason, your visa application is turned down and you are denied a visa? Turn to Chapter 5, Section G.8 *"What To Do If Your Visa Application Is Denied"* (p. 35)

Chapter 13

How To Properly Complete The Visa Application Form

A. THIS FORM IS BASIC FOR YOUR WHOLE APPLICATION.

For almost all non-immigrant visa applications, the basic form that foreign applicants will complete, particularly for applicants filing in U.S. consulates or embassies overseas outside the United State, is the ***Form OF-156.***

The vast majority of requests for nonimmigrant (as well as immigrant) visas are filed in foreign U.S. consulates and embassies. With the U.S. consular and the Immigration and Naturalization Service officials, the Form OF-156, *The Nonimmigrant Visa Application Form,* is what is known as the "primary source" document. Considered to be a legal document, Form OF-156 can come back to haunt you for years and years to come (indeed, forever!), if you were to make any statements that are untrue or misleading in the form or to give an incorrect or improper answer of serious nature to the questions, for the reason that this is the primary source to which the visa processing and immigration officers will refer to again and again in your future history, to check for accuracy or consistency of your statements.

Hence, in this chapter, we shall devote ourselves solely to going through the Non-Immigrant Application Form, step-by-step. We shall primarily examine the information that is required of the alien visa applicant on this basic application form, and go through the underlying considerations and issues that may be considered in answering each question required by the application. ***The underlying idea behind this, is very critical in ultimately determining whether you're to get your visa or not: if you, at least, give some thought beforehand to the process involved in filling out and completing the visa application, you shall have equally enhanced greatly your chances of successfully obtaining a visa.***

NOTE THIS: Like most immigration forms, the specific Form 1-156 used herein for this illustrative demonstration (pp.177-8), may change from time to time, in terms of its format, layout and the numberings assigned to particular questions on the form. But, ***it doesn't matter if the current form you use is different in format or layout, and the like; what is important is this: the principles outlined herein will almost always remain the same*. Additionally, in completing Form 1-156 (and other forms you may have to complete), see also Chapter 18, "Inside The U.S. Immigration Offices: How They Work, How To Get The Best Results in Your Visa Processing,"*** for more on the same issue.

B. NOW, LET'S COMPLETE THE TYPICAL QUESTIONS POSED IN FORM OF-156, THE NON IMMIGRANT VISA APPLICATION FORM, STEP-BY-STEP

(Readers should note that the illustrative answers given here to the questions in the Form, are more particular to the B-2 visa. This visa category is chosen here for purposes of illustration in that the B visa constitutes the nonimmigrant visa category most closely scrutinized by the immigration authorities).

---

*Much of the material used in this Chapter, is excerpted with some updating and modificatons by the present author to better suit the present purposes, from Christopher E. Henry's *How To Win The U.S. Immigration Game*. The present writer and the publisher are deeply indebted to him for granting the use of this material.

Completing the Non-immigrant Visa Application [SAMPLE FORM OF-156 IS REPRODUCED ON PP.177-8].

1. Surname and Family names: (Answer). Enter your last name, exactly as shown in your passport; **First and middle name:** Enter your first name and middle name or initial, as shown in your passport.

2. Other names: If you are a married woman using your husband's name, enter your maiden name. If you have had your name changed legally, enter your former name. If you use another name professionally or for business (as might an actress or musician) enter that name.

3. Nationality: Enter "Nigerian," "Irish," "British," "French," etc. (or "Nigeria," Ireland," "Britain," "France" – the form doesn't really matter) to designate the country in which you hold citizenship. If you hold dual citizenship, be sure that the nationality which you have entered matches the country whose passport you will be submitting with the visa application. (For example, persons who reside in Northern Ireland are entitled to hold both British and Irish pssports).

4. Date of birth: Enter your date of birth numerically in this order: Day, Month, Year (last two numerals). For example, 9 October 1965, would be entered as 9/10/65.

5. Place of birth: Enter the city or town, and country, of your birth. If you were not born in a city or town, enter the appropriate geographic designation, such as "Count Mayo, Ireland".

6-9. Pass number; dates of issue and expiry; place of issue: Enter each exactly as shown in your passport. Make sure that your passport will be valid during the entire time of your anticipated stay in America. If the expiration date will occur during your anticipated stay, you should renew your passport.

10. Home address: Enter your home address as it normally appears on your mail, being sure to show your apartment number, if appropriate. (Remember this: one of the requirements for almost every type of non-immigrant visa is that the applicant continue to maintain a permanent residence abroad to which he or she plans to return).

Home telephone number: Enter your home number if you have one, as it would normally be dialed if calling from the city where the U.S. consulate is located and where you are applying for a visa. If you do not have a telephone at home, enter "None".

11. Have you ever applied for an Immigrant or Non-Immigrant U.S. visa before? This is a very important question which must be understood completely and answered accurately. Many persons who have applied for visas previously and who have been turned down for one reason or another are tempted to answer "No" to this question, and hope that the U.S. consulate won't know the difference. This only adds to their troubles, because by answering untruthfully they have then also committed what is known as VISA FRAUD. The U.S. consulate keeps very good permanent computer records of all visa denials, and *will already know, anyway, if you've been turned down for a visa in the past. Or, sometimes people who have been refused a visa will reapply at a different consulate attempting to hide the fact that they were turned down elsewhere. Whatever the case, just don't compound your troubles by giving a false answer.* If you have never applied for a visa of any type before, put an "X" in front of the "No" box and proceed to the next question. However, if you have applied for a visa in the past, put an "X" in front of the "Yes" box and enter the requested information in the provided space. After "where?", you can simply enter the name of the city where you applied for the visa. After "when?", enter the date in numerical form, as you did in question 4 above. After " type of visas," enter "B'-2," if you applied for a visitor's visa, or the other type of visa that you applied for. After you have provided the requested information, put an "X" in front of one of the two boxes below a "Visa was issued" or "Visa was refused".

12. Name and street address of present employer or school: Enter as requested. If you are not working or going to school, enter "None." **Busness telephone number:** Enter your work telephone number as it would normally be dialed if calling from the city where the U.S. consulate is located and where you are applying for a visa. If you do not have a telephone at your place of work, or if you are unemployed, enter "None".

13. Indicate whether: (a) visa was granted; (b) visa was refused; (c) application was abandoned; or (d) application was withdrawn.

Check off the box that factually applies, if you have ever applied for a U.S. visa of any kind as asked by question 11. Answer must be factual. The U.S. consulates keep a perpetual record of all visa applications, past and present.

14. Has your U.S. visa ever been cancelled?: This is another very important question. If your visa has ever been cancelled, you will undoubtedly find it difficult to be granted another visa in the near future. Don't complicate matters further by answering this question falsely. If you have ever had a visa cancelled by the United States government, enter an "X" in the "Yes" box. If you have NOT ever had a visa cancelled by the United States government, enter an "X" in the "No" box.

15. (A) Has anyone ever filed an Immigrant Visa Petition on your behalf? (B) Has a Labor Certification for employment in the U.S. ever been requested by you or on your behalf? (C) Have you or anyone acting for you ever indicated to a U.S. Consular or Immigration employee a desire to immigrate to the US?: The purpose of the question is to determine if you are, in fact, a true non-immigrant who is planning to come to the United States with the intention of truly leaving at the end of your permitted stay. (See, for example, Chapter 14).

You must answer "Yes" to this question:

- If a brother or sister or other relatives have ever filed an immigrant visa (the Green Card) petition on your behalf, even if that petition has since been withdrawn or rejected or become inactive.
- If any employer or potential employer has ever filed a petition on your behalf with either the U.S. Department of Labor or the Immigration and Naturalization Service, whether for an immigrant visa (which would entitle you to permanent residency) or for a temporary work visa.
- If you or anyone acting on your behalf has ever indicated to any consular official or immigration authority a desire to go live permanently in the United States. Such an indication need not have been on a written applicaton. If you have ever stated during any interview at a U.S. consulate or point-of-entry that you had a desire to immigrate to the US, and that statement was noted by the consular official or immigration authority, then there will be an official notation of your "desire" to immigrate on record.

NOTE: Just because you answer "Yes" to this question, however, does not mean that you will necessarily or automatically be turned down for a non-immigrant visa. But it does create a "presumption", on the part of the consular officials, that you may not be eligible for such a visa and that you are planning to go to America for more than just a visit.

In practical terms, all that this would mean for you, is that there will be a greater burden of proof on you to demonstrate to the consular officials that you are, indeed, a non-immigrant, who has a home and (usually) a job so that you have no intention of abandoning them and that you will leave the United States promptly at the end of your permitted stay there. This, of course, is the same burden of proof which is shared by every applicant for a non-immigrant visa, anyway. But if you answer "yes" to any part of this question (and especially if you answer "yes" to more than one part), your interview will often be much more rigorous and the documentation which is to be submitted with your application will often need to be more extensive. If you answer "NO" to this question when, in fact, a petition has been filed on your behalf or you have indicated a desire to immigrate to a consular official or immigration authority, you will be committing a "visa fraud".

16. Have you ever been in the U.S.?: Sometimes, people answer this question untruthfully just because they have been in the United States, probable illegally, in the past. In most instances, these people would have come to the Unites States on another B-2 visitor's visa, and entered in a perfectly legal manner, but then overstayed their permitted entry period by several months or years. On other occasions, but rarely, people would have come into the Unites States across the Canadian or Mexican border, and may or may not have made a legal entry.

One thing that you can be sure of, is that if you have been in the United States and made a legal entry with a valid visa, there is a record of that entry somewhere. If you walked across one of the land borders, there may or may not be records of your entry or subsequent presence in the country.

The simple fact that you have been in the United States previously in an illegal status will not necessarily prevent you from obtaining another visa. But if you do not answer this question truthfully, that may constitute visa fraud, which can prevent you from getting a visa.

So, if you have never been in the United States, enter "X" in the "NO" box. If you have been in the U.S. at any time, enter "X" in the "Yes" box, and after "When", simply enter the year or years (for example, "1981" or "1981-1983"), and after "For how long?," enter the approximate total period of time spent in the U.S. (for example, "2 years" or "8 months")

17. Present profession or occupation: Enter the name of your usual profession or occupation, if you are cerrently employed or retired. If you are a student, simply enter "student". If you are currently unemployed, enter "Not Working".

18. Sex: There are two boxes – male and female. Put an "X" in the box which describes you, (check only one box).

19. Marital status: You are given a choice of five boxes to check:

- Put an "X" in front of "married" only if you are currently legally married and are not legally separated
- Put an "X" in front of "singl e" only if you have never been married
- Put an "X" in front of "widowed" if you are not currently married and if your most recent marriage ended in the death of your spouse
- Put an "X" in front of "divorced" if you are not currently married and your most recent marriage ended in divorce
- Put an "X" in front of "separated" if you are currently married but are legally separated.

20. Color of hair: Spell out, rather than abbreviate, your hair color. Enter "Brown", "Black", "Blond", Red", etc. Don't put "mixed" or "slightly maroon" or other unusual descriptions.

21. Color of eyes: Spell out, rather than abbreviate, your eye color. Stick to the more mundane hues of the rainbow – "Blue", "Grey" or "Green" are all okey, "speckled" or "purple" won't do.

22. Height: Enter your height numerically. For example, if you are five feet, eight inches tall, this will be entered 5'8"

23. Complexion: This is a roundabout way of finding out what race you are, but an extremely vague way of doing so. If you are white, you will normally enter "Fair" or "Light", but might also enter "Dark" if you have particularly dark skin. Actually, anything you answer will probably be fine, as no one at the consulate is ever likely to read the answer to this question, anyway.

24. Marks of identification: If you have any significant scars, tattoos or similar marks on your body, note them here – for example, "scar, left palm" or "mermaid tattoo, chest."

25. What is the purpose of your trip?: This is another very important question, particularly if you are applying for a B-2 visitor's visa. *If your entry here conflicts with anything you have told or will tell either the consular officials or the immigration authorities during any interview, your visa application may be rejected or you may be granted a visa but refused entry into the United States during your point-of-entry proceedings.* Try to explain the purpose of your trip in a few words, such as "To visit relatives" or "Vacation" or "Sightseeing". But a definite purpose, no matter how simple and straightforward, should be stated. If you answer "There is no purpose" or "Just want to go" or "Nothing better to do," you will arouse the suspicions of the consular officials – they will feel that the reason that you do not seem interested in your "trip", is because there is no trip planned, only a search for employment in America. If, during your interview at the consulate, you seem disinterested or vague about the purpose of your trip, this will confirm those suspicions and your application will likely be denied.

For persons who are applying for other types of visa (B-1, E-1, E-2, H-IB, H-2B, L-1, J and F, etc), the entry here will simply be a short summary of their stated purpose – i.e. "to attend college," "to work temporarily," etc.

26. How long do you plan to stay in the U.S?: This is another very important question, and one that is used to help determine if you fit the "profile" of a potential illegal. The crucial thing to remember about this question – indeed, about almost all B-2 visas – is that, regardless of what your answer is to this question, you will usually be given a visa which is good for a period of one month to one year or more, anyway, and that when you are admitted to the United States, you will in the end almost always be admitted for a combined stay amounting to up to six months. So, it doesn't really matter whether you answer "Two weeks", "Two months" or "Six months", except that many people who have plans of becoming illegals think that the longer period of time they answer, the longer they will stay "legal" in America. When a B-2 visa applicant (particularly one who is young and unmarried) answers "six months" to this question, it is almost like waving a red flag that announces "I want to be allowed off to America to look for work!"

And, of course, if you do answer "six months", another question that will be asked, particularly if you are currently employed, is how can your employer afford to spare you for six months and how secure will your job really be during such a long absence? The only time that a B-2 visa applicant should answer "six months", is if that applicant has a planned documented itinerary for that length of time and can demonstrate that he or she actually needs that much time and has the financial resources to support such a trip without working along the way.

27. At what address will you stay in the US?: If you will be staying with a particular person (or family) or at one address during your stay in the United States, enter the street address, the city and the state of that location. If you will be staying at more than one address, or if you will just be travelling around on a tour, enter "various locations".

28. Name, Relationship, and address of your sponsor, school, or firm in the U.S.A.: Enter the name and full business address of the school you are to be attending in the U.S., or your sponsoring U.S. employer, if applicable, and indicate something like "the school I am to attend" or "the company that I am to work for" or "the company I am to do my training with," and the like.

29. When do you intend to arrive in the US?: The important thing to remember about this question, is that you do not have to commit to a specific date to get your visa. When a visa is issued to you, it will be good for one or more entries during a certain period of time, but as long as you travel during that period, you will be safe. So, all you have to do is make the best estimate of your arrival date in the United States. To avoid confusion, enter the date spelled fully out, e.g., July 15, 2002, in that order.

30. Do you intend to work or to study in the US?: As is stated on the form itself, "Bearers of visitors' visas may not work or study in the US." If you are applying for a B-1 or B-2 visitor's visa, or for an F student visa, or for any visa other than one which expressly permits you to work, and you answer "yes" to this question, your application will immediately be rejected. The only acceptable answer to this question, is "No" – unless you are applying for a visa which allows you to work in the United States, such as an H-1B, H-2B, E-1, E-2 or J visa. And, as stated above, "Bearers of visitors' visas may not work or study in the U.S.," although visiting schools in the United States as a prospective student is a permitted activity for a B-2 visa holder. If you are applying for any visa other than an F (student) visa and you answer "yes" to this question, your application will be rejected. If you will be studying at a school in the United States, you will need to apply for an F student visa (described in Chapter 6).

30a. Do you plan future trips to the US? If so, when?: This question pertains primarily to those applicants seeking B-1 or B-2 visitors' visas. There are several reasons why this question is asked. One of them is entirely innocent; if you have good reason to be travelling to America often, you may receive a "multiple indefinite" visa, which has no set termination date and is good for as many entries into the United States as you may care to make. But this question may also be asked to detect a likely illegal. If you answer that you're planning to go back and forth to America every six months or so, without having an apparently good reason to do this, the only logical assumption that the consular officials could make would be that you were simply an illegal who wants to keep travelling back and forth, just to stay "in status".

31 & 32. Who will furnish financial support, including tickets?: This question is relevant only if someone else will be supporting you in America. For example, if you are applying for a B-2 visa and are going to stay with a husband (wife), or an aunt and uncle in New Jersey, and they will be providing you with living expenses. Very often, young persons applying for the F student visa will be living with American relatives during their stay, who will provide them with food, lodging and spending money.

However, remember that answering this question in the affirmative, that is, giving the names of relatives who will be providing financial support, means in effects, that you will also need to provide an *"Affidavit of Support"* (Form I-134) from each one of these relatives when submitting your Non-immigrant visa Application form. Therefore, if you do say you will be receiving financial support from relatives in America, you will also have to be sure that they will be willing and able to provide you with completed *Affidavit of Support* that they have to document and have certified by a notary public, (see sample of the Form 1-134 on p. 173). The Affidavit of Support will usually require that the person who furnishes it provide and attach supporting papers, such as statements from the banks, stockbrokers and employers of the persons making the affidavits.

However, if you can demonstrate adequate personal means or resources of your own to cover the costs of your trip, this question should simply be answered as follow: "will provide own support, will pay for my own tickets in full"

33. How much money will you take?: Give an estimated amount and state it in the form of a range, such as: "$2,000-$3,500".

34. Are any of the following in the U.S?: (If yes, circle the appropriate relationship and indicate what that person is doing in the US, i.e., studying, working etc): Husband/Wife/Fiancé/Fiancée/Father/Mother/Son/Daughter/Brother/Sister)

This question is very similar in effect to Question 15 above. Recognize, however, that if you were simply to acknowledge that you have a close relative who is living in the United States, that will not necessarily be grounds for the U.S. consulate to deny you a visa, but it will often lead to increased scrutiny of your application, especially if that relative is an illegal in the U.S. If you are engaged to someone who is living in the United States, the consular officials can advise you about obtaining another type of non-immigrant visa which is issued to aliens who are engaged to American citizens. (see Chapter 10). Often, however, a visa applicant will be engaged to someone in America who is either an illegal or even a legal permanent resident there – but is not a citizen of the United States. You should be aware of the fact that if such were to be the case and a visa applicant were to acknowledge that he or she is engaged to someone who is living in America but who is not a U.S., citizen, then that applicant will very likely be denied a visa, because the consular officials will assume that the applicant will plan to stay on indefinitely in America with the fiancé/fiancée.

If you have no relations in the United States, make no entry in this box or simply enter "No".

35. Names and relationships of persons travelling with you: This is a very important part of the application. As is explained on the form, a separate application must be made for each visa applicant, including husbands, wives and children. This is a rather innocent-looking question, but it, too, can be used by consular officials to detect likely illegals. Sometimes, a group of young people will be planning to go to America, usually on B-2 visitors' visas, to look for work. If they fit the profile of typical illegals (young, unmarried, unemployed, or employed in jobs with no real future), and they acknowledge that they will be travelling together, or show up at the U.S. consulate as a group to apply for their visas together, this can lead the consular officials to conclude that they are not simply heading off on a vacation.

36. How Long Have You Lived In This Country (the U.S.A.)?: Give the length of time you've lived or stayed in the U.S. previously, IF you have at any time ever lived or stayed in the country before. If none, enter "None".

37. Please list the countries where you have lived for more than 6 months during the past 5 years:

There are two closely related reasons why this question is asked. First, if you have lived in the United States for more than six months (not by coincidence that usual maximum allowable stay for a non-immigrant), the presumption will be that you overstayed on your previous visit and are likely to do so again. If you have stayed longer than six months in the Unites States on a non-immigrant visa, however, you may have a perfectly good explanation for this – for example, you may have been legitimately granted an extenson by the Immigration and Naturalization Service while you were there, or you may have been ill toward the end of your stay and needed a few weeks to recuperate, or any other number of good reasons. Simple state them.

The second reason this question is asked, is that in order for you to be eligible for a non-immigrant visa, you must have a "permanent" residence abroad to which you will return when your visit to America is over. If you have lived in several different countries during the past five years, this may arouse the suspicions of the consular officials that you either do not have a permanent residence abroad, and/or that you will repeat your recent behavior in other countries and settle in the United States for longer than six months, or that you might be a criminal or fugitive of the law running from one country to another. Hence, if you have lived in another country for more than six months, you should be prepared to answer questions about this and to present documentation (of empolyment or schooling during that period of time) to show that your stay in the other country was both lawful and temporary.

Whatever the circumstances are, you should make sure that the consular officials know about them either on the form or orally, and since this information is not directly requested anywhere on the form, you should explain the circumstances in a separate Cover Letter (if you are mailing your application), or in person, if you are applying at the consulate.

38. To Which Address Do You Wish Your Visa and Passport Sent?:

Enter this, probably as in Question 10 above, but be certain to enter an address that is safe and secure for you to receive important mail.

39. "Important: all applicants must read and answer the following: A visa may not be issued to persons who are within specific categories defined by law as inadmissible to the United States (except when a waiver is obtained in advance). Complete information regarding these categories and whether any of them may be applicable to you, can be obtained from this office. Generally, they include persons:

- afflicted with contagious disease (e.g., tuberculosis), or who have suffered serious mental illness
- arrested, convicted for any offence or crime even though subject of a pardon, amnesty, or other such legal action
- believed to be narcotic addicts or traffickers
- deported from the USA within the last 5 years
- who have sought to obtain a visa by misrepresentation or fraud
- who are or have been members of certain organizations including communist organizations and those affiliated therewith
- who ordered, incited, assisted, or otherwise participated in the persecution of any person because of race, religion, national origin, or political opinion under the control, direct or indirect, of the Nazi Government of Germany, or of the government of any area occupied by, or allied with, the Nazi Government of Germany.

Do any of these appear to apply to you?: If yes, or if you have any question in this regard, personal appearance at this office is recommended. If it is not possible at this time, attach a statement of fact in your case to this application."

This is perhaps the most important question on the Non-Immigrant Visa Application Form. It may also be the question which elicits the lowest percentage of truthful answers (except, of course, for Question 30 , "Do you intend to work [or to study] in the U.S.?"). This is a catch-all question for the "grounds of exclusion", which are all the different legal reasons why a person can be excluded from the United States either by the American consulate when considering a visa application, or by the immigration authorities, when conducting point-of-entry procedures. [see Chapter 17, *"Legal Grounds For Inadmissibility of Aliens To The United States,* in addressing this question]

This is also perhaps the vaguest question on the application. For example, it asks if you're afflicted with contagious disease. Colds are contagious diseases – are you going to answer "Yes" if you have a cold? What about athlete's foot? It also asks if you've been a member of "certain" organizations "including" communist organizations. Well, what are the other ones? How are you supposed to know?

The only way to successfully answer such a vague question is by using some common sense. For example, common sense will tell you that having a cold is no big deal and that that isn't what this part of the question is all about.

But common sense would tell you that if you were given a ticket for speeding ten years ago, and were convicted of this offence, there would still very likely be an official government record of it somewhere, and that your failure to disclose even this very minor crime could be seen as an attempt at a visa fraud. Common sense would also tell you that you would never be denied a visa for one speeding ticket, and that it would be better to report having gotten it than not to report having gotten it.

Suppose you had attended one meeting of a "certain" organization while in college? Would attending such a meeting have made you a "member"? What exactly is a "member", anyway? Would it make sense to report attending that one meeting and then go to all the trouble of trying to explain all of the circumstances? Or, would it be better to use a little common sense and realize that there probably wouldn't be one chance in a thousand that anyone would know or care about such a thing?

The central point here is that you should, of course, never give a misleading answer to any of the questions on the Non-Immigrant Visa Application Form, but you should always exercise some discretion in attempting to understand why a particular question is being asked so that you can give an appropriate answer.

NOTE: If you do answer "Yes" to this question (Queston 39), know that you're in for some very tough questions and possiby a very long wait while facts are been verified. If you answer "No" and are found to be misleading the consulate about an important, or even not so important, matter, you may be denied a visa for good. If you are unsure in the slightest about how to answer this question, this may be one situation where you may be well advised to seek competent legal advise. If you have to answer "Yes" to this question, especially if the "Yes" relates to some past or present criminal matter and you will be seeking a waiver (Chapter 17, Section D), you should definitely have a lawyer prepare the waiver request for you. This may not need to be a "do-it-yourself" project in this particular instances!

40. I certify that I have read and understood all the questions set forth in this application, and the answers I have furnished on this form are true and correct to the best of my knowledge and belief. I understand that possession of a visa does not entitle the bearer to enter the United States of America upon arrival at port of entry, if he or she is found inadmissible.
Date of application. ______________________
Applicant's Signature X______________________

If this application has been prepared by a travel agency or another person on your behalf, the agent should indicate the name and address of agency or person, with appropriate signature shown of individual preparing form.
Signature of person preparing form X____________________

IMPORTANT: From a legal and practical viewpoint, it is extremely unwise to have this form prepared by someone who works at a travel agency that happens to be selling you an airplane ticket. This is not meant to reflect poorly on travel agents, but expertise in immigration law or procedures just isn't one of their strengths.
WHAT YOU DO IS THIS: Take this whole Form OF-156 home with you, prepare it slowly, neatly and carefully. Read it over and over again and check the information to make sure everything is okay. Then sign and date it. Finally, before you file this form with the U.S. consulate, make at least two photocopies of it. Remember, this is a legal document and you should keep one copy of it with your important records. (See Chapter 18 for more on proper documents preparation methods & procedures).

HERE'S THE CENTRAL POINT: whatever you do, just be absolutely certain that everything you say – whether on the Non-Immigrant Visa Application Form, or during your interview at the American consulate, or in your point-of-entry proceedings – is always truthful and consistent.

Chapter 14

Handling The Issue Of The Alien's 'Intent': A Critical Determinant In Whether You Get A Visa In Most Nonimmigrant Visa Situations

A. WHAT IS THE 'ALIEN INTENT' ISSUE?

The concept of the alien's "intent" in U.S. immigration law and procedures, is probably the most critical and tricky issue that any alien seeking an entry visa into U.S., particularly the temporary or nonimmigrant entry visa, may confront at some point along the way. It is certainly one which every alien ought to fully understand and anticipate right from the outset – even before he or she ever fills out the first application form or submits the first application paper. Simply stated, the concept refers to the alien's "true" or underlying intention, his or her real purpose and objective in seeking to be admitted into U.S. – in terms of his intended duration of stay in the country, his actual purpose for coming to the U.S., whether he's intent on seeking employment, and generally complying strictly with the limitations and privileges offered by the specific kind of nonimmigrant visa for whom he is applying. This concept is, indeed, a very critical factor, more particularly for the nonimmigrant visa seeker because of the central importance that is generally attached to the question of the underlying or perceived intention of the nonimmigrant by the U.S. immigration authorities both at the processing stage of the nonimmigrant visa, and at the actual "admission" stage of the alien into the U.S. at the U.S. border port of the entry even after the alien has been granted a visa.

Look at it this way, for an example. The fundamental idea and credo which underlies the granting of all U.S. visas, you should recall from previous Chapters in this manual*, is simply this: an ***immigrant*** type of visa or the Green Card, is issued ONLY to a qualified alien who, it is believed and expected, intends to remain in the U.S. permanently, while a ***nonimmigrant*** (temporary) type of visa, on the other hand, is issued ONLY to a qualified alien who, it is believed and expected, intends to stay in the U.S. for a temporary or specified period of time and then departs. In reality, therefore, if it were so, for example, that the immediate intention of an alien, say Mr. A., is actually to stay PERMANENTLY in the U.S., then it should follow that the only type of visa which he can – and should, rightly – be qualified for, is the IMMIGRANT visa. And, conversely, if the immediate intention of Mr. A is to stay PERMANENTLY in the U.S., then by the same logic he should not be qualified for or entitled to a temporary visa, even if he might otherwise be perfectly qualified to be granted such a temporary visa.

B. HOW THE ALIEN INTENT QUESTION COMES UP IN PRACTICE

Under the U.S. immigration law, in general an alien who meets the specific objective qualifications for a non-immigrant visa, will be denied such a visa or entry into the U.S. even with that visa in hand, if the U.S. consul abroad or the INS examining officer at the border port of entry, merely feels that the alien's "true" intention is to

*See, for example, Chapters 2 and 3.

remain in the U.S. permanently. And, furthermore, all aliens entering the U.S. are "presumed" to be intending immigrants – and thus excludable – unless they have a valid, nonimmigrant visa in their possession, and are entitled to enter the U.S. under that visa. And under the 1996 law known as the Illegal Immigration Reform and Immigrant Responsibility Act (IIRAIRA), it is provided that a person who attempts to enter the U.S. with a visa which is inappropriate for the alien's intended or perceived purpose, can be summarily removed or denied entry by the immigration authorities on the grounds of fraud, and may become even permanently ineligible to enter the U.S.

In practical terms, this results in two practical consequences for the alien visa applicant. First, the U.S. consular officers in foreign countries will only grant a nonimmigrant visa if, and only if, they are satisfied that the alien will return to his home country – regardless of whether the alien may have met all the other conceivable objective qualifications for the issuance of the visa. And secondly, aliens may be "summarily" (i.e., on the spot without trial or hearing) "removed" and denied entry at the border, if the immigration officer believes or feels that their intention for entering the U.S. are different from those envisaged by the type of visa they've been granted, or simply that they are otherwise not entitled to enter the U.S.

From the standpoint of the U.S. immigration authorities, the fundamental problem in dealing with the alien arises from the necessity for the authorities, generally, to be able to determine and uncover what is known as the "immigrant intent" of the alien applicant for a visa – that is, the "real" motives and purposes of the alien for wanting to go to the U.S. As explained earlier in this chapter, the immigration law requires that even if an alien were to meet, perfectly, all the objective qualifications for being granted a non-immigrant type of visa, if the U.S. Embassy abroad were to have cause to believe that the alien's true intention is actually to remain in the U.S. permanently, then that alien should be denied the non-immigrant visa – based on the alien's perceived "true" intent. But what is even more critical in this, is that the law also grants that such critical judgements and determinations, fateful as they are for the fate of the alien's application, are subject solely to the discretion of the U.S. consul or the immigration border inspectors! Within the official culture of the U.S. immigration authorities, the reasoning behind this policy goes roughly like this: to qualify for a nonimmigrant visa, you are required to have the intention to leave the U.S. within a fixed period of time. If you are, therefore, to show or betray any indication whatsoever, overt or concealed, that you are unlikely to leave but would likely remain permanently in the U.S., then the government should not risk giving you the nonimmigrant visa since you are not eligible for a nonimmigrant visa, anyway, if you have the intent to remain permanently in the U.S.!!

Under the immigration law and the rules of operation, there is a simple "basic rule" by which the U.S. consular and immigration authorities determine who is an "immigrant" and who is a "non-immigrant", namely: every alien person of any type or description who is applying for a visa to enter the United States, is simply "presumed" to be, not an intending nonimmigrant, but an intending immigrant (and thus automatically excludable), unless and until he or she can satisfactorily show the consular or immigration officers that he is not one. Which is to say, unless he or she can show that he/she can qualify for a valid non-immigrant visa and is entitled to enter the U.S. under that type of visa.

Here is how Section 214 (b) of the Immigration and Nationality Act [8 U.S.C. 1184 (b)], puts it: *"Every alien shall be [automatically] presumed to be an immigrant until he establishes to the satisfaction of the consular officer at the time of application for a visa, and (to) the immigration officer, at the time of application for admission, that he is entitled to a non-immigrant status under Sec. 101 (a) (15)".*

To sum it up in simple terms, what this "basic rule" has came to mean for the visa applicant in practical terms, is this: you may make all the claims and proclamations you wish to make when you apply for a visa to the effect that you are merely an intending nonimmigrant who harbors no intention to stay permanently in the U.S. But you had better be fully ready and able to establish that claim by good documentations and other means, to the satisfaction of the U.S. officials; otherwise, you simply will not be granted the visa, you simply will be considered ("presumed") to be a probable or intending immigrant, any way, and thus would be denied the visa application!! Or, to put it another way: you can make all the claims in the world you wish that you do not harbor any plans or intention of staying permanently in the U.S. if you're to be admitted, but we simply don't believe you and flat out think you are a liar; in fact, we actually believe you are more likely to do exactly the opposite and stay on permanently in the U.S. – unless you can give us satisfactory proof otherwise!! In short, as an alien applicant for a nonimmigrant visa, if you do not readily appear to the immigration authorities to be truly a non-immigrant, you are automatically "presumed" to be (you are taken to be) an intending immigrant and hence your application will be treated and evaluated accordingly by the same standards as are used for an IMMIGRANT visa (Green Card) applicant!

C. THE THEORY OF "PRECONCEIVED INTENT" OF ALIEN

There is another way the issue of the alien's "intent" arises: namely, in the context of different types of non-immigrant visas. This is the issue of what is known as "preconceived intent". Under the immigration law and procedures, if an alien who holds one type of non-immigrant visa (say, a tourist visa) wishes to change from that nonimmigrant status to another nonimmigrant status (say, to student visa), the INS must believe that at the time the alien originally entered the U.S. as a tourist, he did not intent to apply for a different status before the INS will approve such a change. For example, let's say that you (an alien) entered the U.S. as a tourist with a B-2 visa and then just a month or two after your entry you apply for a change to a student F-1 visa. In such a circumstance, the INS will demand explanation of why you had not originally applied in your home country for that F-1 visa that you now seek to change to. And, unless you can come up with some satisfactory explanation, the INS will likely deny the change of status based on a form of fraud, on the theory of "preconceived intent". Preconceived intent simply means that, as far as the immigration authorities are concerned, you lied about your reasons for coming to the U.S., you misrepresented the facts to them. Thus, in the context of the above example, the INS will simply infer that you gained entry to the U.S. by way of tourist visa with a "preconceived intent" of applying for a different visa status the moment you are allowed into the country, and that your failure to have revealed your "true" reason for going to the U.S. when you first applied for a visa is fraud, pure and simple.

A somewhat famous example of an actual case of an alien who ran afoul of the preconceived intent edict, involves a story often told among immigration lawyers and professionals. As the story goes, there was a young man from an European country who arrived at a U.S. port of entry with a perfectly valid approved nonimmigrant visa in hand seeking to be allowed entry into the U.S. But then, during his brief chat with the border immigration interviewing officer, the young European, nervous and obviously excited and in a friendly and joyous mood for finally getting the opportunity to come to America, chatted idly to the immigration officer to the effect that he was very happy for finally being in the United States, and expressed his unwillingness to ever return to his cold and inhospitable country again. And, at this point, the story goes, the young European was promptly denied entry into the U.S. and sent back to his country – a victim of the immigration officer's conclusion the alien's idle chatter revealed his preconceived intent!

D. THE ALIEN INTENT ISSUE AS A REALITY IN NON-IMMIGRANT VISA PROCESSING

What is central for the alien visa seeker to note, is that ***for the visa applicant, particularly the applicant in nonimmigrant visa situations, the alien intent issue is frequently an inescapable fact of life.*** In fact, on closer scrutiny, the reader or user of this book would soon notice that this issue is one which comes up again and again throughout the book in different ways and contexts, some subtle and others not so subtle. For our purposes here in this chapter, what is important to strongly emphasize – and be well understood by every alien and prospective U.S.

visa applicant – is that the issue of the alien intent is an absolutely critical element in visa application processing, and that it is a factor that, frequently, will almost never be based on any objective criteria, but, usually on the subjective discretion of the consular officer or immigration official involved.

In short, as an alien applying for a visa to U.S., or one already with an approved visa and on the border seekng formal admission into the U.S., you should always bear in mind and anticipate that your mere words, promises and statements (in spoken and/or written form) to the visa processing officials about your purported motivation, purpose, or intention for seeking the entry visa, are generally not going to be enough; that, rather, you must be ready and prepared to prove – by documentations and some hard evidence – that your true intent actually coincides with your words and spoken claims and intentions. Thus, as an alien, perhaps the most important – and ultimately determining – reality you must understand and accept, is this: that your claimed intentions will be under a strict and intense scrutiny by the U.S. immigration and consular authorities when you apply for any type of visa or seek entry into the U.S. That there's just no getting around that reality!*

E. THE INTENT PROBLEM AS APPARENT REFLECTION OF PERHAPS CERTAIN LEGITIMATE CONCERNS AND PAST EXPERIENCES OF THE IMMIGRATION ESTABLISHMENT

It has been observed by some knowledgeable students of the workings of the U.S. immigration process that, given the central position occupied by the issue of attempting to ferret out the alien's intent in the actual administration of the visa processing, and of the alien admission process into the U.S., it might probably be said that "instead of a 'welcome', there is a 'keep out' attitude framed in the [U.S. immigration] law."** Ramon Carrion, a Clearwater Florida immmigration lawyer, noting the awesome power of the U.S. consular and immigration officials to deny an alien a visa or to exclude him from entering the United States, summed up the reputation commonly attributed to U. S. consular and immigration authorities this way:

"It should be noted that many foreign persons complain, [for example], of rudeness on the part of the INS inspectors at the ports of entry... INS inspectors often view themselves as police officials trying to prevent illegal entry into the United States, rather than as goodwill emissaries of the United States. This unfortunate attitude is reinforced by the strong demands for visa to the U.S. and by continuous attempts by certain aliens to circumvent the law and attempt to enter the United States illegally."

Carrion's comments are useful and well-informed. The central point of interest in the comments for our purposes here, is this: that the attitude of arrogance or being overbearing often attributed to the U S. immigration officials, or of acting with some skepticism and distrust about the stated intent or motivation of the visa applicants, are matters not entirely without some good basis or reasons on the part of the immigration officials. The point is that, quite to the contrary, such attitude by immigration officials is, in fact, firmly rooted in some hard realities and historical experiences accumulated over the years by the U.S. immigration establishment in the course of dealings with alien visa applicants from around the world. For one thing, immigration officials have generally believed, as a result of the previous concrete experiences they've had in situations such as the Iranian Revolution of the 1980s and other places, for example, that most people coming to the U.S. from poverty stricken or war-torn or troubled areas of the world, would probably never return to their home countries.

Ramon Carrion, the immigration attorney and author and a long-term Clearwater, Florida practitioner of immi-

---

*There are, under the law, a few nonimmigrant visa categories, however, for which, at least in theory, the immigrant intent is not a factor for their consideration. They include the following: the H-1A, H-1B. L. O. and P visas.

**Roman Carrion, U.S. Immgration Guide, 3rd ed. (Sphinx Publishing Naperville, FL 1998) p. 29

*** Ibid, p. 13

gration law, relates an account of one of many cases in his practice which, he says, demonstrates the "reality" that the U.S. immigration establishment confronts with aliens on a daily basis, and which, he says, forms the basis, as well as the justification, for their attitude of skepticism and lack of trust in the matter of the alien intention. It involved the case of a young Lebanese man in the late 1970s and early 1980s, who was a permanent resident alien in the U.S. married to a U.S. citizen and had sought his (Carrion's) legal assistance in trying to bring his Lebanese parents (they were living in Europe) to visit with him in the U.S. because the parents' application for a B-2 visitors' visa had been denied by various U.S. consuls in Europe. According to Mr. Carrion, from the contacts he made with various U.S. consuls in Europe, it had became crystal clear to him that the central obstacle to overcome, if a visitors' visa was ever to be obtained for the Lebanese parents, was the common belief of the immigration officials that "based upon their experience most business people leaving [the then] war torn Lebanon were doing so with the intention of never returning." Consequently, on the advise of Mr. Carrion, the Lebanese young man eventually traveled to the European country where the parents were staying. He pleaded his case directly with the U.S. consul there and offered to provide (and did provide) a cash bond guaranteeing to the consul that his parents would depart the U.S. at the conclusion of their visit. The young man was able to win the consul's conviction so that his parents were finally granted their visitors' visas.

But here's the point: according to Mr. Carrion, a few months after this meeting, he encountered the young man again in a chance meeting; he inquired of him "how his parents enjoyed their visit to the United States"? But lo and behold, the young man now told him that his parents, after spending some time in the United States, had decided that they were not returning to their home country of Lebanon, and that he (their U.S.-based son) would now be filing a visa petition to obtain a permanent residency visa for them. Mr. Carrion concludes with these words: "This is precisely what the U.S. consul had predicted would happen. Under these circumstances, one can hardly blame U.S. consular officials for being skeptical of a [alien] person's spoken motivations or intentions."

In sum, the central point is that, whether it has come about as a consequence of an accumulation of concrete past experiences and history on the part of U.S. consular and immigration officials, or merely because of some personal bias or subjective thinking on their part, the U.S. consuls and the immigration establishment generally have a common official belief and attitude, some of which are not entirely unrealistic or unjustified by the facts of immigration life, that many aliens who make one claim or the other about their motivations or intentions for seeking entry visa into the United States, actually intend doing (or would wind up doing), a different thing altogether. And that, in consequence of this, alien visa applicants must accept as a central reality of any visa application, the fact that their true, underlying intentions will be questioned and subjected to strict scrutiny of the U.S. consular and immigration authorities whenever they apply for any type of visa, particularly one of nonimmigrant classification.

Chapter 15

The Visa Interview

A. YOU MAY OR MAY NOT BE SUBJECT TO AN INTERVIEW

For all practical purposes, whether you are subjected to a personal interview in your nonimmigrant visa application case, or not, is entirely up to the discretion of the U.S. consulate (or the INS, if applicable). There are no hard-and-fast rules. One application may be immediately approved with little or no questioning, while another identical application will be subjected to a very difficult interview.

One thing is certain, though: if the consular officials have any doubt at all about your eligibility for a visa, they will interview you. The length and difficulty of such interviews vary enormously, but ***all interviews, no matter how short or simple, can very effectively end your chances of getting a visa.*** In any event, whenever an interview is required in a case, the U.S. consulate will usually send you a written notification of the interview appointment.

B. BRING THE ORIGINALS, NOT JUST THE COPIES, OF THE DOCUMENTS WITH YOU FOR VERIFICATION

Generally, whatever forms you'll need to complete for the processing of the application, and whatever documents you might have gathered in support of your application, you should take them with you personally to the interview. Bring, also, with you additional documents you may have been asked to provide by the consular officer. You do not mail the papers this time. This is when you would be expected to present the actual originals (or certified true copies) of the documents for the responsible immigration officials to inspect for accuracy and genuineness.

In the "petition" phase of visa filing in a nonimmigrant visa case involving the filing of the papers by the U.S. sponsor, the Immigration and Naturalization usually holds far fewer interviews, if at all. And when it does, the interview is almost always with the U.S. sponsor (the U.S. employer or institution). Such interviews are requested only if the INS has some doubts that the documents or information contained in the petition forms are genuine or authentic. The same is also true with respect to alien change of status applications in the U.S. in nonimmigrant cases – here, too, interviews are rarely held. And when an alien is called for an interview, the most likely reason is probably that the INS either suspect some type of fraud or believes the alien may be subject to a ground of inadmissibility (Chapter 17). It is in the "application" phase of the visa filing, however, involving the filing of the papers by the alien visa applicant himself, usually in the U.S. consulate abroad, that the vast majority of the interviews are held. Consequently, it is with respect to the visa interviewing procedures in consular filings overseas, that the discussions in this chapter will primarily be focused.

NOTE: If you are ever called for an interview in a visa application case, you must always make sure to report for the interview without fail. Or, at least, contact the interviewer or his office to arrange for another appointment, if you cannot make it. The mere act of applying for a visa and then failing to follow up on it or to report for an interview appointment, may often be viewed negatively by the consulate and can have the same consequences, all the same, as an actual rejection of the visa application by the consulate following an actual interview.

C. THE GENERAL NATURE OF THE INTERVIEW

Briefly summed up, the primary objective of the visa interview is to enable the interviewing consular or INS officer to verify the information already set forth by the alien in the underlying visa petition and application papers (and, where it applies, in the Labor certification papers as well), verifying them as to their accuracy and the genuineness of the supporting documents submitted. The interviewing officer is interested in scrutinizing the alien and the documents submitted for any indication of fraud or misrepresentation of the facts in the application papers. Thus, the interview process basically involves verification of your application's accuracy and inspection of your document to confirm the statements in the application papers. The interviewer basically uses the face-to-face meeting and personal exchanges to counter-check and clarify any questions or apparent contradictions for consistency, with a view to filling in any material gaps or omissions occurring from the papers submitted.

The visa interviewer will closely examine the alien's application papers, from the standpoint as well, of evaluating the alien's real eligibility for admission into the United States. He or she will want answers to question such these: is it clear in the specific case involved, that there are no grounds under the relevant U.S. immigration laws on which this alien can be excluded from entry into, or stay in the U.S.? Does this alien seem to meet the qualifications required for the particular visa applied for? Does this alien exhibit any signs or indications of a preconceived or hidden "intent" to seek employment in the United States, or to disappear into the country and never return to his home country? Evidence of the alien's ties to his home country will usually be checked. The alien in a nonimmigrant visa interview will also certainly be asked how long he intends to remain in the U.S., and any answers betraying an indication that the alien is unsure about his (her) plans to return, or that he has an interest in seeking a Green Card for a permanent residence in America, is almost certain to result in a denial of the visa.

There's another central area of concern for the consular officials particularly in nonimmigrant visa interviews. It involves the issue of the alien's intent (see Chapter 14). First, recall a relevant point we emphasized in a prior Chapter in this manual (Section B of Chapter 14) namely: that one fundamental rule central in all evaluations of nonimmigrant visa applicants, is the basic "presumption" that every alien seeking entry into the United States is an intending IMMIGRANT – until and unless he can satisfactorily establish to the consular official that he is qualified within a nonimmigrant classification.

Simply summarized, it is safe for you to assume that a good deal of the interview you'll have in a nonimmigrant visa case, and one area the consular officer will primarily focus on in such interview, will be largely colored by and related to this fundamental "presumption" under the law. Primarily, the central interest of the interviewing consular officer's probe, and the thrust of his questions, will be aimed at uncovering the answer to this questions: what is your true, underlying "intent?" He will ask question to attempt to uncover, in short, whether you are truly what you claim you are, that is, a non-immigrant who is truly intent on remaining in the U.S. only temporarily; or, on the other hand, if you are actually a fake, a pre-conceived immigrant at heart merely pretending be a nonimmigrant just so that you can secure an easier or fast entry route into the U.S.

D. THE TYPICAL ISSUES IN AN INTERVIEW

Typically, questions posed in an interview would center around some major vital issues and concerns that have for one reason or the other aroused the interest of the visa processing officials. Depending on the length of the interview and the issues involved, the alien may be asked questions regarding his (or her) employment, his education, his work experience and credentials, his finances and means, his living situation and personal background, his plans for the future, etc. The following discussion assumes that the alien has been called in a lengthy, difficult interview. Of course, not everybody will by any means be subjected to that kind of an interview. We merely provide an elaborate scenario of the interviewing process here, however, so that you might as well be quite prepared in the event that your interview turns out to be among the tough ones.

Christopher E. Henry, a New York immigration lawyer who has professionally participated in literally hundreds of visa interviews in a lifetime of immigration work, has catalogued an informed, first-hand scenario of how each of the major issues is typically addressed in consular visa interviews. Henry's depiction of the make-up and workings of the typical nonimmigrant visa interview bears reproducing here as they present a somewhat vivid illustrative picture of the process.

Employment Issue In An Interview

Regarding an interview in which the alien's employment, and albeit indirectly, his underlying "intent", are an issue, Henry presents the following process:*

"You [the alien visa applicant] will also be asked about your employment. Of all the areas of questioning, this is perhaps the most important, because almost all of the illegals now in America went there because of the economic problems in their own countries and the high unemployment rates in those countries. If you have a good job that is secure and well-paid, it will be assumed, usually, that you'll want to return to such a job. But if you are out of work, even temporarily, or if you have a low-paying job that doesn't have much future in it, or if you are working in an occupation (such as barman or construction laborer) for which the pay is sometimes double in America what it is in other countries, then you'll probably be questioned at length, because you'll fit the profile of the typical illegal.

The interviewer's questions will usually be direct and straightforward, but not always. ***Part of the process is to try to trick you into admitting your "real" motives for wanting to go to America.*** For example, [assumimg you are applying for a B visa] you may be asked if you would consider working in America once you got there, or if you would look for work if your money ran out halfway through your trip. If at any point you indicate that you might accept employment for any reason, then you will probably be denied a visa, because you have just admitted that you might violate the terms of the visa. If, on the other hand, you state that you have no intention of working in the United States and that, if faced with any financial emergency, you would contact friends or relatives in America (be sure to have their names and addresses with you), or your own government's consulate, then you will in all likelihood be granted a visa, because you have reaffirmed your intention not to violate the terms of the visa. *The best way to handle any question posed to you, no matter how difficult, is to think before you answer, and ask yourself: "will this answer hurt my chances or help them? Will this answer make it appear that I will or won't volate the terms of the visa?"*

Still staying on the employment issue, Henry asks that the alien, if employed, should come to the interview with a copy of his letter of employment from his employers, and further advises the alien as follows:

"It is a fairly common practice among visa applicants, both those who are unemployed and those who don't want their employers to know of their intentions to leave for America, to submit phoney employer letters, usually prepared by a "friend". Submitting such a letter constitutes an act of visa fraud, and the chances are very good that you will be caught if you do this. The consulate has many ways of detecting phoney employer letters. For example, a young person with a local accent (Irish, English, etc.) will call the employer's number and ask for you, as though you were a friend, and will be told by whoever answers the phone that you don't work there. Don't make the mistake of trying to fool the consulate with a false employer's letter. It is far, far better to provide no letter at all or, if you are unemployed, simply admit the fact.

If you are unemployed at the time you apply for a visa, your situation is made much more difficult because the

---

*Christopher E. Henry, in *How To Win The U.S. Immigration Game* (The O' Brien Press, Dublin, 1989) p.49-50. A good deal of the material in this Section and many of the quoted passages here, are excerpted from, and by courtesy of the author and publisher of the within cited Henry book, to whom the present author and the publisher are immensely indebted.

consular office is likely to assume that you are going to America to find work. It is still possible for you to obtain the visa, though, since there is nothing in the law that requires that you be employed. However, if you are out of work, you will be far more likely to be granted a visa if you are going to America for a specific reason, such as to visit relatives or friends, or to attend a wedding, or to take a vacation. [In answer to the interviewer's question], you should always be as specific as possible in your plans. For example, instead of saying that you want to go to America to "travel around", you might explain exactly what you will be doing there – vacation with relatives in New York City, spending a week in Atlantic City, etc. And then you should be prepared to answer some equally specific questions posed by the interviewer, such as:

- Where will you be staying?
- Whom will you be staying with?
- Who is getting married (if going for a wedding), and how do you know these people?
- What are the names and addresses of the people whom you will be staying with or visiting? How long have you known these people?
- When will you return to your own country?
- Have you made airline reservations? What are the flight numbers?
- Have you paid for the ticket yet?"

Henry adds: "Regarding your travel plans, the most important thing is that you have worked out, in your own mind, all of the details of your trip

- - which begins on a certain date, has a specific reason for occurring, and ends at a set time with your return home. Don't go overboard, however. If you memorize each and every detail of your trip perfectly, your interviewer may become suspicious

- - just know enough about your travel plans to show that you're making a valid visa application. It is helpful to have a letter with you from the relative or friend you will be staying with which confirms that invitation and mentions some of the planned activities or schedule of events in which you will be participating."

Alien's Education & Credential Issues In Interview

For an interview in which the alien's education and academic or other credentials are the focal point, Henry presents the following scenario for the alien:

"You may be questioned about your education for the same reason that you are asked about your employment. Because such a high percentage of the better-education young people in certain countries are not able to find work in their chosen fields, many of them leave within a few months of completing their education. If you have recently finished college and are not employed in the profession for which you were educated, be prepared for a more difficult interview.

One of the ways in which such questions can be handled, is [for you] to have plans to attend graduate school in your own country when you return from America. Naturally, if you have already been accepted at graduate school [in your own country] and can prove this [to the U.S. immigration authorities] by the school's acceptance letter, that will be the best evidence of your plans. Alternatively, a copy of your application or even a clearly-stated plan for pursuing graduate studies, will be helpful. Or, you might be going to the United States to visit a few graduate schools personally so that you could then return home and make applications to those which you found acceptable. As an alternative, you may state simply that you want to see America before you have any long-term responsibilities, and that once you return home you'll be settling down and going to work for good."

Alien's Finance Issue In An Interview

Henry adds this on the often vital issues of the alien's financial position:

"Last but not least, you should be prepared to answer questions about your finances. The interviewer will want to determine if you have enough money to complete the planned trip without violating the terms of the visa by working. Of course, how much money you'll need depends on where you are going and with whom you'll be staying. If you tell the interviewer you'll be renting a car and travelling all around the United States and staying at luxury hotels, you should realize that such a trip could easily cost three hundred dollars a day or more. But if you say you're going to New York City to stay with relatives or friends (preferably relatives, because the ties are presumed to be closer), then forty dollars a day might be sufficient. The important thing is that you demonstrate to the interviewer a realistic understanding of the cost of your proposed trip and ability to cover those costs with the funds you'll be taking with you or have at your disposal once you get to America."

E. THE CENTRAL KEY TO A SUCCESSFUL VISA INTERVIEW: ABSOLUTE TRUTHFULNESS

Many U.S. Immigration lawyers and experts, as well as keen observers of the U.S. immigration and visa application process, have noted the seeming susceptibility of the visa application process to corruption and circumvention of the rules by visa applicants. Some analysts attribute this to the fact of the great demand for the U.S. visa all over the world, and that there is no shortage of applicants for U.S. visa at any time from one year to another. Others, attribute the cause for it to something related to the "cultural habit" of foreign societies to practice and accept bribe-giving and public corruption as a way of life in their common dealings. Whatever the actual causal factor, however, what is crystal clear and far less subject to any doubts or ambiguity, is that the attitude among many aliens to attempt to circumvent the immigration laws and to attempt to enter the United States unlawfully, is a very, very, real one, and indeed quite prevalent.

One team of analysts who are themselves practicing immigration lawyers, accurately summed up this rather pervasive attitude this way:*

> "[There are] stories in circulation about how some people have found shortcuts to the [U.S. immigration] system, legal or illegal. We've been asked about cheating the system an endless number of times. Some people put it more politely than others, but the idea is always the same....[we must say that we are not aware of even an instance where] someone walked into a Consulate and got a Green Card immediately just for the asking, or successfully bribed a U.S. immigration official .... The hard fact is that shortcutting the American immigration system is close to impossible. Moreover, while bribing public officials is generally tolerated in some [foreign] countries, it is not in the U.S..... We point [this attitude] out simply as a cultural reality because, unfortunately, it has [had] the effect of making immigrants from certain countries where bribery is a common practice believe [that] the same tactic will work in the U.S. It won't.... The bottom line is [that the U.S.] immigration officials don't take bribes."

HERE IS THE CENTRAL POINT FOR YOU TO TAKE AWAY IN ALL THIS: ***bribery, lying, cheating, trying to circumvent the law or the regular laid down processing system, or to find an quickie or easy shortcut, just don't work as a method of seeking a U.S. visa; and indeed, quite to the contrary, such methods will usually produce for you exactly the opposite result to what you want – denial of your visa application or physical entry into the United State!*** In truth, the simple reality that every alien visa applicant (or his U.S. sponsor) should quickly internalize and keep to, is that the central key to any alien having a successful and trouble-free visa interview – and visa application – is quite simple. It can be simply summed up in one sentence: absolute honesty and truthfulness on the part of the alien (or, of course, his/her U.S. sponsor). And if there is one thing on which virtually every expert with vast experience in the intricacies of securing a visa under the U.S. immigration laws and system

---

*Quoted from Lawrence A. Canter & Martha S. Siegel. *U.S. Immigration Made Easy* (Nolo Press. 6th Ed.) May 1998. p. 1/2.

are unanimously agreed upon, it is in their common advice that the single, most common underlying factor which generally spells the doom of most alienswho have their application for a visa denied, is misrepresentation of the facts and lack of candor on the part of the alien. ***This point, quite simple and unambiguous, just can't be emphasized enough in any matters having to do with the filing of any U.S. visa of any kind!***

In a visa interview, in particular, the necessity for the alien to be even more meticulously frank and truthful, is especially critical, for the mere fact that a personal interview, if called for by the consulate in a visa application case, is an indication that the consular officials are probably having some doubts and questions already about some aspects of the alien's background, qualifications or character; or about the veracity of his claims and the genuineness of his papers and documentation. And, for the consular official, the interview process is simply the last arena to gather the final facts and information by which to clear up the last remaining lingering doubts and uncertainties in his mind about the alien visa applicant – one way or the other, pro or con. It is not by mere accident, for example, that such is the case that whenever an interview is had in a case, it is usually followed by a prompt decision by the consulate either approving the visa application, or denying it!

Consequently, as one expert put it, "anyone who goes to the U.S. consulate for an interview, or even the possibility of an interview, had better be well-prepared. The interview is not just a formality, but a real decision-making process and its purpose is to catch people who are not telling the truth. The interviewers are experts, and they are well aware that many of the young people who are applying for B-2 visitors' visa, [for example], are planning anything but a "visit" to the United States. They also know that many of these applicants, if granted visa, will join the underground American labor force almost as soon as they reach the U.S..... [The point is that] The consular official who interviews you has probably conducted thousands of these interviews and will not be easily fooled."*

As a visa applicant, the primary reason truthfulness and honesty are the very key to your having a successful visa interview and visa approval, are essentially two-fold: firstly, you are very unlikely to fool the interviewing consular official, but rather, he's more likely to see through your lying and deceitfulness; and secondly, once it ever becomes clear to the consular officer that you have lied or have been less than truthful with him, that act of "visa fraud" alone, automatically spells the death sentence to your visa application there and then!

Again, Chritopher E. Henry, the U.S. Immigration lawyer and specialist, describes the rather life-and-death effect of committing visa fraud on all chances of an alien getting a visa, this way: "Visa fraud [which is defined as any misrepresentation made during the visa application process] is a very serious crime; any person who commits visa fraud may be barred permanently from the United States. Committng visa fraud is often more damaging to a visa applicant than whatever the applicant was trying to cover up in the first place." Henry, pronouncing misrepresentation of the facts and visa fraud the most "exceedingly stupid thing for a visa applicant to do," cites a case in point where he said committing a visa fraud frequently inflicting more damage upon the alien than the very previous crime the alien was trying to cover up. It involves a situation where a visa applicant shall have had a criminal conviction which, in and of itself, isn't really all that serious and may not have been a bar at all to his being granted a visa, but which becomes a serious problem for the alien applicant only "because the alien person is afraid that the visa application will be rejected and therefore lies about the conviction on the application and/or during the interviews." And then, lo and behold, merely on account of the lying, the consulate, which normally has access to all kinds of infornation provided it by the intelligence agencies of other governments any way, uncovers the misrepresentation about the alien's prior conviction, and for that he's denied the visa application – a casualty merely of his

*Henry. Ibid. pp. 47 & 52.

lying about the conviction (the visa fraud), rather than the crime itself, which has not been serious enough to have been a bar to the granting of a visa.

For this reason, given such dire negative consequences of lying even about one's past criminal convictions, Henry concludes with this advice: "So [even] if you do have criminal convictions, it is always best simply to tell the truth. Even if you are rejected initially, it is possible that you may be able to obtain a waiver.... But once you've committed visa fraud, the chances of [your] obtaining a waiver will be virtually nonexistent... You may have closed for good the door to America."

Finally, C. James Cooper, a veteran immigration expert who has been through hundreds of visa interviews in the course of his long professional career as an immigration lawyer, offers this fitting words of advice and wisdom about how to comport oneself at immigration visa interviews:

> "Whatever you do, never let the other side see you get a little nervous when dealing with government officials [at an interview]. This is normal. But remember, immigration officials are law enforcement personnel and have been carefully trained in the art of interviewing foreign nationals. They have been taught that generally, persons who appear to be nervous, ill at ease, who perspire, have sweaty palms and do not make direct eye contact, may be hiding something. Immigration officials are suspicious of anyone who appears to be uptight. Although it is understandable why a person would be nervous and full of anxiety under the scrutinizing eyes of an immigration or consular officer, you will be more successful if you understand the process and know what to expect. Therefore, your composure and mannerism when dealing with an immigration or consular officer are very important. Although you should not act as though you know every thing or be too confident, you should try to be relaxed and appear to be as believable as possible. The impression you make may be the deciding factor on whether or not your visa will be granted."*

F. HOW DO YOU BEST PREPARE FOR AN INTERVIEW?

Bear in mind once again that, basically, the interviewer's main questions and interests will generally center upon the information you have already given in your answers to the questions on the application forms and documents you've submitted to his office, and that his primary task is to review your papers and ask you questions based on all the documents you have submitted in order to verify the accuracy of the facts and the information you've provided. Most of such interviews are actually brief – some 20 to 30 minutes or so long. And sometimes the same questions will be repeated several times, especially in cases where your U.S. employer (or relative) has filed the visa petition for you.

Hence, actually, the most important and best way you can "prepare" for a visa interview, is this: relax, just answer the questions asked you by the interviewer truthfully and simply. Don't try to be smart or clever with the interviewer, he's more than likely to "see through you". If you don't quite understand a question, say so, ask for a clarification before you answer. Or, where you can't understand the English used by the interviewer, or you're confused by his accent or intonation, don't be embarrassed or bashful – ask for a language interpreter.

---

*Cooper in The American Immigration Tapes (Text).

U. S. IMMIGRATION & NATURALIZATION SERVICE

COLOR PHOTOGRAPH SPECIFICATIONS

IDEAL PHOTOGRAPH ◂

IMAGE MUST FIT INSIDE THIS BOX ▸

THE PICTURE AT LEFT IS IDEAL SIZE, COLOR, BACKGROUND, AND POSE. THE IMAGE SHOULD BE 30MM (1 3/16IN) FROM THE HAIR TO JUST BELOW THE CHIN, AND 26MM (1 IN) FROM LEFT CHEEK TO RIGHT EAR. THE IMAGE MUST FIT IN THE BOX AT RIGHT.

<u>THE PHOTOGRAPH</u>

* THE OVERALL SIZE OF THE PICTURE, INCLUDING THE BACKGROUND, MUST BE AT LEAST 40MM (1 9/16 INCHES) IN HEIGHT BY 35MM (1 3/8IN) IN WIDTH.

* PHOTOS MUST BE FREE OF SHADOWS AND CONTAIN NO MARKS, SPLOTCHES, OR DISCOLORATIONS.

* PHOTOS SHOULD BE HIGH QUALITY, WITH GOOD BACK LIGHTING OR WRAP AROUND LIGHTING, AND MUST HAVE A WHITE OR OFF-WHITE BACKGROUND.

* PHOTOS MUST BE A GLOSSY OR MATTE FINISH AND UN-RETOUCHED.

* POLAROID FILM HYBRID #5 IS ACCEPTABLE; HOWEVER SX-70 TYPE FILM OR ANY OTHER INSTANT PROCESSING TYPE FILM IS UNACCEPTABLE. NON-PEEL APART FILMS ARE EASILY RECOGNIZED BECAUSE THE BACK OF THE FILM IS BLACK. ACCEPTABLE INSTANT COLOR FILM HAS A GRAY-TONED BACKING.

<u>THE IMAGE OF THE PERSON</u>

* THE DIMENSIONS OF THE IMAGE SHOULD BE 30MM (1 3/16 INCHES) FROM THE HAIR TO THE NECK JUST BELOW THE CHIN, AND 26MM (1 INCH) FROM THE RIGHT EAR TO THE LEFT CHEEK. IMAGE CANNOT EXCEED 32MM BY 28MM (1 1/4IN X 1 1/16IN).

* IF THE IMAGE AREA ON THE PHOTOGRAPH IS TOO LARGE OR TOO SMALL, THE PHOTO CANNOT BE USED.

* PHOTOGRAPHS MUST SHOW THE ENTIRE FACE OF THE PERSON IN A 3/4 VIEW SHOWING THE RIGHT EAR AND LEFT EYE.

* FACIAL FEATURES **<u>MUST BE IDENTIFIABLE.</u>**

* CONTRAST BETWEEN THE IMAGE AND BACKGROUND IS ESSENTIAL. PHOTOS FOR VERY LIGHT SKINNED PEOPLE SHOULD BE SLIGHTLY UNDER-EXPOSED. PHOTOS FOR VERY DARK SKINNED PEOPLE SHOULD BE SLIGHTLY OVER-EXPOSED.

SAMPLES OF UNACCEPTABLE PHOTOGRAPHS

INCORRECT POSE

IMAGE TOO LARGE

IMAGE TOO SMALL

IMAGE TOO DARK UNDER-EXPOSED

IMAGE TOO LIGHT

DARK BACKGROUND

OVER-EXPOSED

SHADOWS ON PIC

Immigration & Naturalization Service
Form M-378 (6-92)

Chapter 16

Entering The United States: The Process Of Getting Actually "Admitted" Into The Country After You've Got Your Visa

Alright. So, you've gone through all those lengthy formalities and hassles customarily involved in applying or petitioning for a visa to enter the United States. And, at long last, let's say you have been granted the visa; and shortly thereafter, you left your home country and are now at a U.S. border port of entry with your "almighty" U.S. entry permit in your hands seeking to physically enter the United States! Are you automatically guaranteed or entitled to admission just because you have a valid visa in hand?

The answer is a resounding: No! GET THIS POINT VERY CLEAR RIGHT AWAY: think of the process of your whole admission into the U.S. as a TWO-step process; in this two-step process, the issuance of a visa to you is only the first of the two steps! All that your possession of the visa does for you, in practical terms, is entitle you – accord you the right – to come to a border port of entry to the United States. And then, while you are at such border or port of entry, you may then "apply" for actual admission into the country; and, what is more important, you will have to demonstrate your qualification and your eligibility for admission into the U.S. all over again for a second time, to the satisfaction of the immigration officers there at the border. And only then, may you finally be allowed entry into the United States!

The central point here for you to understand, is this: that, ***under the U.S. immigration law and procedures, even with a valid visa stamped in your passport, you can still be turned back at the U.S. "point-of-entry," which is usually an international airport but may also be a land border station on a boundary, such as with Canada or Mexico; that the immigration authorities at an American point-of-entry have the power to, and may, still refuse to admit a visa holder*** if they were to believe or conclude, for any reason, that such a person is not eligible to be admitted into the U.S., or that he or she will be participating in activities (such as employment) which are not permitted by the terms of his or her visa.

A. EVIDENCE OF YOUR VISA ISSUANCE

Upon the approval of your visa petition or application in a foreign country by a U.S. Consul there, if the visa granted you is a NONIMMIGRANT type, the consul shall have typically stamped your passport with a notation indicating the approved visa classification to which you belong, the number of entries you are permitted into the United States. And if the Visa granted you is an IMMIGRANT type of visa, the Consul shall have typically stamped your visa, as well, with a notation thereon about the type of visa granted you.

B. GOING THROUGH INSPECTION AT THE PORT OF ENTRY

In all the time the alien visa seeker is in his home country, or is in any country whatsoever so long as it is outside the United States, the agency of the U.S. Government with the sole jurisdiction or authority over matters concerning the processing of the alien's visa application in the foreign country in question, is the consular office, an arm of the U.S. Department of State. However, once the alien sets his or her foot on a port of entry in the United States (at a land border, an airport or a seaport), from that moment on it is the Immigration and Naturalization Service (INS), an arm of a different agency of the U.S. Government, namely, the Department of Justice, that now takes over and automatically assumes the decision-making powers as to all matters concerning your admission or admissibility, and decides whether you may be admitted or excluded from admission and the grounds thereof. The key point to remember here, is that though you have your visa in hand at a port of entry quite properly issued you by a consulate official abroad, that, nevertheless, is not a guarantee that you will necessarily be allowed entry into the United States.

1. Here's The way the Admission Process Works, in Brief:

• Upon your (the alien's) arrival at the U.S. port of entry, you will have to undergo a "secondary inspection," meaning that you will have to be examined one more time to determine your entitlement to enter the U.S., this time, though, by the INS inspectors as opposed to consular officials. You report for the "inspection and admission" procedure before the INS inspector; you surrender your passport and your visa (and any other relevant or applicable documents, e.g., information on school admission or report of medical examination) to the INS inspector, and, upon the inspector reviewing your documents, he'll probably conduct a kind of mini "interview" with you and ask you a number of questions regarding your eligibility to enter the United States.

• Your name is checked against a "lookout book" that the INS maintains for aliens who may be excludable and for other persons for whom government agencies have requested a "lookout". You may possibly (though not commonly) be required to take a complete medical and physical examination by a Public Health Service Officer, and may be subjected to background investigations.

• In some cases, the immigration inspector may possibly decide that the alien is not eligible for admission. He may determine, for example, that that alien's record, in some way, is in violation of some requirements for which an "exclusion" from entry into the United States is called for under the immigration laws or regulations, or that some material documentation required from the alien has either not been provided or is incomplete or unsatisfactory.

Essentially, to be admitted into the United States, here is what you are required to satisfy the immigration inspector of: that you are "clearly and beyond doubt entitled to land in the United States" – in other words, that you basically meet the necessary qualifications as provided for under the law for the type of visa you hold, and that there truly are no legal barriers that would prevalent you from being admitted into the United States.

2. You May Be Subjected To Long Interview and/or Thorough Inspection, or Little or None At All

NOTE: Be comforted to know that by far the vast majority of visa holders are admitted to the U.S. with very few questions, if any, asked by the immigration officers. The point-of-entry interview vary greatly, and can range from anything like 2 or 3 questions, to extremely difficult, in-depth grilling, which may be accompanied as well by a complete search of the alien (or even a U.S. citizen) and his or her luggage. For most persons, the point-of-entry interview presents no problems. However, the point of the exercise here is that you be prepared for the worse case, involving a case where an alien is assumed selected to be interviewed at length and to be thoroughly searched.

i.) <u>Some Typical Questions & Answers At Port-Of- Entry Inspections</u>

The following are some typical questions that may be asked a person seeking to get into the U.S. in a port-of-entry interview, and samples of possible answers which would be either helpful or harmful to his or her chances of gaining entry to the United States. The section will be useful for all visa holders. However, the questions and answers more particularly concern persons coming to the U.S. with a B-2 visa, as such persons constitute the bulk of persons more likely to be the most closely scrutinized by the immigration authorities.

1. ***How long do you plan to stay in the United States?:*** No matter how you answer this question, you will usually be granted admission generally for six rnonths. (At least this was the common policy until September 11th-2001!). However, illegals often answer "six months", and such will lead the immigration authorities to suspect that they are living and working illegally in the U.S. (or would be doing so in the future), and simply want to obtain "legal" status for as long as possible. The only time that a B-2 visa holder should answer "six months" or "about six months", is if that person has a full schedule planned for that amount of time, and has enough funds with him or available to him to support himself for that length of time without working. (see, also Question 26 of Form 1-156 in Chapter 13, for more on this)

Helpful answers: Give a specific amount of time from two weeks to two months; this would be the usual length of a trip to America by a tourist, since the period will sound "reasonable" for a trip.

Harmful answers: Average, noncommittal reply that indicates you don't have any firm plans.

2. ***Where will you be staying?***

Helpful answer: A specific travel itinerary with names and addresses of relatives or friends (preferably relatives, because they are closer and, in the eyes of the immigration authorities, more likely to help you if you are in financial need) who have invited you to stay with them. It's also helpful to carry with you a letter from the friends or relatives confirming their invitation to you. Occasionally, the immigration authorities will want to telephone whoever you'll be staying with if they have any doubts about your story, so you should have the phone numbers of your hosts with you as well.

Harmful answer: A generalized statement that you will be staying with friends or relatives, but an inability to provide their names, addresses and telephone numbers; or an indefinite answer such as "Just travelling around" or "staying at hotels", or a statement that you'll be staying at a specific hotel where, in fact, you have no reservations.

3. ***What do you plan to do while you're in the United States?***

Helpful answer: Anyone who is legitimately travelling to the United State on a tourist (B-2) visa should usually have some sort of a schedule or itinerary. This doesn't mean that you'll be expected to have every minute of the day planned, but that you should have a general idea of what you'll be doing in America. That's enough. A few specific activities, such as seeing the Empire State Building, watching the Yankees play, going to Atlantic City, or visiting the Metropolitan Museum of Art, are what most vacations are centered around.

Harmful answers: any reply which indicates a lack of knowledge or interest in the usual tourist activities. The most harmful answer that you could give, of course, would be any reply that indicates that you would work, or even look for work, or that you would attend college, conduct any commercial business or engage in any other activity which would violate the terms of your B-2 visitor visa.

4. ***How much money do you have with you?***

Helpful answer: any answer which indicates an approprate amount of money for the stated purpose of your trip. This may take the form of traveler's checks; in addition, you should mention any credit cards that you have that are generally accepted in the United States. Make sure that your answer is a truthful one, however, because if the immigration authorities have any reason to doubt what you say, they will ask you to show them the cash, traveler's checks or credit cards that you claim to have.

Harmful answer: Any reply that is vague or that does not directly answer the question, will arouse the suspicion of the immigration authorities. If you do not seem concerned with the amount of money that you have with you, the immigration authorities can assume only one thing: that you either have a job waiting for you in the U.S., or are planning to find one as soon as you are admitted. Another harmful answer would be any answer which indicates that you had money waiting for you in the United States, either in cash or in a bank account. Again, the assumption would be that you had earned that money from working in the United States during a previous stay there, indicating that you had violated the terms of your visitor's visa in the past and were planning to continue to do so.

5. ***What will you do if you run out of money before your trip is over?***

Helpful answer: "I don't intend to, as I've brought enough money with me, but if I do, the relatives that I'm staying with have said that they will loan me any money that I need," or "My parents told me that if that ever happens they would wire money immediately from home."

Harmful answer: I'm sure I could always find some work to do," or "That's no problem – I'll be getting a pay check every week!"

6. ***Do you have a job you'll be returning to at home?***

Helpful answer: "Yes, I do, and I have brought a letter from my employer;" or "No, I don't, but I'm going to college and will be starting again at the beginning of the next term. Here is my university identification card;" or "No, I don't, but I am studying auto mechanics there and hope to be working in that field shortly."

Harmful answer: "Who needs a job at home? I've got a great one in America!" or any answer, which indicates that you are unemployed and not actively involved in an academic or vocational program which will prepare you for employment. In addition, if you indicate that you have been unemployed for a long period of time and have been on the dole or receiving other similar government benefits, this will be harmful to your chances of admission.

7. ***Where will you be living when you return home?***

Helpful answer: a reply which indicates you'll be returning to a longtime home, such as your parents' home, or another place where you've lived for several years and established roots.

Harmful answer: a vague kind of statement which would lead the immigration authorities to believe that you had no permanent home in your own country that you were planning to return to, or that you had recently closed up your home there. For example, "I was sharing a flat with a few friends, but I guess I'll have to find another place when I go back there," would be a harmful answer

ii.) <u>Possible Searches & Other "Inspections" of You and/or Your Luggage</u>

In addition to the interview, you should anticipate that it is possible that you may be subjected to an extremely thorough search of your luggage and/or of your person. This search serves two purposes. First, it makes sure that you are not carrying any "contraband". (Contrabands may be items which are illegal in themselves, such as marijuana, cocaine or unlicensed handguns, or it may consist of items which are quite legal in themselves but unlawful to bring into the country, such as certain agricultural products). But more important, the search of your person and/or luggage serves to enable the immigration authorities to look for items which may indicate that you are planning to violate the terms of your B-2 visa. For example, items such as the following may present a problem: toolboxes used by tradesmen; letters from U.S. companies offering you employment; classified advertising sections from U.S. newspapers with ads for jobs or apartments; letters from friends in the U.S. who are illegal aliens and may be advising you of how to live the illegal lifestyle; business cards or telephone numbers of employment agencies or immigration attorneys; and certain types of books (such books as even a copy of *How to Obtain Your U.S. Immigration Visa,* which you are now reading), or other literature about immigration, or books about the illegal lifestyle in America.

In addition, your body may physically be searched. This type of search can range from a "pat-down" through your clothes to feel for weapons or drug pouches, to having you remove your shoes or stockings to check for smuggled items in the heels and insoles, to a complete strip search (this, however, is fairly very rare). Regardless of how intrusive any search of your body or luggage may be, however, the best attitude for you will be to simply cooperate. Objecting to such a search will only heighten the suspicions of the immigration authorities.

Last, but far from least, you will be asked to show the ticket for your return flight home (if your point-of-entry is at an airport). Now, make sure that the date of your return flight matches the other information that you have provided to the immigration authorities.

C. ADMISSION OR DENIAL OF ADMISSION

In the end, assuming that all goes well and the immigration inspector approves your being admitted, in that event if you are being admitted in one of the nonimmigrant classifications, the immigration inspector will at that time grant you the specific length of time you will be allowed to stay in the U.S. in accordance with the particular type of visa you were issued. (This, and various other types of information designed to stand as evidence of the alien's lawful admission into the U.S., is either stamped in your passport or, more typically, it is entered in a FORM 1-94, Arrival/Departure Card, and stapled to the inside of your passport). If, on the other hand, you are admitted as an immigrant, you may either be issued an Alien Registration Receipt Card (the "GREEN CARD") on the spot, or a rubber stamp will be placed in your passport to serve as your temporary Green Card; the actual card will then be manufactured and sent to you thereafter by mail at your designated address in the United States.

FINALLY, NOW: YOU CAN REALLY HEAR IT – "WELCOME TO THE UNITED STATES OF AMERICA!!"

D. IF DENIED ADMISSION, YOU COULD SEEK A REVIEW: AN "EXCLUSION" HEARING.

What happens if the immigration inspector conducting the initial examination at your port of entry inspection were to determine that you are not admissible, and therefore "exclude" you – that is, deny you entry into the United States? Usually, you would probably be advised to appear for a *"secondary"* (i.e., more formal) *examination,* if the port of entry at which you arrived is a land border; or, if your place of arrival is at an INS office other than at an airport or seaport, you may be given a *"deferred inspection"*. Thereafter, if you are still found inadmissible, you are ordered "excluded" (i.e., barred from entry), at which point you are given a choice: either voluntarily return to your home country at your own expense, or your case is referred to an immigration judge for a hearing, the so-called **EXCLUSION HEARING PROCEDINGS.**

An "exclusion" hearing is the hearing of relevance to an alien who is refused entry at a port of entry, as opposed to *"deportation"* hearing (Section F below). In a word, an EXCLUSION hearing is one held to determine an alien's right merely to enter the United States; it takes place BEFORE the right to enter is officially granted. It technically differs from a DEPORTATION hearing, in that deportation has to do with determining the alien's right to remain in the U.S. AFTER he shall have already been admitted into the U.S. by an immigration officer and has probably lived in the country for a while.

E. RIGHTS OF DETAINED ALIENS & THE PROCEDURES IN EXCLUSION HEARINGS

To be sure, exclusion proceedings (and, in deed, the relative subject of deportation proceedings) are clearly beyond the very limited scope of the present book, and an alien faced with such a circumstance may well be better advised, anyway, to seek the help of a competent immigration lawyer and immigration social services organizations. Here, therefore, we can only present ***a brief outline of the alien's rights and the procedures involved:***

1. In exclusion hearings, it is the alien himself, and NOT the Immigration Service (INS), that has the burden of proving that he or she is otherwise eligible for admission to the U.S. and that he has actually not violated any immigration laws. And he or she must make this proof by a "clear and convincing evidence"

2. Basically, under the premise that the alien in an exclusion hearing is a person merely "at the door" but who is not yet in, aliens in exclusion hearings are viewed as a group not entitled to the usual constitutional guarrantees; hence, the normal constitutional protections do not apply in exclusion hearings, inasmuch as admitting foreigners to the U.S. is said to be a "privilege" granted only at the pleasure of, and on the terms and conditions set by, the U.S. government.

3. The INS District Director has a right to, if he so chooses, and may in his discretion, either hold you in an immigration detention facility pending the conclusion of the hearing, or release you on a bond or on your own personal recognizance.

4. The hearing takes place before a U.S. immigration judge; and you may (you have a right to, if you wish) represent yourself in the case, or be represented by a friend or a lawyer of your choice, providing you can pay such a lawyer out of your own resources.

5. You are entitled to be told the charges made against you, and to be given the opportunity to present evidence in defense of yourself, and to confront and question any evidence presented or any witnesses who appear or testify against you.

6. Aside from other remedies you may consider, one thing you may do at this hearing is to make an application for political asylum (political asylum procedures are outlined in Chapter 18 of Volume 2 of this manual).

7. In the end, whatever the decision arrived at by the hearing judge, it must be based solely on the evidence presented at the hearing and must be adequately supported by such evidence, and be supported in such a way that it can be rationally inferred that you (the alien) are not entitled to admission.

8. If the decision of the judge is that you be excluded from admission, he will issue an ORDER FOR EXCLUSION (ORDER OF DEPORTATION, if in a deportation case) against you to that effect.

9. You have a right (except if you are a crewman, stowaway or a person excluded on security or medical disqualification grounds) to appeal the decision of the immigration judge to the next level, namely, to the Board of Immigration Appeals in Washington D.C. (To appeal, you must do so immediately, at the conclusion of the hearing, if the decision is oral, or within 10 days of the decision, if the decision is a written one. Initiate the process by serving a written NOTICE OF APPEAL upon the INS promptly).

10. If you fail to appeal the immigration judge's ORDER FOR EXCLUSION (or DEPORTATION), or fail to do so on time, you will immediately be deported – returned, in this instance, to the country from which you came to the U.S.

11. The judge may, at his "discretion", either decide to allow you to post a bail bond, or to release you on parole with or without a bond.

12. On appeal, the following are a few grounds on which you can base your claim that the decision of the immigration judge deserves to be reversed or set aside: **(i)** that there were "improper procedures" at the hearing (i.e. that you had an unfair hearing or that it did not follow the legal and agency requirements set for such hearings); **(ii)** that the judge's ORDER OF EXCLUSION (or Deportation) was based on "mistake of fact" or "errors of law" (i.e., that the judge applied an incorrect meaning or interpretation of the relevant laws and regulations); **(iii)** that the decision did not have "adequate support in the evidence" or was rendered with "unwarranted disregard of the evidence" or was not based on "proper standard of evidence" (i.e., not having a substantial and reasonable basis in the evidence); and **(iv)** that there was on the part of the judge an "arbitrary exercise of discretion" or "failure to exercise discretion" (i.e., that either no reason is given for the decision rendered, or the reason given is irrational or out of keeping with established policy, or discriminatory or based on improper grounds).

13. In exclusion hearings, if you appeal an immigration judge's decision to the Board of Immigration Appeals and the Board's decision still remains unfavorable to you, you have only one final right of appeal: the right to petition a court of law for a judicial review. This petition, called a ***WRIT OF HABEAS CORPUS,*** is filed with the U.S. District Court in the hearing area, the object being for the court to review the administrative action taken in the exclusion hearings and to establish that the Order of Exclusion is valid.

F. IF DENIED THE RIGHT TO REMAIN IN THE U.S., YOU COULD SEEK A REVIEW: DEPORTATION PROCEEDINGS

A "deportation" proceeding, as previously explained in Section D above, is primarily concerned with determining the alien's rights (or lack of it) to remain in the United States AFTER he shall have already been duly admitted into the U.S. by the inmmigration officials. In short, whereas you'll seek an exclusion hearing if you have a valid visa but are denied entry into the U.S., a deportation hearing is what you seek to have when you are denied or threatened with denial of the right to remain in the U.S. at any time after you have gained formal admisson into the country. Usually, a deportation proceeding comes about because the immigration service, probably contending that an alien who had been duly admitted to the country has committed some act which violate certain immigration laws or the terms upon which the alien had been granted his visa, has initiated a move to send the alien back to his home country.

G. RIGHTS OF ALIENS & PROCEDURES IN DEPORTATION HEARINGS

The following is a brief outline summarizing the alien's rights and procedures involved in *deportation hearings:*

(1.) An important preface is appropriate here: aside from a few important areas of differences, by and large the rights of the aliens involved in deportation hearings and the procedures thereof, are essentially the same as those of aliens involved in exclusion hearings, and the procedures thereof. In the interest of brevity and to avoid unnecessary repetition, here's what to do: simply read all the rights and hearing procedures outlined in Section E above for the alien facing an "exclusion" hearing, and treat the said facts therein as equally applicable with respect to the alien facing deportation hearings, except for just a few differences as specified below.

(2.) The significant points of departure regarding the alien involved in deportation proceedings, are as follows:

i) Contrary to the situation prevailing in exclusion proceedings (see paragraph 2 of Section E above), the alien involved in deportation hearing is entitled to, and is accorded, all constitutional rights, protections and privileges that a U.S. citizen has, such as the right not to self-incriminate oneself. In deed, this is probably the overriding distinguishing factor between the two types of hearings.

ii) One manifest way by which the deportation-bound alien enjoys superior constitutional privileges not extended to the exclusion-bound alien, is this: in deportation hearing, it is the immigration service, and NOT the alien, as in the case of aliens facing exclusion, that has the burden of proving, by a "clear and convincing evidence," that the alien is deportable and/or has actually violated specific immigration laws.

iii) Among the remedies open for consideration to the alien in a deportation preceding, are the following "discretionary relief": aside from being able to apply for political asylum in the U.S., you may apply for a "stay (suspension) of deportation" (File Immigration FORM 1-256); and you may apply to have your status adjusted from nonimmigrant to immigrant status, if qualified. (See Chapter 20 of Volume 2 on adjustment of status procedures).

iv) Just as in exclusion hearings, you can appeal a decision by a U.S. immigration judge in a deportation hearing to the ***Board of Immigration Appeal*** in Washington, D.C. under basically the same grounds and ground rules as in Section E above. However, the final appeal in deportation proceedings is not from the Board's decision to the area's U.S. District Court, but to the area's ***U.S. Court of Appeals***. You file for such review of the Board's decision by filing within 6 months after the Board's ruling *a **"PETITION TO REVIEW DEPORTATION ORDER"**.*

NOTE: The Court of Appeals in this instance, will look only at the previously assembled record of the appealed proceedings, with no new evidence submitted or considered. To apply for suspension of deportation, you need to be able to show: that you were continuously present in the U.S. for the previous 7 years or that you performed honorable service in the U.S. armed forces for at least 24 months; that you are of good moral character; how and why your deportation would result in "exceptional and extremely unusual hardship" to yourself or to a U.S. citizen or permanent resident to whom you are closely related by blood or marriage. As usual, massive documentations of sorts would have to be assembled and be presented to the judge at the hearing to prove such contentions: police records, affidavits of good character from respectable U.S. citizens, and of employment from an employer, records of permanent entry into the U.S., birth and/or marriage certificate, bank books, rent receipts, lease, licenses, church and school records, tax receipts, etc, showing continuous residence in the U.S.

v) If you should fail to appeal the INS Board's **FINAL ORDER OF DEPORTATION** (or, before that, the INS judge's Order), or fail to appeal on time, you have a right in deportation hearing to, upon application during the procceding, be deported to any country of your choice (this contrasts with an alien's right in an exclusion case), or you may be granted a right to depart voluntarily (an **ORDER OF VOLUNTARY DEPARTURE)** at your own expense, and thus avoid being deported. This is a very important right, the difference being that an alien who is deported requires a special permission by the INS to return to the U.S. in the future, but an alien who leaves voluntarily does not.

vi) If all else fails, there's still one ultimate relief that a person facing deportation may seek: you may contact your area's Congressman or Senator and request him or her to introduce a "private immigration bill" in Congress to relieve you from deportation or otherwise permit you to "stay" the deportation or otherwise permit you to stay in the U.S. Upon the introduction of such a bill in Congress for an alien, as a rule, the INS will usually stay the deportation of the alien, and, if the bill is neither voted down nor tabled nor withdrawn, and is acted upon favorably at the close of Congress and signed by the president, the alien beneficiary of the bill is rendered eligible to remain in the United States.

H. A WORD OF ADVICE FOR PERSONS SEEKING ENTRY OR FACING EXCLUSION OR DEPORTATION

To conclude this chapter, certain words of caution seem fitting as a guide for aliens in dealing with the immigration officials at the port of entry for purposes of admission, or in going through an exclusion or deportation proceeding, if need be. Much is often made about the supposed "imperial" powers said to be possessed by immigration officers (and even more so, by the consular officers) over decisions as to whether a visa application is to be granted, or about whether a visa-holding alien gets admitted into the country. True, the fact that the powers granted the immigration officers to exclusively decide on such matters are officially sweeping, cannot at all be disputed. Nevertheless, that aside, it is still most important that an alien facing an official encounter with the immigration officer in any of the above treated contexts should have the proper attitude and the right psychological mind-set for productively dealing with the immigration personnel.

To begin with, it is most important that the alien bears in mind that most immigration officials they encounter at the port of entry (or at exclusion or deportation proceedings or elsewhere) are generally fairminded; that they are simply workers with no special axe to grind who are employed to do a job, and are honestly attempting to do just that the best way they can.

Sure, the decision as to whether to admit or to exclude a particular alien may often be "discretionary", even "subjective", and is for the most part based on the immigration official's past experiences which are necessarily limited. Nevertheless, in practice, the factual reality has been that by and large in those instances where aliens appear to have been granted special discretionary relief or favorable rulings by immigration officials, certain common denominators appear to have been present. Typically, to approve an admission, the INS officials would look for a showing of certain objective attributes* – such as a good moral character, close bona fide family ties in the United States, the existence of certain humanitarian reasons for which admission could be allowed, such as probability of hardship resulting to the alien or close relatives in the event of the alien being excluded or deported, and the like. On the other hand, most denials of entry into the U.S. have by and large been based on objective reasons, among the most common of them being the following: violation of immigration requirements (such as engaging in unauthorized work in the U.S.); being previously excluded or deported from the U.S., entering the U.S. as a visitor but with the seeming intention to remain permanently, making false or contradictory statements and misrepresentations to consular and immigration officers or in connection with present or previous applications for visa, failure to make full disclosure of information regarding political or other associations with those having an ideology deemed unacceptable by the U.S. (e.g., past membership in the Communist or Nazi party), likelihood of an alien becoming a "public charge" and not being able to financially support himself, physical or mental disease, alcoholism., drug convictions, a record or history of immorality or of unacceptable criminal convictions (or conduct), especially if involving "moral turpitude" (defined as "a crime of baseness, vileness or depravity in the private or social duties" of a person), and so on.

The point of all this, simply, is that aliens facing the port-of-entry admission process should approach the process with the proper attitude calculated to enhance, not hurt, their cause: they should have the psychological mind-set, and project the attitude that in the final analysis, the decision of the border immigration officer regarding one's admission to (or exclusion from) the United States, will by and large be based on the objective qualities possessed by the alien himself and on the image and background the alien projects to the officer. It is most important that you be absolutely open and truthful with the immigration inspectors (or interviewers); that you be patient, polite, positive and cooperative with them, and be forthcoming in answering their questions. And, though it cannot be said that such attitude will necessarily guarantee that admission will materialize, it will nevertheless guarantee that you will enhance your case and minimize your potential losses and frustrations with the immigration officials.

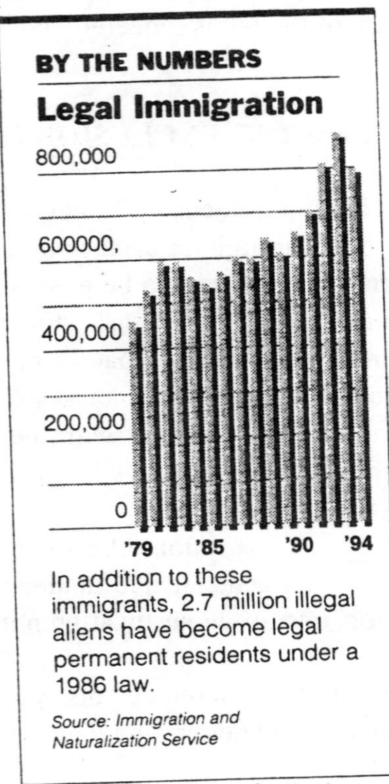

In addition to these immigrants, 2.7 million illegal aliens have become legal permanent residents under a 1986 law.

Source: Immigration and Naturalization Service

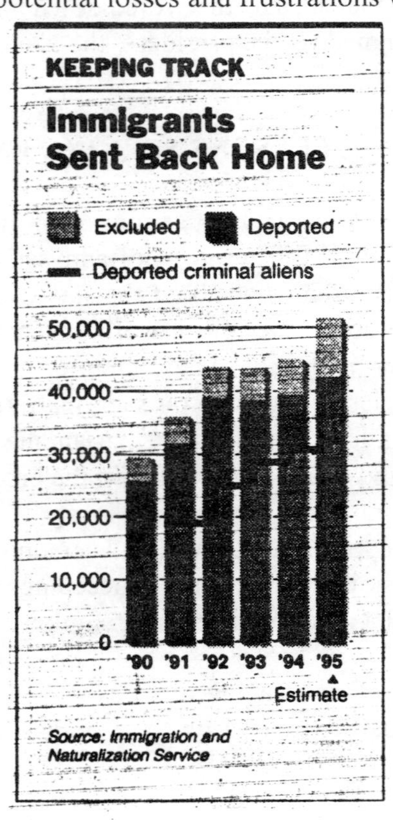

Source: Immigration and Naturalization Service

*In deed, the long-standing policy of the INS has been to grant an alien's application for the relief requested, except where there are specific reasons for it to be rejected. And such policy has been reinforced by a widely influential decision by the Board of Immigration Appeals. (See In Matter of Aral, 13 I & N Dec. 49)

Chapter 17

Legal Grounds For Inadmissibility Of Aliens To The Unite States

A: WHAT IS INADMISSIBILITY?

The Illegal Immigration Reform And Immigrant Responsibility Act (IIRAIRA)* enacted by U.S. Congress in Septembe. 1996, enacted a broad and complex series of changes in the U.S. immigration law, and punitive measures against many typical visa violations, and created some new violations. Move particularly, it enacted major changes in the grounds for the removal of aliens from the U.S. and the rights and powers of the U.S. immigration authorities to bar aliens from admission into the U.S. The law of inadmissibility basically gives the ground and conditions for which the U.S. Consular and immigration authorities may consider an alien as being undesirable and unfit to be admissible into the United.

The basic restrictive element of the 1996 Immigration Reform Law, is what is called the *"summary exclusion"* provision of the law. This provision, which is widely viewed as the one element with probably the most profound and far-reaching impact on aliens planning or seeking to emigrate or gain entry to the U.S., basically empowers an INS inspector at the border to "summarily" exclude and deport an alien requesting admission to the U.S. – that is, the inspector may do so without being subject to a judicial review or an appeal from the inspector's decision – if certain conditions exist. The INS inspector may do so if, in the judgement of the inspector, either <u>one</u> of these conditions are true:

- if the INS inspector is of the opinion that you (the alien) have been untruthful or have made a misrepresenta tion of the facts about almost anything connected to your application for an immigrant or nonimmigrant visa to the U.S., such as your purpose for going, or your intent to return or to stay in the U.S., or your prior personal history or immigration history, or the use or suspected use of false documents, etc; or
- if the INS inspector is of the view that even if you are qualified for another type of visa, you do not have the proper documentation to support your entry to the U.S. in the specific visa category that you are requesting.

An alien who is excluded (for the first time) from entry by border inspector for whatever reason, is barred from making another application for entry for the next 5 years, unless a special waiver is granted. And if an alien has made his entry into the U.S. and subsequently had to be removed from the country, he is barred from entering the U.S. again for a period of 10 years from the date of the departure or removal (or for a period of 20 years in the case of a second or subsequent removal, or in the case of an alien convicted of an aggravate felony).

**It's often referred to as the Immigration Reform Law of 1996, for short.*

B. THE NEW "SUMMARY EXCLUSION" LAW AGAINST ALIENS WHO ARE UNLAWFULLY PRESENT IN THE U.S.

A major new ground of inadmissibility which gives the INS officers and inspectors a sweeping administrative tool, is one provided under the 1996 Immigration Reform Law which subjects aliens who are "unlawfully present" in the United States for 6 months after April 1, 1997, who subsequently left the U.S. voluntarily before there was any removal proceedings and who now seek to be admitted into the U.S. (whether by Adjustment of Status, or by applying for an immigrant or nonimmigrant visa), to a stringent restriction: they are barred from re-entering the U.S. for 3 years; and if the unlawful presence has lasted for one year or move, the waiting period for which the alien is barred from reentering the U.S. is 10 years from the date of the alien's departure from the U.S. For purposes of counting the period of an alien's unlawful presence or overstay, the INS will only consider relevant or applicable a continuous, uninterrupted block of time which continuously runs up to 6 months or 1 year; it will not count or add up a few months (or weeks) during one stay, and few months during another, to be able to come up your "unlawful presence" period.

Who is an "unlawfully present" alien? As interpreted under the immigration regulations, the term "unlawfully present" has a complex definition, but it generally means the overstay by an alien of the time authorized him by the INS, as usually noted on the alien's Arrival-Departure Record (Form 1-94), for him or her to person to remain in the U.S. As interpreted by the INS, such time is defined to include also the time after the INS or the immigration court has determined that an alien has violated the conditions of his admission, as well as the time the alien is required to remain in the U.S. while in formal removal proceedings.

In addition, an alien will not be deemed to be unlawfully present for the purposes of the 3 and 10-year bars to re-entry, for any period of time in which the alien:

- was under the age of 18 years
- had a 'bona-fide' asylum application pending, or any related administrative or judicial review, unless the alien had been employed without authorization
- was the beneficiary of a family unity protection application
- was a 'battered woman or child' who demonstrates a reasonable connection between the status violation or unlawfully entry and the abuse claimed
- undertook a change or extension of status for a maximum period of 120 days, providing the alien had been lawfully admitted and had filed a bona-fide change or extension application and had not been employed without authorization.

For an alien who entered the U.S. after inspector who is admitted to the U.S. for "duration of status" (such as those holding the nonimmigrant A, F, G, or J visas), an unlawful presence will begin to be counted only if an immigration judge determines that the alien is unlawfully present and is deportable, or the INS, in the course of adjudicating on a visa application determines that the alien has violated his status. For an alien admitted until a specified date, unlawful presence will begin to be counted only as from the date designated on his Form 1-94 (or any extensions), or, when applicable, as from the date determined by the INS or an immigration judge to be when the status violation by the alien began. When an alien is granted a voluntary departure, unlawful presence for the purposes of overstay bar begins to be counted as from the date specified for departure in the voluntary departure order, if the alien fails to depart.

C. NATURE OF GROUNDS OF INADMISSIBILITY

Typically, an alien would encounter the issue of exclusion or removal (i.e., inadmissibility) into the U.S. on two primary occasions – first, when he (or she) appears at the U.S. Consulate in his home country to apply for a visa, and, then, when he arrives at the U.S. port of entry attempting to enter the United States. Thus, at the U.S. Consulate office in a foreign country, an alien might have his visa petition denied if the consular officer believes that this particular alien falls under one or more of the grounds of inadmissibility (chart on p. 188). And then, at the U.S. border or port of entry, an alien who already has been granted a visa in his home country and has a valid U.S. visa in his hands, may still be denied entry into the United States by the border Immigration and Naturalization inspectors on the basis that the alien falls under one or more of the grounds of inadmissibility.

The grounds of inadmissibility fall into various categories. They range from health related grounds (e.g. persons found to have a communicable disease of public health significance, such as HIV, tuberculosis, or those who failed to be vaccinated against certain diseases, or who are serious drug abusers or drug addicts etc.); to grounds related to past criminal activities and convictions by an alien; and grounds related to national security interests of the U.S. or to protection of the U.S. labor market, or aliens who have previously entered the U.S. without being properly admitted or paroled, and so on.

The following is a chart summarizing the legal grounds for exclusion ("inadmissibility") of an alien into the United States, and the related conditions under which a WAIVER may be available or unavailable for a given ground.

D. BASIS FOR POSSIBLY REVERSING AN INADMISSIBILITY FINDING

As a practical matter, most decisions made by the U.S. Consular officers on the exclusion or admission of an alien are very difficult, if not virtually impracticable, to reverse since such officers have broad discretion under the immigration rules in interpreting the factual circumstances surrounding any particular alien visa petitioner. As explained in Sections, A and B above, the 1996 law, IIRAIRA, made many profound changes in the areas of effecting the removal of an alien from the United States, and, among other things, it gave the border immigration inspector at the port of entry the power of expedited removal – coupled with the elimination of any appeals from any decision made by the border inspector.

Nevertheless, the immigration laws provide for some situations when certain of the grounds of inadmissibility may still be legally excused or waived, or a finding or inadmissibility by an INS officer reversed.

Ways By Which An Inadmissibility Decision May Be Reversed

If you are found inadmissible by a U.S. Consul officer or an INS inspector at the border, there are four basic ways by which you can get the decision of inadmissibility reversed:

1. In a case involving physical or mental illness only, where you have been cured of the condition by the time of your application for a visa, you can seek a reversal of the prior decision on the grounds that the condition has been corrected. Or, the same thing could also apply where you can show, in the case of certain criminal grounds of inadmissibility, that the underlying criminal conviction was unlawfully obtained, or has been "vacated" (i.e., erased or expunged) by the courts.
2. Where you can prove that the category of inadmissibility the INS had attributed to you is really erroneous and actually don't apply to you, you can get a reversal of the inadmissibility decision against you by the immigra tion authorities. This may, perhaps, be quite complicated, perhaps even downright impossible to do, quite alright. And you may very well need an experienced immigration lawyer to be able to do this, especially

when you have a criminal record in your past. This basis of winning a reversal is used mainly with respect to overcoming criminal and ideological grounds of inadmissibility. Different factors will determine whether your past criminal activity will really constitute an applicable ground of inadmissibility or not:

- The type of the crime committed and the nature of the punishment meted out
- Committing an act that is considered a crime of "moral turpitude" – those crimes that are indicative of bad moral character and extreme dishonesty and moral depravity, such as crimes of theft, assault and battery, murder, rape, and the like – is particularly damaging as a factor for consideration in establishing inadmissi bility and can make you inadmissible even if you have not been convicted; if the criminal activities with which you were associated have no element of moral turpitude, however, they may not generally be consid ered legitimate grounds of inadmissibility.

Factors such as the following may be helpful to your case:

- Crimes and charges with which you have been charged but are dropped
- Expungement laws that remove the crime from your record
- Conviction later erased or vacated based on a showing that it was unlawfully obtained
- The length of the prison term
- How long ago the crime was committed, and the nature and character of your conduct and criminal record since then
- The number of convictions in your background
- Evidence, if any, that you (the alien) may have been rehabilitated
- Available pardons

3. In a situation where the situation is such that you can clearly show, through documentation and otherwise, that the facts or basis upon which the immigration officer rendered his determination of inadmissibility is simply incorrect, what you can do to reverse that decision is simple: merely present your documentation and credible evidence showing that the officer's finding of inadmissibility is incorrect. For example, lets say you were found inadmissible on the grounds of your having certain medical conditions, you simply would present medical reports from your doctor or medical experts demonstrating that the first diagnosis of your medical condition was wrong and that you do not have the medical problem which had been attributed to you. Or, lets' say, for another example, that the immigration office had charged that you lied or misrepresented the facts on your visa application. You can simply present some verifiable and credible evidence proving that you actually told the truth, or that any false statements you made were reasonable, honest mistakes uninten tionally made.

4. <u>WAIVERS</u>* An important way specifically provided for under the 1996 Immigration Reform Law by which an alien may reverse or overcome a finding of inadmissibility by the immigration authorities, is the use of a "waiver" or exemptions. By obtaining a waiver, you are, in effect, obtaining an exception or a pardon of the grounds of inadmissibility used. You don't reverse, or eliminate or disprove the grounds of inadmissibil ity or its finding by the INS against you. Rather, you are merely asking the INS to overlook and discount the problem with which you are charged and grant you the visa, anyway, in spite of that.

The waiver remedy applies only with respect to some of the grounds for inadmissibility. You may apply for a waiver of inadmissibility only <u>AFTER</u> the U.S. Consulate or the INS office has made its decision on your visa

*Note that only the INS office, and no court of law, has jurisdiction to review a decision of the INS to grant or deny a waiver.

application or admission effort and rendered a decision that you are, in fact, inadmissible.

A waiver applies to grounds of inadmissibility involving circumstances such as the following, among others:

- For an alien adjudged a drug abuser or addict, if the alien has some vital family ties and can otherwise prove some mitigating circumstances wherein granting him a waiver is likely to keep his family together and to prevent a hardship, and that having a proper family environment on his part would mitigate any danger to the public; or where a bond is provided
- Persons convicted even of crimes of moral turpitude where the crimes are of "minor offenses" (offences for which the sentence imposed is less than 6 months); where the crime was committed when the alien was under the age of 18 at the time of the crime, and was committed more than 5 years before the date of the application for the visa.
- Crimes for which the maximum possible penalty does not exceed one year, and, if the alien was actually convicted of the crime, where the alien was not in fact sentenced to a term of imprisonment in excess of 6 months.
- Non-drug-related crimes, or offence of prostitution or for conviction of a single offence for possession of 30 grams of marijuana or less, providing the following basic conditions are met: there has been a passage either of 15 years from the disqualifying event coupled with proof of the alien's rehabilitation, or there is an extreme hardship to designated U.S. citizens or permanent resident relatives, such as a spouse, parent, or child.
- For persons charged with fraud or material misrepresentation of a material fact in a visa petition or other document relating to a visa, there is a waiver for those persons who are immediate relatives of U.S. citizens or of permanent resident aliens, or for cases where the fraud occurred at least 10 years before the entry to the U.S. (Applies only to aliens seeking to enter the U.S. as immigrants).
- Aliens guilty of smuggling their immediate family members into the United States, providing the alien is not engaged in the smuggling of any person into the U.S. for profit.
- Aliens who do not have a valid visa or entry document or who do not have the required documents in support of their immigration status at the time of their entry.
- An alien who, in the sole discretion of the INS, is able to establish that the imposition of a bar to re-entry into the U.S. against him for being unlawfully present in the U.S. or for overstaying the time authorized by the INS (a bar for a period of 3 years for overstaying for 180 days to 1 year, and 10 years for overstaying for 1 year or more) would create an extreme hardship on a U.S. citizen or permanent resident spouse or child.

Filing For A Waiver

You may apply for a waiver of inadmissibility only if and AFTER the U.S. Consulate or INS office shall have made a decision on your visa or entry application and has determined that you are, in fact, inadmissible.

In some cases, promptly upon the determination by the consulate or INS office that your answers to the questions on your visa application forms clearly show that you are inadmissible, the office would authority you to begin applying for a waiver immediately as soon as you file your application. But in most cases, however, the consulate or INS office will usually conduct its final interview with the alien before ruling that the alien is inadmissible. In any event, however, once the office makes the determination that the alien is inadmissible and that a waiver is necessary, the alien will be notified by mail. You (the alien) will be given Form 1-601, *Application For Waiver on Ground of Excludability Inadmissibility*, to complete and to file it with the appropriate INS office. The filing fee for this as of this writing is $195 (see sample of Form 1-601 on p. 235).

Waivers to Inadmissibility

GROUNDS TO INADMISSIBILITY	WAIVERS AVAILABLE	CONDITIONS OF WAIVER
Health Problems		
People with communicable diseases. The most common diseases are tuberculosis and HIV (AIDS).	Yes	A waiver is available to an individual who is the spouse or the unmarried son or daughter or the unmarried minor lawfully-adopted child of a U.S. citizen or permanent resident, or of an alien who has been issued an immigrant visa; or to an individual who has a son or daughter who is a U.S. citizen, or a permanent resident, or an alien issued an immigrant visa, upon compliance with INS' terms and regulations.
People with physical or mental disorders which threaten the safety of others.	Yes	Special conditions required by INS, at its discretion.
Drug abusers or addicts.	No	
People who fail to show that they have been vaccinated against certain vaccine-preventable diseases.	Yes	The applicant must show that he or she subsequently received the vaccine; that the vaccine is medically inappropriate as certified by a civil surgeon; or that having the vaccine administered is contrary to the applicant's religious beliefs or moral convictions.
Criminal and Related Violations		
People who have committed crimes involving moral turpitude.	Yes	Waivers are not available for commission of crimes such as attempted murder or conspiracy to commit murder or murder, torture or drug crimes, except for simple possession of less than 30 grams of marijuana, or for people previously admitted as permanent residents, if they have been convicted of aggravated felony since such admission or if they have less than seven years of lawful continuous residence before deportation proceedings are initiated aginst them. Waivers for all other offenses are available only if the applicant is a spouse, parent or child of a U.S. citizen or green card holder; or the only criminal activity was prostitution or the actions occurred more than 15 years before the application for a visa or green card is filed and the alien shows that he or she is rehabilitated and is not a threat to U.S. security.
People with multiple criminal convictions.	Yes	
Prostitutes.	Yes	
Criminals involved in serious criminal activity who have received immunity from prosecution.	Yes	
Drug offenders.	No	However, there may be an acception for a first and only offense or for juvenile offenders.
Drug traffickers.	No	
National Security and Related Violations		
Spies or governmental saboteurs.	No	
People intending to overthrow the U.S. government.	No	
Terrorists and representatives of foreign terrorist organizations.	No	

Waivers to Inadmissibility

GROUNDS TO INADMISSIBILITY	WAIVERS AVAILABLE	CONDITIONS OF WAIVER
People whose entry would endanger U.S. foreign policy, unless the applicant is an official of a foreign government, or the applicant's activities or beliefs would normally be lawful in the U.S., under the constitution.	No	
Voluntary members of totalitarian parties.	Yes	Waiver is available if the membership was involuntary, or is or was when the applicant was under 16 years old, by operation of law, or for purposes of obtaining employment, food rations or other "essentials" of living. Waiver is also possible for past membership if the membership ended at least two years prior to the application (five years if the party in control of a foreign state is considered a totalitarian dictatorship). If neither applies, a waiver is available only for an immigrant who is the parent, spouse, son, daughter, brother or sister of a U.S. citizen, or a spouse, son or daughter of a permanent resident.
Nazis	No	
People Likely to Become Dependent on Public Welfare	No	
Family-sponsored immigrants and employment-sponsored immigrants where a family member is the employment sponsor (or such a family member owns 5% of the petitioning business) whose sponsor has not executed an Affidavit of Support (Form I-864).	No	But an applicant may cure the ground of inadmissibility by subsequently satisfying affidavit of support requirements.
Nonimmigrant public benefit recipients (where the individual came as nonimmigrant and applied for benefits when he or she was not eligible or through fraud). Five-year bar to admissibility.	No	But ground of inadmissibility expires after five years.
Labor Certifications& Employment Qualifications	No	
People without approved labor certifications, if one is required in the category under which the green card application is made.	No	
Graduates of unaccredited medical schools, whether inside or outside of the U.S., immigrating to the U.S. in a category based on their profession, who have not both passed the foreign medical graduates exam and shown proficiency in English. (Physicians qualifying as special immigrants who have been practicing medicine in the U.S. with a license since January 9, 1978 are not subject to this exclusion.)	No	
Uncertified foreign healthcare workers (not including physicians).	No	But applicant may show qualifications by submitting a certificate from the Commission on Graduates of Foreign Nursing Schools or the equivalent.

Waivers to Inadmissibility

GROUNDS TO INADMISSIBILITY	WAIVERS AVAILABLE	CONDITIONS OF WAIVER
Immigration Violators		
People who are present in the U.S. without proper paperwork ("Admission or parole").	Yes	Available for certain battered women and children who came to the U.S. escaping such battery or who qualify as self-petitioners. Also available for individuals who had visa petitions or labor certifications on file before January 14, 1998 ($1,000 penalty required for latter waiver). Does **not** apply to applicants outside of the U.S.
People who were previously deported.	Yes	Discretionary with INS.
People who have failed to attend removal (deportation) proceedings (unless they had reasonable cause for doing so). Five-year bar to inadmissibility.	Yes	Advance permission to apply for readmission. Discretionary with INS.
People who made misrepresentations during the immigration process.	Yes	The applicant must be the spouse or child of a U.S. citizen or green card holder. A waiver will be granted if the refusal of admission would cause extreme hardship to that relative.
People who made a false claim to U.S. citizenship.	No	
Individuals subject to a final removal (deportation) order under the Immigration and Naturalization Act §274C (Civil Document Fraud Proceedings).	Yes	Available to permanent residents who voluntarily left the U.S., and for those applying for permanent residence as immediate relatives or other family-based petitions if the fraud was committed solely to assist the person's spouse or child and provided that no fine was imposed as part of the previous civil proceeding.
Student visa abusers (person who improperly obtains F-1 status to attend a public elementary school or adult education program, or transfers from a private to a public program except as permitted.) Five-year bar to admissibility.	No	
Certain individuals previously removed (deported). Twenty-year bar to admissibility. Five-year bar to admissibility for aggravated felons and for second and subsequent removal.	Yes	Discretionary with INS (advance permission to apply for readmission).
Individuals unlawfully present (time counted only after April 1, 1997). Presence for 180-364 days, results in three-year bar to admissibility. Presence for 365 or more days creates ten-year bar to admissibility. Bars kick in only if the individual departs the U.S. and seeks reentry after a period of unlawful presence.	Yes	One is not considered "unlawfully present" for up to 120 days if, after a lawful admission, an individual filed a valid change or extension of status before the end of the authorized stay (but then subsequently fell out of status) as long as the individual did not work without authorization. Similarly, time spent as a minor, as an asylum applicant (provided the person had a bona fide asylum claim and did not work without authorization), beneficiaries of family unity legislation and claimants under the battered spouse/child provisions do not accrue time in unlawful presence. Individuals admitted for "duration of status" are not unlawfully present until INS or an immigration judge makes such a determination. A waiver is provided for an immigrant who has a U.S. citizen or permanent resident spouse or parent to whom refusal of the application would cause extreme hardship.

Waivers to Inadmissibility

Grounds to Inadmissibility	Waivers Available	Conditions of Waiver
Individuals unlawfully present after previous immigration violations. (Applies to individuals present unlawfully for an aggregate period over one year, who subsequently reenter without being properly admitted. Also applies to anyone ordered removed who subsequently attempts entry without admission.)	No	A permanent ground of inadmissibility. However, after being gone for ten years an applicant can apply for advance permission to reapply for admission.
Stowaways.	No	
Smugglers of illegal aliens.	Yes	Waivable if the applicant was smuggling in people who were immediate family members at the time, and either is a permanent resident or is immigrating under a family or employment-based visa petition.
Document Violations		
People without required current passports or visas.	Yes	Discretionary with INS. Under new "summary removal" procedures, INS may quickly deport people for five years who arrive without proper documents or make misrepresentations during the inspection process.
Draft Evasion and Ineligibility for Citizenship		
People who are permanently ineligible for citizenship.	No	
People who are draft evaders, unless they were U.S. citizens at the time of evasion or desertion.	No	
Miscellaneous Grounds		
Practicing polygamists.	No	
Guardians accompanying excludable aliens.	No	
International child abductors. (The exclusion does not apply if the applicant is a national of a country that signed the Hague Convention on International Child Abduction.)	No	
Unlawful voters (voting in violation of any federal, state or local law or regulation).	No	
Former U.S. citizens who renounced citizenship to avoid taxation.	No	

Chapter 18

Inside The Immigration Offices: How They Work, How To Get The Best Results In Your Visa Processing

To be sure, the U.S. government agencies that process your immigration applications – principally the Embassies or Consulates abroad, and the Immigration and Naturalization Service - and the workers and bureaucrats who work in those agencies in the processing of the visa application, have a reputation for being a bunch of tough-minded, unfeeling, no-nonsense bureaucrats whose primary concern and interest is often in merely laying down the immigration law and enforcing the rules, and not in delivering services. Nevertheless, ***there are a number of things you can do as a visa applicant in order to insure that your dealings with those agencies that process your immigration application move as smoothly and problem-free as possible.***

In this chapter, we provide a general idea of some of such measures.

A. FINDING OUT ABOUT YOUR LOCAL IMMIGRATION OFFICE'S PROCEDURES

As a practical matter, the factual reality is that the nature and extent of the documentation which will be required to support an alien's visa application often vary, even significantly, from one U. S. consulate (or INS) office to another. Hence, even before you begin your application, it is best to contact your local US Consulate or INS office, as the case may be, to inquire about and get the basic information about its office procedures – its work hours, whether it accepts personal inquiries, personal filing of petitions and applications, information on where specifically to file or mail the forms, and inquiry about any special forms or procedures that the office may utilize and about what type of supporting documents are required. For example, some immigration offices may only allow you to file by mail, while others insist may insist that the papers be filed personally in case of questions about the information given or documents submitted.

Unless these questions can be adequately answered for you by the office's recordings on the telephone answering machine, you would probably have to get such answers by making a personal visit to the office, or perhaps possibly by phone or letter. Contact or seek to speak with the person in charge of the processing of immigration application and be sure you get and note the officer's name.

B. IMMIGRATION FORMS PROCEDURES

A few pointers about the proper immigration forms procedures:

● Never give false answers! ***This is the most fundamental, governing rule to bear in mind in filling out and answering any and all questions whatsoever on the immigration forms: HONESTY IS THE VERY BEST POLICY!!*** Answer any questions asked on the forms truthfully as well as fully – your previous (or present) marital situation and children by present or previous marriage or relationship, list of any brothers and sisters (list then all, including full and half siblings or step siblings, but be fully prepared, as in all other matters with the immigration, to present good documentation for any claims).

This is the time to be absolutely certain that you are accurate and truthful; once you submit these forms, its' too late to try to change your answers after that!

• Check with your local INS office or the American Consulate in your country of residence, whichever is applicable, before submitting the immigration forms, about the most recent or current forms, and counter-check the filing fee amount.

• Whenever you file your papers by mail with the consulate or INS office, always do so by *certified* or *registered* mail with return receipt requested. This way, you will have a written confirmation that your papers were received. Keep both the receipt of mailing from the post office, and copies of other papers you submit, in your files for future reference and confirmation. For papers submitted in person, always obtain a written proof of receipt from the office recipient. (See Appendix A for the U.S. Embassy/Consulate contact offices around the world, and Appendix B for a complete list of the INS offices).

C. HERE'S THE BASIC KEY IN CORRECTLY FILLING OUT THE FORMS

A few general rules in regard to completing the immigration forms. A truly important aid to anyone preparing all such forms, are the "blocks" provided on the forms; such blocks are generally self-explanatory and would explicitly indicate the exact information required to be entered for a particular question, and the order in which such information is to be entered in the spaces provided. Secondly, almost every immigration form has a set of "INSTRUCTIONS" on the body of the form, clearly telling the reader the purpose(s) for which the form is appropriate, and giving some pointers on how to complete or file them, and guidelines on the information and supporting documents required to be furnished.

Hence, the first rule in completing the forms is this: in all instances, always be absolutely sure first, to read the forms and to thoroughly understand the information required of you before filling them out. BE DELIBERATELY CAREFUL. Remember this: that the initial batch of forms you complete and submit are what is known as the "primary" documents, meaning that this is the documentary source which the consular and immigration authorities will probably go back to and refer to again and again, and against which they will cross-check any future documents and information from you for consistency.

D. DO NOT SEND THE ORIGINALS OF YOUR DOCUMENTS

When sending or submitting any documents to the consulate or the INS, never send your originals. Rather, simply make a photocopy of the documents and send them. Originals of documents, often irreplaceable, sent to such offices have been known to be lost or misplaced in the crowded offices and massive paperwork of the vast immigration bureaucracy. Hence, always retain the originals, and take them in person to the immigration or consular officers for their own personal inspection and verification on the spot at the proper time.

E. KEEP A COMPLETE FILE OF YOUR OWN

Always make photocopies of each and every form and document you submit to the consular and immigration authorities (quite apart and separate from your originals). The same with every receipt (or cancelled check) the consulate or INS issues you for any fees you pay. Make a separate file and retain such papers in this file for your own records.

As a rule, the same set of papers that are submitted in the filing of the original "petition" (plus more), may have to be submitted for the filing of the visa "application," proper, in the American Consulate abroad, or when you attend the visa interview. And, quite important, these immigration offices do sometimes misplace or lose documents!

F. THE PROPER VISA PHOTO SPECIFICATIONS TO OBTAIN

The INS imposes a number of strict specifications for the photographs and the poses it will accept from applicants for immigration purposes. See sample FORM M-378 on p. 117 for information on the kind of photograph that meets the proper INS specifications.

NOTE: There are professional photographers who specialize in doing INS photos that comply with the INS strict requirements for size, lighting and clarity. They are usually located near and around the INS offices.

G. EVALUATION CENTERS FOR THE ALIEN'S FOREIGN DIPLOMAS

There are many immigrant visa preferences (as well as nonimmigrant visa classifications) that require some United States advanced degrees and academic qualification or its foreign equivalent.

Generally, for the American Consulate or INS to accept a diploma earned in a foreign country, it requires that the university transcripts of the schooling be sent to an accredited academic evaluator for the agency's assessment. Their fees for the evaluation service range from $90 to $170. Here are some of such INS-recognized academic evaluators you may send your school transcripts to in the United States:

World Education Services
P. O. Box 745 Old Chelsea Station
New York, N.Y. 10113-0745
Phone: 212-966-6311

Educational Credential Evaluators Inc
P. O. Box 17499
Milwaukee, WI 53217
Phone: 414-964-0477

Cultural House, Inc.
29 John St., Suite 503
New York, N.Y. 10038
Phone: 212-285-1022
Fax: 212-285-1366

Credentials Evaluation Service
International Education Research Foundation
P. O. Box 66940
Los Angeles, CA 90066
Phone: 310-390-6276

Chapter 19

How To Get An Extention On Your Visa For An Extra Stay

A. THE VISA EXTENSION PROCESS FOR MORE LIFE FOR AN EXPIRED VISA

As fully explained in several passages elsewhere in this book (see Chapters 2 and 3, for example), there are two basic kinds of U.S. entry visas that an alien can receive from the American government – either an ***immigrant*** type of visa (the green card), or a ***nonimmigrant*** type of visa. Basically, with respect to the nonimmigrant type of visa, one major characteristics which distinguishes it, is that it enables the alien to stay in the U.S. on temporary or limited basis. Indeed, if you are an alien holding a non-immigrant visa, upon your being admitted into the country, the immigration officer would have affixed a stamp on your passport (and/or on an immigration Form 1-94 or 1-94W, *Records of Arrival and Departure,* that is attached to your passport), designating your port of entry and the date by which you were admitted and by which your visa is to expire and you are required to leave the U.S.

However, if you are a holder of a nonimmigrant (temporary) visa, and you want, for one reason or the other, to stay legal in the U.S. beyond the specific time limit originally granted you for your visa, what steps do you have to take?

Under the immigration law and procedures, if you were properly admitted to the United States under nonimmigrant classifications as, for example, a temporary business or tourist visitor (person with B-1 or B-2 visas), or as a student or temporary worker or entertainer (person with F-1, H-2A, H-2B, H-3 and M-1 visas, for example), you can apply to the Immigration and Naturalization Service and request for an extension of your stay. You may need to have an extension of your stay in the U.S. for any number of good and reasonable reasons that may be necessitated by your business or professional circumstances or your family reasons. For example, it may be that as a tourist in the United States you feel you have yet more places or site to see or to visit, or that you simply want to visit some new, additional places. Or, as a tourist or visitor, you may come to decide while in the U.S. you need to spend more time for business purposes or with relatives. Whatever your reason, just be sure that you include a detailed explanation of such reasons in the submission you make to the INS in filing your application for an extension.

B. HOW TO FILE FOR AN EXTENSION OF STAY

1. First, prepare the following papers for filing:

- Form 1-539, *Application to Extend/Change Nonimmigrant Status.* (see sample of Form on p. 181)
- Form 1-94, *Record of Arrival and Departure.* Submit a copy. (This form is your official proof of having had lawful entry into the U.S. In the event it has been lost, stolen or damaged, or otherwise not available, you may get the necessary documentation from the INS by filing Form 1-102, *Application forReplacement of Initial Nonimmigrant Arrival-Departure Documents.*)
- Statement of your reason for desiring and requesting the extension, including any supporting, documentations thereof. For example, you may cite as your reason the need to continue medical treatment (or to commence a

new procedure), or to attend the wedding of your best friend, or to finalize a contract for your company on a business deal, or the need for you to make a more extended visit to family members or an old friend previously not included. Whatever your reason, just be sure to attach some pertinent documentations from independent parties that verify your claims, if you can. You may include these facts and information on a separate sheet of paper which you may attach to the application form.

- Evidence supporting the conclusion that the stay and intent of the alien regarding the stay still continues to be temporary, such as evidence of financial support (purchase of travelers' checks, a bank letter), evidence of continued employment or residence overseas by the alien, a return ticket and the like.
- A $140 filing fee for the filing of the Form 1-539, made payable either by personal check or money order to the Immigration and Naturalizaton Service.

2. Personally submit or mail the application and the supporting documents (the above items), directly to the INS office closest to where you (the applicant) live. Always send such application preferably by certified mail, with Return Receipt requested, so that you'll have proof of its being received. You can file a request for extension within 60 days of the expiration date of your stay, but not latter than 15 days before the expiration date.

IMPORTANT: One certain cause for which requests for visa extensions are often denied by the INS, is related to what is known by the INS establishment as the theory of the alien's "preconceived intent." Simply stated, this means that the INS officers would often conclude outright that most – at least many – non-immigrant aliens lie about their reason for coming to the U.S.; that they had probably lied to and decived the American consul who issued them their temporary visa into believing that they wished to be a temporary visitor, when they, in fact, had all along intended to stay permanently in the U.S. upon entering the country. Consequently, to avoid the likelihood of your application for visa extension being readily denied, there's one thing that is very, very central: that you make every effort to maintain your nonimmigrant legal status and not violate the conditions of your stay in the U.S. at any time while you are in the country. You must not have overstayed your visa, for example; you must not have worked when you are not authorized to do so, you must not have changed schools or employer without a prior application to and permission from the INS to do so, and so on. If you do any of these in contravention of the INS rules, you seriously diminish your chances of being granted an extension, among other consequences which could even be more serious. Secondly, if you happen to want to apply for a change of your slatus from one nonimmigrant category to another one (say, from a tourist visa to student visa), try not to do so only within a relatively short time after you just arrived in the country. Doing so would only work to confirm to the INS officials their theory of "preconceived intent" about you – namely, that you had intended all along to become a student in the U.S., for example, when you applied for tourist visa at the American Embassy in your native country. That would be deemed by the INS to be an act of misrepresentation and "visa fraud" on your part, an almost certain ground to deny your request for the new visa, or even to extend your existing visa. (see Chapter 14 for full discussion of the issue of the alien "intent" in visa application matters).

Appendix A

U.S. Embassies and Consulates

Albania
U.S. Embassy
Ruga E. Labinoti 103
PSC 59 Box 100 (A)
APO AE 09624
Tirana
Telephone: 355-42-32875
Fax: 355-42-32222

Algeria
U.S. Embassy
4 Chemin Cheich Bachir Brahimi
Algiers
Telephone: 691255
Fax: 693979

Angola
U.S. Embassy
Rua Houari Boumedienne No. 32
Miramar, Luanda
Telephone: 244-2-346-418/
244-2-345-481
Fax: 244-2-346-924

Argentina
U.S. Embassy
4300 Colombia, 1425
Buenos Aires
Telephone: 777-4533
Fax: 777-0197

Armenia
U.S. Embassy
18 Gen Bagramian
Yerevan
Telephone: 3742-151-144
Fax: 3742-151-550

Australia
U.S. Embassy
Moonah PL
Canberra ACT 2600
Telephone: 270-5000
Fax: 270-5970

U.S. Consulate
553 St. Kilda Road
South Melbourne, Victoria 3004
Telephone: 03-9526-5900
Fax: 03-9529-6774

U.S. Consulate
59th Floor
MLC Centre
19-29 Martin Place
Sydney, NSW 2000
Telephone: 61-2-373-9200
Fax: 61-2-373-9125

U.S. Consulate
246 St. George's Terrace
Perth, WA 6000
Telephone: 61-9-231-9400
Fax: 61-9-231-9444

Austria
U.S. Embassy
Boltzmanngasse 16
A-1091
Vienna
Telephone: 43-1-313-39
Fax: 43-1-310-0682

Azerbaijan
U.S. Embassy
Azadliq Prospekti 83
Baku
Telephone: 9-9412-98-03-35
Fax: 9-9412-98-37-55

Bahamas
U.S. Embassy
Mosmar Building
Queen Street
Nassau
Telephone: 809-322-1181
Fax: 809-356-0222

Bahrain
U.S. Embassy
Shaikh Isa Road
Manama
Telephone: 973-273-300
Fax: 973-275-418

Bangladesh
U.S. Embassy
Diplomatic Enclave
Madani Avenue
Baridhara Model Town
Dhaka
Telephone: 880-2-884700-22
Fax: 880-2-883744-22

Barbados
U.S. Embassy
P.O. Box 302
Bridgetown
Telephone: 246-436-4950
Fax: 246-429-5246

Belarus
U.S. Embassy
Starovilenskaya #46-220002
Minsk
Telephone: 375-172-31-50-00
Fax: 375-172-34-78-53

Belgium
U.S. Embassy
27 Boulevard du Regent
Brussels
Telephone: 32-2-508-2111
Fax: 32-2-511-2725

Belize
U.S. Embassy
Gabourel Lane & Hutson Streets
Belize City
Telephone: 501-2-77161
Fax: 501-2-30802

Benin
U.S. Embassy
Rue Caporal Anani Bernard
Cotonou
Telephone: 30-06-50
Fax: 30-14-39

Bermuda
U.S. Consulate
Crown Hill 16
Middle Road
Devonshire
Hamilton
Telephone: 441-295-1342
Fax: 441-295-1592

Bolivia
U.S. Embassy
Ave. Arce No. 2780
La Paz
Telephone: 591-2-430251
Fax: 591-2-433900

Bosnia
Herzegovina
43 Ul. Duře Dakovica
Sarajevo
Telephone: 387-71-445-700
or 387-71-667-391
Fax: 387-71-659-722

Botswana
U.S. Embassy
P.O. Box 90
Gaborone
Telephone: 267-353-982
Fax: 267-356-947

Brazil
U.S. Embassy
Avenida das Nocoes
Lote 3
Brasilia
Telephone: 55-61-321-7272
Fax: 55-61-321-2833

U.S. Consulate
Avenida Presidente Wilson, 147
Rio de Janeiro
Telephone: 55-21-292-7117
Fax: 55-21-220-0439

U.S. Consulate
Rua Padre Joao Manoel, 933
Sao Paulo
Telephone: 55-11-881-6511
Fax: 55-11-852-1395

U.S. Consulate
Rua Coronel Genuino, 421
9th Floor
Porto Alegre
Telephone: 55-51-226-4288
Fax: 55-51-221-2213

U.S. Consulate
Rua Goncalves Maia, 163
Recife
Telephone: 55-81-421-2441
Fax: 55-81-231-1906

Brunei
U.S. Embassy
P.O. Box B
Bandar Seri Begawan
Telephone: 29670
Fax: 225-293

Bulgaria
U.S. Embassy
1 Sabrona St.
Sofia
Telephone: 980-5241
Fax: 981-8977

Burkina Faso
U.S. Embassy
B.P. 35
Ouagadougou
Telephone: 30-67-23
Fax: 30-38-90

Burma
U.S. Embassy
581 Merchant Street
Rangoon
Telephone: 282055
Fax: 280409

Burundi
U.S. Embassy
B.P. 1720
Avenue du Zaire
Bujumbura
Telephone: 22-29-86
Fax: 22-29-26

Cambodia
U.S. Embassy
27 EO Street 240
Phnom Penh
Telephone: 885-23-426-436
Fax: 885-23-426-437

Cameroon
U.S. Embassy
Rue Nachtigal
Yaounde
Telephone: 237-23-05-12
Fax: 237-23-07-53

Canada
U.S. Embassy
100 Wellington St
Ottawa K1P 5T1
Telephone: 613-238-5335
Fax: 613-238-5720

U.S. Consulate
615 Macleod Trail S.E.
Calgary, Alberta T2G 4T8
Telephone: 403-266-8962
Fax: 403-264-6630

U.S. Consulate
Suite 910, Cogswell Tower
Scotia Square
Halifax, NS B3J 3K1
Telephone: 902-429-2480
Fax: 902-423-6861

U.S. Consulate
1155 St. Alexandre St.
Montreal, Quebec H2Z 1Z2
Telephone: 514-398-9695
Fax: 514-398-0973

U.S. Consulate
P.O. Box 939
Quebec City, Quebec G1R 4T9
Telephone: 418-692-2095
Fax: 418-692-4640

U.S. Consulate
360 University Ave
Toronto, Ontario M5G 1S4
Telephone: 416-595-1700
Fax: 416-595-0051

U.S. Consulate
1095 West Pender St.
Vancouver, B.C. V6E 2M6
Telephone: 604-685-4311
Fax: 604-685-5285

Cape Verde
U.S. Embassy
Rua Abilio Macedo 81
Praia
Telephone: 238-61-56-16
Fax: 238-61-13-55

Central African Republic
U.S. Embassy
Avenue President Dacko
Bangui
Telephone: 236-61-02-00
Fax: 236-61-44-94

Chad
U.S. Embassy
Ave. Felix Eboue
N'Djamena
Telephone: 235-51-70-09
Fax: 235-51-56-54

Chile
U.S. Embassy
Ave. Andres Bello 2800
Santiago
Telephone: 56-2-232-2600
Fax: 56-2-330-3710

China, Mainland
U.S. Embassy
Xiu Shui Bei Jie 3
Beijing
Telephone: 86-10-6532-3831
Fax: 86-10-6532-6422

U.S. Consulate
No. 1 Shamian St. South
Guangzhou
Telephone: 86-20-8188-8911
Fax: 86-20-8186-2341

U.S. Consulate
1469 Huai Hai Middle Road
Shanghai
Telephone: 86-21-6433-6880
Fax: 86-21-6433-4122

U.S. Consulate
52 14th Wei Road
Heping District, 110003
Shenyang
Telephone: 86-24-322-1198
Fax: 86-24-322-2374

U.S. Consulate
4 Lingshiguan Road
Chengdu 610041, Sichuan
Telephone: 86-28-558-3992
Fax: 86-28-558-3520

China, Taiwan
American Institute in Taiwan
7 Lane 134
Hsin Yi Road
Section 3
Taipei
Telephone: 886-2-709-2000
Fax: 886-2-702-7675

Colombia
U.S. Embassy
Calle 22D-BIS No. 47-51
Apartado Aero 3831
Bogota
Telephone: 57-1-315-0811
Fax: 57-1-315-2197

U.S. Consulate
Calle 77 Carrera 68
Centro Comercial Mayorista
Barranquilla
Telephone: 95-353-0970
Fax: 95-353-5216

Comoro Islands
(See Mauritius)

Congo, Democratic Republic of the
(Formerly Zaire)
U.S. Embassy
310 Avenue Des Aviateurs
Kinshasa
Telephone: 243-12-21533
Fax: 243-88-43805

Congo, Republic of
U.S. Embassy
Avenue Amilcar Cabral
Brazzaville
Telephone: 242-83-20-70
Fax: 243-88-43805

Costa Rica
U.S. Embassy
Pavas Road
San Jose
Telephone: 506-220-3939
Fax: 506-220-2305

Cote D'Ivoire
(Formerly Ivory Coast)
U.S. Embassy
5 Rue Jesse Owens
Abidjan
Telephone: 225-21-09-79
Fax: 225-22-32-59

Croatia
U.S. Embassy
Andrije Hebranga 2
Zagreb
Telephone: 385-1-455-55-00
Fax: 385-1-455-85-85

Cuba
U.S. Interest, Swiss Embassy
Calzada entre L & M
Vedado Seccion
Havana
Telephone: 53-7-33-3551/9
Fax: 53-7-33-3700

Cyprus
U.S. Embassy
Metochiou and Ploutarchou Streets
Engomi, Nicosia
Telephone: 357-2-476100
Fax: 357-2-465944

Czech Republic
U.S. Embassy
Trziste 15-12548 Praha
Prague
Telephone: 420-2-5732-0663
Fax: 420-2-5732-0614

Denmark
U.S. Embassy
Dag Hammarskjolds Alie 24
Copenhagen
Telephone: 45-31-42-31-44
Fax: 45-35-43-02-23

Djibouti
U.S. Embassy
Plateau de Serpent
Blvd. Marechal Joffre
Djibouti
Telephone: 35-3995
Fax: 35-3940

Dominican Republic
U.S. Embassy
Calle Cesar Nicolas Penson & Calle Leopoldo Navarro
Santo Domingo
Telephone: 809-221-2171
Fax: 809-686-7437

Ecuador
U.S. Embassy
Avenida 12 de Octubre y Avenida Patria
Quito
Telephone: 593-2-562-890
Fax: 593-2-502-052

U.S. Consulate
9 de Octubre y Garcia Moreno
Guayaquil
Telephone: 593-4-323-570
Fax: 593-4-324-558

Egypt
U.S. Embassy
8, Kamal El-Din Salah St.
Garden City
Cairo
Telephone: 20-2-355-7371
Fax: 20-2-357-3200

U.S. Consulate
3 El Fardaha Street
Alexandria
Telephone: 20-3-472-1009
Fax: 20-3-483-3811

El Salvador
U.S. Embassy
Final Blvd. Santa Elena
Antiguo Cuscatlan
San Salvador
Telephone: 503-278-4444
Fax: 503-278-6011

Eritrea
U.S. Embassy
Franklin D. Roosevelt St.
Asmara
Telephone: 291-1-120004
Fax: 291-1-127584

Estonia
U.S. Embassy
Kentmanni 20, EE 0001
Tallinn
Telephone: 372-6-312-021
Fax: 372-6-312-025

Ethiopia
U.S. Embassy
Entoton Street
Addis Ababa
Telephone: 251-1-550-666
Fax: 251-1-552-191

Fiji
U.S. Embassy
31 Loftus Street
Suva, Fiji
Telephone: 679-314-466
Fax: 679-303-872

Finland
U.S. Embassy
Itainen Puistotie 14A
Helsinki
Telephone: 358-9-171931
Fax: 358-9-635332

France
U.S. Embassy
2 Avenue Gabriel
75382 Paris Cedex 08
Telephone: 33-1-4312-2222
Fax: 33-1-4312-2172

U.S. Consulate
Boulevard Paul Peytral 12
13286 Marseille
Telephone: 33-91-549-200
Fax: 33-91-550-947

U.S. Consulate
15 Avenue d'Alsace
67082 Strasbourg
Telephone: 33-88-35-31-04
Fax: 33-88-24-06-95

Gabon
U.S. Embassy
Blvd. de la Mer
Libreville
Telephone: 241-762-003 or 241-762-004
Fax: 241 745-507

The Gambia
U.S. Embassy
Fajara East-
Kairaba Ave.
Banjul
Telephone: 220-392-856
Fax: 220-392-475

Georgia
U.S. Embassy
25 Atoneli
Tbilisi
Telephone:
SWBD 995-32-989-67 or 995-32-933-803
Fax: 995-32-933-759 or 995-32-938-951

Germany
U.S. Embassy (Branch Office)
108 Berlin
Neustaedtischee Kirchstrasse 4-5
Berlin
Telephone: 49-30-238-5174
Fax: 49-30-238-6290

U.S. Embassy
Deichmanns Ave
53170 Bonn
Telephone: 49-228-3391
Fax: 49-339-2663

U.S. Consulate
Kennedydamm 15-17
40476 Dusseldorf
Telephone: 49-211-47061-0
Fax: 49-211-43-14-48

U.S. Consulate
Siesmayerstrasse 21
60323 Frankfurt
Telephone: 49-69-7535-0
Fax: 49-69-748-204

U.S. Consulate
Alsterufer 27/28
20354 Hamburg
Telephone: 49-171-351269
Fax: 49-40-443004

U.S. Consulate
Wilhelm-Seyfferth-Strasse 4
04107 Leipzig
Telephone: 49-341-213-840
Fax: 49-341-213-8417

U.S. Consulate
Koeniginstrasse 5
80539 Muenchen
Telephone: 49-171-815-4805
Fax: 49-171-283-047

Ghana
U.S. Embassy
Ring Road East
Accra
Telephone: 233-21-775348
Fax: 233-21-776008

Greece
U.S. Embassy
91 Vasilissis Sophias Blvd.
10160 Athens
Telephone: 30-1-721-2951
Fax: 30-1-721-8660

U.S. Consulate
59 Leoforos Nikis
GR-546-22 Thessaloniki
Telephone: 30-31-242905 or
30-31-720-2400
Fax: 30-31-242927 or
30-31242915

Grenada
U.S. Embassy
Box 54
St. Georges
Telephone: 809-444-1173
Fax: 809-444-4820

Guatemala
U.S. Embassy
7-01 Avenida de la Reforma
Zone 10
Guatemala City
Telephone: 502-2-31-15-41
Fax: 502-2-32-04-95

Guinea
U.S. Embassy
Rue KA 038 B.P. 603
Conakry
Telephone: 224-41-15-20 or
224-41-15-21 or
224-41-15-23
Fax: 224-41-15-22

Guinea-Bissau
U.S. Embassy
1 Rua Ulysses S. Grant
Bairro de Penha
Bissau
Telephone: 245-25-2273
Fax: 245-25-2282

Guyana
U.S. Embassy
99-100 Young and Duke Sts.
Kingston, Georgetown
Telephone: 592-2-54900-9
Fax: 592-2-58497

Haiti
U.S. Embassy
5 Harry Truman Blvd.
Port-au-Prince
Telephone: 509-22-0354
Fax: 509-23-1641

The Holy See
U.S. Embassy
Villa Domiziana
Via Delle Terme Deciane 26
00153 Rome, Italy
Telephone: 396-46741
Fax: 396-575-8346 or
396-573-0682

Honduras
U.S. Embassy
Avenido La Paz
Tegucigalpa
Telephone: 504-36-9320
Fax: 504-36-9037

Hong Kong
U.S. Consulate
26 Garden Road
Hong Kong
Telephone: 852-2523-9011
Fax: 852-2845-4845

Hungary
U.S. Embassy
V. Szabadsag Ter 12
Budapest
Telephone: 36-1-267-4400
Fax: 36-1-269-9326

Iceland
U.S. Embassy
Laufasvegur 21
Reykjavik
Telephone: 354-5629100
Fax: 354-5629118

India
U.S. Embassy
Shanti Path
Chanakyapuri 110021
New Delhi
Telephone: 91-11-688-9033
Fax: 91-11-687-2391

U.S. Consulate
Lincoln House
78 Bhulabhai Desai Rd.
Mumbai 400026
Telephone: 91-22-363-3611
Fax: 91-22-363-0350

U.S. Consulate
5/1 Ho Chi Minh Sarani
Calcutta 700071
Telephone: 91-33-282-3611
Fax: 91-33-282-2335

U.S. Consulate
220 Mount Road 600006
Madras
Telephone: 91-44-827-3040
Fax: 91-44-826-2538

Indonesia
U.S. Embassy
Merdeka Selatan 5
Jakarta
Telephone: 62-21-344-2211
Fax: 62-21-386-2259

U.S. Consular Agency
Jalan Segara Ayu No. 5
Sanur 00228
Bali
Telephone: 62-361-88478
Fax: 62-361-87760

U.S. Consulate
Jalan Raya Dr. Sutomo 33
Surabaya
Telephone: 62-31-582287
Fax: 62-31-574492

Iraq
U.S. Embassy
Opp. For. Ministry Club
Masbah Quarter
Baghdad
Telephone: 964-1-719-6138/9
Fax: 964-1-718-9297

Ireland
U.S. Embassy
42 Elgin Road
Ballsbridge
Dublin
Telephone: 353-1-6688777
Fax: 353-1-6670056

Israel
U.S. Consulate
18 Agron Road
Jerusalem 94190
Telephone: 9726-2-253288
Fax: 9726-2-59270

U.S. Embassy
71 Hayarkon St.
Tel Aviv
Telephone: 973-3-519-7575
Fax: 973-3-510-7215

Italy
U.S. Embassy
Via Veneto 119/A
00187 Rome
Telephone: 39-6-46741
Fax: 39-488-2672

U.S. Consulate
Banca d'America e
d'Italia Bldg.
Piazza Poheilo 6
Genoa
Telephone: 39-10-282-741
Fax: 39-10-543-877

U.S. Consulate
Via Principe Amedeo 2
20121 Milano
Telephone: 39-2-290-351
Fax: 39-2-2900-1165

U.S. Consulate
Piazza della Repubblica
80122 Naples
Telephone: 39-81-583-8111
Fax: 39-81-761-1869

U.S. Consulate
Via Re Federico
No. 18 BIS
Palermo
Telephone: 39-091-611-00-20

U.S. Consulate
Lungarno Amerigo Vespucci 38
Florence 50123
Telephone: 39-55-239-8276
Fax: 39-55-216-531

U.S. Consulate
Via Roma 15
Trieste 34132
Telephone: 39-0-040-660-177
Fax: 39-0-040-631-240

Ivory Coast
(See Cote d'Ivoire)

Jamaica
U.S. Embassy
Jamaica Mutual Life Center
2 Oxford Road, 3rd Floor
Kingston
Telephone: 809-929-4850
Fax: 809-926-6743

U.S. Consulate
St. James Place, 2nd Floor
Gloucester Ave.
Montego Bay
Telephone: 809-952-0160/5050

Japan
U.S. Embassy
10-5 Akasaka 1-chome
Minato-ku 107-
Tokyo
Telephone: 81-3-3224-5000
Fax: 81-3-3505-1862

U.S. Consulate
2564 Nishihara
Urasoe City, Okinawa 90121
Telephone: 81-98-876-4211
Fax: 81-98-876-4243

U.S. Consulate
11-5 Nishitenma 2-chome
Kita-Ku
Osaka 530
Telephone: 81-6-315-5900
Fax: 81-6-315-5930

U.S. Consulate
5-26 Ohori 2-chome, Chuo-ku
Fukuoka 810
Telephone: 81-92-751-9331
Fax: 81-92-713-9222

U.S. Consulate
Nishiki SIS Building 6F 10-33
Nishiki 3-chome
Nagoya 460
Telephone: 81-52-203-4011
Fax: 81-52-201-4612

U.S. Consulate
Kita I-Jo
Nisi 28-chome
Chuo-ku
Sapporo 061
Telephone: 81-11-641-1115/7
Fax: 81-11-643-1283

Jordan
U.S. Embassy
Box 354
Amman 11118
Telephone: 962-6-820-101
Fax: 962-820-163

Kazakstan
U.S. Embassy
99/97 Furmanova St.
Almaty
Republic of Kazakstan 4800 12
Telephone: 7-3272-63-39-05
Fax: 7-3272-63-38-83

Kenya
U.S. Embassy
Moi/Haile Selassie Ave
Nairobi
Telephone: 254-2-334141
Fax: 254-2-340838

Korea
U.S. Embassy
82 Sejong-Ro
Chongro-Ku
Seoul
Telephone: 82-2-397-4111
Fax: 82-2-738-8845

Kuwait
U.S. Embassy
P.O. Box 77 SAFAT
Kuwait
Telephone: 965-539-5307
Fax: 965-538-0282

Kyrgyzstan
U.S. Embassy
Erkindik Prospect #66
Bishkek 720002
Telephone: 7-3312-22-29-20
Fax: 7-3312-22-35-51

Laos
U.S. Embassy
Rue Bartholonie
B.P. 114
Vientiane
Telephone: 856-21-212-581
Fax: 856-21-212-584

Latvia
U.S. Embassy
Raina Boulevard 7, LV-1510
Riga
Telephone: 371-2-721-0005
Fax: 371-2-782-0047

Lebanon
U.S. Embassy
P.O. Box 70-840
Antelias
Beirut
Telephone: 961-1-402-200
Fax: 961-1-403-313

Lesotho
U.S. Embassy
P.O. Box 333
Maseru
Telephone: 266-312-666
Fax: 266-310-116

Liberia
U.S. Embassy
1111 United Nations Drive
Monrovia
Telephone: 231-226-370
Fax: 231-226-148

Lithuania
U.S. Embassy
Akmenu
Vilnius 2600
Telephone: 370-2-223-031
Fax: 370-670-6084

Luxembourg
U.S. Embassy
22 Blvd Emmanuel-Servais
2535 Luxembourg
Telephone: 352-460123
Fax: 352-461401

Macedonia
(The former Yugoslav Republic of)
U.S. Embassy
Bul. Ilinden bb
9100 Skopje
Telephone 389-91-116-180
Fax: 389-91-117-103

Madagascar
U.S. Embassy
14 and 16 Rue Raintovo
Antsahavola
Antannanarivo
Telephone: 2612-212-57
Fax: 2612-345-39

Malawi
U.S. Embassy
P.O. Box 30016
Lilongwe
Telephone: 265-783-166
Fax: 265-780-471

Malaysia
U.S. Embassy
376 Jalan Tun Razak
50400 Kuala Lumpur
Telephone: 603-248-9011
Fax: 603-242-2207

Mali
U.S. Embassy
Rue Rochester NY and Rue
Mohamed V, B.P.34
Bamako
Telephone: 223-225-470
Fax: 223-223-712

Malta
U.S. Embassy
2d Floor, Development House
St. Anne Street
Floriana, Valletta
Telephone: 356-235-960
Fax: 356-246-917

Marshall Islands
U.S. Embassy
Oceanside Mejen Loeto
Long Island
Majuro, Republic of the
Marshall Islands
Telephone: 692-247-4011
Fax: 692-247-4012

Mauritania
U.S. Embassy
B.P. 222
Nouakchott
Telephone: 222-2-526-60
Fax: 222-2-515-92

Mauritius
U.S. Embassy
Rogers Building, 4th Floor
John Kennedy Street
Port Louis
Telephone: 230-208-2347
Fax: 230-208-9534

Mexico
U.S. Embassy
Paseo de la Reforma 305
Mexico City
Telephone: 525-211-0042
Fax: 525-208-3373

U.S. Consulate
924 Avenue Lopez Mateos
Ciudad Juarez
Telephone: 52-16-11300
Fax: 52-16-169056

U.S. Consulate
Progreso 175
Guadalajara, Jalisco
Telephone: 52-3-825-2998
Fax: 52-3-826-6549

U.S. Consulate
Monterrey 141 Pre;
Hermosillo 83260, Sonora
Telephone: 52-62-17-2375
Fax: 52-62-17-2578

U.S. Consulate
Tapachula 96
Tijuana, B.C.
Telephone: 52-66-81-7400
Fax: 52-66-81-8016

U.S. Consulate
Paseo Montejo 453
Merida, Yucatan
Telephone: 52-99-25-5011
Fax: 52-99-25-6219

U.S. Consulate
Avenide Constitucion
411 Poniente
Monterrey, N.L.
Telephone: 52-8-345-2120
Fax: 52-8-342-0177

U.S. Consulate
Calle Allende 3330
Col. Jardin
88260 Nuevo Laredo, Tamps.
Telephone: 52-87-14-0152
Fax: 52-87-14-7984

U.S. Consulate
Ave. Primera 2002
87330 Matamoros, Tamps.
Telephone: 52-88-12-44-02
Fax: 52-88-12-21-71

Micronesia
U.S. Embassy
P.O. Box 1286
Kolonia
Telephone: 691-320-2187
Fax: 691-320-2186

Moldova
U.S. Embassy
Strada Alexei Mateevicie #103
277014 Chisinau
Telephone: 373-2-23-37-72
Fax: 373-223-30-44

Mongolia
U.S. Embassy
Ulaanbaatar
Telephone: 976-1-329-095
Fax: 976-1-320-776

Morocco
U.S. Embassy
2 Ave de Marrakech
Rabat
Telephone: 212-7-76-2265
Fax: 212-7-76-5621

U.S. Consulate
8 Blvd. Moulay Youssef
Casablanca
Telephone: 212-2-264-550
Fax: 212-2-204-127

Mozambique
U.S. Embassy
Avenida Kenneth Kaunda
Maputo
Telephone: 258-1-49-27-97
Fax: 258-1-49-01-14

Namibia
U.S. Embassy
Ausplan Building
14 Lossen St.
Private Bag 12029 Ausspannplatz
Windhoek
Telephone: 264-61-221-601
Fax: 264-61-229-792

Nepal
U.S. Embassy
Pani Pokhari
Kathmandu
Telephone: 977-1-411179
Fax: 977-1-419963

Netherlands
U.S. Embassy
Lange Voohout 102
2514 EJ, Den
The Hague
Telephone: 31-70-310-9209
Fax: 31-70-361-4688

U.S. Consulate
Museumplein 19
Amsterdam
Telephone: 31-20-5755-309
Fax: 31-20-5755-310

Netherlands Antilles
U.S. Consulate
J.B. Gorsiraweg #1
Curacao
Telephone: 599-9-613066
Fax: 599-9-616489

New Zealand
U.S. Embassy
29 Fitzherbert Ter.
Thorndon
Wellington
Telephone: 64-4-472-2068
Fax: 64-4-471-2380

U.S. Consulate
4th Floor Yorkshire
General Bldg.
Shortland and O'Connel Sts.
Auckland
Telephone: 64-9-303-2724
Fax: 64-9-366-0870

Nicaragua
U.S. Embassy
Km. 4-1/2 Carretera Sur
Managua
Telephone: 505-2-666010
Fax: 505-2-669074

Niger
U.S. Embassy
B.P. 11201
Niamey
Telephone: 227-72-26-61
Fax: 227-73-31-67

Nigeria
U.S. Embassy
2 Eleke Crescent
Lagos
Telephone: 234-1-261-0097
Fax: 234-1-261-0257

Norway
U.S. Embassy
Drammensveien 18
Oslo 2
Telephone: 47-22-44-85-50
Fax: 47-22-44-33-63

Oman
U.S. Embassy
P.O. Box 50202
Muscat
Telephone: 968-698-989
Fax: 968-699-779

Pakistan
U.S. Embassy
Diplomatic Enclave
Ramna 5
Islamabad
Telephone: 92-51-826-161
Fax: 92-51-214-222

U.S. Consulate
8 Abdullah Haroon Rd
Karachi
Telephone: 92-21-568-5170
Fax: 92-21-568-0496

U.S. Consulate
50 Shahrah-E Bin Badees
Lahore
Telephone: 92-42-636-5530
Fax: 92-42-636-5177

U.S. Consulate
11 Hospital Road
Peshawar
Telephone: 92-521-279801
Fax: 92-521-276712

Palau
P.O. Box 6028
Koror
Telephone: 680-488-2920
Fax: 680-488-2911

Panama
U.S. Embassy
Apartado
6959 Panama City
Telephone: 507-227-1777
Fax: 507-227-1964

Papua New Guinea
U.S. Embassy
Douglas St.
Port Moresby
Telephone: 675-321-1455
Fax: 675-321-3423

Paraguay
U.S. Embassy
1776 Mariscal Lopez Ave.
Asuncion
Telephone: 595-21-213-715
Fax: 595-21-213-728

Peru
U.S. Embassy
Avenida Encalada
Cuadra 17
Monterrico, Lima
Telephone: 51-1-434-3000
Fax: 51-1-434-3037

Philippines
U.S. Embassy
1201 Roxas Blvd.
Manila
Telephone: 63-2-523-1001
Fax: 63-2-522-4361

U.S. Consulate
3rd Floor
Philippine American Life Ins. Bldg.
Jones Ave.
Cebu
Telephone: 63-32-310-261/2
Fax: 63-32-310-174

Poland
U.S. Embassy
Aleje Ujazdowskle 29/31
Warsaw
Telephone: 48-22-628-3041
Fax: 48-22-628-8298

U.S. Consulate
Ulica Stolarska 9
31043 Krakow
Telephone: 48-12-229764
Fax: 48-12-218292

Portugal
U.S. Embassy
Avenida das Forcas Armadas
1600 Lisbon
Telephone: 351-1-727-3300
Fax: 351-1-726-9109

U.S. Consulate
Avenida D. Henrique
Ponta Delgada, Sao Miguel
Azores
Telephone: 351-96-22216
Fax: 351-96-27216

Qatar
U.S. Embassy
Fariq Bin Omran
Doha
Telephone: 974-864701
Fax: 974-861669

Romania
U.S. Embassy
Strada Tudor Argheze 7-9
Bucharest
Telephone: 40-1-210-4042
Fax: 40-1-210-0395

Russia
(New embassies for former Soviet states will be opening soon)
U.S. Embassy
Novinskiy Bul'var 19/23
Moscow
Telephone: 7-095-252-2451
Fax 7-095-956-4261

U.S. Consulate
Ulitsa
Petra Lavrova St. 15
St. Petersburg
Telephone: 7-812-275-1701
Fax: 7-812-110-7022

Rwanda
U.S. Embassy
Blvd de la Revolution
B.P. 28
Kigali
Telephone: 301-985-9339
Fax: 301-250-72128

Saudi Arabia
U.S. Embassy
Collector Road M
Riyadh Diplomatic Quarter
Riyadh
Telephone: 966-1-488-3800
Fax: 966-1-488-3989

U.S. Consulate
Between Aramco Hqrs & Dhahran Int'l Airport
Dharhran
Telephone: 966-3-891-3200
Fax: 933-3-891-6816

U.S. Consulate
Palestine Rd.
Ruwais
Jeddah
Telephone: 966-2-667-0080
Fax: 966-2-669-2991

Senegal
U.S. Embassy
B.P. 49
Avenue Jean XXIII
Dakar
Telephone: 221-23-42-96
Fax: 221-22-29-91

Serbia–Montenegro
U.S. Embassy
Belgrade
Telephone: 381-11-645-655
Fax: 381-11-645-332

Seychelles
(See Mauritius)

Sierra Leone
U.S. Embassy
Walpole & Siaka Stevens Sts.
Freetown
Telephone: 232-22-226-481
Fax: 232-22-225-471

Singapore
U.S. Embassy
30 Hill Street
Singapore 0617
Telephone: 65-338-0251
Fax: 65-338-4550

Slovak Republic
U.S. Embassy
Hviezdoslavovo Namestie 4
81102 Bratislava
Telephone: 421-7-533-3338
Fax: 421-7-533-5439

Slovenia
U.S. Embassy
Box 254
Prazakova 4
1000 Ljubljana
Telephone: 386-61-301-427
Fax: 386-61-301-401

South Africa
U.S. Consulate
Broadway Industries Center
Heerengracht, Foreshore
Cape Town
Telephone: 27-21-21-4280
Fax: 27-21-25-3014

U.S. Consulate
Durban Bay House, 29th Floor
333 Smith Street
Durban 4001
Telephone: 27-31-304-4737
Fax: 27-31-301-8206

U.S. Consulate
11th Floor, Kine Center
Commissioner & Krulis Streets
Johannesburg
Telephone: 27-11-331-1681
Fax: 27-11-331-6178

U.S. Consulate
877 Pretorius St.
Arcadia 0083
Pretoria
Telephone: 27-12-342-1048
Fax: 27-12-342-2244

South Korea
(See Korea)

Spain
U.S.Embassy
Serrano 75
Madrid
Telephone: 34-1-587-2200
Fax: 34-1-587-2303

U.S. Consulate
Reina Elisenda 23
Barcelona 08034
Telephone: 34-3-280-2227
Fax: 34-3-205-7764

Sri La
U.S. ssy
210 Galle Rd.
Colombo 3
Telephone: 94-1-448007
Fax: 94-1-437-345

Sudan
U.S. Embassy
Sharia Ali Abdul Latif
Khartoum
Telephone: 249-11-774461
Fax: 249-11-873-151-6770

Suriname
U.S. Embassy
Dr. Sophie Redmondstraat 129
Paramaribo
Telephone: 472900
Fax: 42800

Swaziland
U.S. Embassy
Central Bank Buiding
P.O. Box 199, Warner Street
Mbabane
Telephone: 268-46441
Fax: 268-45959

Sweden
U.S. Embassy
Strandvagen 101
Stockholm
Telephone: 46-8-783-5300
Fax: 46-8-661-1964

Switzerland
U.S. Embassy
Jubilaeumstrasse 93
3005 Bern
Telephone: 41-31-357-7011
Fax: 41-31-357-7344

U.S. Consulate
11, Route de Pregny
1292 Chambesy
Geneva
Telephone: 41-22-749-4111
Fax: 41-22-749-4880

Syria
U.S. Embassy
Abu Rumaneh
Al Mansur St. No. 2
Damascus
Telephone: 963-11-333-2814
Fax: 963-11-224-7938

Tajikistan
U.S. Embassy
Octyabrskaya Hotel
105A Prospect Rudaki
Dushanbe, Tajikistan 734001
Telephone: 7-3772-21-03-56
Fax: 7-3772-20-03-62

Tanzania
U.S. Embassy
36 Laibon Rd.
Dar es Salaam
Telephone: 255-51-666010
Fax: 255-51-666701

Thailand
U.S. Embassy
95 Wireless Rd.
Bangkok
Telephone: 66-2-205-4000
Fax: 66-2-255-2915

U.S. Consulate
Vidhayanond Rd.
Chiang Mai
Telephone: 66-53-252-629
Fax: 66-53-252-633

Togo
U.S. Embassy
Rue Pelletier Caventou & Rue Vouban
Lome
Telephone: 228-21-77-17
Fax: 228-21-79-52

Trinidad and Tobago
U.S. Embassy
15 Queens Park West
Port of Spain
Telephone: 809-622-6372
Fax: 809-628-5462

Tunisia
U.S. Embassy
144 Ave. de la Liberte
Tunis
Telephone: 216-1-782-566
Fax: 216-1-789-719

Turkey
U.S. Embassy
110 Ataturk Blvd.
Ankara
Telephone: 90-312-468-6110
Fax: 90-312-467-0019

U.S. Consulate
Ataturk Caddesi
Adana
Telephone: 90-322-454-2145
Fax: 90-322-457-6591

U.S. Consulate
104-108 Mesrutiyet Cadesi
Tepebasi
Istanbul
Telephone: 90-212-251-3602
Fax: 90-212-251-2554

Turkmenistan
U.S. Embassy
9 Pushkin Street
Ashgabat
Telephone: 9-9312-35-00-45
Fax: 9-9312-51-13-05

Uganda
U.S. Embassy
Parliament Avenue
Kampala
Telephone: 256-41-259792
Fax: 256-41-259794

Ukraine
U.S. Embassy
10 Yuria Kotsubynskoho
254053 Kiev
Telephone: 380-44-244-7345
Fax: 380-44-244-7350

United Arab Emirates
U.S. Embassy
Al-Sudan St.
Abu Dhabi
Telephone: 971-2-436-691
Fax: 971-2-434-771

U.S.Consulate
Dubai International Trade Ctr
Dubai
Telephone: 971-2-314-043
Fax: 971-2-434-771

United Kingdom
U.S. Embassy
24/31 Grosvenor Square
London, W1A 1AE
Telephone: 44-171-499-9000
Fax: 44-171-409-1637

U.S. Consulate
Queen's House
14 Queen Street
Belfast, Northern Ireland
Telephone: 44-1232-241279
Fax: 44-1232-248482

Uruguay
U.S. Embassy
Lauro Muller 1776
Montevideo
Telephone: 598-2-23-60-61
Fax: 592-2-48-86-11

Uzbekistan
U.S. Embassy
82 Chilanzarskaya
Tashkent
Telephone: 7-3712-77-14-07
Fax: 7-3712-40-63-35

Venezuela
U.S. Embassy
Colle F con Calle Suapure
Colinas de Valle Arriba
Caracas
Telephone: 58-2-977-2011
Fax: 58-2-977-3253

Vietnam
U.S. Embassy
7 Lang Ha Road
Ba Dinh District
Hanoi
Telephone: 84-4-843-1500
Fax: 84-4-835-0484

Western Samoa
U.S. Embassy
P.O. Box 3430
Apia
Telephone: 685-21-631
Fax: 685-22-030

Yemen–Republic of
U.S. Embassy
Dhahr Himyar Zone
Sheraton Hotel District
Sanaa
Telephone: 967-1-238-843
Fax:967-1- 251-563

Zaire
(See Congo, Democratic Republic of the)

Zambia
U.S. Embassy
Independence & United Nations Avenues
Lusaka
Telephone: 260-1-250-955
Fax: 260-1-252-225

Zimbabwe
U.S. Embassy
172 Herbert Chitepo Ave.
Harare
Telephone: 263-4-794-521
Fax: 263-4-796-488

Appendix B

Directory of INS Offices

INS Central Office

Immigration & Naturalization Service
Justice Department
425 Eye St. N.W.
Washington, D.C. 20536
Information: 202-514-2648
Form Requests: 800-870-3676
Fax: 202-514-3296

INS Regional Offices

California Service Center
Immigration & Naturalization Service
24000 Avila Road
P.O. Box 30080
Laguna Niguel, CA 92677-8080
Telephone: 714-306-2995
Fax: 714-306-3081

Nebraska Service Center
Immigration & Naturalization Service
850 S Street
Lincoln, NE 68508
Telephone: 402-437-5218

Texas Service Center
Immigration & Naturalization Service
Room 2300
7701 N. Stemmons Freeway
Dallas, TX 75247
Telephone: 214-767-7020
Fax: 214-767-7477

Vermont Service Center
Immigration & Naturalization Service
70 Kimball Ave.
South Burlington, VT 05403-6813
Telephone: 802-660-5000
Fax: 802-660-5114

INS District Offices

Anchorage, Alaska
620 E. 10th Avenue
Suite 102
Anchorage, AK
907-271-3524

Atlanta, Georgia
77 Forsythe Street, SW
Room G-85
Atlanta, GA 30303
404-331-0253

Baltimore, Maryland
100 S. Charles St.
Baltimore, MD 21201
410-962-2010

Boston, Massachusetts
John F. Kennedy Federal Bldg.
Government Center, Room 700
Boston, MA 02203
617-565-4214

Buffalo, New York
130 Federal Center
Buffalo, NY 14202
716-651-4741

Chicago, Illinois
10 W. Jackson Blvd.
Chicago, IL 60604
312-886-6770

Cleveland, Ohio
1240 E. 9th St., Room 1917
Cleveland, OH 44199
216-522-4766

Dallas, Texas
8101 N. Stemmons Freeway
Dallas, TX 75247
214-655-3011

Denver, Colorado
4730 Paris Street
Denver, CO 80209
303-371-0986

Detroit, Michigan
333 Mount Elliott St.
Detroit, MI 48207
313-586-6000

El Paso, Texas
1545 Hawkins Blvd., Suite 167
El Paso, TX 79901
915-540-7341

Harlingen, Texas
2102 Teege Road
Harlingen, TX 78550
210-427-8592

Helena, Montana
2800 Skyway Drive
Helena, MT 59601
406-449-5220

Honolulu, Hawaii
595 Ala Moana Blvd.
Honolulu, HI 96813
808-449-5220

Houston, Texas
509 N. Belt Drive
Houston, TX 77060
713-847-7950

Kansas City, Missouri
9747 North Conant Ave.
Kansas City, MO 64153
816-891-0684

Los Angeles, California
300 N. Los Angeles Street
Los Angeles, CA 90012
213-894-2780

Miami, Florida
7880 Biscayne Blvd.
Miami, FL 33138
305-530-7657

New Orleans, Louisiana
701 Loyola Avenue
Room T-8005
New Orleans, LA 70113
504-589-6521

New York, New York
Jacob K. Javits Federal Building
26 Federal Plaza
New York, NY 10278
212-206-6500

Newark, New Jersey
Federal Building
970 Broad Street
Newark, NJ 07102
201-645-2269

Omaha, Nebraska
3736 S. 132nd Street
Omaha, NE 68144
402-697-9155

Philadelphia, Pennsylvania
1600 Caldwell St.
Philadelphia, PA 19130
215-656-7150

Phoenix, Arizona
2035 N. Central Ave.
Phoenix, AZ 85004
602-379-3114

Portland, Maine
739 Warren Avenue
Portland, ME 04103
207-780-3399

Portland, Oregon
Federal Building
511 N.W. Broadway
Portland, OR 97209
503-326-3962

St. Paul, Minnesota
2901 Metro Drive
Bloomington, MN 55425
612-335-2211

San Antonio, Texas
727 E. Durango
San Antonio, TX 78206
210-871-7000

San Diego, California
880 Front Street
San Diego, CA 92188
619-557-5645

San Francisco, California
Appraisers Building
630 Sansome Street
San Francisco, CA 94111
415-705-4411

San Juan, Puerto Rico
Carlos E. Chardon Street
Room 359
Hato Rey, PR 00918
809-766-5380

Seattle, Washington
815 Airport Way South
Seattle, WA 98134
206-553-0070

Washington, D.C.
4420 N. Fairfax Drive
Arlington, VA 22003
203-307-1642

Appendix C

Regional Department of Labor Offices

Region	States
Atlanta 100 Alabama St. SW Suite 6M12 Atlanta, GA 30367 Tel: 404-562-2092 Fax: 404-562-2149	Alabama, Florida, Georgia, Kentucky, Mississippi, North Carolina, South Carolina, Tennessee
Boston JFK Federal Building Room E-350 Boston, MA 02203 Tel: 617-565-3630 Fax: 617-565-2229	Connecticut, Maine, Massachusetts, New Hampshire, Rhode Island, Vermont
Chicago 230 South Dearborn St. 6th Floor Chicago, IL 60604 Tel: 312-353-1053 Fax: 312-353-4474	llinois, Indiana, Michigan, Minnesota, Ohio, Wisconsin
Dallas 525 Griffin Street Room 317 Dallas, TX 75202 Tel: 214-767-8263 Fax: 214-767-5113	Arkansas, Louisiana, New Mexico, Oklahoma, Texas
Denver 1999 Broadway Suite 1780 Denver, CO 80202 Tel: 303-844-1650 Fax: 303-844-1685	Colorado, Montana, North Dakota, South Dakota, Utah, Wyoming
Kansas City 1100 Main St., Suite 1050 City Center Square Kansas City, MO 64106 Tel 816-426-3796 Fax: 816-426-2929	Iowa, Kansas, Missouri, Nebraska
New York 201 Varick Street Room 755 New York, NY 10014 Tel: 212-337-2185 Fax: 212-337-2144	New York, New Jersey, Puerto Rico, Virgin Islands
Philadelphia 3535 Market St. Philadelphia, PA 19101 Tel: 215-596-6363 Alien Certification Fax: 215-596-0480 Administrator Fax: 215-596-0329	Delaware, District of Columbia, Maryland, Pennsylvania, Virginia, West Virginia
San Francisco P.O. Box 193767 San Francisco, CA 94119-3767 Tel: 415-975-4610 Fax: 415-975-4612	Arizona, California, Guam, Hawaii, Nevada
Seattle 1111 Third Avenue Suite 900 Seattle, WA 98101 Tel: 206-553-7700 Fax: 206-553-0098	Alaska, Idaho, Oregon, Washington

APPENDIX D

Glossary Of Terms & Some Relevant Definitions

ACCOMPANYING OR FOLLOWING TO JOIN: Immediate family members who travel to the U.S. with the principal alien, or who arrive in the U.S. after the principal alien. Does not include those who come to the U.S. before the principal alien.

ADMITTED: An alien who has been inspected and allowed to enter the U.S. in an Immigrant or non-Immigrant status.

ADJUSTMENT OF STATUS: The procedure for changing an alien's non-Immigrant status to an Immigrant status while in the U.S. (see Chapter 20 of text)

ADVISORY OPINION: A procedure which allows the Visa Office in Washington, D.C. (part of the U.S. State Department) to review the decision of a U.S. Consul. A Consul is generally not obligated to change the decision even after an Advisory Opinion is issued.

ALIEN: A person who is NOT a citizen or national of the U.S. (Chapter 2, Section A the text).

APPEAL: A procedure allowed in certain cases for a superior person or board to review the decision and papers in a case. After review, the person or board can return the papers for further action, allow the original decision to stand, change the decision in whole or in part.

ATTORNEY: A lawyer admitted to practice law in any jurisdiction in the United States.

BOARD OF IMMIGRATION APPEALS: The part of the U.S. Justice Department responsible for review of decisions on Preference Petitions and for certain other appeals from decisions or actions of the Immigration and Naturalization Service.

BRIEF. The paper or letter accompanying an appeal or motion which contains the facts or rebuttal.

BUSINESS NECESSITY: A justification for requiring a Combination of Duties, foreign language requirement, or other special requirement not found in the Dictionary of Occupational Titles. Business Necessity arises when the absence of the requirement would tend to undermine the business. Business Necessity can also refer to a situation in a private household when a Live-in requirement for a domestic worker is essential to the household.

CERTIFYING OFFICER: The employee of the U.S. Labor Department responsible for issuing the Labor Certificate and for affixing the Certification Stamp to the Application Form.)

DICTIONARY OF OCCUPATIONAL TITLES: A publication of the U.S. Government listing job titles and descriptions. It is used as a guide by the local Employment Service offices and the U.S. Department of Labor. It is available for examination in many public libraries and government agencies. The Dictionary is for sale by the Superintendent of Documents in Washington,
D.C., and in U.S. Government Book Stores in larger U.S. cities.

EXCEPTIONAL ABILITY: (See discussion in text at Chapter 14)

EXCLUDABLE: An excludable alien is barred from entering the U.S. Some excludable aliens are barred permanently; others may enter after receiving a waiver. (See discussion in Chap. 22 and 24 of text)

GREEN CARD: A card identifying the holder as being registered as a Permanent Resident of the U.S. The color of the card is no longer green, but the name has remained. The Green Card is officially a Form 1-551

"Alien Registration Receipt."

IMMEDIATE FAMILY: An alien's spouse and children. The spouse must be the legal spouse. The children must be under 21 years of age, unmarried, and be considered legitimate by the Immigration Service or U.S Consul.

IMMIGRANT: An alien who intends to remain in the U.S. permanently or for an indefinite time.

IMMIGRANT VISA: The type of Visa issued to persons who are qualified for U.S. Permanent Residence.

IMMIGRATION AND NATURALIZATION SERVICE (INS): A part of the U.S. Department of Justice responsible for implementing and enforcing most of the immigration laws.

IMMIGRATION SERVICE: See Immigration and Naturalization Service.

INS: See Immigration and Naturalization Service.

INSPECTION: The procedure which occurs when an alien is questioned (or allowed to pass without questioning) by an Officer of the U.S. Immigration Service at a port of entry. No "Inspection" occurs if the alien falsely claims to be a U.S. Citizen or evades a proper examination.

LABOR CERTIFICATE: Issued by the U.S. Department of Labor after it finds that U.S. workers will not be adversely affected if an alien fills a particular job. The finding is shown by the placement of a special stamp upon the application form. The stamp contains the words of the Certificate and the Signature of the Certifying Officer. (See Chap. 23 of text)

LIVE-IN JOB: A job which requires the employee to live on the employer's premises as a condition of employment.

LOCAL EMPLOYMENT SERVICE OFFICE: The unit responsible for the initial receipt and processing of applications for Labor Certificates except for Schedule A Occupations. These offices are part of a State or other non-Federal employment service (except in Washington, D.C.). It is distinct (separate) from the U.S. Department of Labor but acts as a preprocessor of Labor Certificate applications on behalf of the U.S. Department of Labor. (See Chapter 23 of text)

MOTION: A written request made to a government agency as part of an application procedure.

NON-IMMIGRANT: An alien on a temporary visit or stay who intends to depart from the U.S. after completing the purpose of his trip of limited duration.

NOTICE OF FINDING: (See discussion in text at p.)

NUMERICAL, LIMITATION: (See Chap. 5 of text)

PAROLE: A status granted by the Immigration Service to an alien who has been inspected and who is allowed to enter the U.S. for a particular purpose even though the alien lacks required documents or visa. For an example, parole status may be granted by the Immigration Service at the port of entry to allow an alien to apply for political asylum, or to testify at a judicial proceeding, or receive necessary medical treatment. It may also be granted to allow an alien to complete a pending Adjustment of Status application upon his return to the U.S. if the alien had been given Advance Parole before departing.

PETITION: A form used to apply for a preference under the immigration law. Refers to the Form I- 140, Petition for First, Second and Third Preferences, or Form I-130 for family-based petitions.

PREFERENCE: One of the categories in which an alien may qualify for an Immigrant Visa (Permanent Residence).

PREFERENCE DATE: The date which determines an alien's place on the list for a Preference. (See discussion in Chapter 5 of text).

PRINCIPAL ALIEN: An alien who has qualified for U.S. Permanent Residence directly and not derivatively. As an example, the alien who has an approved Labor Certificate and an approved Preference Petition is the "principal alien", while his or her spouse and minor unmarried children are not principal aliens but obtain their right to the Immigrant (Resident) Visa only derivatively. The derivative aliens are usually those who will

accompany, or follow to join, the Principal Alien.
PRIORITY DATE: See Preference Date.
REBUTTAL: The written response to a Notice of Finding by the U.S. Labor Department. (See discussion in Chapter 23, Section E of text)
RECONSIDERATION: The procedure for having the papers in a case re-examined by the appropriate government agency so that a more favorable decision will be made.
REOPENING: The procedure which allows additional facts or papers to be added to the record of a case.
REGIONAL OFFICE: An office of the Employment and Training Administration of the U.S. Department of Labor responsible for final processing and issuing regular Labor Certificates. The Certifying Officer is an employee in the Regional Office. There are several Regional Offices in the U.S.
REGULAR LABOR CERTIFICATE: A Labor Certificate for a job *not* on Schedule A (see Chapter 23 of text)
SCHEDULE A. A list of occupations for which an alien employee need not receive a Labor Certificate. (See Section A of Chapter 23)
SCHEDULE B: A list of occupations for which an alien employee cannot receive a Labor Certificate unless with a waiver.
TRWOV or TWOV: *T*Ransit *W*ith*O*ut Visa. Refers to an alien who is allowed to enter the U.S. without a visa while in transit between airplane flights or between ships.
U.S.: United States.
U.S. CONSUL: An employee of the U.S. State Department posted at a Consulate or Embassy of the U.S. abroad, responsible for approving and issuing Immigrant or non-Immigrant Visas.
U.S. DEPARTMENT OF LABOR: Refers to the section of the U.S. Labor Department responsible for processing and issuing Labor Certificates. It is part of the Labor Department's Employment and Training Administration.
U.S. EMPLOYER: Any person with a U.S. location authorized to offer a job to an alien for Labor Certificate purposes. Can be an individual, corporation, or other legal person. Does not include an alien temporarily in the U.S. even though authorized to work.
U.S. WORKER: A person who is authorized to work in the U.S. including U.S. citizens and U.S. permanent residents. Does not include an alien temporarily in the U.S. even though authorized to work.
VISA APPOINTMENT: The procedure which occurs when an applicant for U.S. immigrant (residence) status appears before a U.S. Consul abroad to allow the Consul to determine if the alien is qualified for an Immigrant Visa.
VISA BULLETIN: A publication issued by the U.S. State Department which gives the status of the Immigrant Visa priority dates. (See Chap 5 of text)
WAIVER: Special permission issued by a U.S. government agency to allow an alien to receive a privilege or benefit that the alien could not otherwise have received. For example, a Labor Certificate cannot be issued for a job on Schedule B without special permission (a waiver) from the Labor Department. Some excludable aliens can be admitted to the U.S. but only if they receive a waiver.

Appendix E

Sample Immigration Forms Listed In The Manual (Where To Find Them)

(Forms are listed in their numerical order)

Number/Name of Form — **Page Where Found**

Other Forms or Special Documents Listed In The Manual

U.S. Department of Justice
Immigration and Naturalization Service
Please Read Instructions on Page 2

Certificate of Eligibility for Nonimmigrant (F-1) Student Status - For Academic and Language Students

OMB No. 1115-0051

Form 1-20A-B Page 1

This page must be completed and signed in the U.S. by a designated school official.

1. Family Name (surname)

First (given) name (do not enter middle name)

Country of birth	Date of birth (mo./day/year)
Country of citizenship	Admission number (Complete if known)

2. School (school district) name

School official to be notified of student's arrival in U.S. (Name and Title)

School address (include zip code)

School code (including 3-digit suffix, if any) and approval date
______________ 214F ______________ approved on ______________

For Immigration Official Use

Visa issuing post	Date Visa issued

Reinstated, extension granted to:

3. This certificate is issued to the student named above for:
(Check and fill out as appropriate)
a. ☐ Initial attendance at this school.
b. ☐ Continued attendance at this school.
c. ☐ School transfer.
Transferred from ______________.
d. ☐ Use by dependents for entering the United States.
e. ☐ Other ______________.

4. Level of education the student is pursuing or will pursue in the United States: (check only one)
a. ☐ Primary
b. ☐ Secondary
c. ☐ Associate
d. ☐ Bachelor's
e. ☐ Master's
f. ☐ Doctorate
g. ☐ Language training
h. ☐ Other

5. The student named above has been accepted for a full course of study at this school, majoring in ______________.
The student is expected to report to the school not later than (date) ______________ and complete studies not later than (date) ______________
The normal length of study is ______________.

6. ☐ English proficiency is required:
☐ The student has the required English proficiency.
☐ The student is not yet proficient, English instructions will be given at the school.
☐ English proficiency is not required because ______________
____

7. This school estimates the student's average costs for an academic term of _______ (up to 12) months to be:
a. Tuition and fees $ ______________
b. Living expenses $ ______________
c. Expenses of dependents $ ______________
d. Other (specify): $ ______________
Total $ ______________

8. This school has information showing the following as the student's means of support, estimated for an academic term of _____ months (Use the same number of months given in item 7).
a. Student's personal funds $ ______________
b. Funds from this school $ ______________
(specify type) ______________
c. Funds from another source $ ______________
(specify type and source) ______________
d. On-campus employment (if any) $ ______________
Total $ ______________

9. Remarks: ______________

10. School Certification I certify under penalty of perjury that all information provided above in items 1 through 8 was completed before I signed this form and is true and correct, I executed this form in the United States after review and evaluation in the United States by me or other officials of the school of the student's application, transcripts or other records of courses taken and proof of financial responsibility, which were received at the school prior to the execution of this form; the school has determined that the above named student's qualifications meet all standards for admission to the school; the student will be required to pursue a full course of study as defined by 8 CFR 214.2(f)(6); I am a designated official of the above named school and I am authorized to issue this form.

Signature of designated school offical | Name of school offical (print or type) | Title | Date issued | Place issued (city and state)

11. Student Certification I have read and agreed to comply with the terms and conditions of my admission and those of any extension of stay as specified on page 2. I certify that all information provided on this form refers specifically to me and is true and correct to the best of my knowledge. I certify that I seek to enter or remain in the United States temporarily, and solely for the purpose of pursuing a full course of study at the school named on Page 1 of this form. I also authorize the named school to release any information from my records which is needed by the INS pursuant to 8 CFR 214.3(g) to determine my nonimmigrant status

Signature of student | Name of student | Date

Signature of parent or guardian if student is under 18 | Name of parent/guardian (Print or type) | Address(city) | (State or province) | (Country) | (Date)

Form I-20 A-BA-20ID (Rev 04-27-88)N

For official use only
Microfilm Index Number

I-20 SCHOOL

Authority for collecting the information on this and related student forms is contained in 8 U.S.C. 1101 and 1184. The information solicited will be used by the Department of State and the Immigration and Naturalization Service to determine eligibility for the benefits requested.

INSTRUCTIONS TO DESIGNATED SCHOOL OFFICIALS

1. **The law provides severe penalties for knowingly and willfully falsifying or concealing a material fact, or using any false document in the submission of this form.** Designated school officials should consult regulations pertaining to the issuance of Form I-20 A-B at 8 CFR 214.3 (K) before completing this form. Failure to comply with these regulations may result in the withdrawal of the school approval for attendance by foreign students by the Immigration and Naturalization Service (8 CFR 214.4).

2. **ISSUANCE OF FORM I-20 A-B.** Designated school officials may issue a Form I-20 A-B to a student who fits into one of the following categories, if the student has been accepted for full-time attendance at the institution: a) a prospective F-1 nonimmigrant student; b) an F-1 transfer student; c) an F-1 student advancing to a higher educational level at the same institution; d) an out of status student seeking reinstatement. The form may also be issued to the dependent spouse or child of an F-1 student for securing entry into the United States.

When issuing a Form I-20 A-B, designated school officials should complete the student's admission number whenever possible to ensure proper data entry and record keeping.

3. **ENDORSEMENT OF PAGE 4 FOR REENTRY.** Designated school officials may endorse page 4 of the Form I-20 A-B for reentry if the student and/or the F-2 dependents is to leave the United States temporarily. This should be done only when the information on the Form I-20 remains unchanged. If there have been substantial changes in item 4, 5, 7, or 8, a new Form I-20 A-B should be issued.

4 **REPORTING REQUIREMENT.** Designated school official should always forward the top page of the Form I-20 A-B to the INS data processing center at P.O. Box 140, London, Kentucky 40741 for data entry except when the form is issued to an F-1 student for initial entry or reentry into the United States, or for reinstatement to student status. (Requests for reinstatement should be sent to the Immigration and Naturalization Service district office having jurisdiction over the student's temporary residence in this country.)

The INS data processing center will return this top page to the issuing school for disposal after data entry and microfilming.

5. **CERTIFICATION.** Designated school officials should certify on the bottom part of page 1 of this form that the Form I-20 A-B is completed and issued in accordance with the pertinent regulations. The designated school official should remove the carbon sheet from the completed and signed Form I-20 A-B before forwarding it to the student.

6. **ADMISSION RECORDS.** Since the Immigration and Naturalization Service may request information concerning the student's immigration status for various reasons, designated school officials should retain all evidence which shows the scholastic ability and financial status on which admission was based, until the school has reported the student's termination of studies to the Immigration and Naturalization Service.

INSTRUCTIONS TO STUDENTS

1. **Student Certification.** You should read everything on this page carefully and be sure that you understand the terms and conditions concerning your admission and stay in the United States as a nonimmigrant student before you sign the student certification on the bottom part of page 1. **The law provides severe penalties for knowingly and willfully falsifying or concealing a material fact, or using any false document in the submission of this form.**

2. **ADMISSION.** A nonimmigrant student may be admitted for duration of status. This means that you are authorized to stay in the United States for the entire length of time during which you are enrolled as a full-time student in an educational program and any period of authorized practical training plus sixty days. While in the United States, you must maintain a valid foreign passport unless you are exempt from passport requirements.

You may continue from one educational level to another, such as progressing from high school to a bachelor's program or a bachelor's program to a master's program, etc., simply by invoking the procedures for school transfers

3.**SCHOOL.** For initial admission, you must attend the school specified on your visa. If you have a Form I-20 A-B from more than one school, it is important to have the name of the school you intend to attend specified on your visa by presenting a Form I-20 A-B from that school to the visa issuing consular officer. Failure to attend the specified school will result in the loss of your student status and subject you to deportation.

4. **REENTRY.** A nonimmigrant student may be readmitted after a temporary absence of five months or less from the United States, if the student is otherwise admissible. You may be readmitted by presenting a valid foreign passport, a valid visa, and either a new Form I-20 A-B or a page 4 of the Form I-20 A-B (the I-20 ID Copy) properly endorsed for reentry if the information on the I-20 form is current.

5. **TRANSFER.** A nonimmigrant student is permitted to transfer to a different school provided the transfer procedure is followed. To transfer school, you should first notify the school you are attending of the intent to transfer, then obtain a Form I-20 A-B from the school you intend to attend. Transfer will be effected only if you return the Form I-20 A-B to the designated school official within 15 days of beginning attendance at the new school. The designated school official will then report the transfer to the Immigration and Naturalization Service.

6. **EXTENSION OF STAY.** If you cannot complete the educational program after having been in student status for longer than the anticipated length of the program plus a grace period in a single educational level, or for more than eight consecutive years, you must apply for extension of stay. An application for extension of stay on a Form I-538 should be filed with the Immigration and Naturalization Service district office having jurisdiction over your school at least 15 days but no more than 60 days before the expiration of your authorized stay.

7. **EMPLOYMENT.** As an F-1 student, you are not permitted to work off-campus or to engage in business without specific employment authorization. After your first year in F-1 student status, you may apply for employment authorization on Form I-538 based on financial needs arising after receiving student status, or the need to obtain practical training.

8. **Notice of Address.** If you move, you must submit a notice within 10 days of the change of address to the Immigration and Naturalization Service. (Form AR-11 is available at any INS office.)

9. **Arrival/Departure.** When you leave the United States, you must surrender your Form I-94 Departure Record. Please see the back side of Form I-94 for detailed instructions. You do not have to turn in the I-94 if you are visiting Canada, Mexico, or adjacent islands other than Cuba for less than 30 days.

10. **Financial Support.** You must demonstrate that you are financially able to support yourself for the entire period of stay in the United States while pursuing a full course of study. You are required to attach documentary evidence of means of support.

11. **Authorization to Release Information by School.** To comply with requests from the United States Immigration & Naturalization Service for information concerning your immigration status, you are required to give authorization to the named school to release such information from your records. The school will provide the Service your name, country of birth, current address, and any other information on a regular basis or upon request

12. **Penalty.** To maintain your nonimmigrant student status, you must be enrolled as a full-time student at the school you are authorized to attend. You may engage in employment only when you have received permission to work. Failure to comply with these regulations will result in the loss of your student status and subject you to deportation.

Form 1-20A

FORM I-20A

Page 3

CERTIFICATE BY NONIMMIGRANT STUDENT UNDER SECTION 101 (a) (15) (F) (i) OF THE IMMIGRATION AND NATIONALITY ACT

1. I seek to enter or remain in the United States temporarily and solely for the purpose of pursuing a full course of study at the school named on page 1 of this form.

2. Please print name in full	3. My maximum anticipated stay is (Months)
4. My educational objective is	
5. I am financially able to support myself for the entire period of my stay in the United States while pursuing a full course of study. (State source and amount of support:) (Documentary evidence of means of actual support must be attached to this form)	
6. I last attended (Name of School) (City) (State) (Country)	
7. My major field of studies was	8. I completed such studies on (Date)
9. The person most closely related to me who lives outside the United States is: (Name) (Relationship) (Address)	
10. The person most closely related to me who lives in the United States is: (If you have no relative in the United States, give the name of a friend.) (Name) (Relationship) (Address)	

To Be completed by the student.

11. I understand the following:

a. A nonimmigrant student applying for admission to the United States for the first time after being issued an F-1 (student's) visa, will not be admitted unless he intends to attend the school specified in that visa. Therefore, if before he departs for the United States the student decides to attend some other school, he should communicate with the issuing American consular office for the purpose of having such other school specified in the visa. Any other nonimmigrant student will not be admitted to the United States unless he intends to attend the school specified in the Form I-20 or Form I-94 which he presents to the immigration officer at the port of entry.

b. A nonimmigrant student is not permitted to work off-campus for a wage or salary or engage in business while in the United States unless permission to do so has first been granted by the Immigration and Naturalization Service. A student who requires employment (1) because of economic necessity due to unforeseen circumstances arising after admission, or (2) to obtain practical training, may apply to the Immigration and Naturalization Service on Form I-538 for permission to accept such employment. Additional information concerning employment is set forth in Form I-538. The alien spouse or child accompanying or following to join a nonimmigrant student is not permitted to work in the United States.

c. A nonimmigrant student is permitted to remain in the United States only while maintaining nonimmigrant student status, and in any event not longer than the period fixed at the time of admission (or change to student classification) unless he applies to the Immigration and Naturalization Service on Form I-538 in accordance with the instructions on that form between 15 and 30 days prior to the expiration of the period of his authorized stay and obtains an extension of his stay.

d. Each year, every nonimmigrant student in the United States on the first day of January must submit by the 31st of January a written notice of his address to the Immigration and Naturalization Service. In addition, a notice must be sent within 10 days after every change of address. Regardless of whether he moves, each nonimmigrant student is required to file written notice of his address every 3 months. Printed forms obtainable at the United States immigration office or post office should be used in making the annual address report, the change of address report, and the 3-month address report.

e. At the time a nonimmigrant student departs from the United States, his temporary entry permit (Form I-94) is to be surrendered to a representative of the steamship or airline if he leaves via a seaport or airport, to a Canadian immigration officer if he leaves across the Canadian border, or to a United States immigration officer if he leaves across the Mexican border.

f. A nonimmigrant student may remain in the United States temporarily only for the purpose of pursuing a full course of study at a specified school. If, after being admitted, the student desires to transfer to another school, he must make written application on Form I-538 for permission to make such a transfer. The application must be submitted to the office of the Immigration and Naturalization Service having jurisdiction over the area in which the school from which he wishes to transfer is located. The application must be accompanied by Form I-20 completed by the school to which he wishes to transfer. He may not transfer until his application is approved. The application will be denied if the student failed to actually take a full course of study at the school he was last authorized by the Service to attend, unless he establishes that his failure to do so was due to circumstances beyond his control or was otherwise justified.

g. A student who seeks to re-enter the United States as a nonimmigrant student after a temporary absence must be in possession of the following documents: (i) A valid unexpired student visa (unless exempt from visa requirements), (ii) A passport valid for six months beyond the period of readmission (unless exempt from passport requirements); (iii) A current copy of Form I-20 (A and B). However, only the "A" copy of Form I-20 is required in the case of a nonimmigrant student returning from temporary absence outside the United States to continue attendance at the same school which the Immigration and Naturalization Service last authorized him to attend, in such case, Form I-20A may be retained by the student and used by him for any number of reentries within twelve months from the date of issuance, the certificate on page 2 of Form I-20A need not be completed, and Form I-20B should be destroyed.

h. A nonimmigrant student who does not register at the school specified in his temporary entry permit (Form I-94), or whose school attendance is terminated, or who takes less than a full course of study, or who accepts unauthorized employment, thereby fails to maintain his status and must depart from the United States immediately.

I CERTIFY THAT THE ABOVE IS CORRECT. I hereby agree to comply with the above and any other terms and conditions of my admission and any extension of stay. I hereby authorize the named school and any school to which I may subsequently transfer to release to the Immigration and Naturalization Service any information from my education records which the Service needs to know in order to determine if I am maintaining the lawful nonimmigrant status in which I was admitted to the United States under the immigration law. More specifically, I authorize the school to report, in writing, to the Immigration and Naturalization Service if I fail to register within 60 days of the time expected, if I fail to carry a full course of study, if I fail to attend classes to the extent normally required, if I am failing courses, if I become employed or if I terminate attendance at the named school and to provide the Service upon demand with my latest address.

SAMPLE SHEET

Signature of Student	Address (City)	(State or Province)	(Country)		(Date)
X					
(Signature of Parent or Guardian if Student is Under 18 Years of Age)			(Address)	(Relationship)	(Date)

To Be completed by the student.

IF YOU NEED MORE INFORMATION CONCERNING YOUR F-1 NONIMMIGRANT STUDENT STATUS AND THE RELATING IMMIGRATION PROCEDURES, PLEASE CONTACT EITHER YOUR FOREIGN STUDENT ADVISOR ON CAMPUS OR A NEARBY IMMIGRATION AND NATURALIZATION SERVICE OFFICE.

THIS PAGE, WHEN PROPERLY ENDORSED, MAY BE USED FOR ENTRY OF THE SPOUSE AND CHILDREN OF AN F-1 STUDENT FOLLOWING TO JOIN THE STUDENT IN THE UNITED STATES OR FOR REENTRY OF THE STUDENT TO ATTEND THE SAME SCHOOL AFTER A TEMPORARY ABSENCE FROM THE UNITED STATES.

For reentry of the student and/or the F-2 dependents (EACH CERTIFICATION SIGNATURE IS VALID FOR ONLY ONE YEAR.)

Signature of Designated School Official	Name of School Official (print or type)	Title	Date
Signature of Designated School Official	Name of School Official (print or type)	Title	Date
Signature of Designated School Official	Name of School Official (print or type)	Title	Date
Signature of Designated School Official	Name of School Official (print or type)	Title	Date
Signature of Designated School Official	Name of School Official (print or type)	Title	Date
Signature of Designated School Official	Name of School Official (print or type)	Title	Date

Dependent spouse and children of the F-1 student who are seeking entry/reentry to the U.S.

Name family (caps) first	Date of birth	Country of birth	Relationship to the F-1 student

Student Employment Authorization and other Records

FORM DSP-66
Presently, FORM IAP-66

CERTIFICATE OF ELIGIBILITY FOR EXCHANGE VISITOR (J-1) STATUS

Completed by the school

PLEASE DO NOT STAPLE THIS FORM (FILLED OUT BY SCHOOL)

DEPARTMENT OF STATE
BUREAU OF EDUCATIONAL AND CULTURAL AFFAIRS
CERTIFICATE OF ELIGIBILITY FOR EXCHANGE VISITOR (J - 1) STATUS

Form Approved
OMB No. 47-R0144

PART I — IT IS HEREBY CERTIFIED THAT:

1. ______ (Family Name of Exchange Visitor) ______ (First Name) ______ (Middle Name) ______ ( ) Male; ( ) Female

born ___ (Mo.) ___ (Day) ___ (Yr.) in ______ (City), ______ (Country)

a legal permanent resident of ______ (Country) ___ (Code), whose position in that country is ______ ___ (Pos Code) and whose U.S. address is or will be

THE PURPOSE OF THIS FORM IS TO:
1 ( ) Begin a new program
2 ( ) Extend an on going program
3 ( ) Transfer to a different program
4 ( ) Replace a lost form
5 ( ) Permit the visitor's family to enter the U.S. separately.

2. will be sponsored by University of ______ to participate in Exchange Visitor Program No. P- 1- 168 , which is still valid and is officially described as follows:

A program to provide courses of study (undergraduate or graduate level), training, research, teaching, lecturing, or a combination thereof, in all the fields of study available at the University or institutions and installations under its control, for foreign students, trainees, guest instructors, visiting professors, and leaders in fields of specialized knowledge or skill.

3. This form covers the period from ___ (Mo.) ___ (Day) ___ (Yr.) to ___ (Mo.) ___ (Day) ___ (Yr.) (one year maximum.)
[Th]is form is for family travel or replaces a lost form, the expiration date on the exchange visitor's I-94 is ______

4. The category of this visitor is 1 ( ) Student, 2 ( ) Trainee, 3 ( ) Teacher, 4 ( ) Professor, 5 ( ) Research Scholar or Specialist, 6 ( ) International Visitor, 7 ( ) Professional Trainee, and the specific educational field or non-study activity to be engaged in is Code No. ______ (Subj/Field Code), verbally described as follows:

5. During the period covered by this form, it is estimated that the following financial support (in U.S. $) will be provided to this exchange visitor by:

a. ( ) The Program Sponsor in item 2 above $______.
Financial support from organizations other than the sponsor will be provided by one or more of the following:
b1. ( ) U.S. Government Agency(ies): ______ (Agency Code), $______; b2.______ (Agency Code), $______.
c1. ( ) International Organization(s): ______ (Int. Org. Code), $______; c2.______ (Int. Org. Code), $______.
d. ( ) The Exchange Visitor's Government $______.
e. ( ) The binational Commission of the visitor's Country $______.
f. ( ) All other organizations providing support $______.
g. ( ) Personal funds $______.

(If necessary, use above spaces for funding by multiple U.S. Agencies or Intl. Organizations)

6. I.N.S. USE

7. ______ (Name of Official Preparing Form) ______ (Title)
______ (Address)
______ (Signature of Responsible Officer or Alternate R.O.) ______ (Date)

PART II — ENDORSEMENT OF CONSULAR OR IMMIGRATION OFFICER REGARDING SECTION 212(e) OF THE I.N.A.

I, ______ (Name)
______ (Title)
have determined that this alien in the above program
1. ( ) is not subject to the two year residence requirement;
2. ( ) is subject, based on: A. ( ) government financing and/or
B. ( ) the Exchange Visitor Skills List.

______ (Signature of Officer) ______ (Date)

PART III — STATEMENT OF RESPONSIBLE OFFICER FOR RELEASING SPONSOR (FOR TRANSFER OF PROGRAM)

Date ______, Transfer of this exchange visitor from program No. ______ sponsored by ______
to the program specified in item (2) is necessary or highly desirable and is in conformity with the objectives of the Mutual Educational and Cultural Exchange Act of 1961.

______ (Signature of Officer) ______ (Date)

FORM DSP-66
(6-75)

Copy 1 - For Immigration and Naturalization Service

Page 1

SAMPLE SHEET

Form 1-126

United States Department of Justice
Immigration and Naturalization Service

Form approved
OMB No. 43-RO297

SAMPLE FORM I-126

REPORT OF STATUS BY TREATY TRADER OR INVESTOR

NOTE: Refer to "Explanatory Note" on p. 37, especially paragraph 6.

p. 1.

Registration Number

Read instructions on other side before filling out this report

1. Name (Last, in capital letters) [redacted] (First) Jules (Middle) Renaud
2. Date of Birth: Dec. 2, 1951
3. Place of Birth (City or Town) [redacted] (State or Province) (Country) French West Indies
4. Present Nationality: French
5. United States Mailing Address (Apt. No.) (No. and Street) [redacted] Main Avenue, (City or Town) [redacted], (State) Colorado (Zip Code) 81301
6. Foreign Residence (Street) [redacted], (City or Town) St. Barthelemy (State or Province) (Guadeloupe) 97133 (Country) F.W.I.
7. Resided at above foreign address (Month, day, year) From 12/2/51 To (Month, day, year) present
8. Date of Entry (Month, day, year): August 7, 1983
9. Port of Entry (City) Miami (State) Florida
10. Name of vessel or other conveyance: Eastern Airlines
11. Visa: 007[redacted] Issued on (Mo., day, year): 8/5/83 Visa Issued at (City) Martinique (Country) F.W.I.
12. Passport Number: 4[redacted] Issued on (Mo., day, year): 7/27/83 Issued at (City) (Country) St. Barthelemy, F.W.I. Expiration Date: 7/26/88

13. Information Concerning Business Engaged in Pursuant to Treaty of Commerce and Navigation with the United States:

A. Name of Country Signatory to Treaty with United States
France

B. Name and address of business or enterprise in which engaged or employed
[redacted] Restaurant, [redacted] Main Avenue, [redacted], Colorado, 81301

C. Nature of business or enterprise
French and Caribbean restaurant

D. List all countries engaged in trade with the company named in item B and the amount derived from each country

U.S. gross sales - projected, $500,000.00

E. Percentage of Business or Enterprise Owned by Nationals of Country of Which You Are a National: 100 %. Are such Nationals residing abroad? YES ____ NO XX . If such Nationals are residing in the United States, list their immigration status.

F. Title of My Position or Occupation
Master Chef

G. Brief Description of My Duties
Preparation of all Caribbean dishes, which involve knowledge of the recipes which are proprietary secrets of [redacted]; baking daily French bread; preparing all patés and pastries (see approval of fellow employee dated 11/1/82 - ALPHA-L)

H. (Check box and fill in blank as appropriate)

[XX] I am an employee of the business or enterprise named in item 13B.

[XX] I am an independent developer or director of operations of the business or enterprise named in item 13B, in which I have personally invested or am in the process of investing cash or other capital in the amount of $ $35,000.00

14. Documents attached in support of this report (See Instructions)

[XX] Arrival-Departure Record (Form I-94)
[XX] Letter from Employer
[ ] Application for Extension of Stay (Form I-539)
[XX] Application for Change of Nonimmigrant Status (Form I-506)

OVER

OVER→

Form I-126 (Rev.6-26-78)N

p.2

Form 1-126

15. Marital status

[X] Married [ ] Divorced [ ] Widowed [ ] Never Married

Name of Spouse: Anne Gertrude [redacted]

Nationality of Spouse	Passport Issued By (Country)	Expires on (Date)
French	Franch	July 26, 1988

Present Address of Spouse: [redacted], St. Barthelemy, F.W.I.

16.

Name of Children	Date of Birth	Country of Birth	Passport Issued by (Country) and Expires on (Date)	
Fabienne Anne [redacted].	1/8/78	F.W.I.	None	
Donatienne [redacted]	1/12/80	F.W.I.	None	

Note: If the children for whom you are seeking extension or change of nonimmigrant status do not residue with you, give their complete address on a separate attachment to this application.

17. I certify that all information furnished in this report is true and correct.

Date 9/30/83 ______ [signature]
Signature of Treaty Trader or Investor or applicant seeking such status

18. Signature of person preparing form, if other than Treaty Trader or Investor or applicant seeking such status

I declare that this document was prepared by me at the request of the Treaty Trader or Investor or applicant seeking such status and is based upon all information of which I have any knowledge.

[signature]
Signature

Date 10/3/83 Address 110 16th St., 14th Floor, Denver, Colorado 80202

INSTRUCTIONS

If you were admitted to this country as a Treaty Trader prior to December 24, 1952, this report must be submitted annually, 30 days prior to each anniversary of your entry, to the immigration office having jurisdiction over your place of residence; and, in that case, no application for extension of temporary stay need be submitted.

If you are seeking to acquire status as a Treaty Trader or Investor, this report must be attached to your Application for Change of Nonimmigrant Classification, Form I-506.

If you acquired status as a Treaty Trader or Investor on or after December 24, 1952, this report must be attached to your Application for Extension of Temporary Stay (Form I-539).

Submit with this report your temporary entry permit (Form I-94, Arrival-Departure Record). If your temporary entry permit is attached to your passport, the permit should be removed for this purpose. DO NOT SEND IN YOUR PASSPORT. However, you must be in possession of a passport valid for at least six (6) months beyond the date to which your stay may be extended.

If you are employed, submit with this report a letter from your employer stating your present and intended position and duties. Name and title or position of person signing the letter should be clearly indicated. If your employer is a person and not an organization, the letter from your employer should indicate whether or not he is an E-1 or E-2 nonimmigrant.

A Treaty Trader or Investor may include in this report any alien dependent spouse and unmarried, minor children who are in the United States. If this application includes your wife and children, their Forms I-94 must be submitted with the application. They too must be in possession of passports valid for at least six months beyond the expiration date of the extensions requested. In all other cases separate reports must be made.

DO NOT WRITE IN THIS SPACE

(For use of Immigration and Naturalization Service Officer)

[ ] Status maintained [ ] Status not maintained [ ] See Form I-506 for action taken.

Date ______ ______
District Director

GPO 930-77

SAMPLE SHEET

(End of Form)

SAMPLE FORM I-129B

NOTE: See "Explanatory Note" on p.37, first, especially item 2 therein.

UNITED STATES
DEPARTMENT OF JUSTICE
Immigration and Naturalization Service

Form approved
OMB No. 43-R0348

Date Filed

Fee Stamp

File No.

PETITION TO CLASSIFY NONIMMIGRANT AS TEMPORARY WORKER OR TRAINEE

(To be submitted in duplicate, with supplementary documents described in instructions, to the District Director having administrative jurisdiction over the place in the United States in which it is intended the alien(s) be employed or trained)

(THIS BLOCK NOT TO BE FILLED OUT BY PETITIONER)

The Secretary of State is hereby notified that the alien(s) for whom this petition was filed is (are) entitled to the nonimmigrant status checked below:

☐ H-1 ☐ H-3
☐ H-2 ☐ L-1

The validity of this petition will expire on______________. The admission of the alien(s) may be authorized to the above date.

DATE OF ACTION DD

REMARKS:

DISTRICT

(PETITIONER NOT TO WRITE ABOVE THIS LINE)
(PLEASE FILL IN WITH TYPEWRITER OR PRINT IN BLOCK LETTERS IN INK)

I hereby petition, pursuant to the provisions of section 214(c) of the Immigration and Nationality Act, for the following: (Check one.)

H-1 ☒ Alien(s) of distinguished merit and ability to perform services of an exceptional nature requiring such merit and ability.

H-2 ☐ Alien(s) to perform temporary service or labor for which a bona fide need exists. (One who is to perform duties which are themselves temporary in nature.)

H-3 ☐ Alien trainee(s). (One who seeks to enter at the invitation of an individual, organization, firm, or other trainer for the purpose of receiving training in any field of endeavor. Incidental production necessary to the training is permitted provided a United States worker is not thereby displaced.)

L-1 ☐ Intra-company transferee. (One who has been employed continuously for one year and who seeks to enter in order to continue to render services to the same employer or a subsidiary or affiliate thereof in a managerial or executive capacity or in a capacity which involves specialized knowledge.)

1. NAME OF PETITIONER
Inc.

2. DATE BUSINESS ESTABLISHED
February 19, 1976

3. ADDRESS (NUMBER, STREET, CITY, STATE, ZIP CODE)
Parkway, , Englewood, Colorado

4. DESCRIPTION OF PETITIONER'S BUSINESS, INCLUDING ITS NATURE, NUMBER OF EMPLOYEES, AND GROSS ANNUAL INCOME
Importers and distributors in wearing apparel;
Employees, 19;
Gross annual income, $2,400,000.00

5. LOCATION OF AMERICAN CONSULATE AT WHICH ALIEN(S) WILL APPLY FOR VISA(S): (City in Foreign Country) Hong Kong (Foreign Country)

(If petition is to be made for more than one H alien and application for visas will be made at more than one American Consulate, a separate petition must be submitted for each consulate at which H visa applications will be made. Separate petition must be filed for each L-1 alien.)

6. THE ALIEN(S) WILL PERFORM SERVICES OR LABOR FOR OR RECEIVE TRAINING FROM THE FOLLOWING ESTABLISHMENT IN THE U.S.:
(Name of Establishment) , Inc.
DTC Parkway, Suite , Englewood, Colorado,
(Street and Number) (City or Town) (State) (Zip Code)

7. PERIOD REQUIRED TO COMPLETE SERVICES OR TRAINING
From (date) Date of approval
To (date) 24 mos thereafter
No. of days or months 24 mos.

8. WAGES PER ~~week~~ year
$42,000.00

8A. HOURS PER WEEK
40

9. OVERTIME RATE
--

10. OTHER COMPENSATION (Explain)
none

10A. VALUED AT
$ -- WEEKLY

11. BY WHOM PAID?
Employer, Inc.

RECEIVED	TRANS. IN	RET'D-TRANS. OUT	COMPLETED

Form I-129B
(Rev. 6-20-80)N

FORM I-129B

P.1 of 3 pgs.

SAMPLE SHEET

(Page 2)

ALL PETITIONERS COMPLETE ITEMS 12A THROUGH 22. If petition is for more than one H alien, give required information for each additional alien in space provided on page 3. If the identity of the H aliens is not known at present, you must furnish information concerning them as soon as that information becomes known to you

12A. ALIEN'S NAME (Family name in capital letters) [redacted] (First name) Dawning (Middle name) Zing Fong

12B. OTHER NAMES (Show all other past and present names, including maiden name if married woman.) none

12C. NUMBER OF ALIENS INCLUDED IN THIS PETITION 1

13. ADDRESS TO WHICH ALIEN WILL RETURN (Street and Number) (City) (Province) (Country)
Flat B, 10th Flr., [redacted] Sheung Shing St., [redacted], Hong Kong

14. PRESENT ADDRESS Same as #13 above

15. PROPOSED PORT OF ENTRY San Francisco, CA.

16. DATE OF BIRTH 5/21/58

17. PLACE OF BIRTH Hong Kong

18. PRESENT NATIONALITY OR CITIZENSHIP Hong Kong

19. PRESENT OCCUPATION Merchandiser

20. HAS AN IMMIGRANT VISA PETITION EVER BEEN FILED ON THE ALIEN'S BEHALF? [ ] YES [X] NO
If "Yes", where was it filed?

21. HAS THE ALIEN EVER APPLIED FOR AN IMMIGRANT VISA OR PERMANENT RESIDENCE IN THE U.S.? [ ] YES [X] NO
If "Yes", where did he apply?

22. TO YOUR KNOWLEDGE, HAS ANY VISA PETITION FILED BY YOU OR ANY OTHER PERSON OR ORGANIZATION FOR THE NAMED ALIEN(S) BEEN DENIED? [ ] YES [X] NO
If you answered "yes", complete the following: Date of filing of each denied petition
Place of filing of each denied petition (city)
TO YOUR KNOWLEDGE, HAVE ANY OF THE NAMED ALIEN(S) EVER BEEN IN THE U.S.? [ ] YES [ ] NO (If "yes" identify each on Page 3)

23. NONTECHNICAL DESCRIPTION OF SERVICES TO BE PERFORMED BY OR TRAINING TO BE RECEIVED BY ALIEN(S) (THIS BLOCK NEED NOT BE COMPLETED IF PETITION IS FOR H-2 WORKERS) As an Apparel Account Executive, to supervise all overseas buying of fabric, samples and production, and to coordinate all fabrics and accessories with each factory for production.

24. (If you are petitioning for an H-1 physician or nurse, complete this block.)
DOES THE LAW GOVERNING THE PLACE WHERE THE ALIEN'S SERVICES WILL BE PERFORMED RESTRICT HIM/HER FROM PERFORMING ANY OF THE DESIRED SERVICES? [ ] YES [ ] NO If the answer is "yes", attach statement listing the restricted services and setting forth the reason for the restriction. (See instructions for Physicians and Nurses.)

25. (If you are petitioning for a trainee complete this block.)
A. IS SIMILAR TRAINING AVAILABLE IN ALIEN'S COUNTRY? [ ] YES [ ] NO
B. WOULD ALIEN'S TRAINING RESULT IN DISPLACEMENT OF UNITED STATES WORKER? [ ] YES [ ] NO

26. (If you are petitioning for an L-1 alien, complete this block.) (Check appropriate boxes.)
a. The alien has been employed in an [ ] executive; [ ] managerial capacity; [ ] in a capacity which involves specialized knowledge
by (name and address of employer) since (date)
b. The petitioner is [ ] the same employer [ ] subsidiary [ ] an affiliate of the employer abroad.

FILL IN ITEMS 27 THROUGH 31 INCLUSIVE ONLY IF PETITION IS FOR H-2 ALIEN(S)

27. DESCRIPTIVE JOB TITLE OF WORK TO BE PERFORMED BY ALIEN(S) (Use title which corresponds to that used in job order placed with state Employment Service or Agency by petitioner for same type of labor. Where work in more than one job classification is to be performed by aliens, state number to be employed in each job classification.)

28. IS (ARE) ALIEN(S) SKILLED IN WORK TO BE PERFORMED? [ ] YES [ ] NO [ ] UNKNOWN

29. IS ANY LABOR ORGANIZATION ACTIVE IN THE LABOR FIELD(S) SPECIFIED IN ITEM 27? [ ] YES [ ] NO
(If yes specify organization(s) and labor field(s).)

30. IS THE PETITIONER INVOLVED IN, OR ARE THERE THREATENED, ANY LABOR RELATIONS DIFFICULTIES, INCLUDING STRIKES OR LOCK-OUTS? (Specify)

31. I HAVE NOT BEEN ABLE TO FIND IN THE UNITED STATES ANY UNEMPLOYED PERSON(S) CAPABLE OF PERFORMING THE DUTIES OF THE POSITION(S) TO BE FILLED. THE FOLLOWING EFFORTS HAVE BEEN MADE TO FIND SUCH PERSON(S): (Complete only if labor certification not attached.)

ALL PETITIONERS FILL IN ITEMS 32 THROUGH 34B.

32. LIST DOCUMENTS SUBMITTED IN SUPPORT OF THIS PETITION. Petitioner's supporting letter; beneficiary's diplomas and school transcripts, resume

SAMPLE SHEET

FORM I-129B

P.2 of 3 pgs.

(Page 3)

33. THE DOCUMENTS SUBMITTED HEREWITH ARE HEREBY MADE A PART OF THIS PETITION.

I am willing [illegible] any bond required as a condition to the approval of this petition.
I agree that as soon as known I shall furnish the District Director to whom this petition is being submitted with the names of those alien(s) not named herein.
If the petition is for temporary worker(s), I certify that I have a bona fide need of such worker(s).
If the petition is for trainee(s), I certify he/she is coming to the United States to participate in a bona fide training program.
I certify that the statements and representations made in this petition are true and correct to the best of my knowledge and belief.

34A. SIGNATURE OF PETITIONER	DATE	34B. TITLE (Must be petitioner or authorized agent of petitioner)
William R. [redacted]	5-15-84	Pres

SIGNATURE OF PERSON PREPARING FORM, IF OTHER THAN PETITIONER

35. I declare that this document was prepared by me at the request of the petitioner and is based on all information of which I have any knowledge.

(Signature)	(Address)	(Date)
C. James Cooper, Jr.	999 18th St., #3220 Denver, Colorado 80202	2/7/84

If this petition is for more than one alien of distinguished merit and ability (H-1) or trainee (H-3), use spaces below to give required information. If additional space is needed, attach separate sheet executed in same general manner.

NAME	DATE OF BIRTH	PLACE OF BIRTH	NATIONALITY	OCCUPATION

PRESENT ADDRESS

ADDRESS TO WHICH ALIEN WILL RETURN

NONTECHNICAL DESCRIPTION OF SERVICES TO BE PERFORMED BY OR TRAINING TO BE RECEIVED BY ALIEN

NAME	DATE OF BIRTH	PLACE OF BIRTH	NATIONALITY	OCCUPATION

PRESENT ADDRESS

ADDRESS TO WHICH ALIEN WILL RETURN

NONTECHNICAL DESCRIPTION OF SERVICES TO BE PERFORMED BY OR TRAINING TO BE RECEIVED BY ALIEN

NAME	DATE OF BIRTH	PLACE OF BIRTH	NATIONALITY	OCCUPATION

PRESENT ADDRESS

ADDRESS TO WHICH ALIEN WILL RETURN

NONTECHNICAL DESCRIPTION OF SERVICES TO BE PERFORMED BY OR TRAINING TO BE RECEIVED BY ALIEN

If this petition is for more than one (H-2) alien to perform temporary service or labor, use spaces below to give required information. If additional space is needed, attach separate sheet executed in same general manner. Identify each alien who has been in the U.S., by placing an "X" in the last column.

NAME	NATIONALITY	DATE AND PLACE OF BIRTH	PRESENT ADDRESS	X

FORM I-129B

(End of Form)

P. 3 of 3 pgs.

SAMPLE FORM I-129B

UNITED STATES
DEPARTMENT OF JUSTICE
Immigration and Naturalization Service

Form approved
OMB No. 43-R0348

PETITION TO CLASSIFY NONIMMIGRANT AS TEMPORARY WORKER OR TRAINEE

Date Filed

NOTE: See "Explanatory Note" on p.37 first — especially Paragraph No. 3 therein.

Fee Stamp

File No.

(To be submitted in duplicate, with supplementary documents described in instructions, to the District Director having administrative jurisdiction over the place in the United States in which it is intended the alien(s) be employed or trained)

(THIS BLOCK NOT TO BE FILLED OUT BY PETITIONER)

The Secretary of State is hereby notified that the alien(s) for whom this petition was filed is (are) entitled to the nonimmigrant status checked below:

☐ H-1 ☐ H-3
☐ H-2 ☐ L-1

The validity of this petition will expire on ______________.
The admission of the alien(s) may be authorized to the above date.

DATE OF ACTION
DD
DISTRICT

REMARKS:

(PETITIONER NOT TO WRITE ABOVE THIS LINE)
(PLEASE FILL IN WITH TYPEWRITER OR PRINT IN BLOCK LETTERS IN INK)

I hereby petition, pursuant to the provisions of section 214(c) of the Immigration and Nationality Act, for the following: (Check one.)

H-1 ☐ Alien(s) of distinguished merit and ability to perform services of an exceptional nature requiring such merit and ability.

H-2 ☒ Alien(s) to perform temporary service or labor for which a bona fide need exists. (One who is to perform duties which are themselves temporary in nature.)

H-3 ☐ Alien trainee(s). (One who seeks to enter at the invitation of an individual, organization, firm, or other trainer for the purpose of receiving training in any field of endeavor. Incidental production necessary to the training is permitted provided a United States worker is not thereby displaced.)

L-1 ☐ Intra-company transferee. (One who has been employed continuously for one year and who seeks to enter in order to continue to render services to the same employer or a subsidiary or affiliate thereof in a managerial or executive capacity or in a capacity which involves specialized knowledge.)

SAMPLE SHEET

1. NAME OF PETITIONER: Rocky [redacted] Co., Inc., a Colo. corp.

2. DATE BUSINESS ESTABLISHED: 1950s

3. ADDRESS (NUMBER, STREET, CITY, STATE, ZIP CODE): [redacted] Brighton Boulevard, Denver, Colorado, [redacted]

4. DESCRIPTION OF PETITIONER'S BUSINESS, INCLUDING ITS NATURE, NUMBER OF EMPLOYEES, AND GROSS ANNUAL INCOME
All processes involving tin;
Employees, 4;
Gross annual income, $150,000.00

5. LOCATION OF AMERICAN CONSULATE AT WHICH ALIEN(S) WILL APPLY FOR VISA(S): (City in Foreign Country) Juarez, (Foreign Country) Mexico

(If petition is to be made for more than one H alien and application for visas will be made at more than one American Consulate, a separate petition must be submitted for each consulate at which H visa applications will be made. Separate petition must be filed for each L-1 alien.)

6. THE ALIEN(S) WILL PERFORM SERVICES OR LABOR FOR OR RECEIVE TRAINING FROM THE FOLLOWING ESTABLISHMENT IN THE U.S.:
(Name of Establishment) Rocky [redacted]g Co., Inc.
[redacted] Brighton Boulevard, Denver, Colorado [redacted]
(Street and Number) (City or Town) (State) (Zip Code)

7. PERIOD REQUIRED TO COMPLETE SERVICES OR TRAINING — From (date)	To (date)	No. of days or months	8. WAGES PER WEEK	8A. HOURS PER WEEK	9. OVERTIME RATE
12/23/81	12/31/82	12 mos.	$200.00	40	--

10. OTHER COMPENSATION (Explain)	10A. VALUED AT	11. BY WHOM PAID?
None	$ -- WEEKLY	Rocky [redacted] Co.

RECEIVED	TRANS. IN	RET'D-TRANS OUT	COMPLETED

Form I-129B
(Rev. 6-20-80)N

FORM I-129B

P.1 of 3 pgs.

(Page 2)

ALL PETITIONERS COMPLETE ITEMS 12A THROUGH 22. If petition is for more than one H alien, give required information for each additional alien in space provided on page 3. If the identity of the H aliens is not known at present, you must furnish information concerning them as soon as that information becomes known to you.

12A. ALIEN'S NAME (Family name in capital letters) [redacted] (First name) Arturo (Middle name) NMN

12B. OTHER NAMES (Show all other past and present names, including maiden name if married woman.) None

12C. NUMBER OF ALIENS INCLUDED IN THIS PETITION 1

13. ADDRESS TO WHICH ALIEN WILL RETURN (Street and Number) (City) (Province) (Country)
c/o Petro [redacted], [redacted] Flacc Lourdes, Chihuahua, Chihuahua, Mexico

14. PRESENT ADDRESS Same as #13 above

15. PROPOSED PORT OF ENTRY El Paso, Texas

16. DATE OF BIRTH 1/7/46

17. PLACE OF BIRTH Chihuahua, Chihuahua, Mexico

18. PRESENT NATIONALITY OR CITIZENSHIP Mexican

19. PRESENT OCCUPATION Tin hand-wiper

20. HAS AN IMMIGRANT VISA PETITION EVER BEEN FILED ON THE ALIEN'S BEHALF? ☐ YES ☒ NO
If "Yes", where was it filed?

21. HAS THE ALIEN EVER APPLIED FOR AN IMMIGRANT VISA OR PERMANENT RESIDENCE IN THE U.S.? ☐ YES ☒ NO
If "Yes", where did he apply?

22. TO YOUR KNOWLEDGE, HAS ANY VISA PETITION FILED BY YOU OR ANY OTHER PERSON OR ORGANIZATION FOR THE NAMED ALIEN(S) BEEN DENIED? ☐ YES ☒ NO
If you answered "yes", complete the following: Date of filing of each denied petition
Place of filing of each denied petition (city)
TO YOUR KNOWLEDGE, HAVE ANY OF THE NAMED ALIEN(S) EVER BEEN IN THE U.S.? ☐ YES ☐ NO (If "yes" identify each on Page 3)

23. NONTECHNICAL DESCRIPTION OF SERVICES TO BE PERFORMED BY OR TRAINING TO BE RECEIVED BY ALIEN(S) (THIS BLOCK NEED NOT BE COMPLETED IF PETITION IS FOR H-2 WORKERS)

24. (If you are petitioning for an H-1 physician or nurse, complete this block.)
DOES THE LAW GOVERNING THE PLACE WHERE THE ALIEN'S SERVICES WILL BE PERFORMED RESTRICT HIM/HER FROM PERFORMING ANY OF THE DESIRED SERVICES? ☐ YES ☐ NO If the answer is "yes", attach statement listing the restricted services and setting forth the reason for the restriction. (See instructions for Physicians and Nurses.)

25. (If you are petitioning for a trainee, complete this block.)
A. IS SIMILAR TRAINING AVAILABLE IN ALIEN'S COUNTRY? ☐ YES ☐ NO
B. WOULD ALIEN'S TRAINING RESULT IN DISPLACEMENT OF UNITED STATES WORKER? ☐ YES ☐ NO

26. (If you are petitioning for an L-1 alien, complete this block.) (Check appropriate boxes.)
a. The alien has been employed in an ☐ executive; ☐ managerial capacity; ☐ in a capacity which involves specialized knowledge
by ______ (name and address of employer) since ______ (date)
b. The petitioner is ☐ the same employer ☐ subsidiary ☐ an affiliate of the employer abroad.

FILL IN ITEMS 27 THROUGH 31 INCLUSIVE ONLY IF PETITION IS FOR H-2 ALIEN(S)

27. DESCRIPTIVE JOB TITLE OF WORK TO BE PERFORMED BY ALIEN(S) (Use title which corresponds to that used in job order placed with state Employment Service or Agency by petitioner for same type of labor. Where work in more than one job classification is to be performed by aliens, state number to be employed in each job classification.)
Hand-wiping of tin

28. IS (ARE) ALIEN(S) SKILLED IN WORK TO BE PERFORMED? ☒ YES ☐ NO ☐ UNKNOWN

29. IS ANY LABOR ORGANIZATION ACTIVE IN THE LABOR FIELD(S) SPECIFIED IN ITEM 27? ☐ YES ☒ NO
(If "yes", specify organization(s) and labor field(s).)

30. IS THE PETITIONER INVOLVED IN, OR ARE THERE THREATENED, ANY LABOR RELATIONS DIFFICULTIES, INCLUDING STRIKES OR LOCK-OUTS? (Specify)
No

31. I HAVE NOT BEEN ABLE TO FIND IN THE UNITED STATES ANY UNEMPLOYED PERSON(S) CAPABLE OF PERFORMING THE DUTIES OF THE POSITION(S) TO BE FILLED. THE FOLLOWING EFFORTS HAVE BEEN MADE TO FIND SUCH PERSON(S): (Complete only if labor certification not attached.)

ALL PETITIONERS FILL IN ITEMS 32 THROUGH 34B.

32. LIST DOCUMENTS SUBMITTED IN SUPPORT OF THIS PETITION.
Labor certification; employer's letter

SAMPLE SHEET

FORM I-129B

P. 2 of 3 pgs.

33. THE DOCUMENTS SUBMITTED HEREWITH ARE HEREBY MADE A PART OF THIS PETITION.

I am willing (unwilling) to post any bond required as a condition to the approval of this petition.
I agree that as soon as known I shall furnish the District Director to whom this petition is being submitted with the names of those alien(s) not named herein.
If the petition is for temporary worker(s), I certify that I have a bona fide need of such worker(s).
If the petition is for trainee(s), I certify he/she is coming to the United States to participate in a bona fide training program.
I certify that the statements and representations made in this petition are true and correct to the best of my knowledge and belief.

34A. SIGNATURE OF PETITIONER	DATE	34B. TITLE (Must be petitioner or authorized agent of petitioner)
Peter [redacted]	1/5/82	President

SIGNATURE OF PERSON PREPARING FORM, IF OTHER THAN PETITIONER

35. I declare that this document was prepared by me at the request of the petitioner and is based on all information of which I have any knowledge.

C. James Cooper, Jr. (Signature)
110 16th St., 14th Floor
Denver, Colorado 80202 (Address)
1/5/82 (Date)

If this petition is for more than one alien of distinguished merit and ability (H-1) or trainee (H-3), use spaces below to give required information. If additional space is needed, attach separate sheet executed in same general manner.

NAME	DATE OF BIRTH	PLACE OF BIRTH	NATIONALITY	OCCUPATION

PRESENT ADDRESS

ADDRESS TO WHICH ALIEN WILL RETURN

NONTECHNICAL DESCRIPTION OF SERVICES TO BE PERFORMED BY OR TRAINING TO BE RECEIVED BY ALIEN

NAME	DATE OF BIRTH	PLACE OF BIRTH	NATIONALITY	OCCUPATION

PRESENT ADDRESS

ADDRESS TO WHICH ALIEN WILL RETURN

NONTECHNICAL DESCRIPTION OF SERVICES TO BE PERFORMED BY OR TRAINING TO BE RECEIVED BY ALIEN

NAME	DATE OF BIRTH	PLACE OF BIRTH	NATIONALITY	OCCUPATION

PRESENT ADDRESS

ADDRESS TO WHICH ALIEN WILL RETURN

NONTECHNICAL DESCRIPTION OF SERVICES TO BE PERFORMED BY OR TRAINING TO BE RECEIVED BY ALIEN

If this petition is for more than one (H-2) alien to perform temporary service or labor, use spaces below to give required information. If additional space is needed, attach separate sheet executed in same general manner. Identify each alien who has been in the U.S., by placing an "X" in the last column

NAME	NATIONALITY	DATE AND PLACE OF BIRTH	PRESENT ADDRESS	X

FORM I-129B

(End of Form)

FORM I-129B

UNITED STATES
DEPARTMENT OF JUSTICE
Immigration and Naturalization Service

Date Filed

Form approved
OMB No. 43-R0348

Fee Stamp

NOTE: See "Explanatory Note" on p.37, especially item 4

PETITION TO CLASSIFY NONIMMIGRANT AS TEMPORARY WORKER OR TRAINEE

File No.

(To be submitted in duplicate, with supplementary documents described in instructions, to the District Director having administrative jurisdiction over the place in the United States in which it is intended the alien(s) be employed or trained)

(THIS BLOCK NOT TO BE FILLED OUT BY PETITIONER)

The Secretary of State is hereby notified that the alien(s) for whom this petition was filed is (are) entitled to the nonimmigrant status checked below:

☐ H-1 ☐ H-3
☐ H-2 ☐ L-1

The validity of this petition will expire on ____________.
The admission of the alien(s) may be authorized to the above date.

DATE OF ACTION
DD
DISTRICT

REMARKS:

(PETITIONER NOT TO WRITE ABOVE THIS LINE)
(PLEASE FILL IN WITH TYPEWRITER OR PRINT IN BLOCK LETTERS IN INK)

I hereby petition, pursuant to the provisions of section 214(c) of the Immigration and Nationality Act, for the following: (Check one.)

H-1 ☐ Alien(s) of distinguished merit and ability to perform services of an exceptional nature requiring such merit and ability.

H-2 ☐ Alien(s) to perform temporary service or labor for which a bona fide need exists. (One who is to perform duties which are themselves temporary in nature.)

H-3 ☒ Alien trainee(s). (One who seeks to enter at the invitation of an individual, organization, firm, or other trainer for the purpose of receiving training in any field of endeavor. Incidental production necessary to the training is permitted provided a United States worker is not thereby displaced.)

L-1 ☐ Intra-company transferee. (One who has been employed continuously for one year and who seeks to enter in order to continue to render his services to the same employer or a subsidiary or affiliate thereof in a managerial or executive capacity or in a capacity which involves specialized knowledge.)

1. NAME OF PETITIONER: [redacted] Co. (a division of the [redacted] Corporation)

2. DATE BUSINESS ESTABLISHED: 1854

3. ADDRESS (NUMBER, STREET, CITY, STATE, ZIP CODE): [redacted] 28th Street, Boulder, Co. [redacted] (local [redacted])
[redacted] Washington Avenue, Saginaw, Michigan [redacted] (home office)

4. DESCRIPTION OF PETITIONER'S BUSINESS, INCLUDING ITS NATURE, NUMBER OF EMPLOYEES, AND GROSS ANNUAL INCOME
Petitioner is engaged in the business of the retailing of lumber and building materials. Petitioner is a division of an international corporate conglomerate with many divisions in the fields of agricultural machinery, credit and other enterprises throughout the world. employees: 7,151. Gross Annual Income: $25,809,692

5. LOCATION OF AMERICAN CONSULATE AT WHICH ALIEN(S) WILL APPLY FOR VISA(S): (City in Foreign Country) Zurich (Foreign Country) Switzerland

(If petition is to be made for more than one H alien and application for visas will be made at more than one American Consulate, a separate petition must be submitted for each consulate at which H visa applications will be made. Separate petition must be filed for each L-1 alien.)

6. THE ALIEN(S) WILL PERFORM SERVICES OR LABOR FOR OR RECEIVE TRAINING FROM THE FOLLOWING ESTABLISHMENT:
(Name of Establishment) [redacted] Co. (a division of the [redacted] Corporation)
[redacted] 28th Street (Street and Number) Boulder (City or Town) Colorado (State) [redacted] (Zip Code)

7. PERIOD REQUIRED TO COMPLETE SERVICES OR TRAINING From (date)	To (date)	No. of days or months	8. WAGES PER WEEK	8A. HOURS PER WEEK	9. OVERTIME RATE
February 15.	August 15.	6 months	$175.00	48 hrs.	None

10. OTHER COMPENSATION (Explain)	10A. VALUED AT	11. BY WHOM PAID?
None	$ N/A WEEKLY	N/A

RECEIVED	TRANS. IN	RET'D-TRANS. OUT	COMPLETED

Form I-129B
(Rev. 2-25-76)N

FORM I-129B

P. 1 of 3 pgs

SAMPLE SHEET

SAMPLE SHEET

(Page 2)

ALL PETITIONERS COMPLETE ITEMS 12A THR[illegible] 22. If petition is for more than one H alien, give requ[illegible]nformation for each additional alien in space provided on page 3. If the identity of the H al[illegible] is not known at present, you must furnish information concerning them as soon as that information becomes known to you.

12A. ALIEN'S NAME (Family name in capital letters) [redacted] (First name) Andreas (Middle name) Willi

OTHER NAMES (Show all other past and present names, including maiden name if married woman.) None

12C. NUMBER OF ALIENS INCLUDED IN THIS PETITION 1

13. ADDRESS TO WHICH ALIEN WILL RETURN (Street and Number) [redacted] (City) 8157 Dielsdorf (Province) Zurich (Country) Switzerland

14. PRESENT ADDRESS [redacted] Green Place Longmont, Colorado [redacted]

15. ~~PROPOSED~~ PORT OF ENTRY Chicago 8-15-77

16. DATE OF BIRTH 1-30-53

17. PLACE OF BIRTH Zurich, Switzerland

18. PRESENT NATIONALITY OR CITIZENSHIP Swiss

19. PRESENT OCCUPATION Trainee

20. HAS AN IMMIGRANT VISA PETITION EVER BEEN FILED ON THE ALIEN'S BEHALF? ☐ YES ☒ NO
If "Yes", where was it filed?

21. HAS THE ALIEN EVER APPLIED FOR AN IMMIGRANT VISA OR PERMANENT RESIDENCE IN THE U.S.? ☐ YES ☒ NO
If "Yes", where did he apply?

22. TO YOUR KNOWLEDGE, HAS ANY VISA PETITION FILED BY YOU OR ANY OTHER PERSON OR ORGANIZATION FOR THE NAMED ALIEN(S) BEEN DENIED? ☐ YES ☒ NO
If you answered "yes", complete the following: Date of filing of each denied petition ________
Place of filing of each denied petition (city) ________

TO YOUR KNOWLEDGE, HAVE ANY OF THE NAMED ALIEN(S) EVER BEEN IN THE U.S.? ☒ YES ☐ NO (If "yes" identify each on Page 3)
(as a tourist for 5 wks. from 7/76 to 8/27/76)

23. NONTECHNICAL DESCRIPTION OF SERVICES TO BE PERFORMED BY OR TRAINING TO BE RECEIVED BY ALIEN(S) (THIS BLOCK NEED NOT BE COMPLETED IF PETITION IS FOR H-2 WORKERS)

Training for management of lumber retail business.

24. (If you are petitioning for an H-1 physician or nurse, complete this block.)
DOES THE LAW GOVERNING THE PLACE WHERE THE ALIEN'S SERVICES WILL BE PERFORMED RESTRICT HIM FROM PERFORMING ANY OF THE DESIRED SERVICES? ☐ YES ☒ NO If the answer is "yes", attach statement listing the restricted services and setting forth the reason for the restriction. (See instructions for Physicians and Nurses.)

(If you are petitioning for a trainee, complete this block.)
A. IS SIMILAR TRAINING AVAILABLE IN ALIEN'S COUNTRY? ☐ YES ☒ NO
B. WOULD ALIEN'S TRAINING RESULT IN DISPLACEMENT OF UNITED STATES WORKER? ☐ YES ☒ NO

26. (If you are petitioning for an L-1 alien, complete this block.) (Check appropriate boxes.) not applicable
a. The alien has been employed in an ☐ executive, ☐ managerial capacity; ☐ in a capacity which involves specialized knowledge
by ________ (name and address of employer) since ________ (date)
b. The petitioner is ☐ the same employer ☐ subsidiary ☐ an affiliate of the employer abroad.

FILL IN ITEMS 27 THROUGH 31 INCLUSIVE ONLY IF PETITION IS FOR H-2 ALIEN(S)

27. DESCRIPTIVE JOB TITLE OF WORK TO BE PERFORMED BY ALIEN(S) (Use title which corresponds to that used in job order placed with state Employment Service or Agent or petitioner for same type of labor. Where work in more than one job classification is to be performed by aliens, state number to be employed in each job classification.)

28. IS (ARE) ALIEN(S) SKILLED IN WORK TO BE PERFORMED? ☐ YES ☐ NO ☐ UNKNOWN

29. IS ANY LABOR ORGANIZATION ACTIVE IN THE LABOR FIELD(S) SPECIFIED IN ITEM 27? ☐ YES ☐ NO
(If "yes", specify organization(s) and labor name)

30. IS THE PETITIONER INVOLVED IN, OR ARE THERE THREATENED, ANY LABOR RELATIONS DIFFICULTIES, INCLUDING STRIKES OR LOCK-OUTS? (Specify)

31. I HAVE NOT BEEN ABLE TO FIND IN THE UNITED STATES ANY UNEMPLOYED PERSON(S) CAPABLE OF PERFORMING THE DUTIES OF THE POSITION(S) TO BE FILLED. THE FOLLOWING EFFORTS HAVE BEEN MADE TO FIND SUCH PERSONS: (Complete only if labor certification not attached.)

ALL PETITIONERS FILL IN ITEMS 32 THROUGH 34B.

32. LIST DOCUMENTS SUBMITTED IN SUPPORT OF THIS PETITION 1. Letter from [redacted] regarding Training program. 2. Letter from Swiss Embassy 3. Letter from AIESEC-U.S.

FORM I-129B

P. 2 of 3 pgs.

33. THE DOCUMENTS SUBMITTED HEREWITH ARE HEREBY MADE A PART OF THIS PETITION.
I am willing (unwilling) to post any bond required as a condition to the approval of this petition.
I agree that as soon as known I shall furnish the District Director to whom this petition is being submitted with the names of those alien(s) not named herein.
If the petition is for temporary worker(s), I certify that I have a bona fide need of such worker(s).
If the petition is for trainee(s), I certify he is coming to the United States to participate in a bona fide training program.
I certify that the statements and representations made in this petition are true and correct to the best of my knowledge and belief.

34A. SIGNATURE OF PETITIONER	DATE	34B. TITLE (Must be petitioner or authorized agent of petitioner)
[redacted] CO. By: [signature]	Jan. 31, 1979	ZONE MANAGER

SIGNATURE OF PERSON PREPARING FORM, IF OTHER THAN PETITIONER

35. I declare that this document was prepared by me at the request of the petitioner and is based on all information of which I have any knowledge.

(Signature)	(Address)	(Date)

If this petition is for more than one alien of distinguished merit and ability (H-1) or trainee (H-3), use spaces below to give required information. If additional space is needed, attach separate sheet executed in same general manner.

NAME	DATE OF BIRTH	PLACE OF BIRTH	NATIONALITY	OCCUPATION
PRESENT ADDRESS				
ADDRESS TO WHICH ALIEN WILL RETURN				
NONTECHNICAL DESCRIPTION OF SERVICES TO BE PERFORMED BY OR TRAINING TO BE RECEIVED BY ALIEN				

NAME	DATE OF BIRTH	PLACE OF BIRTH	NATIONALITY	OCCUPATION
PRESENT ADDRESS				
ADDRESS TO WHICH ALIEN WILL RETURN				
NONTECHNICAL DESCRIPTION OF SERVICES TO BE PERFORMED BY OR TRAINING TO BE RECEIVED BY ALIEN				

NAME	DATE OF BIRTH	PLACE OF BIRTH	NATIONALITY	OCCUPATION
PRESENT ADDRESS				
ADDRESS TO WHICH ALIEN WILL RETURN				
NONTECHNICAL DESCRIPTION OF SERVICES TO BE PERFORMED BY OR TRAINING TO BE RECEIVED BY ALIEN				

If this petition is for more than one (H-2) alien to perform temporary service or labor, use spaces below to give required information. If additional space is needed, attach separate sheet executed in same general manner. Identify each alien who has been in the U.S., by placing an "X" in the last column.

NAME	NATIONALITY	DATE AND PLACE OF BIRTH	PRESENT ADDRESS	X

Form I-129B

(End of Form)

P. 3 of 3 pgs.

U.S. Department of Justice
Immigration and Naturalization Service (INS)

Form I-129F

OMB #1115-0054

Petition for Alien Fiancé(e)

DO NOT WRITE IN THIS BLOCK

Case ID#

A#

G-28 or Volag #

The petition is approved for status under Section 101(a)(15)(k). It is valid for four months from date of action.

Action Stamp

Fee Stamp

AMCON: ______

☐ Personal Interview
☐ Document Check
☐ Field Investigations
☐ Previously Forwarded

Remarks:

A. Information about you

1. **Name** (Family name in CAPS) (First) (Middle)
2. **Address** (Number and Street) (Apartment Number)
   (Town or City) (State/Country) (ZIP/Postal Code)
3. **Place of Birth** (Town or City) (State/Country)
4. **Date of Birth** (Mo/Day/Yr)
5. **Sex** ☐ Male ☐ Female
6. **Marital Status** ☐ Married ☐ Single ☐ Widowed ☐ Divorced
7. **Other Names Used** (including maiden name)
8. **Social Security Number**
9. **Alien Registration Number** (if any)
10. **Names of Prior Husbands/Wives**
11. **Date(s) Marriages(s) Ended**
12. **If you are a U.S. citizen, complete the following:**
    My citizenship was acquired through (check one)
    ☐ Birth in the U.S.
    ☐ Naturalization
    Give number of certificate, date and place it was issued
    ☐ Parents
    Have you obtained a certificate of citizenship in your own name?
    ☐ Yes ☐ No
    If "Yes", give number of certificate, date and place it was issued
13. Have you ever filed for this or any other alien fiancé(e) or husband/wife before? ☐ Yes ☐ No
    If you checked "yes," give name of alien, place and date of filing, and result

B. Information about your alien fiancé(e)

1. **Name** (Family name in CAPS) (First) (Middle)
2. **Address** (Number and Street) (Apartment Number)
   (Town or City) (State/Country) (ZIP/Postal Code)
3. **Place of Birth** (Town or City) (State/Country)
4. **Date of Birth** (Mo/Day/Yr)
5. **Sex** ☐ Male ☐ Female
6. **Marital Status** ☐ Married ☐ Single ☐ Widowed ☐ Divorced
7. **Other Names Used** (including maiden name)
8. **Social Security Number**
9. **Alien Registration Number** (if any)
10. **Names of Prior Husbands/Wives**
11. **Date(s) Marriages(s) Ended**
12. **Has your finance(e) ever been in the U.S.?**
    ☐ Yes ☐ No
13. **If your finance(e) is currently in the U.S., complete the following:**
    He or she last arrived as a (visitor, student, exchange alien, crewman, stowaway, temporary worker, witout inspection, etc.)

Arrival/Departure Record (I-94) Number

Date arrived (Month/Day/Year)

Date authorized stay expired, or will expire, as shown on Form I-94 or I-95

INITIAL RECEIPT	RESUBMITTED	RELOCATED		COMPLETED		
		Rec'd	Sent	Approved	Denied	Returned

B. (continued) Information about your alien finance (e)

14. List all children of your alien financé(e) (if any)

(Name)	(Date of Birth)	(Country of Birth)	(Preesent Address)

15. Address in the United States where your financé(e) intends to live

(Number and Street) (Town or City) (State)

16. Your financé (e)'s address abroad

(Number and Street) (Town or City) (Province) (Country) (Phone Number)

17. If your financé (e)'s native alphabet is other than Roman letters, write hs or her name and address abroad in the native alphabet:

(Name) (Number and Street) (Town or City) (Province) (Country)

18. Your financé (e) is related to you. ☐ Yes ☐ No

If you are related, state the nature and degree of relationship, e.g., third cousin or maternal uncle, etc.

19. Your financé (e) has met and seen you. ☐ Yes ☐ No

Describe the circumstances under which you met. If you have not personally met each other, explain how the relationship was established, and explain in detail any reasons you may have for requesting that the requirement that you and your financé (e) must have met should not apply to you.

20. Your financé (e) will apply for a visa abroad at the American Consulate in ______________ (City) ______________ (Country)

(Designation of a consulate outside the country of your financé(e)'s last residence does not guarantee acceptance for processing by that consulate. Acceptance is at the discretion of the designated consulate.)

C. Other Information

If you are serving overseas in the armed forces of the United States, please answer the following:

I presently reside or am stationed overseas and my current mailing address is ______________

I plan to return to the United States on or about ______________

Penalties: **You may, by law be imprisoned for not more than five years, or fined $250,000, or both, for entering into a marriage contract for the purpose of evading any provision of the immigration laws and you may be fined up to $10,000 or imprisoned up to five years or both, for knowingly and willfully falsifying or concealing a material fact or using any false document in submitting this petition.**

Your Certification

I am legally able to and intend to marry my alien financé(e) within 90 days of his or her arrival in the United States. I certify, under penalty of perjury under the laws of the United States of America, that the foregoing is true and correct. Furthermore, I authorize the release of any information from my records which the Immigration and Naturalizaton Service needs to determine eligibility for the benefit that I am seeking.

Signature ______________ Date ______________ Phone Number ______________

Signature of Person Preparing Form if Other than Above

I declare that I prepared this document at the request of the person above and that it is based on all information of which I have any knowledge.

Print Name ______________ (Address) ______________ (Signature) ______________ (Date) ______________

G-28 ID Number ______________

Volag Number ______________

For sale by the Superintendent of Documents, U.S. Government Printing Office
Washington, D.C. 20402

*U.S.GPO:1996-405-024/34021

U. S. Department of Justice
Immigration and Naturalization Service

Form I-134 Affidavit of Support 173

(ANSWER ALL ITEMS: FILL IN WITH TYPEWRITER OR PRINT IN BLOCK LETTERS IN INK.)

I, ______________________ (Name), *residing at* ______________________ (Street and Number)

______________________ (City) (State) (ZIP Code if in U.S.) (Country)

BEING DULY SWORN DEPOSE AND SAY:

1. I was born on ______ (Date) at ______ (City) (Country)

 If you are ***not*** a native born United States citizen, answer the following as appropriate:

 a. If a United States citizen through naturalization, give certificate of naturalization number ______

 b. If a United States citizen through parent(s) or marriage, give citizenship certificate number ______

 c. If United States citizenship was derived by some other method, attach a statement of explanation.

 d. If a lawfully admitted permanent resident of the United States, give "A" number ______

2. That I am______years of age and have resided in the United States since (date) ______

3. That this affidavit is executed in behalf of the following person:

Name			Sex	Age
Citizen of—(Country)	Marital Status	Relationship to Deponent		
Presently resides at—(Street and Number)	(City)	(State)	(Country)	

Name of spouse and children accompanying or following to join person:

Spouse	Sex	Age	Child	Sex	Age
Child	Sex	Age	Child	Sex	Age
Child	Sex	Age	Child	Sex	Age

4. That this affidavit is made by me for the purpose of assuring the United States Government that the person(s) named in item 3 will not become a public charge in the United States.

5. That I am willing and able to receive, maintain and support the person(s) named in item 3. That I am ready and willing to deposit a bond, if necessary, to guarantee that such person(s) will not become a public charge during his or her stay in the United States, or to guarantee that the above named will maintain his or her nonimmigrant status if admitted temporarily and will depart prior to the expiration of his or her authorized stay in the United States.

6. That I understand this affidavit will be binding upon me for a period of three (3) years after entry of the person(s) named in item 3 and that the information and documentation provided by me may be made available to the Secretary of Health and Human Services and the Secretary of Agriculture, who may make it available to a public assistance agency.

7. That I am employed as, or engaged in the business of ______ (Type of Business) with ______ (Name of concern)

 at ______ (Street and Number) (City) (State) (Zip Code)

 I derive an annual income of *(if self-employed, I have attached a copy of my last income tax return or report of commercial rating concern which I certify to be true and correct to the best of my knowledge and belief. See instruction for nature of evidence of net worth to be submitted.)* $______

 I have on deposit in savings banks in the United States $______

 I have other personal property, the reasonable value of which is $______

I have stocks and bonds with the following market value, as indicated on the attached list which I certify to be true and correct to the best of my knowledge and belief. $ ____________
I have life insurance in the sum of $ ____________
With a cash surrender value of $ ____________
I own real estate valued at $ ____________
With mortgages or other encumbrances thereon amounting to $ ____________

Which is located at ____
(Street and Number) (City) (State) (Zip Code)

8. That the following persons are dependent upon me for support: *(Place an "X" in the appropriate column to indicate whether the person named is **wholly or partially** dependent upon you for support.)*

Name of Person	Wholly Dependent	Partially Dependent	Age	Relationship to Me

9. That I have previously submitted affidavit(s) of support for the following person(s). If none, state ***"None"***

Name	Date submitted

10. That I have submitted visa petition(s) to the Immigration and Naturalization Service on behalf of the following person(s). If none, state none.

Name	Relationship	Date submitted

11. ***(Complete this block only if the person named in item 3 will be in the United States temporarily.)***
That I ☐ do intend ☐ do not intend, to make specific contributions to the support of the person named in item 3. *(If you check "do intend", indicate the exact nature and duration of the contributions. For example, if you intend to furnish room and board, state for how long and, if money, state the amount in United States dollars and state whether it is to be given in a lump sum, weekly, or monthly, or for how long.)*

____

____

____

OATH OR AFFIRMATION OF DEPONENT

I acknowledge at that I have read Part III of the Instructions, Sponsor and Alien Liability, and am aware of my responsibilities as an immigrant sponsor under the Social Security Act, as amended, and the Food Stamp Act, as amended.

I swear (affirm) that I know the contents of this affidavit signed by me and the statements are true and correct.

Signature of deponent ____

Subscribed and sworn to (affirmed) before me this ________ ***day of*** ______________________, 19______

at ______________________________________ ***My commission expires on*** ____________________

Signature of Officer Administering Oath ______________________ ***Title*** ____________________

If affidavit prepared by other than deponent, please complete the following: I declare that this document was prepared by me at the request of the deponent and is based on all information of which I have knowledge.

____

(Signature) ***(Address)*** ***(Date)***

FORM I-140
(Good till June 1986; after that date, you must use new Form sampled pp.)

Form I-140

UNITED STATES DEPARTMENT OF JUSTICE
IMMIGRATION AND NATURALIZATION SERVICE

OMB No. 1115-0061
Approval expires 4-86

p. 1 of 2 pgs.

PETITION TO CLASSIFY PREFERENCE STATUS OF ALIEN ON BASIS OF PROFESSION OR OCCUPATION

DATE RECEIVED	FEE STAMP
NOTE: Refer to "Explanatory Note" on p. 37, especially item 2, 3 + 4.	

SAMPLE SHEET

TO THE SECRETARY OF STATE

Petition was filed on ______

Beneficiary's file number: A ______

Petition is approved for status under section ☐ 203(a)(3). ☐ 203(a)(6)

☐ Sec. 212(a)(14) certification attached.

☐ Blanket Sec. 212(a)(14) certification issued.

DATE OF ACTION

DD

DISTRICT

REMARKS

PETITIONER IS NOT TO WRITE ABOVE THIS LINE

Read this form and the attached instructions carefully before filling in petition

Petition is hereby made to classify the status of the alien beneficiary named herein for issuance of an immigrant visa as ("X" one)

☒ A THIRD PREFERENCE IMMIGRANT—An alien who is a member of the professions, or who because of his exceptional ability in the sciences or arts will substantially benefit prospectively the national economy, cultural interests or welfare of the United States, and whose services are sought by an employer. (Sec. 203(a)(3), Immigration and Nationality Act, as amended.)

☐ A SIXTH PREFERENCE IMMIGRANT—An alien who is capable of performing skilled or unskilled labor, not of a temporary or seasonal nature, for which a shortage of employable and willing persons exists in the United States. (Sec. 203 (a) (6), Immigration and Nationality Act, as amended.)

(If you need more space to answer fully any questions on this form, use a separate sheet, identify each answer with the number of the corresponding question and sign and date each sheet.)

PART I—INFORMATION CONCERNING ALIEN BENEFICIARY

1. NAME (Last, in CAPS) (First) (Middle): [redacted] Arun NMN
2. ALIEN REGISTRATION NO. (If any):
3. PROFESSION OR OCCUPATION: Development Engineer
4. OTHER NAMES USED (Married woman give maiden name): None
5. DO NOT WRITE IN THIS SPACE
6. DOES BENEFICIARY INTEND TO ENGAGE IN HIS/HER PROFESSION OR OCCUPATION IN THE UNITED STATES? ☒ YES ☐ NO. IF "NO," EXPLAIN
7. PLACE OF BIRTH (Country): United Kingdom
8. DATE OF BIRTH (Month, day, year): 9/17/61
9. NAME OF PETITIONER (Full name of organization; if petitioner is an individual give full name with last in capital letters): [redacted] Co., Colorado [redacted]k Operation
10. NUMBER OF YEARS OF BENEFICIARY'S EXPERIENCE (If none explain why.): Approx. 1 year
11. CITY AND STATE IN THE UNITED STATES WHERE ALIEN INTENDS TO RESIDE: Ft. Collins, Colorado (City) (State)
12. BENEFICIARY'S PRESENT ADDRESS (Number and street) (City or town) (State or province) (Country) (ZIP Code, if in U.S.): [redacted] Shields Street, [redacted], Ft. Collins, Colorado [redacted]
13. TO YOUR KNOWLEDGE, HAS A VISA PETITION EVER BEEN FILED BY OR ON BEHALF OF THIS BENEFICIARY BASED ON HIS/HER PROFESSION OR OCCUPATION? ☐ Yes ☒ No. If "Yes," give name of each petitioner and date and place of filing.
14. IF BENEFICIARY IS NOW IN THE U.S. (a) HE/SHE LAST ARRIVED ON 8/20/83 (Month) (Day) (Year) AS A F-1 (Visitor, student, exchange alien, temporary worker, crewman, stowaway, etc.) SHOWN ON FORM I-94 OR I-95 (b) SHOW DATE BENEFICIARY'S STAY EXPIRED OR WILL EXPIRE AS (Show latest date) 12-2-87 H-1

15. BENEFICIARY'S SPOUSE (If Unmarried, State Unmarried)

NAME (Last name)	(First name)	(Middle name)	(Maiden name, if married women)
Not married			
COUNTRY OF BIRTH	DATE OF BIRTH	PRESENT ADDRESS (No. and Street) (City or town) (State or Province) (Country)	

16. BENEFICIARY'S CHILDREN (If None State None)

NAME (Show M or S for married or single)	M.S.	BIRTHDATE	COUNTRY OF BIRTH	ADDRESS
None				

RECEIVED	TRANS. IN	RET'D-TRANS. OUT	COMPLETED

Form I-140 (Rev. 5-5-83)N

-OVER- →

FORM I-140 (Expired June 1986)

p. 2 of 2 pgs.

17. "X" THE APPROPRIATE BOX BELOW AND FURNISH THE INFORMATION REQUIRED FOR THE BOX MARKED.

☐ Alien will apply for a visa abroad at the American Consulate in ______ (City in foreign country) ______ (Foreign country)

☒ Alien is in the United States and will apply for adjustment of status to that of a lawful permanent resident in the office of the Immigration and Naturalization Service at Denver (City) Colorado (State) If the application for adjustment of status is denied the alien will apply for a visa abroad at the American Consulate in Calgary, Alberta, Canada (City in foreign country) (Foreign country)

PART II—INFORMATION CONCERNING EMPLOYER AND POSITION

18. NAME OF PETITIONER (Full name of organization, if petitioner is an individual give full name with last in capital letters): [redacted] Co., Colorado [redacted] Operation — TELEPHONE NUMBER: 303-[redacted]

19. ADDRESS (Number and street) (Town or city) (State) (ZIP code): [redacted] Harmony Road, Ft. Collins, Colorado [redacted]

20. PETITIONER IS (X one): ☐ U.S. CITIZEN ☐ PERMANENT RESIDENT ALIEN ("A" NUMBER ______) ☐ NONIMMIGRANT ☒ ORGANIZATION

21. NET ANNUAL INCOME: Excess of $6 Billion

22. WILL BENEFICIARY BE EMPLOYED AT THE ABOVE ADDRESS? ☒ YES ☐ NO IF "NO," GIVE ADDRESS WHERE THE ALIEN WILL WORK.

23. DO YOU DESIRE AND INTEND TO EMPLOY THE BENEFICIARY ☒ YES ☐ NO

24. HAVE YOU EVER FILED A VISA PETITION FOR AN ALIEN BASED ON PROFESSION OR OCCUPATION? ☐ YES ☐ NO. IF "YES," HOW MANY SUCH PETITIONS HAVE YOU FILED?

25. ARE SEPARATE PETITIONS BEING SUBMITTED AT THIS TIME FOR OTHER ALIENS? ☐ YES ☒ NO. IF "YES," GIVE NAME OF EACH ALIEN.

26. THE FOLLOWING DOCUMENTS ARE SUBMITTED WITH THIS PETITION AND ARE MADE A PART THEREOF.

Labor Certification and attached documents showing alien's qualifications for third preference status;
Employer's offer of employment letter;
Employer's latest annual report

PART III—CERTIFICATION OF PETITIONER OR AUTHORIZED REPRESENTATIVE

27. This petition was prepared by: ("X" one) ☐ the petitioner ☐ another person

If petition was prepared by another person, Item 29 below must also be completed.

The petition may be completed and signed only by the following persons:

In third preference cases — by the beneficiary or by the person filing the petition on the beneficiary's behalf. If the petition is being filed by a person on behalf of the alien beneficiary, Item 28 below must be completed by that person.

In sixth preference cases — by the employer who desires and intends to employ the beneficiary. If the employer is an organization, the petition must be completed and signed by a high level officer or employee of the organization.

I certify, under penalty of perjury under the laws of the United States of America that the foregoing is true and correct.

Executed on (date) 12/31/85 Signature Marlene [redacted]

If petitioner is an organization, print full name and title of authorized official who is signing petition in behalf of organization:

Name and Title: Marlene [redacted] Personnel Representative Date 12/31/85

28. **DECLARATION OF PERSON FILING PETITION FOR THIRD PREFERENCE ON BEHALF OF ALIEN BENEFICIARY**

I declare that I have been requested [redacted] by the alien beneficiary to file this petition on his (her) behalf.

Marlene (Signature) [redacted] Harmony Road Ft.Collins (Address—Number, Street, City, State and ZIP Code) 12/31/85 (Date)

29. **SIGNATURE OF PERSON PREPARING FORM, IF OTHER THAN PETITIONER**

I declare that this document was prepared by me at the request of the petitioner and is based on all information of which I have any knowledge

(Signature) 999 Eighteenth St.Denver,CO (Address—Number, Street, City, State and ZIP Code) 12/31/85 (Date)

TO PETITIONER: DO NOT FILL IN THIS BLOCK — FOR USE OF IMMIGRATION OFFICER

a. Corrections numbered ( ) to ( ) were made by me or at my request. ______ (Date) ______ (City)

______ (Signature of petitioner or authorized member of petitioner's organization) ______ (Title)

b. The person whose signature appears immediately above was interviewed under oath and affirmed all allegations contained herein.

______ (Date) ______ (City) ______ (Signature and Title)

(End of Form)

SAMPLE SHEET

Form OF-156

SAMPLE OF FORM 156

p. 1 of 2 pgs.

SAMPLE SHEET

SAMPLE
VISITOR (NONIMMIGRANT) VISA APPLICATION

Form Approved
O.M.B. No. 47-R0166

NONIMMIGRANT VISA APPLICATION

PART I

IMPORTANT: *ALL APPLICANTS MUST READ AND ANSWER THE FOLLOWING:*

(1) U.S. law prohibits the issuance of a visitor visa to persons who plan to remain in the United States indefinitely or who will accept employment there. A VISITOR MAY NOT WORK.

(2) A visa may not be issued to persons who are within specific categories defined by law as inadmissible to the United States (except when a waiver is obtained in advance). Complete information regarding these categories and whether any may be applicable to you can be obtained from this office. Generally, they include persons afflicted with contagious diseases (such as tuberculosis) or who have suffered serious mental illness; persons with criminal records involving offenses of certain kinds, including offenses against public morals; narcotic addicts or traffickers; persons who have been deported from the U.S.A.; persons who have sought to obtain a visa by means of misrepresentation or fraud; and persons who are, or have been members of certain organizations, including communist organizations and those affiliated therewith.

DO ANY OF THE FOREGOING RESTRICTIONS APPLY TO YOU?

☐ YES ☒ NO

If YES, or if you have any question in this regard, personal appearance at this office is recommended. If it is not possible at this time, attach a statement of facts in your case to this application.

PART II

PLEASE PRINT THE FOLLOWING INFORMATION

1. LAST NAME: Bermanti — FIRST NAME: Samieu — MIDDLE NAME:
2. OTHER NAMES (*Maiden, Professional, Religious, Aliases*): None
3. NATIONALITY: Malaysia
4. DATE OF BIRTH (*Month, day, year*): 11/8/52
5. PLACE OF BIRTH (*City, State, Country*): Kuala Lumpur, Selangor,
6. PASSPORT NUMBER: 011111
7. DATE PASSPORT ISSUED: 3/14/75
8. DATE PASSPORT EXPIRES: 3/14/80
9. PASSPORT ISSUED AT: KualaLumpur

DO NOT WRITE IN THIS SPACE

B-1, B-2, OTHER ______

MULTIPLE OR ______ APPLICATIONS

INDEF., 48 MOS., OR ______ MOS.

LO ______ VISA NO. ______

ISSUED/REFUSED ON ______ BY ______

REFUSED: SECTION ______ INA

REVIEWED BY ______

Leave Blank

10. RESIDENTIAL ADDRESS (*Include apartment number and postal zone*)
14, Talan 21/32
Kuala Lumpur, Selangor
Malaysia
Home Telephone Number:

11. HAVE YOU EVER APPLIED FOR A UNITED STATES VISA OF ANY KIND? ☐ Yes ☒ No
(*If YES, state where, when and type of visa*)

12. NAME AND ADDRESS OF EMPLOYER OR SCHOOL
Food Universal Co.
Kuala Lumpur, Malaysia
Business Telephone Number:

13. INDICATE WHETHER:
☐ Visa was granted
☐ Visa was refused
☐ Application was abandoned
☐ Application was withdrawn

14. HAS YOUR U.S. VISA EVER BEEN CANCELED? ☐ Yes ☒ No

15. HAVE YOU EVER BEEN THE BENEFICIARY OF AN IMMIGRANT VISA PETITION OR INDICATED TO A U.S. CONSULAR OFFICER A DESIRE TO IMMIGRATE TO THE U.S.A.? ☐ Yes ☒ No

16. HAVE YOU EVER BEEN IN THE UNITED STATES? (*If YES, when and for how long?*) ☐ Yes ☒ No

OPTIONAL FORM 156 (Rev. 2-76)
(Formerly Form FS-257a)
Department of State
50156-102

COMPLETE ALL QUESTIONS ON REVERSE OF FORM →

OVER →

SAMPLE SHEET

Form 156 is reproduced herein for illustrative purposes, courtesy of and from "Immigrating to the U.S.A" by Dan P. Danilov (Self-Counsel Press, Inc.), pp.98-99.

FORM OF 156

p. 2 of 2 pgs.

SAMPLE
(Back)

SAMPLE SHEET

17. PRESENT PROFESSION OR OCCUPATION (*If retired, state past profession*) mechanic

18. SEX ☐ Female ☒ Male

19. MARITAL STATUS ☒ Married ☐ Single ☐ Widowed ☐ Divorced ☐ Separated

20. COLOR OF HAIR Black

21. COLOR OF EYES Brown

22. HEIGHT 5'4"

23. COMPLEXION Olive

24. MARKS OF IDENTIFICATION scar on left cheek

25. WHAT IS THE PURPOSE OF YOUR TRIP? to visit brother in Chicago, Ill.

26. HOW LONG DO YOU PLAN TO STAY IN U.S.A.? 6 months

27. AT WHAT ADDRESS WILL YOU RESIDE IN THE U.S.? 1827 Broadmore St. Chicago, Illinois 60607

28. NAME, RELATIONSHIP, AND ADDRESS OF SPONSOR, SCHOOL, OR FIRM IN U.S.A.

29. WHEN DO YOU INTEND TO ARRIVE IN THE U.S.A.? February 10, 79

30. DO YOU INTEND TO WORK OR STUDY IN THE U.S.A.? ☐ Yes ☒ No

31. WHO WILL PAY FOR YOUR TICKETS TO LEAVE THE U.S. AT THE END OF YOUR TEMPORARY VISIT? I will pay for my tickets

32. WHO WILL FURNISH FINANCIAL SUPPORT? I will

33. HOW MUCH MONEY WILL YOU TAKE? $2000 U.S.

34. ARE ANY OF THE FOLLOWING IN THE U.S.A.? (*If YES, what is their status, i.e., student, working, etc?*)

☐ HUSBAND/WIFE no ☐ FIANCE/FIANCEE no ☒ BROTHER/~~SISTER~~ working
☐ FATHER/MOTHER no ☐ SON/DAUGHTER no

35. NAMES AND RELATIONSHIPS OF PERSONS TRAVELING WITH YOU none

36. HOW LONG HAVE YOU LIVED IN THIS COUNTRY? (*Country where you are applying for nonimmigration visa*) 6 years

37. PLEASE LIST THE COUNTRIES WHERE YOU HAVE LIVED FOR MORE THAN SIX MONTHS DURING THE PAST FIVE YEARS

Countries	*Cities*	*Approximate Dates*
Malaysia	Kuala Lumpur	April, 1972-present

38. TO WHICH ADDRESS DO YOU WISH YOUR VISA AND PASSPORT SENT? 14, Talan 21/32, Kuala Lumpur, Malaysia

39. IMPORTANT: ALL APPLICANTS MUST READ AND ANSWER THE FOLLOWING:

A visa may not be issued to persons who are within specific categories defined by law as inadmissible to the United States (except when a waiver is obtained in advance). Complete information regarding these categories and whether any may be applicable to you can be obtained from this office. Generally, they include persons

- Afflicted with contagious diseases (i.e., tuberculosis) or who have suffered serious mental illness;
- Arrested, convicted for any offense or crime even though subject of a pardon, amnesty, or other such legal action;
- Believed to be narcotic addicts or traffickers;
- Deported from the U.S.A. within the last 5 years;
- Who have sought to obtain a visa by misrepresentation or fraud;
- Who are or have been members of certain organizations including Communist organizations and those affiliated therewith;
- Who ordered, incited, assisted, or otherwise participated in the persecution of any person because of race, religion, national origin, or political opinion under the control, direct or indirect, of the Nazi Government of Germany, or of the government of any area occupied by, or allied with, the Nazi Government of Germany.

DO ANY OF THESE APPEAR TO APPLY TO YOU? ☒ No ☐ Yes
If YES, or if you have any question in this regard, personal appearance at this office is recommended. If it is not possible at this time, attach a statement of facts in your case to this application.

40. I certify that I have read and understood all the questions set forth in this application and the answers I have furnished on this form are true and correct to the best of my knowledge and belief. I understand that possession of a visa does not entitle the bearer to enter the United States of America upon arrival at port of entry if he or she is found inadmissible.

DATE OF APPLICATION 6/9/89

APPLICANT'S SIGNATURE [signature]

If this application has been prepared by a travel agency or another person on your behalf, the agent should indicate name and address of agency or person with appropriate signature of individual preparing form.

SIGNATURE OF PERSON PREPARING FORM ____________

DO NOT WRITE IN THIS SPACE

37 mm x 37 mm
PHOTO
Glue or staple photo here

OPTIONAL FORM 156 (Rev. 6/82) PAGE 2
Department of State

SAMPLE SHEET

FINGERPRINTS

Form FD-258

APPLICANT — LEAVE BLANK

TYPE OR PRINT ALL INFORMATION IN BLACK

LAST NAME NAM [redacted] FIRST NAME Sang MIDDLE NAME Kil

FBI — LEAVE BLANK

SIGNATURE OF PERSON FINGERPRINTED [redacted]

ALIASES AKA Sung [redacted]

ORI COINSDNOO USINS DENVER, CO

RESIDENCE OF PERSON FINGERPRINTED [redacted] Clinton Street [redacted], Colorado, 80010

DATE OF BIRTH DOB Month 3 Day 3 Year 45

CITIZENSHIP CTZ Korea

SEX	RACE	HGT.	WGT.	EYES	HAIR	PLACE OF BIRTH POB
M	-	5'7"	160	Brn	Blk	Korea

DATE / SIGNATURE OF OFFICIAL TAKING FINGERPRINTS [signature]

YOUR NO. OCA

LEAVE BLANK

EMPLOYER AND ADDRESS of fingerprinter
Aurora Police Department
Alameda Avenue
Aurora, Colorado

FBI NO. FBI

CLASS

ARMED FORCES NO. MNU

REF.

REASON FINGERPRINTED
Permanent Resident Applicant

SOCIAL SECURITY NO. SOC

MISCELLANEOUS NO. MNU

SAMPLE SHEET

1. R. THUMB | 2. R. INDEX | 3. R. MIDDLE | 4. R. RING | 5. R. LITTLE

6. L. THUMB | 7. L. INDEX | 8. L. MIDDLE | 9. L. RING | 10. L. LITTLE

LEFT FOUR FINGERS TAKEN SIMULTANEOUSLY | L. THUMB | R. THUMB | RIGHT FOUR FINGERS TAKEN SIMULTANEOUSLY

NOTE: Upon filling in the applicable information in the upper part of this form, the actual "fingerprinting" is to be done by an appropriate official (e.g. a police officer or other law enforcement personnel). See instructions on the back side of this Form.

U.S. Department of Justice
Immigration and Naturalization Service

For G-325A
BIOGRAPHIC INFORMATION

OMB No. 1115-0066

(Family name) (First name) (Middle name)	☐ MALE ☐ FEMALE	BIRTHDATE (Mo.-Day-Yr.)	NATIONALITY	FILE NUMBER A-
ALL OTHER NAMES USED (Including names by previous marriages)	CITY AND COUNTRY OF BIRTH			SOCIAL SECURITY NO. (If any)

	FAMILY NAME	FIRST NAME	DATE, CITY AND COUNTRY OF BIRTH (If known)	CITY AND COUNTRY OF RESIDENCE
FATHER				
MOTHER (Maiden name)				

HUSBAND (If none, so state) OR WIFE	FAMILY NAME (For wife, give maiden name)	FIRST NAME	BIRTHDATE	CITY & COUNTRY OF BIRTH	DATE OF MARRIAGE	PLACE OF MARRIAGE

FORMER HUSBANDS OR WIVES (if none, so state)

FAMILY NAME (For wife, give maiden name)	FIRST NAME	BIRTHDATE	DATE & PLACE OF MARRIAGE	DATE AND PLACE OF TERMINATION OF MARRIAGE

APPLICANT'S RESIDENCE LAST FIVE YEARS. LIST PRESENT ADDRESS FIRST.

STREET AND NUMBER	CITY	PROVINCE OR STATE	COUNTRY	FROM MONTH	FROM YEAR	TO MONTH	TO YEAR
						PRESENT TIME	

APPLICANT'S LAST ADDRESS OUTSIDE THE UNITED STATES OF MORE THAN ONE YEAR

STREET AND NUMBER	CITY	PROVINCE OR STATE	COUNTRY	FROM MONTH	FROM YEAR	TO MONTH	TO YEAR

APPLICANT'S EMPLOYMENT LAST FIVE YEARS. (IF NONE, SO STATE.) LIST PRESENT EMPLOYMENT FIRST

FULL NAME AND ADDRESS OF EMPLOYER	OCCUPATION (SPECIFY)	FROM MONTH	FROM YEAR	TO MONTH	TO YEAR
				PRESENT TIME	
Show below last occupation abroad if not shown above. (Include all information requested above.)					

THIS FORM IS SUBMITTED IN CONNECTION WITH APPLICATION FOR: ☐ NATURALIZATION ☐ STATUS AS PERMANENT RESIDENT ☐ OTHER (SPECIFY):	SIGNATURE OF APPLICANT	DATE
Are all copies legible? ☐ **Yes**	IF YOUR NATIVE ALPHABET IS IN OTHER THAN ROMAN LETTERS, WRITE YOUR NAME IN YOUR NATIVE ALPHABET IN THIS SPACE:	

PENALTIES: SEVERE PENALTIES ARE PROVIDED BY LAW FOR KNOWINGLY AND WILLFULLY FALSIFYING OR CONCEALING A MATERIAL FACT.

APPLICANT: BE SURE TO PUT YOUR NAME AND ALIEN REGISTRATION NUMBER IN THE BOX OUTLINED BY HEAVY BORDER BELOW.

COMPLETE THIS BOX (Family name)	(Given name)	(Middle name)	(Alien registration number)

SAMPLE FORM I-506

UNITED STATES DEPARTMENT OF JUSTICE
IMMIGRATION AND NATURALIZATION SERVICE

P.I.

Form Approved
OMB No. 43-R0342

Fee Stamp

NOTE: Refer to "Explanatory Note" on p.37, especially Paragraph 6 thereof

APPLICATION FOR CHANGE OF NONIMMIGRANT STATUS

(Under Section 248 of the Immigration and N

→ Please read the instructions o

I hereby apply to have my status in the U changed to that of a nonimmigrant E-2 (Student, visitor, etc.)

I wish to remain in the United States in that new status ~~until~~ as long as I am eligible (Month, Day, Year)

This application is submitted together with the required documents which are made a part hereof, and if applicable the fee of $10.

PRESS FIRMLY—LEGIBLE COPY REQUIRED. PRINT OR TYPE YOUR NAME EXACTLY AS IT APPEARS ON YOUR ARRIVAL-DEPARTURE RECORD FORM I-94. IF YOUR MAILING ADDRESS IN THE U.S. IS WITH SOMEONE WHOSE FAMILY NAME IS DIFFERENT FROM YOURS, INSERT THAT PERSON'S NAME IN THE C/O BLOCK.

1. YOUR NAME — FAMILY NAME (Capital Letters): [redacted] FIRST: Jules MIDDLE: Renaud

IN CARE OF — C/O: Dominique A. [redacted] FILE NUMBER (If Known):

2. MAILING ADDRESS IN U.S. — NUMBER AND STREET (Apt. No.): [redacted] Main Avenue
CITY: [redacted] STATE: Colorado ZIP CODE: 81301

3. DATE OF BIRTH (Month, Day, Year): Dec. 2, 1951 COUNTRY OF BIRTH: F.W.I. COUNTRY OF CITIZENSHIP: France

4. PRESENT NONIMMIGRANT CLASSIFICATION: B-2 DATE ON WHICH AUTHORIZED STAY EXPIRES: Jan. 6, 1984

5. DATE AND PORT OF LAST ARRIVAL IN UNITED STATES: 8/7/83 - Miami, Fla. NAME OF VESSEL, AIRLINE, OR OTHER MEANS OF LAST ARRIVAL IN U.S.: Eastern Airlines

6. THE PERMIT NUMBER ON MY FORM I-94 IS [redacted]

7. I AM IN POSSESSION OF PASSPORT NUMBER:* 4[redacted]
ISSUED BY (Country): French West Indies
WHICH EXPIRES ON: (Month, Day, Year): July 26, 1988

8. I AM ATTACHING MY TEMPORARY ENTRY PERMIT FORM I-94

9. I ENTERED WITH PASSPORT VISA NO. 007[redacted]

10. MY NONIMMIGRANT STATUS IN THE UNITED STATES ☐ HAS ☒ HAS NOT BEEN CHANGED SINCE MY ENTRY (If changed, give details)

FOR GOVERNMENT USE ONLY

Reclassification to

☐ STAY GRANTED TO (Date)

☐ Application DENIED V.D. TO (Date)

DATE OF ACTION

DO OR OIC OFFICE

11. MY PERMANENT ADDRESS OUTSIDE THE UNITED STATES IS: (Street) (City or Town) (County, District, Province or State) (Country)

Petit [redacted], St. Barthelemy [redacted] (Guadeloupe) F.W.I.

12. I RESIDED AT THE ADDRESS IN ITEM 11 FROM: (Month, Day, Year) December 2, 1951 TO: (Month, Day, Year) present

13. SINCE MY ENTRY INTO THE UNITED STATES I HAVE RESIDED AT THE FOLLOWING PLACES:

(Street and No.) (City or Town) (State)	FROM: (Month, Day, Year)	TO: (Month, Day, Year)
[redacted] Main Avenue, [redacted] Colorado	August 8, 1983	Present Time

14. I DESIRE TO HAVE MY NONIMMIGRANT STATUS CHANGED FOR THE FOLLOWING REASONS:

See attached

15. I DID NOT APPLY TO THE AMERICAN CONSUL FOR A VISA IN THE NONIMMIGRANT STATUS WHICH I AM NOW SEEKING FOR THE FOLLOWING REASONS:

See attached

16. I SUBMIT THE FOLLOWING DOCUMENTARY EVIDENCE TO ESTABLISH THAT I WILL MAINTAIN THE NONIMMIGRANT CLASSIFICATION TO WHICH I WISH TO BE CHANGED:

Form I-126 with supporting documentation.

ATTACH YOUR FORM I-94 — *DO NOT SEND YOUR PASSPORT

RECEIVED	TRANS. IN	RET'D-TRANS OUT	COMPLETED

FORM I-506 (REV. 9-12-77)Y

FORM I-506 P.2.

17. (COMPLETE THIS BLOCK ONLY IF YOU ARE APPLYING FOR CHANGE TO STUDENT STATUS) THE COUNTRY IN WHICH I INTEND TO LIVE AND WORK AFTER I COMPLETE MY SCHOOLING IN THE UNITED STATES IS ______

(IF YOU ARE SEEKING TO ATTEND A VOCATIONAL OR BUSINESS SCHOOL, COMPLETE THE FOLLOWING ADDITIONAL STATEMENTS BY CHECKING THE APPROPRIATE BOXES.)
THE SCHOOLING I AM SEEKING ☐ IS ☐ IS NOT AVAILABLE IN MY COUNTRY.

☐ INTEND ☐ DO NOT INTEND TO ENGAGE IN THE OCCUPATION FOR WHICH THAT SCHOOLING WILL PREPARE ME.

18. MY OCCUPATION IS: Chef | 19. SOCIAL SECURITY NO. (If none, state "none") None

20. ☐ HAVE ☒ HAVE NOT BEEN EMPLOYED OR ENGAGED IN BUSINESS SINCE ENTERING THE UNITED STATES. IF ANSWER IS IN AFFIRMATIVE, COMPLETE THE FOLLOWING:
NATURE OF OCCUPATION OR BUSINESS IN WHICH I ☐ AM ☐ WAS EMPLOYED:

NAME OF EMPLOYER OR BUSINESS FIRM | ADDRESS

MY EMPLOYMENT OR ENGAGEMENT IN BUSINESS BEGAN ON: (Month, Day, Year) | AND ENDED ON: (Month, Day, Year)

MY MONTHLY INCOME FROM EMPLOYMENT OR BUSINESS ☐ IS ☐ WAS:

21. IF NOT EMPLOYED OR ENGAGED IN BUSINESS IN THE UNITED STATES, DESCRIBE FULLY THE SOURCE AND AMOUNT OF YOUR INCOME ABROAD AND HOW SUPPORTED WHILE IN THE UNITED STATES: (If applying for change to student status, see Instruction #4.)
Am employed by [redacted] in St. Barthelemy, F.W.I. - on leave of absence - salary is $250/weekly plus bonus; savings of $9,000

22. ☒ I AM ☐ AM NOT MARRIED

Name of Spouse	Present address	Citizenship (Country)
Anne Gertrude [redacted]	[redacted] St. Barthelemy, F.W.I.	France

23. I HAVE two (Number) CHILDREN: (List children below)

Name	Age	Place of Birth	Present Address
Fabienne Anne [redacted]	5	F.W.I.	[redacted]
Donatienne [redacted]	3	F.W.I.	St. Barthelemy, FWI

I HAVE four (Number) OTHER RELATIVES IN THE UNITED STATES: (List relatives below)

Name	Relationship	Immigration Status	Present Address
Roger [redacted]	Half-brother	Perm.Res.	[redacted] SW 256 St., Homestead, Miami, Fl.
Leon [redacted]	Half-brother	Perm.Res.	Address unknown
Ribert [redacted]	Half-brother	Perm.Res.	Address Unknown
Ginette [redacted]	Sister-in-Law	E-2	[redacted] Main Ave., [redacted], CO

N/A ... COMPLIED WITH THE ADDRESS REPORTS REQUIRED BY THE ALIEN REGISTRATION ACT OF 1940 AS AMENDED AND BY SECTION 265 OF THE IMMIGRATION AND NATIONALITY ACT.

☐ HAVE ☒ HAVE NOT BEEN ARRESTED OR CONVICTED OF ANY CRIMINAL OFFENSE IN THE UNITED STATES OR IN ANY FOREIGN COUNTRY. IF ANSWER IS IN THE AFFIRMATIVE, GIVE DETAILS:

I certify that the above is true and correct to the best of my knowledge and belief. (If form prepared by other than applicant, that person must execute item 25.)

[signature] 9/30/83
(Signature of Applicant) (Date)

SIGNATURE OF PERSON PREPARING FORM, IF OTHER THAN APPLICANT
I declare that this document was prepared by me at the request of the applicant and is based on all information of which I have any knowledge.

[signature] 110 Sixteenth St., 14th Flr. Denver, Colorado 80202 10/3/83
(Signature) (Address) (Date)

SAMPLE SHEET

Response to Items 14 and 15 on Form I-506: [Attached To Form I-506]

14. I became associated with Dominique A. [redacted] and his wife, Josseline M.L. [redacted], as an employee in their restaurant, [redacted], in St. Barthelemy in the French West Indies in 1975 as their master chef. I prepared the specialized Caribbean dishes, the pates, the pastries, the recipes for which are proprietary to the [redacted] Restaurant, and the French bread, and was with them until early 1982.

15. Recently, I was invited by Mr. and Mrs. [redacted]s to visit their new restaurant in [redacted], Colorado, with the possibility of investing in it and possibly going back to work for them. I felt I could not make a decision about investing in the restaurant, or accepting their offer of employment until I took a look at their restaurant, the city of [redacted] and Colorado in general.

After seeing the [redacted] Restaurant and much discussion with Mr. and Mrs. [redacted], I concluded that my investing in their restaurant would be a wise, financial move for me and, because I always enjoyed working with them in the past, I would like to work with them again.

FORM I-539

NOTE → IMPORTANT Please read attached instructions before filling out application. Use typewriter or print in block letters with ball-point pen. Be sure this application and the attached Form I-539A and address mailing label are legible. Do not leave any question unanswered. When appropriate, insert "none" or "not applicable". If you need more space to answer fully any question on this form use a separate sheet of paper this size, and identify each answer with the number of the corresponding question.

UNITED STATES DEPARTMENT OF JUSTICE
IMMIGRATION AND NATURALIZATION SERVICE

READ INSTRUCTIONS CAREFULLY
FEE WILL NOT BE REFUNDED

OMB No. 1115—0093
Expires 1-94

FEE STAMP

APPLICATION TO EXTEND TIME OF TEMPORARY STAY

I HEREBY APPLY TO EXTEND MY TEMPORARY STAY IN THE UNITED STATES

PRESS FIRMLY — LEGIBLE COPY REQUIRED. PRINT OR TYPE YOUR NAME EXACTLY AS IT APPEARS ON YOUR ARRIVAL—DEPARTURE RECORD FORM I-94. IF YOUR MAILING ADDRESS IN THE U.S. IS WITH SOMEONE WHOSE FAMILY NAME IS DIFFERENT FROM YOURS, INSERT THAT PERSON'S NAME IN THE C/O BLOCK.

1. YOUR NAME — FAMILY NAME (CAPITAL LETTERS) FIRST MIDDLE

IN CARE OF — C/O

2. MAILING ADDRESS IN U.S. — NUMBER AND STREET (APT. NO.) — FILE NUMBER — CITY — STATE — ZIP CODE

3. DATE OF BIRTH (MO./DAY/YR.) — COUNTRY OF BIRTH — COUNTRY OF CITIZENSHIP

4. PRESENT NONIMMIGRANT CLASSIFICATION — DATE ON WHICH AUTHORIZED STAY EXPIRES

5. DATE AND PORT OF LAST ARRIVAL IN U.S. — NAME OF VESSEL, AIRLINE, OR OTHER MEANS OF LAST ARRIVAL IN U.S.

THE ADMISSION NUMBER FROM MY I-94 IS:

6. DATE TO WHICH EXTENSION IS REQUESTED

7. REASON FOR REQUESTING EXTENSION

TELEPHONE NUMBER

8. REASON FOR COMING TO THE U.S.

9. HAS AN IMMIGRANT VISA PETITION EVER BEEN FILED IN YOUR BEHALF? ☐ YES ☐ NO IF "YES", WHERE WAS IT FILED?

FOR GOVERNMENT USE ONLY

☐ EXTENSION GRANTED TO (DATE) — DATE OF ACTION

☐ EXTENSION DENIED V.D. TO (DATE) — DD OR OIC OFFICE

SAMPLE SHEET

10. HAVE YOU EVER APPLIED FOR AN IMMIGRANT VISA OR PERMANENT RESIDENCE IN THE U.S.? ☐ YES ☐ NO IF "YES", WHERE DID YOU APPLY?

11. I INTEND TO DEPART FROM THE U.S. ON (DATE) — I AM IN POSSESSION OF A TRANSPORTATION TICKET FOR MY DEPARTURE ☐ YES ☐ NO

12. PASSPORT NO. * — EXPIRES ON (DATE) — ISSUED BY (COUNTRY) — 13. NUMBER, STREET, CITY, PROVINCE (STATE) AND COUNTRY OF PERMANENT RESIDENCE

14. MY USUAL OCCUPATION IS: — 15. SOCIAL SECURITY NO. (IF NONE, STATE "NONE")

16. I ☐ AM ☐ AM NOT MARRIED. IF YOU WISH TO APPLY FOR EXTENSION FOR YOUR SPOUSE AND CHILDREN, GIVE THE FOLLOWING: (SEE INSTRUCTIONS # 1)

NAME OF SPOUSE AND CHILDREN	DATE OF BIRTH	COUNTRY OF BIRTH	PASSPORT ISSUED BY (COUNTRY) AND EXPIRES ON (DATE)	

NOTE IF SPOUSE AND CHILDREN FOR WHOM YOU ARE SEEKING EXTENSION DO NOT RESIDE WITH YOU, GIVE THEIR COMPLETE ADDRESS ON A SEPARATE ATTACHMENT TO THIS APPLICATION.

17. I (INSERT "HAVE" OR "HAVE NOT") ________ BEEN EMPLOYED OR ENGAGED IN BUSINESS IN THE UNITED STATES. (IF YOU HAVE BEEN EMPLOYED OR ENGAGED IN BUSINESS IN THE UNITED STATES, COMPLETE THE REST OF THE BLOCK.)

NAME AND ADDRESS OF EMPLOYER OR BUSINESS	INCOME PER WEEK	DATES EMPLOYMENT OR BUSINESS BEGAN AND ENDED

I certify that the above is true and correct

SIGNATURE OF APPLICANT X (Alien signs here) — DATE

SIGNATURE OF PERSON PREPARING FORM, IF OTHER THAN APPLICANT

I declare that this document was prepared by me at the request of the applicant and is based on all information on which I have any knowledge.

SIGNATURE — ADDRESS — DATE

ATTACH YOUR FORM I-94 OR I-144—*DO NOT SEND YOUR PASSPORT

RECEIVED	TRANS. IN	RET'D. TRANS. OUT	COMPLETED

Form I-539 (Rev. 5-4-89)N

U.S. Department of Justice
Immigration and Naturalization Service

Form I-601

Application for Waiver of Ground of Excludability

OMB No. 1115-0048

DO NOT WRITE IN THIS BLOCK

☐ 212 (a) (1) ☐ 212 (a) (10) Fee Stamp
☐ 212 (a) (3) ☐ 212 (a) (12)
☐ 212 (a) (6) ☐ 212 (a) (19)
☐ 212 (a) (9) ☐ 212 (a) (23)

A. Information about applicant -

1. Family Name (Surname in CAPS) (First) (Middle)
2. Address (Number and Street) (Apartment Number)
3. (Town or City) (State/Country) (ZIP/Postal Code)
4. Date of Birth *(Month/Day/Year)* 5. I&N File Number A-
6. City of Birth 7. Country of Birth
8. Date of visa application 9. Visa applied for at:

10. Applicant was declared inadmissible to the United States for the following reasons: (List acts, convictions, or physical or mental conditions. If applicant has active or suspected tuberculosis, the reverse of this page must be fully completed.)

11. Applicant was previously in the United States, as follows:

City & State	From (Date)	To (Date)	I&NS Status

12. Social Security Number

B. Information about relative, through whom applicant claims eligibility for a waiver -

1. Family Name (Surname in CAPS) (First) (Middle)
2. Address (Number and Street) (Apartment Number)
3. (Town or City) (State/Country) (ZIP/Postal Code)
4. Relationship to applicant 5. I&NS Status

C. Information about applicant's other relatives in the U.S. *(List only U.S. citizens and permanent residents)*

1. Family Name (Surname in CAPS) (First) (Middle)
2. Address (Number and Street) (Apartment Number)
3. (Town or City) (State/Country) (ZIP/Postal Code)
4. Relationship to applicant 5. I&NS Status

1. Family Name (Surname in CAPS) (First) (Middle)
2. Address (Number and Street) (Apartment Number)
3. (Town or City) (State/Country) (ZIP/Postal Code)
4. Relationship to applicant 5. I&NS Status

1. Family Name (Surname in CAPS) (First) (Middle)
2. Address (Number and Street) (Apartment Number)
3. (Town or City) (State/Country) (ZIP/Postal Code)
4. Relationship to applicant 5. I&NS Status

***Signature** (of applicant or petitioning relative)*

Relationship to applicant Date

Signature** (of person preparing application, if not the applicant or petitioning relative) **I declare that this document was prepared by me at the request of the applicant, or petitioning relative, and is based on all information of which I have any knowledge.

Signature

Address Date

Initial receipt	Resubmitted	Relocated		Completed		
		Received	Sent	Approved	Denied	Returned

SAMPLE FORM ETA 750A

U.S. DEPARTMENT OF LABOR
Employment and Training Administration

P.1. OMB Approval No. 44-R1301

APPLICATION FOR TEMPORARY ALIEN EMPLOYMENT CERTIFICATION

IMPORTANT: READ CAREFULLY BEFORE COMPLETING THIS FORM

PRINT legibly in ink or use a typewriter. If you need more space to answer questions on this form, use a separate sheet. Identify each answer with the number of the corresponding question. SIGN AND DATE each sheet in original signature.

To knowingly furnish any false information in the preparation of this form and any supplement thereto or to aid, abet, or counsel another to do so is a felony punishable by $10,000 fine or 5 years in the penitentiary, or both (18 U.S.C. 1001).

NOTE: Refer to "Explanatory Note" on p. 37, especially the No. 3 paragraph therein.

PART A. OFFER OF EMPLOYMENT

1. Name of Alien (Family name in capital letter, First, Middle, Maiden): [redacted], Arturo N.M.N.

2. Present Address of Alien (Number, Street, City and Town, State ZIP Code or Province, Country): c/o Pedro [redacted], [redacted] Flacc Lourdes, Chihuahua, Chihuahua, Mexico

3. Type of Visa (If in U.S.): None

The following information is submitted as evidence of an offer of employment.

4. Name of Employer (Full name of organization): Rocky [redacted]., Inc.

5. Telephone (Area Code and Number): 303-[redacted]

6. Address (Number, Street, City or Town, Country, State, ZIP Code): [redacted] Brighton Boulevard, Denver, Colorado [redacted]

7. Address Where Alien Will Work (if different from item 6): N/A

8. Nature of Employer's Business Activity	9. Name of Job Title	10. Total Hours Per Week a. Basic	10. b. Overtime	11. Work Schedule (Hourly)	12. Rate of Pay a. Basic	12. b. Overtime
All processes involving tin	Hand-wiping of tin	40	N/A	7:30 a.m. 4:00 p.m.	$ 5.00 per hour	$ N/A per hour

13. Describe Fully the Job to be Performed (Duties)

The hand-wiping of tin on copper cooking ware and other types of copper utensils; the application of tin to heated and fluxed copper surfaces, either by a stick of pure tin, or in the molten state from a ladle, and then wiped and swirled over the surface by hand.

14. State in detail the MINIMUM education, training, and experience for a worker to perform satisfactorily the job duties described in Item 13 above.

EDUCATION (Enter number of years)	Grade School: 6	High School: 6	College: 0	College Degree Required (specify): None; Major Field of Study: None
TRAINING	No. Yrs.: 1	No. Mos.:		Type of Training: Hand-wiping of tin
EXPERIENCE	Job Offered — Number Yrs.: 9	Job Offered — Mos.:	Related Occupation — Yrs.: -- Mos.:	Related Occupation (specify): --

15. Other Special Requirements: None

16. Occupational Title of Person Who Will Be Alien's Immediate Supervisor: Owner/President

17. Number of Employees Alien will Supervise: 0

1. QUALIFIED WORKERS CANNOT BE FOUND IN THE UNITED STATES.
2. EMPLOYMENT SERVICE POLICIES HAVE BEEN OBSERVED.
3. THIS CERTIFICATION IS VALID FROM 12/23/81 THROUGH 12/31/82

12/23/81
(DATE)

Charles B. Vigil for
(CERTIFYING OFFICER)
RAYMOND P. LAMB

ENDORSEMENTS (Make no entry in this section - for government use only)

Date Forms Received	
L.O. 8-5-81	S.O. 12/3/81
R.O. 12-17-81	N.O.
Ind. Code 5051	Occ. Code 56228 1014
Occ. Title HAND TINNER	

P.1 of 2 pgs.

FORM ETA 750A P.2

18. COMPLETE ITEMS ONLY IF JOB IS TEMPORARY

a. No. of Openings To Be Filled By Aliens Under Job Offer	b. Exact Dates You Expect To Employ Alien — From	To
1	1/1/82	12/31/82

19. IF JOB IS UNIONIZED *(Complete)*

a. Number of Local	b. Name of Local	c. City and State
N/A		

20. STATEMENT FOR LIVE-AT-WORK JOB OFFERS *(Complete for Private Household Job ONLY)* N/A

Description of Residence ("X" one)	Number of Rooms	b. No. Persons Residing at Place of Employment — Adults		Children	Ages	c. Will free board and private room not shared with anyone be provided? ("X" one)
☐ House			BOYS			☐ YES ☐ NO
☐ Apartment			GIRLS			

21. DESCRIBE EFFORTS TO RECRUIT U.S. WORKERS AND THE RESULTS. *(Specify Sources of Recruitment by Name)*

Prior to filing ETA 750, inquiries within the industry; newspaper advertisements.

Subsequent to filing of ETA 750, job offer filed with local Job Service Center; advertisements in The Denver Post, Denver, Colorado, and in the Phoenix Gazette of Phoenix, Arizona.

22. Applications require various types of documentation. Please read PART II of the instructions to assure that appropriate supporting documentation is included with your application.

23. EMPLOYER CERTIFICATIONS

By virtue of my signature below, I HEREBY CERTIFY the following conditions of employment.

a. I have enough funds available to pay the wage or salary offered the alien.

b. The wage offered equals or exceeds the prevailing wage and I guarantee that, if a labor certification is granted, the wage paid to the alien when the alien begins work will equal or exceed the prevailing wage which is applicable at the time the alien begins work.

c. The wage offered is not based on commissions, bonuses, or other incentives, unless I guarantee a wage paid on a weekly, bi-weekly or monthly basis.

d. I will be able to place the alien on the payroll on or before the date of the alien's proposed entrance into the United States.

e. The job opportunity does not involve unlawful discrimination by race, creed, color, national origin, age, sex, religion, handicap, or citizenship.

f. The job opportunity is not:

(1) Vacant because the former occupant is on strike or is being locked out in the course of a labor dispute involving a work stoppage.

(2) At issue in a labor dispute involving a work stoppage.

g. The job opportunity's terms, conditions and occupational environment are not contrary to Federal, State or local law.

h. The job opportunity has been and is clearly open to any qualified U.S. worker.

24. DECLARATIONS

DECLARATION OF EMPLOYER ➤ *Pursuant to 28 U.S.C. 1746, I declare under penalty of perjury the foregoing is true and correct.*

SIGNATURE	DATE
X [signature]	July 28, 1981

NAME (Type or Print)	TITLE
Peter [redacted]	President/Owner

AUTHORIZATION OF AGENT OF EMPLOYER ➤ I HEREBY DESIGNATE the agent below to represent me for the purposes of labor certification and I TAKE FULL RESPONSIBILITY for accuracy of any representations made by my agent.

SIGNATURE OF EMPLOYER	DATE
X [signature]	July 28, 19[illegible]

NAME OF AGENT (Type or Print) [if applicable]	ADDRESS OF AGENT (Number, Street, City, State, ZIP Code)
C. James Cooper, Jr.	110 16th Street, 14th Floor Denver, Colorado 80202

FORM ETA750A (End of Form) P.2 of 2 pgs.

p.1

ETA 750A (Part A)

SAMPLE

U.S. DEPARTMENT OF LABOR
Employment and Training Administration

FORM ETA 750A APPLICATION FOR ALIEN EMPLOYMENT CERTIFICATION

IMPORTANT: READ CAREFULLY BEFORE COMPLETING THIS FORM

PRINT legibly in ink or use a typewriter. If you need more space to answer questions on this form, use a separate sheet. Identify each answer with the number of the corresponding question. SIGN AND DATE each sheet in original signature.

To knowingly furnish any false information in the preparation of this form and any supplement thereto or to aid, abet, or counsel another to do so is a felony punishable by $10,000 fine or 5 years in the penitentiary, or (18 U.S.C. 1001).

PART A. OFFER OF EMPLOYMENT

1. Name of Alien (*Family name in capital letter, First, Middle, Maiden*)
[redacted] Arun

2. Present Address of Alien (*Number, Street, City and Town, State ZIP Code or Province, Country*)
[redacted] Shields [redacted], Fort Collins, Colorado, [redacted], USA

3. Type of Visa (*If in U.S.*)
F-1 (practical training)

The following information is submitted as evidence of an offer of employment.

4. Name of Employer (*Full name of organization*)
[redacted]., Colorado [redacted] Operation

5. Telephone (*Area Code and Number*)
303-[redacted]

6. Address (*Number, Street, City or Town, Country, State, ZIP Code*)
[redacted] Harmony Road, Fort Collins, [redacted] Colorado, [redacted]

NOTE: Refer to "Explanatory Note" on p. 37, esp. paragraph 3

7. Address Where Alien Will Work (*if different from item 6*)
N/A

8. Nature of Employer's Business Activity	9. Name of Job Title	10. Total Hours Per Week a. Basic	10. b. Overtime	11. Work Schedule (Hourly)	12. Rate of Pay a. Basic	12. b. Overtime
Manufacturer of computers, peripherals & software, electronic equip, etc.	Development Engineer (Software)	40	--	8:00 a.m. 5:00 p.m.	$ 30,240 per year	$ -- per hour

13. Describe Fully the Job to be Performed (*Duties*)

Architect, design and develop advanced networking and operating system software on UNIX-based technical workstations, using C language; apply strong academic background in operating systems, networking, UNIX and C language to 2K NCSS (2,000 Non-Commented Source Statement) operating system and networking-related software products.

D.O.T. 003.167-062

14. State in detail the MINIMUM education, training, and experience for a worker to perform satisfactorily the job duties described in Item 13 above.

	Grade School	High School	College	College Degree Required (*specify*)
EDUCATION (*Enter number of years*)	6	6	6	Bachelor and Master
				Major Field of Study: Computer Science

	No. Yrs.	No. Mos.	Type of Training
TRAINING			

	Job Offered Yrs.	Job Offered Mos.	Related Occupation Yrs.	Related Occupation Mos.	Related Occupation (*specify*)
EXPERIENCE	0				

15. Other Special Requirements

16. Occupational Title of Person Who Will Be Alien's Immediate Supervisor: Project Manager

17. Number of Employees Alien will Supervise: 0

ENDORSEMENTS (*Make no entry in section - for government use only*)

Date Forms Received	
L.O. MAY 02 1985	S.O.
R.O. 6/19/85	N.O.
Ind. Code 35	Occ. Code 003167062
Occ. Title: Development Engineer	

CERTIFICATION
PURSUANT TO THE PROVISIONS OF SECTION 212(A) (14) OF THE IMMIGRATION AND NATIONALITY ACT AS AMENDED I HEREBY CERTIFY THAT THERE ARE NOT SUFFICIENT U. S. WORKERS AVAILABLE AND THE EMPLOYMENT OF THE ABOVE WILL NOT ADVERSELY AFFECT THE WAGES AND WORKING CONDITIONS OF WORKERS IN THE U. S. SIMILARLY EMPLOYED.

10/18/85 Charles B. Vigil
(Certifying Officer)

Replaces MA 7-50A, B and C (Apr. 1970 edition) which is obsolete.

ETA 750 (Oct. 1979)

-OVER- →

FORM ETA 750-A P.2

18. COMPLETE ITEMS ONLY IF JOB IS TEMPORARY			19. IF JOB IS UNIONIZED (Complete)	
a. No. of Openings To Be Filled By Aliens Under Job Offer	b. Exact Dates You Expect To Employ Alien — From	To	a. Number of Local	b. Name of Local
N/A				c. City and State

20. STATEMENT FOR LIVE-AT-WORK JOB OFFERS (Complete for Private Household Job ONLY)

a. Description of Residence ("X" one)	Number of Rooms	b. No. Persons Residing at Place of Employment — Adults	Children		Ages	c. Will free board and private room not shared with any-one be provided? ("X" one)
☐ House			BOYS			☐ YES ☐ NO
☐ Apartment	N/A		GIRLS			

21. DESCRIBE EFFORTS TO RECRUIT U.S. WORKERS AND THE RESULTS. (Specify Sources of Recruitment by Name)

Employer has and will conduct such recruitment efforts as are appropriate and normal to the industry and customary for this company.

SAMPLE

22. Applications require various types of documentation. Please read PART II of the instructions to assure that appropriate supporting documentation is included with your application.

23. EMPLOYER CERTIFICATIONS

By virtue of my signature below, I HEREBY CERTIFY the following conditions of employment.

a. I have enough funds available to pay the wage or salary offered the alien.

b. The wage offered equals or exceeds the prevailing wage and I guarantee that, if a labor certification is granted, the wage paid to the alien when the alien begins work will equal or exceed the prevailing wage which is applicable at the time the alien begins work.

c. The wage offered is not based on commissions, bonuses, or other incentives, unless I guarantee a wage paid on a weekly, bi-weekly or monthly basis.

d. I will be able to place the alien on the payroll on or before the date of the alien's proposed entrance into the United States.

e. The job opportunity does not involve unlawful discrimination by race, creed, color, national origin, age, sex, religion, handicap, or citizenship.

f. The job opportunity is not:

(1) Vacant because the former occupant is on strike or is being locked out in the course of a labor dispute involving a work stoppage.

(2) At issue in a labor dispute involving a work stoppage.

g. The job opportunity's terms, conditions and occupational environment are not contrary to Federal, State or local law.

h. The job opportunity has been and is clearly open to any qualified U.S. worker.

24. DECLARATIONS

DECLARATION OF EMPLOYER — *Pursuant to 28 U.S.C. 1746, I declare under penalty of perjury the foregoing is true and correct.*

SIGNATURE	DATE
[signature]	4-22-85
NAME (Type or Print) [redacted] Company By Marlene [redacted]	TITLE Personnel Representative

AUTHORIZATION OF AGENT OF EMPLOYER — *I HEREBY DESIGNATE the agent below to represent me for the purposes of labor certification and I TAKE FULL RESPONSIBILITY for accuracy of any representations made by my agent.*

SIGNATURE OF EMPLOYER	DATE
[signature]	4-22-85
NAME OF AGENT (Type or Print) C. James Cooper, Jr.	ADDRESS OF AGENT (Number, Street, City, State, ZIP Code) 999 Eighteenth Street, Suite 3220 Denver, Colorado 80202

-OVER-

ETA 750B (Part B)

p.3

PART B. STATEMENT OF QUALIFICATIONS OF ALIEN

FOR ADVICE CONCERNING REQUIREMENTS FOR ALIEN EMPLOYMENT CERTIFICATION: *If alien is in the U.S., contact nearest office of Immigration and Naturalization Service. If alien is outside U.S., contact nearest U.S. Consulate.*

IMPORTANT: READ ATTACHED INSTRUCTIONS BEFORE COMPLETING THIS FORM.

...int legibly in ink or use a typewriter. If you need more space to fully answer any questions on this form, use a separate sheet. Identify each answer with the number of the corresponding question. Sign and date each sheet.

1. Name of Alien *(Family name in capital letters)* — [redacted] | *First name* Arun | *Middle name* NMN | *Maiden name* N/A

2. Present Address *(No., Street, City or Town, State or Province and ZIP Code)* — [redacted]. Shields, [redacted], Fort Collins, Colorado, [redacted] | *Country* USA

3. Type of Visa *(If in U.S.)* — F-1 (prac. training)

4. Alien's Birthdate *(Month, Day, Year)* — 9/17/61

5. Birthplace *(City or Town, State or Province)* — Southampton | *Country* United Kingdom

6. Present Nationality or Citizenship *(Country)* — Indian

7. Address in United States Where Alien Will Reside — [redacted]. Shields, Rd, Fort collins, Colorado, [redacted], USA

8. Name and Address of Prospective Employer if Alien has job offer in U.S. — [redacted]., Colorado [redacted] Operation

9. Occupation in which Alien is Seeking Work — Development Engineer (Software)

10. "X" the appropriate box below and furnish the information required for the box marked

a. ☐ Alien will apply for a visa abroad at the American Consulate in → | City in Foreign Country | Foreign Country

b. ☒ Alien is in the United States and will apply for adjustment of status to that of a lawful permanent resident in the office of the Immigration and Naturalization Service at → | City: Denver | State: Colorado

11. Names and Addresses of Schools, Colleges and Universities Attended *(Include trade or vocational training facilities)*	Field of Study	FROM Month	FROM Year	TO Month	TO Year	Degrees or Certificates Received
Ohio State University Columbus, Ohio	Computer Science	Sept.	1983	Dec.	1984	M.S.
Indian Inst. of Tech. Kanpur, India	Computer Science	Aug.	1978	May	1983	B.Tech.
Colvin Talugdars Coll. Lucknow, India	Maths, Science	July	1975	July	1977	Graduated

SPECIAL QUALIFICATIONS AND SKILLS

12. Additional Qualifications and Skills Alien Possesses and Proficiency in the use of Tools, Machines or Equipment Which Would Help Establish if Alien Meets Requirements for Occupation in Item 9.

N/A

13. List Licenses *(Professional, journeyman, etc.)*

N/A

14. List Documents Attached Which are Submitted as Evidence that Alien Possesses the Education, Training, Experience, and Abilities Represented

Diploma - school transcript

Endorsements | DATE REC. DOL | O.T. & C.

(Make no entry in this section — FOR Government Agency USE ONLY)

(Items continued on next page)

-OVER- →

FORM ETA 750-B

P.4

15. WORK EXPERIENCE. List all jobs held during past three (3) years. Also, list any other jobs related to the occupation ... seeking certification as indicated in item 9.

a. NAME AND ADDRESS OF EMPLOYER

[redacted]co., Colorado [redacted] Operation
[redacted]. Harmony Road, Fort Collins, Colorado, [redacted]

NAME OF JOB	DATE STARTED Month / Year	DATE LEFT Month / Year	KIND OF BUSINESS
Development Engineer (Software)	Jan. 1985	to present	Design & Mfg. of computers, etc.

DESCRIBE IN DETAILS THE DUTIES PERFORMED, INCLUDING THE USE OF TOOLS, MACHINES, OR EQUIPMENT

Creates software; responsible for assignments involving research, development, or design of new products or maintaining existing products, which includes development of standards, algorithms, architectures, specifications, languages, networking, as well as problem analysis, planning, scheduling, establishing operating data, and conducting tests.

NO. OF HOURS PER WEEK: 40

b. NAME AND ADDRESS OF EMPLOYER

NAME OF JOB	DATE STARTED Month / Year	DATE LEFT Month / Year	KIND OF BUSINESS

DESCRIBE IN DETAIL THE DUTIES PERFORMED, INCLUDING THE USE OF TOOLS, MACHINES, OR EQUIPMENT

NO. OF HOURS PER WEEK

c. NAME AND ADDRESS OF EMPLOYER

NAME OF JOB	DATE STARTED Month / Year	DATE LEFT Month / Year	KIND OF BUSINESS

DESCRIBE IN DETAIL THE DUTIES PERFORMED, INCLUDING THE USE OF TOOLS, MACHINES, OR EQUIPMENT

NO. OF HOURS PER WEEK

16. DECLARATIONS

DECLARATION OF ALIEN ➤➤ Pursuant to 28 U.S.C. 1746, I declare under penalty of perjury the foregoing is true and correct.

SIGNATURE OF ALIEN [redacted] — DATE 3/19/85

AUTHORIZATION OF AGENT OF ALIEN ➤➤ I hereby designate the agent below to represent me for the purposes of labor certification and I take full responsibility for accuracy of any representations made by my agent.

SIGNATURE OF ALIEN [redacted] — DATE 3/19/85

NAME OF AGENT (Type or print)	ADDRESS OF AGENT (No., Street, City, State, ZIP Code)
C. James Cooper, Jr.	999 Eighteenth Street, Suite 3220 Denver, Colorado 80202

(End of Form)

Form ETA-9035

Labor Condition Application for H-1B Nonimmigrants

U.S. Department of Labor
Employment and Training Administration
U.S. Employment Service

OMB Approval No.: 1205-0310
Expiration Date: 11-30-97

1. Full Legal Name of Employer

2. Federal Employer I.D. Number

3. Employer's Telephone No.
( )

4. Employer's FAX No.
( )

5. Employer's Address (No., Street, City, State, and ZIP Code)

6. Address Where Documentation is Kept (If different than item 5)

7. OCCUPATIONAL INFORMATION (Use attachment if additional space is needed)

(a) Three-digit Occupational Group Code (From Appendix 2): ________ (b) Job Title (Check Box if Part-Time): ________ ☐

(c) No. of H-1B Nonimmigrants	(d) Rate of Pay	(e) Prevailing Wage Rate and its Source (see instructions)	(f) Period of Employment From	To	(g) Location(s) Where H-1B Nonimmigrants Will Work (see instructions)
________	$________	$________ ☐SESA ☐Other: ________	________	________	________
________	$________	$________ ☐SESA ☐Other: ________	________	________	________

8. EMPLOYER LABOR CONDITION STATEMENTS (Employers are required to develop and maintain documentation supporting labor condition statements 8(a) and 8(d). Employers are further required to make available for public examination a copy of the labor condition application and necessary supporting documentation within one (1) working day after the date on which the application is filed with DOL. Check **each** box to indicate that the employer will comply with **each** statement.)

☐ (a) H-1B nonimmigrants will be paid at least the actual wage level paid by the employer to all other individuals with similar experience and qualifications for the specific employment in question or the prevailing wage level for the occupation in the area of employment, whichever is higher.

☐ (b) The employment of H-1B nonimmigrants will not adversely affect the working conditions of workers similarly employed in the area of intended employment.

☐ (c) On the date this application is signed and submitted, there is not a strike, lockout or work stoppage in the course of a labor dispute in the occupation in which H-1B nonimmigrants will be employed at the place of employment. If such a strike or lockout occurs after this application is submitted, I will notify ETA within 3 days of the occurrence of such a strike or lockout and the application will not be used in support of petition filings with INS for H-1B nonimmigrants to work in the same occupation at the place of employment until ETA determines the strike or lockout has ceased.

☐ (d) A copy of this application has been, or will be, provided to each H-1B nonimmigrant employed pursuant to this application, and, as of this date, notice of this application has been provided to workers employed in the occupation in which H-1B nonimmigrants will be employed: (check appropriate box)

☐ (i) Notice of this filing has been provided to the bargaining representative of workers in the occupation in which H-1B nonimmigrants will be employed; or

☐ (ii) There is no such bargaining representative; therefore, a notice of this filing has been posted and was, or will remain, posted for 10 days in at least two conspicuous locations where H-1B nonimmigrants will be employed.

9. DECLARATION OF EMPLOYER. Pursuant to 28 U.S.C. 1746, I declare under penalty of perjury that the information provided on this form is true and correct. In addition, I declare that I will comply with the Department of Labor regulations governing this program and, in particular, that I will make this application, supporting documentation, and other records, files and documents available to officials of the Department of Labor, upon such official's request, during any investigation under this application or the Immigration and Nationality Act.

Name and Title of Hiring or Other Designated Official ________ Signature ________ Date ________

Complaints alleging misrepresentation of material facts in the labor condition application and/or failure to comply with the terms of the labor condition application may be filed with any office of the Wage and Hour Division of the United States Department of Labor.

AN APPLICATION CERTIFIED BY DOL MUST BE FILED IN SUPPORT OF AN H-1B VISA PETITION WITH THE INS.

FOR U.S. GOVERNMENT AGENCY USE ONLY: By virtue of my signature below, I acknowledge that this application is hereby certified and will be valid from ________ through ________.

Signature and Title of Authorized DOL Official ________ ETA Case No. ________ Date ________

Subsequent DOL Action: Suspended ________ (date) Invalidated ________ (date) Withdrawn ________ (date)

The Department of Labor is not the guarantor of the accuracy, truthfulness or adequacy of a certified labor condition application.

Public reporting burden for this collection of information is estimated to average 1 hour per response, including the time for reviewing instructions searching existing data sources, gathering and maintaining the data needed, and completing and reviewing the collection of information. Send comments regarding this burden estimate or any other aspect of this collection of information, including suggestions for reducing this burden, to the Office of U.S. Employment Service, Department of Labor, Room N-4470 and/or the Office of IRM Policy, DOL, Room N-1301, 200 Constitution Avenue, N.W., Washington, DC 20210. (1205-0310).

DO NOT SEND THE COMPLETED FORM TO EITHER OF THESE OFFICES

GPO 784-977/59058

ETA 9035 (Rev. Dec. 1994)

FROM:

, INC.

EMPLOYER OFFER OF EMPLOYMENT LETTER

TO:

Miss Dawning
Flat B, 10th Flr.
n
Sheung Shing St.
Hong Kong

April 3, 1984

Dear Dawning:

As we have discussed, I have offered you the position of Apparel Account Executive with our company on a temporary basis, until we are able to locate, hire and train an individual to fill this position on a permanent basis.

This letter is to confirm this offer and your acceptance of this position at an annual salary of $42,000.00. This position's responsibilities include the handling of all our clothing orders with each of the factories in Hong Kong and Taiwan, coordinating all piece goods with each factory, setting up production schedules that can be met, and setting up a file and production system in our office that will correlate with those factories.

I became quite impressed with your experience and abilities in handling our account with your employer in Hong Kong, and feel that you will add greatly to the efficient organization of the development and production areas of our business which will help increase our productivity.

As you are aware, the offer of the position of Apparel Account Executive is subject to approval of our petition by the Immigration and Naturalization Service.

Sincerely,

Bill
Bill

BG:jcb

NOTE: See "Explanatory Note" on P.37, especially the No. 2 paragraph thereof.

Parkway Englewood, Colorado 80111
Cable: • TWX • FAX (303)

FROM:

■■■■, INC.

NOTE: See "Explanatory Note" on p. 37, especially the No. 2 paragraph thereof.

April 9, 1984

(EMPLOYER'S JOB DESCRIPTION)

TO WHOM IT MAY CONCERN:

As our Account Executive, Miss Dawning ■■■ will be responsible for the management and coordination of all areas related to the development and production of our product lines. At the current time, we have five lines of skiwear fashions for a total of approximately 300 styles. We work a year in advance in this industry, and for each season our development and production encompass the following sequence of activities:

1. Research the current market and trends.
2. Identify design concept, price point, and style catagories for each line.
3. Anticipate trends for the coming season by working with fabric, trim, and color resources. (To include: Arthur Kahn, Seatex, Toray, Gore-Tex, Y.K.K. zippers, Sumitomo, Schoeller Textil, Pottendorfer, and AuMan.)
4. Select fabrics and colors for the new season, and order greige goods and lab dips from each vendor.
5. Coordination of trim and hardware colors with these resources to complement fabric colors.
6. Design, sketch, and detail styles for each line.
7. Adopt styles from sketches to be made into prototype samples.
8. Select factory to make prototype based upon equipment necessary to produce this style of garment.
9. Send designer sketch with detailed specification sheet to factory.
10. Upon receipt of prototype from factory, each style is reviewed and comments are made on the fit, detail, construction, and design elements. These comments are sent back to the factory.
11. Each prototype style that is considered for adoption into the line is then priced from the factory.
12. All fabrics, knit, trim, hardware, and accessories are coordinated to be delivered to the factory for sample production.
13. Styles are selected for each line, and details regarding fabric, insulation, knit, hardware, etc. are sent to the factory. Sample colors are selected, labeling defined, sizing established, and prices are set for our catalog.
14. Sample production is coordinated to meet the scheduled selling shows for our industry.
15. Sales for each style are projected and greige goods are booked for each fabric for production. Production space with each factory is also booked in anticipation of our needs for the coming season.
16. Based on sales and early projections, all elements for production are coordinated for delivery to the factory so that the product ship dates meet the delivery requirements of our customers.

Miss ■■■'s education, experience, and ability to communicate in Chinese make her a most desireable candidate for this position. Her knowledge of textiles and garment construction, as well as, her experience in working in the same factories we use in Hong Kong and Taiwan will provide us with the strong communication link we do not currently have. Since she has been managing our account in Hong Kong, we feel she can help us to more efficiently organize our development and production areas (as listed) to meet the needs of our factories. We expect that her contribution will help us to increase productivity and effect more timely delivery of samples and production for better business. Miss ■■■ salary will be $42,000.

Sincerely,

Bill ■■■

■■■ Suite 2000 ■■■ Englewood, Colorado 80111
Cable: ■■■ • TWX ■■■ • FAX ■■■

FROM:

Rocky Co. Inc.
Brighton Boulevard, Denver, Colorado
303
NOTE: Refer to "Explanatory Note" on p. 37, especially the No. 3 paragraph therein.

Hot Dip Tinning -- Handwipe Tinning -- Electro Tin Plating

<u>EMPLOYER LETTER</u> (Letter of Business Necessity)

January 5, 1982

<u>TO</u>:

Immigration and Naturalization Service
1961 Stout Street
Denver, Colorado 80202

Re: Mr. Arturo ← Name of the alien Beneficiary

Gentlemen:

This letter is being written in support of the H-2 classification petition being filed herewith on behalf of Arturo to be employed by this company on a temporary basis as a hand-wiper of tin.

The Department of Labor has certified this individual to work temporarily in the United States for our company. As evidenced by such certified Alien Employment Application, ads were placed in newspapers in the United States, which resulted in no applicants for the job of the hand-wiping of tin.

Mr. abilities in the art of tin hand-wiping will be of benefit to our company, in that his sole purpose will be to train a U. S. citizen in this little-known art.

Yours very truly,

ROCKY CO., INC.

Peter s, President

Name of the Employing company

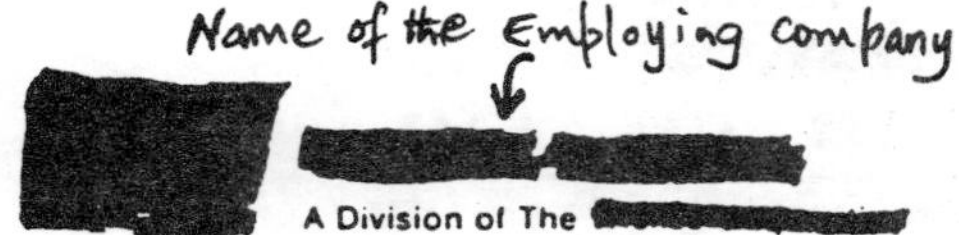

A Division of The

TRAINING
PROGRAM LETTER

To Whom It May Concern:

Andreas , an exchange student from Switzerland is requesting an "H-3" visa which would enable him to complete Management Training Programm. We have encouraged him to do so, since it would be a tremendous value for him.

Andreas will be trained in marketing and sales of lumber and building-products. Approximately 25% of his time will be devoted to productive work while training. 75% will be training.

Classroomtraining or selfstudiing of slideshows, books and other company materials will take about 8 to 10 hrs. per week. (48-hour work week.) The trainee will be instructed in construction and architecture of american housing which is entirly different from the one in Switzerland. Much time will also be devoted to productknowledge and the operating procedures of the Company.

Approximately 24 to 26 hrs. are spent on the job training. The trainee will get acquainted with

- Warehousing: Stocking of materials, general operations of a warehouse and lumberyard
- Sales: Salestechniques and displays
- Advertising: specialtechniques involved in the lumberbusiness
- Inventory management: Management of stock and ordering materials.

This Training will enable Andreas to sell and market Lumber and other Buildingmaterials, also make him capable of managing smaller operations.

special trainingprogramm is considered to be the industries best. With 260 Lumberyards alone in the United States we are the true leaders in this field and today the world's largest lumber retailer. Hence our training provided in the United States cannot be duplicated anywhere else.

signed: ______________________, date: 2-5-1979

Kaj (Zonemanager of in Colorado, a division of The

SAMPLE SHEET

SAMPLE SHEET

NOTE: Refer to "Explanatory Note" on p.37, especially Paragraph 4 therein.

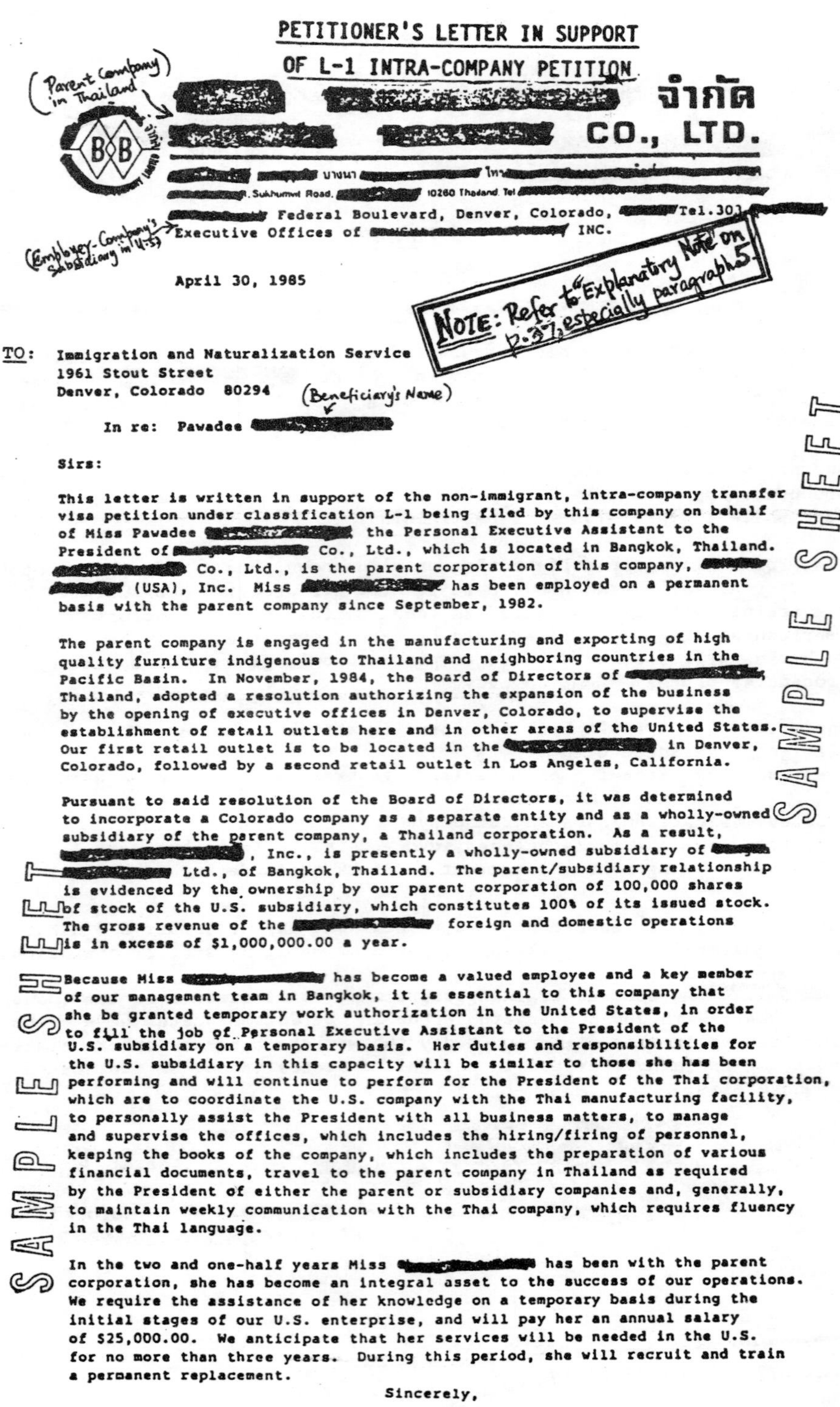

PETITIONER'S LETTER IN SUPPORT

OF L-1 INTRA-COMPANY PETITION

(Parent Company in Thailand)

จำกัด

CO., LTD.

บางนา ไทย

Sukhumvit Road, 10260 Thailand Tel

Federal Boulevard, Denver, Colorado, Tel.303
Executive Offices of INC.

(Employer-Company's subsidiary in U.S.)

April 30, 1985

NOTE: Refer to Explanatory Note on p. 37, especially paragraph 5.

TO: Immigration and Naturalization Service
1961 Stout Street
Denver, Colorado 80294

In re: Pawadee (Beneficiary's Name)

Sirs:

This letter is written in support of the non-immigrant, intra-company transfer visa petition under classification L-1 being filed by this company on behalf of Miss Pawadee the Personal Executive Assistant to the President of Co., Ltd., which is located in Bangkok, Thailand. Co., Ltd., is the parent corporation of this company, (USA), Inc. Miss has been employed on a permanent basis with the parent company since September, 1982.

The parent company is engaged in the manufacturing and exporting of high quality furniture indigenous to Thailand and neighboring countries in the Pacific Basin. In November, 1984, the Board of Directors of Thailand, adopted a resolution authorizing the expansion of the business by the opening of executive offices in Denver, Colorado, to supervise the establishment of retail outlets here and in other areas of the United States. Our first retail outlet is to be located in the in Denver, Colorado, followed by a second retail outlet in Los Angeles, California.

Pursuant to said resolution of the Board of Directors, it was determined to incorporate a Colorado company as a separate entity and as a wholly-owned subsidiary of the parent company, a Thailand corporation. As a result, , Inc., is presently a wholly-owned subsidiary of Ltd., of Bangkok, Thailand. The parent/subsidiary relationship is evidenced by the ownership by our parent corporation of 100,000 shares of stock of the U.S. subsidiary, which constitutes 100% of its issued stock. The gross revenue of the foreign and domestic operations is in excess of $1,000,000.00 a year.

Because Miss has become a valued employee and a key member of our management team in Bangkok, it is essential to this company that she be granted temporary work authorization in the United States, in order to fill the job of Personal Executive Assistant to the President of the U.S. subsidiary on a temporary basis. Her duties and responsibilities for the U.S. subsidiary in this capacity will be similar to those she has been performing and will continue to perform for the President of the Thai corporation, which are to coordinate the U.S. company with the Thai manufacturing facility, to personally assist the President with all business matters, to manage and supervise the offices, which includes the hiring/firing of personnel, keeping the books of the company, which includes the preparation of various financial documents, travel to the parent company in Thailand as required by the President of either the parent or subsidiary companies and, generally, to maintain weekly communication with the Thai company, which requires fluency in the Thai language.

In the two and one-half years Miss has been with the parent corporation, she has become an integral asset to the success of our operations. We require the assistance of her knowledge on a temporary basis during the initial stages of our U.S. enterprise, and will pay her an annual salary of $25,000.00. We anticipate that her services will be needed in the U.S. for no more than three years. During this period, she will recruit and train a permanent replacement.

Sincerely,

(USA), INC.

Vichol , President

SAMPLE SHEET

JOSSELINE
DOMINIQUE

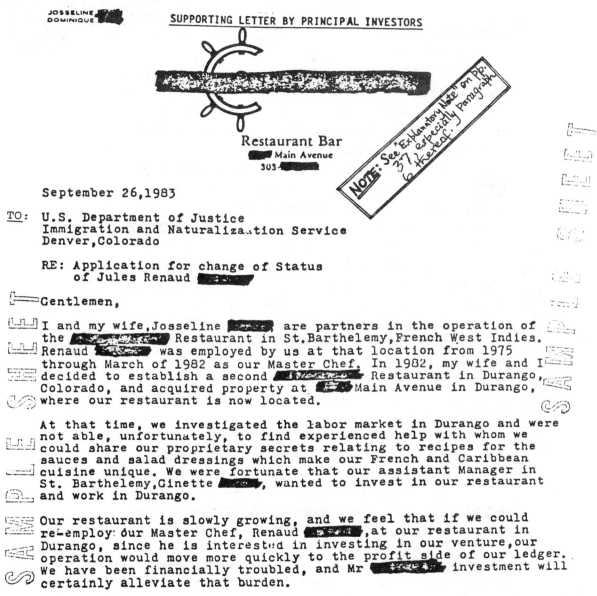

SUPPORTING LETTER BY PRINCIPAL INVESTORS

Restaurant Bar
Main Avenue
303-

NOTE: See "Explanatory Note" on pp. 37, especially paragraph 6 thereof.

September 26,1983

TO: U.S. Department of Justice
Immigration and Naturalization Service
Denver,Colorado

RE: Application for change of Status
of Jules Renaud

Gentlemen,

I and my wife,Josseline are partners in the operation of the Restaurant in St.Barthelemy,French West Indies. Renaud was employed by us at that location from 1975 through March of 1982 as our Master Chef. In 1982, my wife and I decided to establish a second Restaurant in Durango, Colorado, and acquired property at Main Avenue in Durango, where our restaurant is now located.

At that time, we investigated the labor market in Durango and were not able, unfortunately, to find experienced help with whom we could share our proprietary secrets relating to recipes for the sauces and salad dressings which make our French and Caribbean cuisine unique. We were fortunate that our assistant Manager in St. Barthelemy,Ginette , wanted to invest in our restaurant and work in Durango.

Our restaurant is slowly growing, and we feel that if we could re-employ our Master Chef, Renaud ,at our restaurant in Durango, since he is interested in investing in our venture,our operation would move more quickly to the profit side of our ledger. We have been financially troubled, and Mr investment will certainly alleviate that burden.

Attached hereto is a copy of the menu offered in St.Barthelemy, and a copy of the menu offered at our Durango restaurant, utilizing our proprietary secrets in the preparation of the various sauces, etc...

We are very anxious to have Mr with us again, and request that you favorably consider his request for change of his status in the U.S. Thank you.

Very truly yours,

Dominique

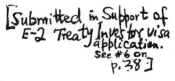

[Submitted in Support of E-2 Treaty Investor visa application. See #6 on p.38]

STATE OF COLORADO)
) ss.
COUNTY OF LA PLATA)

AFFIDAVIT

DOMINIQUE A. [redacted], being first duly sworn, deposes and states as follows:

1. That he is the holder of a non-immigrant "E-2" visa issued at Martinique, French West Indies, on February 16, 1982, which expires on February 16, 1986.

2. That the affiant and his spouse, JOSSELINE [redacted] who is also the holder of a non-immigrant "E-2" visa which expires on February 16, 1986, are the owners of real property located in Durango, Colorado, with a street address of [redacted] Avenue. A copy of the deed to this property is attached hereto.

3. That the affiant and his spouse have established a restaurant located at the above address known as the [redacted]t Restaurant, specializing in French and Caribbean cuisine.

4. That Jules Renaud [redacted] had been employed by the affiant and his wife at their [redacted] in St. Barthelemy, French West Indies, as their primary chef from November, 1975, to March 15, 1982, which position required specialized knowledge and training in the method of the operation of the restaurant.

5. That [redacted] is currently in the United States as a visitor, which non-immigrant status expires on January 6, 1984. A copy of his I-94 is attached hereto.

6. That the affiant and his wife wish to re-employ Mr. [redacted] as the master chef of [redacted] in Durango, and that Mr. Laplace wishes to invest in said restaurant.

7. That Jules Renaud [redacted] is the brother-in-law of Ginette Josephe [redacted] who is an employee of the [redacted] Restaurant and an investor therein, and who was granted E-2 status on November 1, 1982.

[signature]
Dominique A. [redacted]

Subscribed and sworn to before me this 19th day of September, 1983.

My commission expires 11-1-86.

[signature]
Notary Public
949 Second Ave.
Durango, Co. 81301

EMPLOYER LETTER IN SUPPORT OF H-1 PETITION

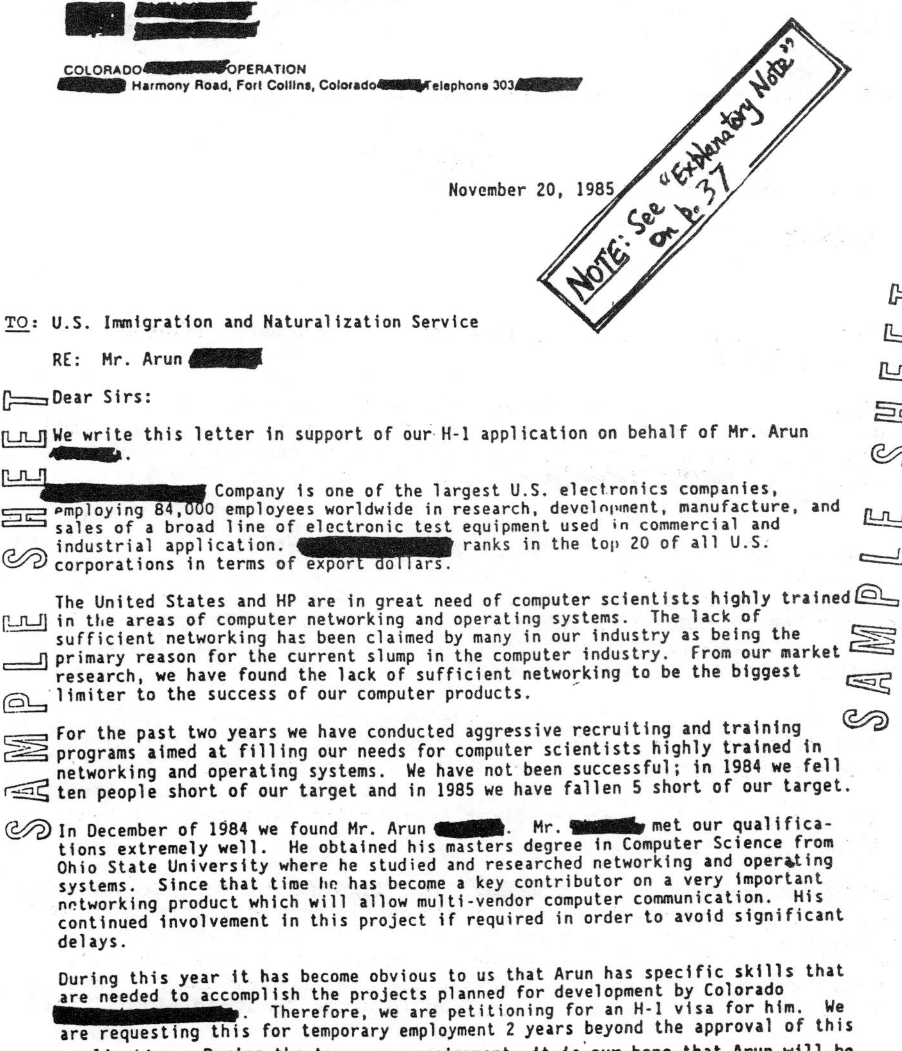

COLORADO OPERATION
Harmony Road, Fort Collins, Colorado Telephone 303

November 20, 1985

TO: U.S. Immigration and Naturalization Service

RE: Mr. Arun

Dear Sirs:

We write this letter in support of our H-1 application on behalf of Mr. Arun .

Company is one of the largest U.S. electronics companies, employing 84,000 employees worldwide in research, development, manufacture, and sales of a broad line of electronic test equipment used in commercial and industrial application. ranks in the top 20 of all U.S. corporations in terms of export dollars.

The United States and HP are in great need of computer scientists highly trained in the areas of computer networking and operating systems. The lack of sufficient networking has been claimed by many in our industry as being the primary reason for the current slump in the computer industry. From our market research, we have found the lack of sufficient networking to be the biggest limiter to the success of our computer products.

For the past two years we have conducted aggressive recruiting and training programs aimed at filling our needs for computer scientists highly trained in networking and operating systems. We have not been successful; in 1984 we fell ten people short of our target and in 1985 we have fallen 5 short of our target.

In December of 1984 we found Mr. Arun . Mr. met our qualifications extremely well. He obtained his masters degree in Computer Science from Ohio State University where he studied and researched networking and operating systems. Since that time he has become a key contributor on a very important networking product which will allow multi-vendor computer communication. His continued involvement in this project if required in order to avoid significant delays.

During this year it has become obvious to us that Arun has specific skills that are needed to accomplish the projects planned for development by Colorado . Therefore, we are petitioning for an H-1 visa for him. We are requesting this for temporary employment 2 years beyond the approval of this application. During the temporary assignment, it is our hope that Arun will be able to train or recruit individuals to carry on these responsibilities.

Thank you for your time and consideration for this petition.

Sincerely,

Sandy L.
R&D Section Manager

EMPLOYER'S OFFER OF EMPLOYMENT LETTER

(Name of Employing company)

COLORADO OPERATION
3404 East Harmony Road, Fort Collins, Colorado 80525, Telephone 303 226-3800

December 31, 1985

NOTE: See "Explanatory Note" on p. 37.

TO: U.S. Immigration and Naturalization Service

RE: Mr. Arun

Dear Sirs:

We write this letter in support of our application for permanent residency on behalf of Mr. Arun .

Company is one of the largest U.S. electronics companies, employing 84,000 employees worldwide in research, development, manufacture, and sales of a broad line of electronic test equipment used in commercial and industrial application. ranks in the top 20 of all U.S. corporations in terms of export dollars.

The United States and are in great need of computer scientists highly trained in the areas of computer networking and operating systems. The lack of sufficient networking has been claimed by many in our industry as being the primary reason for the current slump in the computer industry. From our market research, we have found the lack of sufficient networking to be the biggest limiter to the success of our computer products.

For the past two years we have conducted aggressive recruiting and training programs aimed at filling our needs for computer scientists highly trained in networking and operating systems. We have not been successful; in 1984 we fell ten people short of our target and in 1985 we have fallen 5 short of our target. Considering this, we obtained labor certification from the Department of Labor for this position.

In December of 1984 we found Mr. Arun . Mr. met our qualifications extremely well. He obtained his masters degree in Computer Science from Ohio State University where he studied and researched networking and operating systems. Since that time he has become a key contributor on a very important networking product which will allow multi-vendor computer communication. His continued involvement in this project if required in order to avoid significant delays.

Upon approval by the Immigration Service, the company intends to hire Mr. Chandra permanently at a yearly salary of $32,640.00.

Thank you for your time and consideration for this petition.

Sincerely,

COMPANY

Thomas J.
Personnel Section Manager

TJL/lb

FROM:
U.S. Department of Labor

Employment and Training Administration
1961 Stout Street
Denver, Colorado 80294

(DOL'S LETTER APPROVING CERTIFICATION)

NOTE: Refer to "Explanatory Note" on P. 37, especially item 3

Date: October 18, 1985

TO: Mr. C. James Cooper, Jr.
Attorney at Law for the Alien
999 - 18th Street, Suite #3220
Denver, Colorado 80202

Employer: [redacted] Co.
Fort Collins, Colorado

NAME OF THE ALIEN
[redacted], ARUN

OCCUPATION OF THE ALIEN
Development Engineer (Software)

DATE APPLICATION SUBMITTED FOR PROCESSING
5/2/85

The U. S. Department of Labor has made a determination on your Application for Alien Employment Certification pursuant to Title 20, Code of Federal Regulations, Section 656.21, and as required by the Immigration and Nationality Act, as amended.

Form ETA 7-50A has been certified, and it is enclosed with the supporting documents.

All enclosures should be submitted to the Immigration and Naturalization Service District Office for consideration of the alien's application for adjustment of status (I-485), or with your petition (Form I-140).

Sincerely,

Becky Stuart
for CHARLES C. VIGIL
Certifying Officer

Attachments

cc: State Agency for State of Colorado;
Alien - Mr. Arun [redacted], [redacted] Shields, [redacted], Ft. Collins, CO [redacted]

EXPLANATORY NOTE

This is Certification from the Department of Labor which is used by the Department of Labor office in Denver. Although the form is dated October 18, 1985, the alien's priority date for a visa number was May 2, 1985, which was the date the Application for Labor Certification was received by the State agency.

CONTRACT OF EMPLOYMENT (A SAMPLE)

This is a contract of Employment between Mr/Ms ________, who resides at _(address?)__, City of_______, State of______, (hereinafter called "EMPLOYER"), and Mr/Ms________________who resides at__________, city/town of__________, State of_______ Zip____(hereinafter called "EMPLOYER").

The Employer hereby agrees to employ the Employee as a live-in domestic worker in the Employer's home at the above address, at a salary of $_______ per hour for the first forty (40) hours worked, and $_______per hour, for the next four (4) hours worked, if any, up to the required forty-four (44) hours per week. The Employer also agrees to pay the Employee at the same "overtime" rate of $_____per hour for all time worked over forty-four (44) hours per week. The regular weekly wage (i.e., without overtime) is $________ The Employee will be given private room and board at no expense to the Employee.

The duties of the Employee will consist of the following: general household work, cleaning, laundry, shopping, cooking and serving meals, child care, answering the door and phone, and running general errands, lawn tending.

Household equipment, which the Employee will operate, are: dishwasher, vacuum cleaner, washing machine and dryer, lawn mower.

The hours of employment will be forty-four (44) per week, from_____A.M. to_____P.M.; daily, 5 days per week, with a 2 hour rest period and 2 hours for meals each day. The Employee will work a guaranteed minimum of four (4) hours overtime per week at an hourly rate of $_____. The Employee agrees to live on the premises of the Employer. Employee is totally free to leave the premises at all times which are not working hours.

The Employer and the Employee, each agrees to give the other a two-week notice of intent to terminate the employment herein.

The Employer and the Employee, each acknowledges the receipt of a duplicate of this Contract, and each asserts that he/she entered into and signed this document freely, willingly, and voluntarily, after having first read, considered, and understood the contents thereof.

S IGNED:	SIGNED:
______________	____________
(Employer)	(Employee)
Dated:_____200___.	Dated:_____200___.

"BUSINESS NECESSITY" LETTER (A SAMPLE)
(On the Employer's Letterhead)

Date:__________

Local Employment Service
Address:__________
City.______ State ______
Zip.__________

Re: Business Necessity
Employee: Jozef Braun
Employer: Castle Export Corp.
Job: Supervisor, Export Department

Gentlemen:

We have required that the person who is in the position of Supervisor in the Export Department be able to speak French fluently.

This requirement is necessary for us since about 70% of our business is to buyers in France. The buyers do not speak English very well and always prefer to deal in French, their native language.

We have two other people in the Export Department who will be supervised by Mr. Braun. Both of these people speak some French but are not fluent. Our business has suffered in the past because of the language problem.

In addition to his supervisory duties, you will also note that his job includes receiving and processing orders, shipping documents, and other papers related to the export function. Many of these documents are in French. We have attached samples of documents we have received in the past. Sometimes we have had the documents translated by outside personnel at great cost of time and money.

Unless the Supervisor can speak and write French fluently, it will hurt our business very much and make it not possible for us to continue to compete.

Very truly yours,

Roger Perter
President

NOTE: This sample letter is cited, with permission for which we are most grateful to the Publisher, from the "Green Card Book".

NOTICE OF JOB OFFERING

COOK, GREEK STYLE FOOD. A job is open for a cook of Greek style food. Prepare Greek dishes such as spanakopita, keftedakia, stuffed grape leaves, and others. Requires two years experience in a similar job. Uses commercial cooking equipment including ovens, mixers, food processors, and other restaurant kitchen equipment. 40 hours per week at $250.00 per week. Call Mr.__________ at phone No:__________, if interested. Phone between the hours of ______ and ______

To the Labour Department: this notice was posted on the Bulletin Board of the Greek Spoon Restaurant from __________ to __________ There were no responses.

Signed: __________
Name Signed & Your Title:__________

CERTIFICATE OF APPROVED LABOUR CERTIFICATION (OR, OF DENIED LABOUR CERTIFICATION)

U.S. DEPARTMENT OF LABOR
EMPLOYMENT AND TRAINING ADMINISTRATION
1515 Broadway
New York, N.Y. 10036

Date: _______

In reply refer to DD/CB

TO: ABC Restaurant, Inc
Address: _______________

John Doe , SPECIALTY COOK FRENCH/THAI
Alien's name and occupation

DEC 15, 1980
Date of acceptance for processing

The Department of Labor has made a determination on your application for alien employment pursuant to Title 20, Code of Federal Regulations, Section 656.21 and as required by the Immigration and Nationality Act, as amended. Final action has been taken as follows:

☑ 1. Form ETA 7-50 has been certified and is enclosed with the supporting documents. All enclosures should be submitted to the Immigration and Naturalization Service District Office for consideration of alien's application for adjustment of status (I-485) or with your petition (Form I-140).

☐ 2. Form ETA 7-50 has been certified and forwarded to the .... Consulate at which the alien has indicated he will file a visa application. The Consular Officer will inform the alien of any additional documents to be submitted and steps to be taken in order to apply for an immigrant visa.

☐ 3. Form ETA 7-50 has not been certified and is being returned. A certification cannot be issued as required by Section 212(a)(14) of the Immigration and Nationality Act, as amended, on the basis of information available for the following reasons:

☐ a. There are U.S. workers available who are able, willing, and qualified for the job.

☐ b. The employment of aliens would have an adverse effect on wages and/or working conditions of U.S. workers similarly employed.

The wage offer of .... is below the prevailing rate of .... for this occupation in the proposed area of employment.

Prevailing wage was determined by ....

....

Sincerely,

Bette F. Roy

BETTE F. ROY
Certifying Officer

cc: State ES Agency

CC: John Doe

> Request for a review of a denial of certification may be made. A request for review of a denial may only be made in writing addressed to the Chief Administrative Law Judge, Department of Labor, and submitted by certified mail to the Certifying Officer who denied certification within 35 days of date of this denial for transmittal and shall: (1) Clearly identify the particular certification determination for which review is sought; (2) set forth the particular grounds on which the request is based; and (3) include all documents which accompanied the denial of certification.

ETA 7-145 (Dec. 1976)

SAMPLE SHEET

Form ETA 7-145

NOTE: The above document, set forth herein for illustrative purposes, is reproduced here by courtesy of and from "The Greencard Book," by Richard Madison (Visa Publishing Co., New York N.Y.), p.73. A few minor modifications have been made herein by the present publisher.

NOTICE OF FINDINGS

U.S. DEPARTMENT OF LABOR
EMPLOYMENT AND TRAINING ADMINISTRATION
1515 Broadway
New York, N.Y. 10036

Date: ______ In reply refer to: DD/CB

John Doe /Spec. Cook French/Thai
Alien's name and occupation

12/15/80
Date of acceptance for processing

TO: ABC Restaurant, Inc.
Address: ____________________

The Department of Labor has considered your application. In accordance with Title 20, Code of Federal Regulations, Section 656.25(C)(3), we hereby issue our Notice of Findings. You have until September 20, 1981..... to submit documentary evidence to rebut the finding outlined below by certified mail on or before the date specified above. If the rebuttal evidence is not received by certified mail on or before, this Notice of Findings automatically becomes the final decision to deny labor certification.

(1) Pursuant to 20 CFR 656.21(b)(7) the Revised Federal Requirements employer must document that if labor certification is granted, the wage rate paid will equal or exceed the prevailing wage applicable at that time. The statement will equal or exceed. The said prevailing wage at the time "is not satisfactory,
(2) Pursuant to 20 CFR 656.21(b)(15) employer has documented that he will be able to place the alien on the payroll on or before his date of proposed entry into U.S. It is noted that alien has been employed since March 1, 1978, therefore employer should document that alien is presently on the payroll.
(3) Pursuant to 20 CFR 656.21(b)(9) employer has documented "subsequent to filing with my local employment service office. I placed a further advertisement in a newspaper of general circulation directing applicants to report to the local office of the employment service." This documentation was signed on 10/4/80 the job order was not placed until 11/30,/80 and the additional ad on May 23, 1981, therefore this is not a bonafide statement.
(4) Pursuant to 20 CFR 656.21(b)(10) employer has stated he posted a notice. A copy of this notice and the results of its posting must be submitted.
(5) Item 31, Form MA 7-50B, pertaining to education and training requirements, have not been answered. If none required so state.
(6) Items 5 and 6 of Form MA 7-50A, pertaining to names of schools attended or special qualifications and skills has not been answered.
(7) Should employer choose to comply with the above and/or rebut these findings he may address his letter to this office.

Sincerely,

BETTE F. ROY
Certifying Officer
cc. State E. S. Agency

ETA 7-145A

ETA 7-145A (Dec. 1976)

NOTE: The above document, set forth herein for illustrative purposes, is reproduced here by courtesy of and from "The Greencard Book," by Richard Madison (Visa Publishing Co.), p.72 . A few minor modifications have been made by the present Publisher herein.

Appendix F

LIST OF OTHER PUBLICATIONS FROM DO-IT-YOURSELF LEGAL PUBLISHERS

Please DO NOT tear our this page. Consider others!

The following is a list of books obtainable from the Do-It-Yourself Publishers/Selfhelper Law Press of America.

(Customers: For your convenience, just make a photocopy of this page and send it along with your order. All prices quoted here are subject to change without notice.)

1. How To Draw Up Your Own Friendly Separation/Property Settlement Agreement With Your Spouse
2. Tenant Smart: How To Win Your Tenants' Legal Rights Without A Lawyer (New York Edition)
3. How To Probate & Settle An Estate Yourself Without The Lawyers' Fees ($35)
4. How To Adopt A Child Without A Lawyer
5. How To Form Your Own Profit/Non-Profit Corporation Without A Lawyer
6. How To Plan Your 'Total' Estate With A Will & Living Will, Without a Lawyer
7. How To Declare Your Personal Bankruptcy Without A Lawyer ($29)
8. How To Buy Or Sell Your Own Home Without A Lawyer or Broker ($29)
9. How To File For Chapter 11 Business Bankruptcy Without A Lawyer ($29)
10. How To Legally Beat The Traffic Ticket Without A Lawyer (forthcoming)
11. How To Settle Your Own Auto Accident Claims Without A Lawyer ($29)
12. How To Obtain Your U.S. Immigration Visa Without A Lawyer ($30) Vol. 1 or 2
13. How To Do Your Own Divorce Without A Lawyer [10 Regional State-Specific Volumes] ($35)
14. How To Legally Change Your Name Without A Lawyer
15. How To Properly Plan Your 'Total' Estate With A Living Trust, Without The Lawyers' Fees ($35)
16. Legally Protect Yourself In A Gay/Lesbian Or Non-Marital Relationship With A Cohabitation Agreement
17. Before You Say 'I do' In Marriage Or Co-Habitation, Here's How To First Protect Yourself Legally
18. The National Home Mortgage reduction Kit (forthcoming) ($26.95)
19. The National Home Mortgage Qualification Kit ($28.95)

Prices: Each book, except for those specifically priced otherwise, costs $26, plus $4.00 per book for postage and handling. New Jersey residents please add 6% sales tax. **ALL PRICES ARE SUBJECT TO CHANGE WITHOUT NOTICE**

CUSTOMERS: Please make and send a zerox copy of this page with your orders)

ORDER FORM

TO: **Do-it-Yourself Legal Publishers**
60 Park Place # Suite **1013**, Newark, NJ 07102

Please send me the following:

1.__________copies of ____

2.__________copies of ____

3.__________copies of ____

4.__________copies of ____

Enclosed is the sum of $_____________ to cover the order. *Mail my order to:*

Mr./Mrs.//Ms/Dr. ____

Address (include Zip Code please): ____

____

Phone No. and area code: ( ) ______________________ Job: ( ) ______________________

*New Jersey residents enclose 6% sales tax.

IMPORTANT: Please do NOT rip out the page. Consider others! Just make a photocopy and send it.

INDEX